Civil War and State Formation

Mikropolitik der Gewalt – Micropolitics of Violence

Volume 9

Edited by Klaus Schlichte and Peter Waldmann

Felix Gerdes, Dr. phil., is political scientist and specializes in politics of Sub-Saharan Africa and South-East Asia. He currently works as Academic Staff at Zaman University, Phnom Penh, Cambodia.

Felix Gerdes

Civil War and State Formation

The Political Economy of War and Peace in Liberia

Campus Verlag
Frankfurt/New York

Bibliographic Information published by the Deutsche Nationalbibliothek.
Die Deutsche Nationalbibliothek lists this publication in the Deutsche Nationalbibliografie.
Detailed bibliographic data are available in the Internet at http://dnb.d-nb.de.
ISBN 978-3-593-39892-1

Cover illustration © Felix Gerdes, Capitol Hill Legislative Building, view from the social sciences building of the University of Liberia.
Cover design: Campus Verlag GmbH, Frankfurt-on-Main
Printing office and bookbinder: CPI buchbücher.de, Birkach
Printed on acid free paper.
Printed in Germany

For further information:
www.campus.de
www.press.uchicago.edu

Contents

List of Tables viii

Preface ix

1. Introduction 1

2. War, Peace, and Young States 8
   - 2.1. The State and Other Types of Political Organization 9
     - 2.1.1. The Importance of Variance in (Personal) Authority 9
     - 2.1.2. Non-legitimate Domination 15
     - 2.1.3. The Empirical State 17
   - 2.2. State Formation, State Erosion and Society 19
     - 2.2.1. State-Building and State Decay 19
     - 2.2.2. Society and the State 26
     - 2.2.3. A Note on Sequences of Domination 29

3. The First Liberian Civil War: The Rise of Charles Taylor 31
   - 3.1. Collusion, Competition and Military Combat 34
     - 3.1.1. The Actors 34
     - 3.1.2. Elimination Contests 39
     - 3.1.3. Winning a War by Way of Elections 56
     - 3.1.4. Summary: Civil War as State-Building 59

3.2. Political Economy of the NPFL 60
3.2.1. Creation of the NPFL and Imposition of Taylor 60
3.2.2. Politics of the NPFL: Administration and Legitimacy 64
3.2.3. Discipline, Repression and Material Interests 73
3.2.4. Economics of the NPFL 79
3.3. Taylor's Adversaries and their Weaknesses 104
3.3.1. The Doe Government 106
3.3.2. The Interim Government of National Unity 109
3.3.3. The Independent National Patriotic Front of Liberia 115
3.3.4. The ECOWAS Cease-Fire Monitoring Group 117
3.3.5. The United Liberation Movements 123
3.3.6. The Liberia Peace Council 128
3.4. Summary: Taylor and his Rivals 131
3.5. From Warlord to Statesman: Charles Taylor as President 132
3.5.1. Transplanting a System of Domination 134
3.5.2. The Security Sector 139
3.5.3. Revenue Generation in Charles Taylor's Liberia 140
3.5.4. Key Features of Liberia Inc. 150
3.6. Summary: The Rise of Charles Taylor 152

4. Taylor's Fall and the Dawn of a Neo-patrimonial Democracy 154
4.1. The Government: Cracks in the System 154
4.1.1. Disintegration of the Security Sector 154
4.1.2. Repression and the Erosion of a Patrimonial System 158
4.1.3. An Aggressive Regional Policy 161
4.1.4. The Economics of Taylor's Fall 165
4.1.5. The Final Events 167

4.2. The Rebels: LURD and MODEL 168

4.3. The National Transitional Government of Liberia 172

4.3.1. The Erosion of the Former Regime 175

4.3.2. LURD and MODEL: Rebels Falling Apart 182

4.3.3. Political Parties and Civil Society: Dashed Hopes 187

4.4. Elections and a New Regime 191

4.4.1. Presidential Elections: Warring Parties 192

4.4.2. The Leading Candidates and their Networks 194

4.4.3. The Legislature 205

4.5. Liberia under Johnson Sirleaf: Rebuilding the State? 217

4.5.1. Anatomy of a Post-War Regime 218

4.5.2. Major Issues in Institutional Development 222

4.5.3. An Anti-Corruption Policy? 226

4.5.4. New Elections—Reconfigured Alliances 231

4.6. Political Economy of the New Liberia 235

4.6.1. A Peacekeeping and Reconstruction Economy 235

4.6.2. Natural Resources and Political Control 237

4.7. From Taylor to Johnson Sirleaf: Major Issues 249

5. Conclusion 251

Bibliography 263

Index 285

List of Tables

Table 1: State of Disarmament after Deadline February 9, 1997 57
Table 2: Estimates of Value of Iron Ore Exports from Liberia 83
Table 3: Figures on Timber Trade 84
Table 4: Post-War Timber Exports, FOB 84
Table 5: Data on Liberian Rubber Exports and Prices 88
Table 6: Liberian Diamond Exports and Belgian Imports Preface 93
Table 7: Coffee and Cocoa Production, FOB Prices 97
Table 8: Official Development Assistance to Liberia 101
Table 9: Profits Controlled by Taylor 103
Table 10: RUF Diamond Exports (Liberia FOB) and Taylor's Profits 143
Table 11: Post-War Timber Exports, FOB 144
Table 12: Timber Export Volumes and State Timber Revenue 146
Table 13: Rubber Exports 1997–2003 148
Table 14: Presidential Election Results 2005: Top Contenders 204
Table 15: Strongest Parties in the 52nd Legislature 212
Table 16: Strongest Parties in the 53rd Legislature 212
Table 17: Associates of Warring Parties in the Legislature 214
Table 18: Official Development Assistance to Liberia, 1997–2010 236
Table 19: Table 19: UNMIL Budgets August 2003–June 2010..................237

Preface

This book is a revised and updated version of my doctoral thesis, which I submitted in November 2010 at the University of Hamburg. It is the outcome of a contingent path of mine, formed by many coincidences and to which many people and a number of institutions have contributed. My parents' support, the opportunities Hamburg´s academic institutions offered, and scholarship institutions have played a great role in making it possible.

Looking back, my path started when, at the age of sixteen, a relative's NGO job gave me the opportunity to visit a remote and tranquil region in northern Burkina Faso that is, for several years now, off-limits to Westerners because of the activities of Al Qaida-affiliated groups. Since then, I have maintained an interest in Africa, and I have to thank Laurence Marfaing and Leonhard Harding for their personal commitment to the German Academic Exchange Service (DAAD) scholarship program and support that allowed me to study at Dakar's Université Cheikh Anta Diop. My life would not have developed as it did had I not become affiliated with the unique AKUF-project established by Klaus-Jürgen Gantzel, integrating students into research on wars. Urged by Ulf Engel and encouraged by a Guinean student colleague, I later undertook research on the militarization of refugee camps for my *Diplom* (M.A.) thesis in Guinea-Conakry, again greatly supported by the DAAD. This is where I developed a fascination for Liberia and its people. My doctoral thesis and research in Liberia would not have been possible without the scholarship provided by the Friedrich-Ebert-Foundation, to which I am grateful. This book has further profited from my subsequent employment in the project "Formation of Political Elites in Post-war Societies" at the Research Unit of Wars, University of Hamburg, which was funded by the Deutsche Forschungsgemeinschaft (DFG).

I owe much to my supervisors, Cord Jakobeit and Klaus Schlichte, who provided valuable support and encouragement. I would further like to take this occasion to thank all those who supported me along my way, inter alia by providing personal encouragement during times of slow progress, by criticizing my writings, by providing materials and helping me to gain access to informants, and also by helping me to better understand West Africa through personal experience. Among those who need to be named are: Aimé Biagui, Cherif Balde, Eginhard P. Daniel Meijering, Elizabeth Chester, Frank Baumfalk, Heinz Jockers, Jens Siegelberg, Laura Morawek, Magnus Kutz, Max Steinhardt, Maik Schädler, Manfred Zbrzezny, Ousmane Tamboura, Patrick Singh, Sadia Yallah, Sebastian Schiek, Stephan Hensell, Wilhelm Laszlob, Wolfgang Schreiber, and Yvette Sagna (RIP). Nathaniel Ebenezer Daygbor and Mike Jabateh greatly assisted my research in Liberia.

Special thanks go to Bhakti Eike Ohlendorf for her time, criticism and encouragement when these were most needed, and Falk Zirkel, who put his graphic design skills at my disposal for this and other projects despite short deadlines, a busy schedule at work and a newborn baby at home. I apologize to all those I could not or forgot to mention here. Finally, I am deeply grateful to my parents Greta Gerdes and Horst Langner-Gerdes, who supported me throughout in all the ways they could, and my brother Hannes Gerdes for supporting all of us. Of course, all errors and omissions in this book are solely my responsibility.

Felix Gerdes *Phnom Penh, February 2013*

1. Introduction

In late June 2010, the *International Monetary Fund* (IMF) announced debt relief worth some 4.6 billion dollars for Liberia (cf. IMF June 29, 2010). For this tiny country of roughly 3.5 million inhabitants, this did not only represent significantly improved long-term economic perspectives, it was also of great symbolic importance and signaled the definitive readmission of Liberia into the international community. For more than a decade, the country had been best known for its devastating wars, and was widely regarded a "failed state" (cf. Pham 2004). Yet only a few years after the last war ended in 2003, Liberia started being hailed as a success story. More than anything else, observers lauded the country for its political progress as evidenced by the democratic election of President Ellen Johnson Sirleaf in 2005, its maintenance of significant civil liberties thereafter, and the introduction of technocratic economic policy reforms. Hence, the IMF's First Deputy Managing Director stressed that "*it was the sustained implementation of a strong macroeconomic program and ambitious reform agenda by the government of President Johnson Sirleaf*" (IMF June 30, 2010, italics original) which convinced the Bretton Woods Institutions to support debt relief.

The contrast with Liberia's international reputation just a few years earlier is striking. Not only was the state seen as having collapsed, but the country was considered the "eye in the regional storm" (ICG 2003b), wreaking havoc on its neighbors and destabilizing West Africa. This perspective developed and became prominent during the First Liberian War from 1989 to 1996, when the country was the scene of West Africa's bloodiest internal conflict. During these years, some 60,000 to 80,000 people died as a direct result of fighting (Ellis 2007a, 316).[1] As the powers of the central government eroded and the formal economy crumbled, armed factions accumulated powers and traded the country's natural

1 Frequently quoted but questionable estimates put the number of deaths at 200,000 to 250,000 (Ellis 2007a, 316).

resources. At times, it appeared that faction leaders were making fortunes out of war (cf. Reno 1998). The Second Liberian War from 2000 to 2003 only served to reinforce notions of Liberia as a "failed state", i.e. one providing virtually no services to its citizens and subject to political dynamics promoting use of violence as a means of politics (cf. Pham 2004).

The phenomenon of simultaneous destruction and acquisition of wealth apparent in many civil wars prompted academic observers to think of these wars as specific societal systems characterized by specific opportunities to gain power and wealth.[2] Powerful war-time actors, it is argued, are used to realizing their chances within the parameters of these systems. As they are "doing well out of war", the situation is considered to further their economic interests (Collier 2000). Political dynamics arguably work in concert with economic ones. Keen (1998; 2000) argues that war constitutes an environment perfectly suited to both governments and warlords who want to eliminate opponents, repress organized opposition and maintain authoritarian forms of domination. Warring factions may therefore be interested in perpetuating war, rather than winning it.

Neo-liberal economic policies are often considered the background to civil wars, although analysts emphasize different aspects. Reno (1998; 2000) stresses declining state revenues as a result of neo-liberal policy reforms imposed by the Bretton Woods Institutions. In consequence, rulers cut back on social services and patronage transfers, which entails an erosion of legitimacy. In weak states, political elites tend to exert significant personal control over economic and social capital, and these resources can be used to mobilize armed resistance once these elites have been excluded from state patronage. As warlords, these elites commercialize natural resources and generate profits but do not have to shoulder the expenses of states, rendering their informal networks competitive political actors vis-à-vis genuine states.[3] According to Reno's argument, a major structural transformation of the international system has been at the root of the emergence of warlord systems. During the Cold War, the world's superpowers alimented "Third World" rulers and, in consequence, absolved them from the need to build self-sustaining systems of domination. The end of the Cold War and an associated re-ordering of the world on the basis of neo-liberal principles entailed the collapse of weak states and created opportunities for alternative systems of domination.

---

2 See, for instance, Reno (1998); Collier (2000); Keen (2000); Collier/Hoeffler (2004).

3 On Liberia cf. Reno (1995).

Kurtenbach and Lock (2004), by contrast, emphasize socio-economic factors. According to their argument, neo-liberal reforms imposed from outside since the end of the Cold War have led to a massive decline in formal sector employment in less advanced economies, because of public sector retrenchment. As a consequence, the informal sector (rather than competitive formal business) grows. Economic informalization further diminishes the tax base of the state. State capacity is consequently further reduced, resulting in weaker law enforcement. This in turn leads to growth of the criminal economy. Migration, equally reinforced by the retrenchment of the formal sector, enables criminal networks to expand beyond their home countries ("shadow globalization"). Autonomous economic accumulation allows these networks to accumulate power, forge cooperative relations with state agencies, and impose their interests by means of violence (Kurtenbach/Lock 2004, 22–23). Although competition between these clandestine networks does not necessarily or even predominantly take on the form of war, it is associated with levels of violence that may be higher than those experienced during war (cf. Lock 2004, 58–60). While some form of peace may still be achievable, transformation of war-torn states appears impossible in the short term given the global and structural nature of the problem.

It seems that major global trends are working against states remaining the central political entities in their territories. They could consequently hardly be able to pursue "ambitious reforms", and Liberia could in no way have reversed the path it had taken so quickly. Thus, which role did the civil wars really play in the trajectory of the Liberian state?

Arriving at an answer firstly requires investigating to what extent patterns of authority have indeed changed during the wars and thereafter. Subsequently, we will be able to identify causes of change, or of the lack thereof. In the light of the theoretical perspectives quoted above, which stress the opportunities for states and their rivals to obtain resources that will confer political power, the question of how the Liberian state disintegrated and was then restored is a question of emergence of new political actors and transformation of established political actors. More specifically, the question firstly is how and why dissidents could successfully challenge the claim of the state to control the means of military violence and themselves become the major controllers of the use of force. And why and how did a reconfiguration of political actors take place that allowed politics to be conducted in a more civil way, and how and why could control of means of military violence become recentralized? As Zeeuw (2008, 2) has remarked, "despite the importance of the political transformation of non-state armed movements in the settlement of civil wars and in postwar democratization, surprisingly little is known about this process."

Modern theories of states and their formation generally include considerations on wars, regimes and democracy, and frequently adopt a political economy perspective that is useful for the analysis of both regimes and war economies. Applied to a re-emerging state like Liberia, state-building theory may provide interesting insights on democracy by focusing on broader societal processes underlying the creation and functioning of democratic state institutions.

In order to develop an understanding of state formation, Chapter 2 firstly discusses the term "the state", drawing in particular on Max Weber and interpretations of his work prominent in studies on African societies. The chapter introduces Weber's ideal-types of legitimate domination and discusses the term of neo-patrimonial domination, defining the latter as a governance arrangement characterized by patrimonial patterns clashing with relatively weaker but nonetheless enduring legal-rational ones. In more general terms, I define the empirical state as a governance arrangement combining elements of a global ideal with local practices (Schlichte 2005). State formation is defined as the extension of the effective powers of this state over a population within an identifiable geographical area on the one hand, and progressive political integration of the population into the exercise of state powers on the other. Drawing on Charles Tilly, I emphasize the (frequently violent) political competition that is intrinsically associated with competition over the economic resources that are needed for state-building. Norbert Elias' theory of configurations characterized by interdependence, imbalances and political contests, leading to shifts in the distribution of power, is also introduced, in order to help us to explain and analyze the waxing and waning of state power. As proposed by both Tilly and Elias, political economy in a wider sense, i.e. the authoritative acquisition of values and authoritative redistribution of values, is an important concept for investigating the evolution of patterns of authority in general and of the state in particular.

Chapters 3 and 4 form the central part of this study. While chapter 3 traces the ascent of Charles Taylor from senior organizer of an irregular armed faction to sovereign president, chapter 4 analyzes his fall and the emergence of a new political regime. As their overarching issue, the two chapters investigate the fragmentation and re-centralization of political power in Liberia, showing how these phenomena were related to changes in the political economy.

Chapter 3 analyzes political patterns and the political economy of major political actors of the First War. Many of the terms developed for analysis of historic state formation as proposed in chapter 2 are equally helpful to investigating state-forming dynamics in contemporary civil wars. The analysis pays special attention to the *National Patriotic Front of Liberia* (NPFL), the rebel group led by Charles Taylor, but also analyzes in depth his (interlinked) adversaries, i.e. the interim government, the Nigerian-led intervention force,[4] and the diverse armed factions that emanated from the pre-war government. For each of the important political actors, I investigate the basis of their claim to, and their degree of, legitimacy—the latter on the basis of narratives in the absence of more reliable evidence. I further analyze their organizational patterns and control over revenues. Legitimacy, internal organization and control over revenues are the key factors I investigate to explain the relative strength of political actors.

The strength of armed factions and other political actors in the First Liberian War has not been systematically analyzed before, and neither has the available data been compared and checked for plausibility. As I show, high but often implausible estimates of war economy revenues of the NPFL have been widely used in the debate. The chapter entertains the hypothesis that Charles Taylor's rise had much less to do with superior war economy profits than has frequently been argued, and was to a large extent due to his superior, charismatically-based legitimacy and the poor political organization of his rivals. I argue that the profits of war are inadequate an explanation for the destruction of Liberia. Rather, the intermittent breakdown of the Liberian state was a political phenomenon engendered by a severe lack of government legitimacy and sustained by a politically motivated regional intervention. The latter was supported by the developed states of the world and sponsored a host of poorly organized, unrepresentative and illegitimate armed or unarmed political actors.

Chapter 4 investigates the fall of Taylor and the emergence of a new, neo-patrimonial and democratic regime. I apply the same categories used in the previous chapter—political patterns, legitimacy, control over reve-

---

4 The regional intervention force has been widely discussed in academia and I cannot claim to offer a particularly deep analysis of it, although my arranging of the material is innovative.

nues—to the analysis of the Charles Taylor government, the rebels who unseated him, and relevant civilian political forces. The analysis covers three institutionally different phases, i.e. the Second Liberian War, the power-sharing interim government following it, and the rule of newly elected President Ellen Johnson Sirleaf. I show that, faced with a different political situation involving new challenges and constraints, Taylor's legitimacy eroded. While this allowed rebels to gain a temporary military advantage, they were too weak to monopolize power and acted accordingly. The result was a power-sharing government composed of various forces and characterized by fragmentation of powers, as well as a high degree of use of public office for private benefit. Importantly, none of the former armed factions succeeded in accumulating power and legitimacy, and hence opportunities were created for civilian political actors. The democratic elections of 2005, i.e. the line-up of forces, the resources at their disposal and the alliances struck by the final contenders, are analyzed in detail with a view to explaining the eventual poll results. The latter part of the chapter is devoted to dynamics of the Johnson Sirleaf government, arguing that Liberia has entered a new, probably cyclical, phase in its political history that can be conceptualized as "neo-patrimonial democracy."

The conclusion summarizes the key findings of this study. In short, my analysis of the Liberian wars differs fundamentally from prominent other ones (cf. Reno 1995; 1998; cf. Pham 2004). The wars were characterized by many of the classical elements and mechanisms of state-building familiar to us from the European experience. Put differently, the Liberian wars represented processes of state-building rather than state collapse. The conclusion offers some more general reflections on Young States and the international system.

A few notes on primary sources[5] will help the reader to appreciate the basis of this study. A major part of my research involved analyzing Liberian newspaper articles. Liberian journalism is often problematic, and article space is more or less openly up for sale to any interested party. Yet newspapers provide valuable clues on how aspiring elites present them-

5 The available literature has been extensively consulted. Ellis' (2007a) seminal study provides the most complex picture of the First Liberian civil war, analysing the historical, political, economic, international relations and cultural dimensions of the war. If I quote the volume extensively, it is because it provides an invaluably rich reservoir of information on the First Liberian War. This book further owes much to the insights of Reno (1995; 1998) and Utas (2003). This study further heavily draws on reports from the International Crisis Group (ICG), the Panel of Experts, and Global Witness.

selves, who supports whom, what alliances have been concluded, and often contain insider information launched or leaked by the interested parties. Generally, I have checked newspaper articles for plausibility in the light of evidence from other sources.

Further, during four field research trips, I gathered information using different types of interviews.[6] All in all, I conducted about 150 individual interviews with Liberian elites, expatriate experts, Liberian analysts, political or civil society activists, journalists, and rural chiefs. Most of these interviews were conducted in Monrovia, although a significant number occurred in semi-urban and rural settings. Many of these interviews were off-the-record, but all information available to me has been used to select newspaper articles quoted in this study. Most sources have been anonymized in order to protect informants.

In order to gather information on the social background of the warring groups and recent political change, I travelled to their respective heartlands—the Counties of Grand Gedeh, Lofa, Nimba and Bong—during my second trip. I further went to Bomi and Sinoe because of occupations of rubber plantations there by ex-combatants.[7] I held 26 focus group interviews in different settings, mostly with school students between the ages of 16 and 35.[8] The object of discussion was relations between grassroots and power holders at present and in the recent past. Youths (in the African sense) constitute the numerically most important population category and have been a major recruitment reservoir for armed groups. I thus found this population category to be of major interest for my study

6 Field research took place from November 2005 to February 2006; from October 2006 to March 2007; from March to April 2011; and from February to April 2012.

7 In addition, I did several short trips to other destinations relevant for specific reasons, in particular Buchanan, Tubmanburg (Bomi Hills) and Lofa Bridge.

8 Due to the interruption of schooling during the wars, school students often were significantly older in Liberia than in other settings.

2. War, Peace, and Young States[9]

"War made the state, and the state made war"—thus Charles Tilly (1975b, 42) famously summarized the European state-building experience. Correspondingly, internal wars in post-colonial states have been understood as "ex-post consolidation of preordained statehood" (Siegelberg 1994, 138, translation F.G.). By contrast, since the end of the Cold War civil wars in Africa have most often been understood as state failure or decay (Erdmann 2003, 271–272; Schlichte 1998). In a different but related perspective, the phenomena have been analyzed as alternative systems of domination and accumulation.[10] More generally, academics expressed doubts whether the political entities on the continent should ever have been called states at all and, consequently, whether state-building was ever pursued in a more than superficial fashion (Jackson 1990; Chabal/Daloz 1999; 2006).

Yet how can we theoretically frame domination in a country like Liberia? Do these assertions hold true, and "the state" is a category appropriate for understanding neither the dynamics of war nor domination after it? Then, if war was not about imposing, extending, resisting and altering the powers of the state, what are the dynamics of war? And what are the patterns of domination after war? Or should internal wars continue to be considered part of a process of ex-post consolidation of preordained state-

9 The term is applicable to many of the states formerly grouped as "Third World". It is meant to designate states that for historical reasons are strongly patterned by ideal-typical traditional authority, natural resource economies, and weak ideal-typical characteristics of modern statehood. Euphemisms such as "emerging" or "developing" states have little analytic merit and do not constitute an alternative to the "Third World" paradigm. The north-south distinction is little helpful because it does not take account of increasing variance of political-economic systems. We need more, not less than three categories to classify contemporary states.

10 See, for instance, Reno (1998; 2000); Keen (2000); Jung (2003); Collier/Hoeffler (2004)

hood? Developing an answer to these questions requires a discussion of the state and related terms.

This chapter firstly discusses the notion of statehood. Subsequently, I show how statehood relates to empirical states. Then follows an elaboration of state formation theory that clarifies how states came about and further develops the notion of the state by discussing the complementary processes of extension of central authority and societal influence on central power. The chapter finally closes with a few remarks on application of the terms developed here to the empirical object of this study.

2.1. The State and Other Types of Political Organization

When talking about the state we need to distinguish two dimensions. The first one is the state as an empirical phenomenon, i.e. the basic political unit structuring the international system. The second one is that of statehood; an ideal-typical characteristics of modern domination. Three characteristics are widely accepted as integral to statehood. Among these is rule over a defined territory; i.e. statehood requires borders not frontiers. Furthermore, there is a defined permanent resident population. Third, the ideal-typical state features an externally and internally sovereign, centralized apparatus monopolizing the means and legitimate use of violence (cf. Reinhard 1999, VIII). Max Weber further specified the organizational characteristics of that apparatus, which are widely accepted as defining features of modern domination. As the discussion of the state in Africa has paid too little attention to relevant distinctions in Weber's political sociology, the following subsection elaborates on and quotes extensively from Weber's thought.

2.1.1. The Importance of Variance in (Personal) Authority

Weber distinguishes his types of domination on the basis of beliefs in legitimacy, since legitimacy is a necessary condition for enduring rule. This is important as principles of legitimacy are closely related to the way in which domination is administered. Yet for Weber, the belief in legitimacy is, first of all, a quality of the ruler's administrative staff employed to coerce subjects (Weber 1978a, 212–213). The military is a segment of the administration and considered as such in this study. The belief of subjects in legitimacy is a secondary issue, and this study emphasizes relations between ruler and staff to explain domination. Yet to the extent that there is political mass mobilization and that political influence of the populace increases due to democratization, attitudes of those dominated become more important, and this study takes this into account.

The ideal-type of modern domination is legal-rational authority. It is based on the "belief in the legality of enacted rules and the right of those elevated to authority under such rules to issue commands" (ibid., 215). This is possible because of a conception of laws, rules and regulations that considers these not as transcendental imperatives, but as contingent decisions amenable by human beings.

The mode of administration corresponding to legal-rational domination is bureaucratic. A bureaucracy is defined by its impersonal character, and the core characteristics of a bureaucracy are oriented towards upholding that character. Keeping written records, rule-bound decisions informed by records, clear hierarchies, specified spheres of competence, above-average salaries, and staff trained to understand laws and regulations determining administrative decisions are key features of bureaucracy. Officials are subject to systematic control and disciplinary action oriented toward fulfillment of impersonal office obligations (ibid., 218–221).

Statehood is a precondition for modern democracy in a fundamental way. Violence needs to be monopolistically and centrally controlled in order to subject it to democratic control. Just as importantly, administrative staff must be qualified and motivated to impose democratically decided laws uniformly on a population, politics must be a public rather than a secret elite affair, and a functional modern judicial system is integral to modern democracy, to name only the most obvious institutional features (cf. Bendel/Krennerich 2003; cf. Hyden 2000). Ideal-typical patterns of traditional domination thus contradict modern democracy.

"Authority will be called traditional if legitimacy is claimed for it and believed in by virtue of the sanctity of age-old rules and powers. The masters are designated according to traditional rules and are obeyed because of their traditional status (*Eigenwürde*)" (Weber 1978a, 226). Of particular relevance for Liberia, Weber distinguishes two primary ideal-types of traditional domination: gerontocracy and primary patriarchal domination.

"The term gerontocracy is applied to a situation where so far as rule over the group is organized at all it is in the hands of elders—which originally was understood literally as the eldest in actual years, who are the most familiar with the sacred traditions. This is common in groups which are not primarily of an economic or kinship character. 'Patriarchalism' is the situation where, within a group (household) which is usually organized on both an economic and a kinship basis, a particular individual governs who is designated by a definite rule of inheritance. Gerontocracy and patriarchalism are frequently found side by side. The decisive characteristic of both is the belief of the members that domination, even though it is an inherent traditional right of the master, must definitely be exercised as a joint right in the interest of all members and is thus not freely appropriated by the incumbent. In order that this shall be maintained, it is crucial that in both cases there is a complete absence of a personal (patrimonial) staff. Hence the master is still largely dependent upon the willingness of the members to comply with his orders since he has no machinery to enforce them. Therefore, the members (*Genossen*) are not really subjects (*Untertanen*)." (ibid., 231)

Concerning domination in gerontocracies, Weber stressed that his remarks only apply "so far as" there is domination "at all" (ibid.). It is thus typical of this ideal-type that domination is weak. African communities with strong gerontocratic and patriarchal traits have frequently been called acephalous because of this. As the ruler or the ruling elders do not dispose of staff personally loyal to them who could enforce decisions, respect for decisions is dependent on the will of community members. The members have to be convinced of the righteousness of a decision, and forums for the creation of social pressure need to be put in place. As a consequence, decisions are frequently taken collectively (palaver) or by a chief, following discussions of qualified members.[11] Ethnologists concerned with Africa have often categorized these forms of political organization as "democracy" (on Liberia: cf. Moran 2006). What is important is that there is no recognizable staff as such. In the north-west of Liberia, secret traditional elite institutions, such as the "Leopards", who are considered transcendental beings in popular thought, do, however, play an important role in sanctioning challenges to patriarchal and gerontocratic authority. These may be conceptualized as embryonic patrimonial staff. Forms of authority fade over into each other. In empirical politics, there is no irreconcilable antagonism between different types of authority.

Patrimonialism, an ideal-typical sub-type of traditional domination, evolves out of other (typically patriarchal) forms of authority when a

11 Gender, age, initiation, etc., may all be criteria for qualification.

power holder succeeds in establishing personally loyal administrative staff able to enforce decisions. Contrasting patrimonialism and bureaucracies as modes of administration of power, the former is characterized by the absence of a distinction between public and private, as well as the all-dominant importance of personal relations between ruler and staff (Weber 1978a, 231–241). A key defining feature is the treatment of a realm as a private patrimony (ibid., 244). Weber considered the ruler to be "free to do good turns on the basis of his personal pleasure and likes, particularly in return for gifts" in the latter sphere (ibid.).

However, the ruler's discretionary sphere of action tends to become progressively restrained due to the creation of relations of mutual obligations. Reciprocal exchange of unequal goods creating personal ties is a principle universally found in traditional societies. As intermediary staff are institutionalized, exchange takes on the form of granting privileges in return for political loyalty. Exchange of values, regularly taking on the symbolically enriched material form of gifts, may appear as a totally voluntary act, yet traditional rules of reciprocity bind both parties (Mauss 1954, 10–12). Morally, the ruler is not free to reciprocate or not, leading to regularization of domination (Jung 1995, 135). This is due to the gift having more than an economic quality; it remains linked to the giver, and exchange creates a "spiritual bond" with the receiver (Mauss 1954, 11). As for Sub-Saharan Africa, reciprocal exchange has been considered the very foundation of political patterns (Chabal 2009; cf. Bayart 1993).[12]

These considerations are useful for clarifying the notion of patrimonialism. In my interpretation, the core characteristic of patrimonialism is the creation of legitimacy by establishing complex personal bonds of loyalty, making use of the traditional principle of reciprocal exchange of unequal values. This implies that there is no distinction between public and private, that the "authoritative allocation of values" (Easton 1953) takes place through personal relations patterning the administration of power, and that clientelism is an integral feature of patrimonialism. There are no public goods in a modern sense. Patrimonialism further implies that there are no universal rights. Justice means

12 This may be due to comprehensive political changes in the course and aftermath of colonial rule, when an extraordinary variety of political systems was integrated into the uniform model of the (post-)colonial state. Reciprocal exchange may be the major traditional principle that survived.

treating persons differently according to social status rather than respecting their equal rights as citizens (cf. Mungiu-Pippidi 2006).

Variants of patrimonialism diverge strongly in a number of respects. An important difference is that in degrees of centralization of domination. "In the case of pure patrimonialism, there is complete separation of the functionary from the means of carrying out his function" (Weber 1978a, 234). The paramount ruler personally controls all economic opportunities, and private prerogatives are controlled and discretionarily allocated by him. Providing the means of administration both increases the need for the ruler to personally acquire patrimonial revenue and his ability to control patrimonial staff. This correlates with staff subsistence being assured by "living from the lord's table" or receiving discretionary "allowances (usually in kind) from the lord's magazines or treasury" (ibid., 235).

By contrast, in the "estate-type of patrimonialism", the "administrative staff appropriates particular powers and the corresponding economic assets" (ibid., 232) and "has personal control of the means of administration" (ibid., 234). Then, individuals making up the patrimonial staff live "by the appropriation of property income, fees or taxes" or from exploiting fiefs (ibid., 235). Whenever lower ranking holders of authority privately appropriate authority, patrimonial authority tends to disintegrate. Legitimacy is created through the exchange of rights to appropriation against loyalty, but it is compromised and opportunities of the ruler to impose his will are severely limited. "Feudal patrimonialism" and "prebendal patrimonialism" are borderline cases but nevertheless fall under the patrimonial paradigm (cf. ibid., 255–262). Such *decentralized patrimonialism* and the associated weak legitimacy of the central ruler imply deficits in control. It is often (though not necessarily) spatially manifested and more pronounced in the periphery of polities.

Patrimonial rule historically progressively developed legal-rational features. "Bureaucracy has first developed in patrimonial states with a body of officials recruited from extra-patrimonial sources [i.e. individuals not compelled to personal loyalty as enshrined in the traditional social order] but [...] these officials were at first personal servants[13] of their masters" (ibid., 229). As these officials lacked traditional status (*Eigenwürde*), they were prevented from legitimately appropriating governing powers.

13 The term used in the English edition is "followers" to stress the element of legitimacy, but the German original reads "Diener", which is more appropriately translated as "servant" (and here, the element of obedience deserves emphasis).

Patrimonialism, as a subtype and mode of administration of traditionally legitimized domination, needs to be differentiated from charismatic domination. Charismatic domination is legitimized trough the belief of subjects in the extraordinary qualities of a leader (ibid., 241). These qualities may be of different kinds. We can therefore talk of clerical charisma, scientific charisma, warrior charisma, etc. This belief is created as a consequence of the interplay of individuals with charismatic talent and subjects. That is, charismatic leaders have a personal quality that has to be distinguished from charisma. Charismatic talent, e.g. the ability to talk in a fashion that elates crowds or persuades people, enables us to analyze the way in which the belief in charisma is created.

The lack of administrative continuity, cohesion and regularity is a defining feature of charismatic administration (ibid., 243). The relationship between ruler and staff can be likened to that between prophet and disciples. Administrative staff are chosen according to inspirations of the ruler identifying charismatic talent of "disciples". In contrast to traditional and bureaucratic domination, charismatic domination is "specifically revolutionary" (ibid). Charismatic leaders seek to introduce innovations, and thus are typical agents of social and political change. Importantly, the leader maintains an eminent position. The staff is personally loyal to him and does not appropriate governing powers, much less use these as individually appropriated economic advantages (ibid.).

Charismatic domination is incompatible with everyday routine and is a transient phenomenon characterizing periods of accelerated social change. It thus becomes routinized, i.e. "either traditionalized or rationalized, or a combination of both" (ibid., 246). Although charisma was a prominent category for analysis of African politics during the period of decolonization, the transient character of charismatic domination evidenced in the lack of "personal charismatic appeal [or] a sense of mission" (Roth 1968, 196) on the part of most new state elites has led scholars to dismiss it as a useful tool and to turn to patrimonialism instead.

On a higher level of abstraction, the ideal-types of traditional and charismatic domination in fact both follow a traditional "patterning pattern", that of personal relations. The distinction between personal and impersonal, the latter bearing the connotation of rational, formal and abstract, is fundamental to constructing ideal-types of traditional and modern societies (Siegelberg 1994, 37–38).[14] The term *personal relations* designates a structuring principle characterized by social organization around persons or personified forces (e.g. gods, kings and ghosts).

> "The structuring principle of personal relations cannot be equated with so-called face-to-face relations, i.e. direct interactions [or personal ties] [...]. Personal relations may, but do not need to be relations between persons who are personally acquainted. The personal character of traditional societies is not based on actual direct contacts between persons, but on the cognitive realization of society as a pantheon of personifications. [...] Constellations of persons, rather than abstract terms and patterns, do represent social relations of power in traditional societies." (Jung 1995, 158, translation F.G.)

2.1.2. Non-legitimate Domination

Weber's elaborations on different subtypes of patrimonialism can be considered as drawing a continuum between two extreme borderline cases of traditional legitimate domination. On one end of the continuum lies feudalism, an extreme version of estate-type patrimonialism, and on the other sultanism (Hensell 2009, 52). Feudalism is characterized by almost total appropriation of governing powers by intermediary staff who owe their position to traditional social status, absorbing the legitimacy of the paramount ruler (Weber 1978a, 255–256). Although feudal staff's use of power diminishes the power of the center, domination remains legitimate albeit on a local level. In the case of sultanism, there are very few traditional restraints on the ruler's power, and the scope for discretionary action is consequently extremely large (ibid., 232). In order to establish an ideal-type of illegitimate domination, this section isolates techniques of rule that allow for a widening of the sphere of discretion. In reference to Reno (1998), the ideal-type is termed *warlord politics*.

What distinguishes "the warlord from traditional leaders such as tribal chieftains, traditional notables, or landlords [is] the fact that he [... is] not bound to the people under his domination by the reciprocal norms of traditional societies" (Jung 2003, 20, cf. MacKinlay 2000, 49). Ideal-

14 The terms "tradition" and "modernity" as employed in this study are conceived as analytical ideal-types. In this perspective, societies in Europe, North America, parts of Asia-Pacific, and probably elsewhere too, largely work according to modern principles, but are replete with continuously re-invented and remodeled traditional patterns, and often exhibit some features of charismatic rule too.

typically, a patrimonial ruler seeks to integrate the whole populace into clientelistic networks expressing reciprocal relations (Reno 1998).[15] By contrast, a warlord seeks to reduce the number of those benefiting from rule to an absolute minimum. Exclusion from patronage networks is classically associated with a loss of legitimacy. In warlord politics, exclusion is intended to increase the relative value of the spoils of power by causing greater scarcity, optimizing the cost-benefit ratio of patronage. Consequently, decreasing levels of patronage can be reconciled with maintenance of a ruling network.

"To make patronage work as a means of political control, the ruler must prevent all individuals from gaining unregulated access to markets. A […] [warlord] ruler thus logically seeks to make life *less secure* and *more materially impoverished* for subjects. That is, a […] [warlord] ruler will minimize his provision of public goods to a population. Removing public goods, like security or economic stability, that are otherwise enjoyed by all, irrespective of their economic or political station, is done to encourage individuals to seek the ruler's personal favor to secure exemption from these conditions." (Reno 2000, 46–47, italics original)[16]

The withdrawal of security and economic opportunities has stabilizing consequences that may temporarily make up for destabilizing tendencies. By withdrawing security and economic opportunities, social and material capacities for resistance are weakened. As internal sources of economic accumulation and opportunities for social organization are destroyed, insurgents face tremendous difficulties unless they can find external backers. Other warlord techniques include fuelling of conflict between domestic groups and thus reducing security, deliberate destruction of sources of income, and filling security forces with vulnerable strangers without ties to the populace in terms of culture, ethnicity and religion (Weber 1978b, 1017–1018). Further, in order to prevent military staff from overthrowing the ruler, the security apparatus is fragmented and its different segments compete for the ruler's favors. Ideal-typically, staff are tied to the ruler purely by economic incentives, i.e. *zweckrationale* interests. Exchange of

15 Clientelism is a pyramidal system of exchange of unequal values. Its basic units are personal dyadic relations. The values allocated by the higher ranking party are termed patronage.

16 For reasons of congruence, I have replaced the term "shadow state" with "warlord" in the quotation. In the quoted publication, Reno himself stated that "elsewhere" (i.e. in Reno 1998), he used "the term warlord politics [to describe] shadow states" (Reno 2000, 47).

values has the character of economically rational transactions and staff do not believe in the legitimacy of the ruler.

Warlord techniques may stabilize rule for considerable periods of time. However, destruction of economic opportunities implies that that there is little potential for revenue growth, and that warlord rule will encounter financial problems. Further, in practice not all sources of revenues can be controlled or destroyed, and the lack of legitimacy renders warlord rule vulnerable, in particular to external challenges. As warlord politics is inimical to the regularity of bureaucratic and traditional rule, it is likely to be combined with charismatic legitimacy. When charisma erodes, it may be substituted for by routinization, an increase in warlord politics techniques, or both. A disproportionate increase in warlord politics techniques is particularly likely when resources for a routinization of charisma are lacking. As warlord politics, patrimonial authority and charismatic domination share the pattern of personal relations as dominant organizing principles, switches between these types are much easier than the transformation to bureaucracy.

2.1.3. The Empirical State

Ideal-types are heuristic tools and, as analytical abstractions, serve to distinguish principles, but do not, in their pure, unmitigated form exist in real, contemporary social-political life. Thus, the state as structuring the international system deviates from statehood as an analytical ideal.

In studies on Africa and the Middle East especially, the real-type of the neo-patrimonial state is widely used to analyze and describe the real-world dynamics of domination. Yet, despite its extensive use, there is little consensus on its key features.[17] However, the prefix "neo" designates diverging aberrations from patrimonialism (Erdmann/Engel 2007, 95–104) and drawing on Weber's political sociology, neo-patrimonialism thus is a hybrid form of governance featuring patrimonial and bureaucratic patterns, since the latter are specifically modern and thus justify using the prefix (cf. ibid., 105). However, as ideal-types do not, by definition, appear in reality in their pure form, some mixture characterizes most states.

17 Important contributions to the debate are Clapham (1985); Eisenstadt/Lemarchand (1981); Médard (1982); Roth (1968); Theobald (1982); Walle (1994).

Semantically, the term stresses patrimonial features at the expense of a modern element. In neo-patrimonial states, patrimonial patterns are dominant but bureaucratic elements exist. Patrimonial features clash with bureaucratic rationality, engendering the bending, circumvention and violation of bureaucratic norms. Disciplinary action is oriented towards assuring personal loyalty and obedience first and foremost, and not administrative rationality. The role of bureaucratic institutions often is to define spheres of responsibility, which in turn determine realms of appropriation.

The association between traditional legitimacy and patrimonial administration implies that the latter is not just a default option occasioned by a lack of resources to build legal-rational structures. In order to assure stability on the basis of personal connections, these need to be grounded in wider cultural systems of legitimacy-generating reciprocity.

In order to distinguish neo-patrimonial states from essentially bureaucratic ones, a quantification of patrimonial and bureaucratic elements would be helpful. So far, only a few laudable efforts have been made to operationalize patrimonialism (cf. Basedau 2003; cf. Therkildsen 2005), and none of these is fully convincing. For instance, absence of democratic elections and concentration of powers in a paramount ruler (cf. Bratton/Walle 1994) are not defining features of patrimonialism. Patrimonialism is expressed in patterns of authority rather than the way of coming to power and (even) *decentralized patrimonialism* may be combined with legal-rational features of rule. Patrimonial staff may have appropriated wide-ranging powers and the neo-patrimonial president may be of rather symbolic importance. High public sector salaries may indicate patrimonial (cf. Therkildsen 2005) as well as bureaucratic principles.

I do, however, want to propose a few questions that could be useful for operationalizing neo-patrimonialism. When it comes to the crunch and patrimonial and bureaucratic norms conflict, which principles determine administrative or juridical decision (cf. Conrad 2006)? More specifically, when *Big Men* privileges clash with codified law, how often do courts rule against elite interests? To what extent does qualification, merit and, if applicable, seniority play a role in public sector employment and promotion, and to what extent do personal ties take precedence? Which proportion of revenues acquired by governing powers flows through personal channels, and how much goes through formal channels? What proportion of tax revenue is bureaucratically accounted for? As a proportion of the governing powers' revenue, how much is spent on public goods, and how much is privatized? If indicators consistently tend towards the patrimonial side, we may speak of neo-patrimonialism, provided domination is legitimate. The question here is whether patrimonial features effectively stabilize political power, or whether staff do not show loyalty in return for being accorded privileges. Evidently, this data is hard to get, but nonetheless these questions help clarifying the notion of neo-patrimonialism.

Moving away from the narrow focus on Weber's political sociology, in more general terms the empirical state can be characterized as a field of action, the manifestations of which are informed by a global ideal of statehood and national practices of rule. Contemporary political actors themselves exhibit a social habitus that is partly informed by universal modern ideas and principles, and partly by locally specific notions. In consequence, the state is a space within which power is organized and which its principles oscillate between a global ideal of modern statehood and specific national patterns (Schlichte 2005, 84–111).

2.2. State Formation, State Erosion and Society

State formation involves two complementary processes that diverge analytically and in historical sequencing. The first one is extension of central authority, which is a non-linear process intermittently subject to retrenchment. The second one is that of society imposing itself on the state, effectively enhancing its power by strengthening legitimacy.

2.2.1. State-Building and State Decay

Historically, state-building has been a highly violent process. Charles Tilly (1985) analyses European state-building as the unintended outcome of violent actions by self-seeking political entrepreneurs. At the core of his reflections is the widely recognized intrinsic association between the emergence of monopolistic control over the means of violence and the emergence of a centrally-controlled, coherent system of taxation. In his perspective, "war making", "extraction" of values, "protection" of sources of income and "state-making" are interwoven processes entailing a consolidation of central, sovereign power in the long run (ibid., 183). Ideal-typically, four stages of political economy development can be distinguished: A "period of anarchy and plunder" tending to destroy necessary sources of revenue is followed by a "stage in which tribute takers attracted customers and established their monopolies by struggling to create exclusive, substantial states" as extraction becomes more regularized and sustainable (ibid., 176). Likening state-makers to organized crime, Tilly describes those of this stage as a "protection racket" of which the "customer" is a victim (ibid.). Relative security due to these monopolies and consequent economic development is translated into a "stage in which merchants and landlords began to gain more from protection rents than governors did from tribute". Eventually, "technological changes surpassed protection rents as sources of profits for entrepreneurs" (ibid., 177).

Describing similar processes, Elias (1999; 2006a) introduced the terms *configuration*, *survival unit*, and *free competition* into his analysis of state-building processes. A configuration is characterized by interdependencies between the people within it. Of interest here are configurations which universally group human beings and which Elias proposes as *tertium comparationis* for the comparative analysis of societies. Of major importance is the *survival unit* (*Überlebenseinheit*), which is an essentially political entity. It is characterized by the control of the use of violence in relations between its members, as well as relations between the unit and the outside world. Other pertinent units are those of material and symbolic reproduction. In human life, both assuring subsistence and generating symbolic systems that allow communication and cooperation are social matters (Elias 2006b). Linkages between survival units and units of material reproduction constitute what is conventionally called political economy.[18] The configuration analyzed in this study is Liberia, a unit characterized by a political center linking its various elements through competition for sovereign state power as well as an unequal distribution of the costs and benefits of that central power.

Configurations are inherently characterized by internal imbalances, inter alia in terms of power and wealth. These imbalances render internal patterns of configurations dynamic, given that people try to improve their position and thereby force their rivals to re-organize in order to defend

18 My analysis would profit greatly from integrating symbolic reproduction, as thoughts, ideas and attitudes impact heavily on political and economic strategies. I do mention some important elements of Liberian political thought, but providing a history of symbolic reproduction is beyond the scope of this study. Yoder (2003) and Ellis (2007) in particular provide interesting insights in this respect.

their status. Internal competition is a key feature of configurations (Elias 2006a, 170–176). Although directional, political development is a contingent process dependent on the imposition and marginalization of sociopolitical forces. Elias proposes to develop dynamic terms with which to analyze fluctuations of power that both characterize and determine political development, and has criticized the ideal-typical method as static thinking (ibid). However, ideal-types do not represent a static reality. They are heuristic instruments, allowing us to identify principles between which real political life fluctuates. In this study, ideal-types and changes in degree of manifestation are used as markers indicating shifts in the societal distribution of power. The empirical part of this study essentially is an analysis of shifts of power within the Liberian configuration.

Elias conceives early state-building as an elimination contest between competing survival units. This early phase is termed *free competition* (Elias 1999, 163). Violent political conflict during this phase aims at destroying a rival unit, absorbing its resources and expanding one's own unit. Physical insecurity and economic scarcity forces survival units to accumulate resources, entailing violent conflict between them. In terms of political economy, victory enables one of the actors to appropriate economic resources that were formerly controlled by its rival. Military victory thus translates into accumulation of values, which in turn translates into increased military capacities. As a consequence, a self-feeding cycle of monopolization of the means of violence and monopolization of value extraction unfolds. The sequence of war, victory, accumulation of values and renewed war is termed a political *monopoly mechanism*. As it works repeatedly, it shapes societies over extended periods of time, giving direction to political change (Elias 1999, 151–168). This directional process is not, however, a straightforward one. While Elias stresses elimination of rivals as the core process of state-building, Tilly provides a more nuanced view, attributing equal importance to "conquest, alliance, chicanery, argument, [...] administrative encroachment" and co-optation, all being backed up by military power (Tilly 1975a, 636; cf. Tilly 1985).

As authority is becoming more institutionalized, competition is no longer free but framed by prior processes of accumulation of power. Political conflict increasingly is about controlling rather than destroying established structures of power (Elias 1999, 213–230). Greater institutional continuity leads to increasing and more complex interdependencies. Complex interdependencies involve subjects, segments of the populace, and rulers. As a consequence, the ruler becomes more dependent upon those ruled. State-building, hitherto primarily a process of extension and imposition of centralized power on society (*Durchstaatlichung der Gesellschaft*), is complemented by a process of society imposing itself on the state (*Vergesellschaftung des Staates*) (Siegelberg 2000, 12; Elias 1999, 156–157). This may take place through extension of patrimonial clientelistic relationships. The specific modern expressions of *Vergesellschaftung des Staates* are nationalism and liberal democracy. The more power is constrained through complex interdependencies and (consequently) the more the accumulation of values takes place in society rather than at the center of political power, the less political conflict will be about personal control of political power and the more it will concern societal distribution of costs and benefits of the monopoly of violence. This implies a depersonalization of the administration of power.

Liberian state-building was, in one vital aspect, more similar to the European experience than it was to state-building in most other African states. Liberia was not colonized by another state, and extension of sovereign authority proceeded largely without recourse to resources of a developed capitalist economy. While European state-building was characterized by a closely interwoven process of domestic revenue extraction and consolidation of authority, African state-building was, to a large extent, a consequence of European colonialism. More specifically, relatively well-developed domestic economies provided superior resources to European states, which were thus able to conquer African territories. In times of crisis, the center's resources in terms of military technology, economic values and administrative knowledge could be drawn on. Colonial rule did not need to be consolidated to the same extent as state-makers had been forced to do in Europe. However, decolonization, completing a vital step in the emergence of a worldwide state system, can be seen as analogous to a conventional pattern of overstretching and retrenchment of central rule. While "economies of scale in the production of effective force" allow progressive extension of central authority, "diseconomies of scale in control and command" (Tilly 1985, 177) put limits to that extension. State power reaches its limits where "the costs of communication and control exceed the returns from the periphery" (Tilly 1975a, 636).

In the post-colonial states thus created, competition was no longer free, but framed by the colonial legacy. Nonetheless, the dynamics of extension and retrenchment of central authority remain very acute in the 21st century.

The equilibrium, or, in Elias' terms, the unstable balance, between economies and diseconomies of scale is determined by a number of factors. Most important among these are administrative patterns, the state of technology (ibid., 636), location and character of natural resources,[19] world market integration, interdependencies, and degrees of cultural difference and homogeneity of the peoples of a conquered territory (cf. Tilly 1975a; 1992; cf. Elias 1999). It can be argued that colonialism could endure as long as it did because of interdependencies Bayart (2000) termed *extraversion*.

"The leading actors in sub-Saharan societies have tended to compensate for their difficulties in the autonomization of their power and in intensifying the exploitation of their dependents by deliberate recourse to the strategies of extraversion, mobilizing resources derived from their (possibly unequal) relationship with the external environment. The external environment thus turned into a major resource in the process of political centralization and economic accumulation." (Bayart 2000, 218–219)

Access to externally-generated power resources, which, in post-colonial times, has taken on the form of politically motivated transfers from former colonial powers, military and financial Cold War patronage, development assistance, and natural resource rents (cf. Bayart 2000), is widely considered the key political economy variable that engenders weak statehood. Political and economic rents allow rulers to refrain from building legitimacy among lower status strata. There is little need to minimize tax evasion and build costly bureaucratic administrations in order to monitor transactions that could be taxed. By contrast, rents allow the establishing of patrimonial

19 Auty (2001) introduced the distinction between diffuse and point resources. Diffuse resources are spread over large areas, and their extraction does not necessitate control over a particular area. Diffuse resources tend to finance rebel groups who can occupy places at the margins of government control. Billon (2001) extends this typology by adding the dimensions of, from the government's point of view, distant and proximate resources. A resource close to the capital city is less likely to be captured by rebels than is a resource close to a border (ibid., 570). As will become clear in the empirical chapters, investment costs play an important role too. Capital intensive activities, such as iron ore and crude oil extraction, tend not to be undertaken in times of war, as potential losses due to destruction are extremely high. When undertaken in situations of instability, these activities tend to take place under government control and help to finance the sovereign state, because legality offers superior opportunities for ensuring or hedging investment costs. Further, large firms able to mobilize significant capital are vulnerable to lawsuits brought against them by sovereign governments for supporting rebel groups.

clientelistic networks and the financing of a disproportionately strong repressive apparatus.[20] Yet states in Africa are comparatively young, and the population density, low levels of which historically prevented centralization of power and extension of interdependencies (cf. Kelsall 2005), is rising.

In the post-Cold War era, internal wars were often understood as projects of political entrepreneurs who are interested in personal economic benefit and creating legitimacy by asserting sectarian identities that contradict national integration (Kaldor 1999; Münkler 2002; 2006). The perspective of war as a profitable economic enterprise has been argued most prominently by Collier and Hoeffler (Collier 2000; Collier/Hoeffler 2004). Adding a Weberian political economy perspective, Reno argued that internal wars could be understood as—quite likely durable—re-inventions of non-sovereign patrimonial fiefs after the sudden withdrawal of Cold War patronage had engendered the demise of post-colonial neo-patrimonial patterns (Reno 1998; 2000; on Liberia: Reno 1995). Yet internal wars in the 1990s have lasted less long than wars during the Cold War era, indicating that wars based on autonomous natural resource exploitation are economically less sustainable than international patronage-based ones (Staines 2004). After an initial rise in wars as Cold War dependent regimes crumbled and competition for the spoils of power increased, the incidence of civil war has more than halved between 1993 and 2008 (Schreiber 2009).

This makes sense, considering that the production of violence continues to enjoy large economies of scale, and that competition between insecure war actors inevitably compels them to accumulate as many resources as possible. Although warring parties "may have a shared interest in war" (Keen 1998, 73; cf. Keen 2000), cooperation is unlikely to be stable. The least we could say is that "warfare does not automatically lead to a strengthening or weakening of the state" (Schlichte 2003, 38), and often, monopoly mechanism dynamics continue to work.

State formation has historically taken place in parallel with the emergence of the international system of states, which was an evidently international phenomenon. Part of the explanation is that, ever since the Peace of Westphalia, statehood has been an expectation held by the major actors in the international system, and has been rewarded in terms of privileged access to diplomatic resources (cf. Siegelberg 2000).

---

20 Cf. Tilly (1975a, 638); Reno (1998); Ross (1999); Auty (2001); Schlichte (2005, 182–215).

States continue to be important actors in the international system, they and other actors still hold statehood as an expectation, and statehood is still rewarded internationally. This is evident from the privileged diplomatic access of sovereign states, development assistance, bilateral and multilateral state-building support programs, and access to international credit as well as debt relief. Further, warlords and even heads of sovereign states who were considered to have violated principles of statehood and destabilized the international state system have recently been put before international courts.[21] All in all, there remains a premium on the state, giving it a competitive advantage over alternative models of political organization. As international mechanisms supporting the state work repeatedly over extended periods of time, the maintenance of sovereign states as organizations "controlling the principal means of coercion within a given territory, which [are] differentiated from other organizations operating in the same territory, autonomous, centralized and formally coordinated" (Tilly 1975a, 638) is a strong probability.

Concerning bureaucratic institution building, Young States are frequently subject to processes that, although deviating from the European experience, are not altogether different. A major development in the Occident was the disempowerment of traditional local power holders, particularly as a consequence of destruction and flight in the Thirty Years War (Siegelberg 2000, 15). Equally important was the replacement of patrimonial bonds through development of capitalist relations of production, notably in the wake of mass expulsions motivated by capitalist *mise en valeur* of lands (cf. Marx 1987, Chapter 23 + 24). Similar processes characterize natural resource exploitation in Young States, although rents nowadays may offer more opportunities for establishing patrimonial bonds. Further, ongoing interests of rulers in accumulation of power provide incentives to dispossess staff of personal rights to governing powers (Weber 1978a, 229).[22] Probably the most important development in Europe, however, has been the autonomization of the bureaucracy, as civil service staff have become the major social base of the state (cf. Siegelberg 2000, 22; cf. Schlichte 2005). The importance of the modern, "*évolué*" element for state domination in Africa is widely recognized, but the state's reach has not extended far enough for it to circumvent alternative power-holders. There

21 Charles Taylor, prosecuted for supporting rebels in neighboring Sierra Leone (and not for committing human rights violations in Liberia) is a case in point.

22 Rwanda, Ethiopia and Uganda (cf. Tangri/Mwenda 2006) may illustrate dynamics.

are, however, prospects for an extension of central state domination. Furthermore, there is a connection between increasing interdependencies, a shift in the object of political power towards changing the distribution of the costs and benefits of the monopoly on violence, and determining that distribution through universal laws imposed by a bureaucracy.

2.2.2. Society and the State

An important yet historically late dimension of state-building is that of society imposing itself on the state (*Vergesellschaftung des Staates*). Historically, the influence of societal actors on the exercise of governing powers is closely related to the need of the state to tax its population in order to finance rule and legitimize taxation so as to minimize resistance and evasion. The early cultural manifestation of the interlacement of society and the state in Europe has been nationalism, i.e. the process bringing about the "imagined communities" corresponding to the "arbitrary" borders drawn by coercive state-builders (Anderson 2006; Elwert 1989; cf. Siegelberg 2000).[23] Eventually, society's grip on the state has become expressed as liberal democracy in the Occident. In Africa in general and in post-war countries in particular, external democracy support programs, intended to strengthen political legitimacy and consequently promote political stability, have become a major source of revenue. Partly as a consequence of these opportunities offered by external actors, and partly too in response to popular mobilization against governments in power, the incidence of "electoral democracy" has dramatically increased in Africa since the end of the Cold War. In a prominent critique of dynamics of democratization on the continent, Bayart (2000, 226) argues that the "discourse of democracy [...] is no more than yet another source of economic rents, comparable to earlier discourses such as the denunciation of communism or of imperialism in the time of the Cold War, but better adapted to the spirit of the age."

Democratization thus merely allowed the re-establishing of patrimonial patterns, which had been previously put under pressure by the withdrawal of Cold War patronage. Schaffer (1998) proposes that African notions of

23 As Tilly remarked, the fact of Western Europe having been "more culturally homogeneous than any other comparable world area outside of China" since the Roman Empire (Tilly 1992, 4) greatly facilitated the consolidation of "arbitrary" boundaries and the states they contain.

democracy, indeed, refer first of all to integration of ordinary subjects into systems of patronage. The dynamics criticized by Bayart would thus in fact be suitable for African countries. Indeed, democratization in Africa appears to entail an increase in "corruption" (Lindberg 2003; Mungiu-Pippidi 2006; cf. Pech 2009, 22–24). "Corruption" as an inherently normative term is different from patrimonialism, but, inasmuch as it refers to the lack of a distinction between public and private, both do overlap. The increase in corruption is due to an increase in political competition, expressed as "competitive clientelism" (Berg-Schlosser 2005, 319) or "competitive particularism" (Mungiu-Pippidi 2006, 89).

In the long run, democracy appears to entail decreasing levels of corruption (Blake/Martin 2006). As part of this process, the "authoritative allocation of values" (Easton 1953) increasingly takes place in the form of provision of collective and eventually public goods, as opposed to private patronage (Bueno de Mesquita et al. 2002). The basic democratic institution of regular elections entails a mobilization of citizens, supporting democracy in the medium to long run (Lindberg 2006). Political mobilization increases the costs of vote buying and other forms of private patronage provision, engendering superior cost effectiveness of provision of public goods (Bueno de Mesquita et al. 2002). Administering these necessitates bureaucratic institutions. This, however, is dependent on intermediating authorities not holding sufficient power to guarantee the voting patterns of their clients (ibid.). It further necessitates moderate insecurity on the part of the elites, i.e. insecurity sufficient to compel them to generate legitimacy through allocation of values, but not as great as to cause short-term considerations to overshadow longer-term objectives (cf. Pech 2009, 22). There is a relevant degree of individualism in Liberia, and a limited power of intermediate authorities to guarantee election outcomes (cf. Sawyer 2008), but also a high degree of elite insecurity.

As mentioned above, contemporary Western notions of democracy require an effective bureaucracy. However, this has not always been the case. Weber himself considered bureaucratic authority to be a form of administration with possible negative consequences for participation and liberties, and hardly thought about it in terms of democratic potential. Firstly, bureaucratic authority made possible a degree of government control over society hardly imaginable in previous times, and relations of power were devoid of any personal bond between rulers and ruled that could constrain the former. Second, the specific knowledge of bureaucrats could become a superior power resource vis-à-vis an elected government. There was thus a danger of uncontrolled appropriation of powers by bureaucratic staff (Schönberger 2007, 162). There are some similarities to this situation in both Western Europe and Japan.[24] Such a situation would have been diametrically opposed to democratic rule as conceptualized by Weber. Weber tended to assimilate democratic rule to charismatic domination. The democratic ruler whom he imagined was a populist, plebiscitary ruler "who would influence masses in an emotional and irrational way" (ibid., translation F.G.). Weber's notion thus came close to what has been termed "delegative democracy" and is considered an inherently flawed type of democracy (cf. O'Donnell 1994). We may, however, note that notions of democracy that do not presuppose an effective bureaucracy have their precursors in Europe. Similarly, such notions may be particularly attractive at grassroots level in societies with weak bureaucracies. From a normative point of view, "neo-patrimonial democracy" may be an improvement over authoritarian neo-patrimonialism and warlord rule. In order to justify the term, general elections must allow for the possibility of deposition of rulers. Hence this type of democracy may be one of the forms by which society's grip on the state at the periphery is assured in a much more institutionalized way than it has been in classical post-colonial neo-patrimonialism.

Weak bureaucratic institutions imply that the legal-rational arrangements considered defining features of liberal democracy, in particular the rule of law (cf. Dahl 1998), exhibit considerable deficits. This, however, tells little about whether a political system becomes more democratic or not. Rather, we have to investigate processes underlying democratization. Defining a democratic regime in procedural (rather than institutional) terms, it qualifies as "democratic to the degree that political relations between the state and its citizens feature broad, equal, protected and mutually binding consultation" (Tilly 2008, 13–14; italics omitted). Democratization thus means execution of processes promoting the broad, equal, protected and mutually binding character of consultation (ibid., 15). According to Tilly, three major processes underlie democratization. These are an "increase […] of integration between interpersonal networks of trust […] and public politics", an "increase […] in the insulation from public politics of the major categorical inequalities […] around which citizens

24 In this perspective, Japan, frequently termed a society without a state, appears as a very strong bureaucratic state without a government (cf. Boyd 2006).

organize their daily lives", and an "decrease in the autonomy of major power centers (especially those wielding significant coercive means) such as warlords, patron-client chains, armies, and religious institutions with respect to public politics" (ibid., 23).

Historically, trust networks have shielded themselves from power holders in order to avoid seizure of their resources or loss of autonomy but the segregation of trust networks from regimes blocked their members' "commitment to collective democratic enterprises" (ibid., 74). The observation that democracy frequently is stable despite massive but not politically articulated inequalities leads Tilly to conclude that any "democratization process depends not necessarily on diminution of categorical inequalities but on insulation of public politics from categorical inequality" (ibid., 75). Finally, autonomy of power centers undermines the broad, equal, protected and mutually binding character of consultation (ibid., 76). These procedural criteria help to determine whether political integration of dominated people increases in a state with weak bureaucratic institutions and consequently whether the integrative dimension of state-building is being strengthened.

2.2.3. A Note on Sequences of Domination

Political trajectories in Young States cannot be assumed to mirror those experienced in the Occident. As a consequence of the global spread of modernity, *inter alia* through colonialism, and its confrontation with societies organized on the basis of traditional modes of political and economic reproduction, the simultaneous existence of modern and traditional patterns characterizes peripheral societies. This, however, should not lead us to consider these societies as either intrinsically traditional-patrimonial (cf. Chabal/Daloz 1999; 2006) or stubbornly neo-patrimonial. There are important differences between types of neo-patrimonial organization.

As a heuristic tool for analyzing processes of social change, Braudel (1984) proposes to distinguish three layers of historicity. These are the *longue durée* stretching over centuries, *conjonctures* typically rising and falling within decades, and *histoire événementielle*, i.e. singular events and their immediate consequences. Much as did Elias (2006b), he deplored a focus by contemporary social analysis on short-term phenomena and a lack of reflection on how these are embedded in long-term trends.

Braudel hardly offers criteria to distinguish between the layers but proposes to consider the era of trade-based capitalism a distinct *longue durée* period (Braudel 1984, 196). A major feature of that period was accumulation based on trade rather than a cycle of knowledge creation, investment, and superior production (cf. Marx 1987, Chapters 1–3). Natural resource economies realize profits in trade rather than production. In a Marxian sense, natural resources are not produced but extracted. They are generated as a consequence of ecological processes that can be influenced by investment in a very limited way only. Natural resources thus are scarce, which creates rents that are prone to appropriation by way of control over the means of force (cf. Auty 2001). Similarly, agricultural goods are dependent on ecological variables and seasonal cycles that investment has no impact on. Rulers are thus not dependent on promoting conditions that support knowledge creation and investment. Relevant for war economies, capital concerned with natural resource extraction cannot relocate when conditions deteriorate (cf. Billon 2001, 569).

In this sense, Liberia's political economy has been characterized by trade-based capitalism throughout. Political power has been based on appropriation of rents that stabilized patrimonial relations. In this sense, Liberia's *longue durée* pattern has been that of neo-patrimonialism. However, there are important differences in political organization below the *longue durée* abstraction. Each of the empirical chapters analyzes a distinct *conjuncture*: the first is *Warlord Rule* and the second *Democratic Neo-patrimonialism.*

3. The First Liberian Civil War: The Rise of Charles Taylor

As I already mentioned, Liberia was not colonized by another state. It was the creation of US American "free men of color" sent to a supposed homeland by private organizations. In the 1820s, first settlements in contemporary Liberia were established. As I have argued elsewhere, Liberian state-building proceeded at break-neck speed, starting from very low foundations. The "Americo-Liberian" project evolved into successively higher, i.e. more extensive and consolidated, domination regimes or *conjonctures*, and in long-term perspective, the civil wars investigated here fit neatly into Liberia's history of state formation (Gerdes 2013). A few features and events providing the background to the civil wars need to be understood.

The formation of the Liberian state was violent and evolved around the antagonism between the "Americo-Liberian" and indigenous groups on its territory. Numerous small-scale indigenous polities were located there and constituted anything but a united force. "Americo-Liberian" hegemony and *de-facto* one-party rule of the *True Whig Party* (TWP) became challenged in the 1970s. "Progressive" organizations, in particular the *Movement for Justice in Africa* (MOJA) and a rival *Progressive Alliance of Liberia* (PAL), formed in settler society and teamed up with modernized indigenous elites. Against the background of the political crisis, President William Tolbert was overthrown in a military coup by indigenous non-commissioned officers in 1980. The coup brought Master-Sergeant Samuel K. Doe to power and started the *conjuncture* of warlord rule. The military government soon split, as internal rivalries developed and army chief Thomas Quiwonkpa was driven into exile by the increasingly repressive ruler. The conflict took on an ethno-regional dimension, as Doe concentrated power in his Krahn originating from eastern Grand Gedeh County, and Mandingo. Quiwonkpa loyalists staged a small raid in 1983 and members of his Gio group from northern Nimba County started being pushed out of the military and the government. Charles Taylor, associated with the "progressive" movement and Quiwonkpa, had held a senior cabinet post and similarly fled the country amid allegations of embezzlement. Doe took the title of president after rigged elections in 1985, and Quiwonkpa tried to fight his way to power the same year. The attack, however, failed and cost him his life. Repression increased, turned more violent and often arbitrarily targeted Nimbaians. Legitimacy of the president eroded further. Eventually in December 1989, Charles Taylor's NPFL attacked the severely weakened government. Doe's Krahn are one of the smallest ethnic groups of Liberia, constituting some five percent of the population, while Nimba is the second-most populous County (after Montserrado containing the capital city Monrovia).

The first Liberian civil war has frequently been perceived as a breakdown of social order and an example of the "coming anarchy" (Kaplan 1994). Scholars, politicians and observers argued that faction leaders and in particular Charles Taylor, did not have an interest in ending the war, as instability offered superior opportunities for accumulation (Montclos 1999, 242; Prkic 2005, 133).

Yet the first Liberian war ended with the (temporary) re-establishment of a central political authority, internationally recognized as the 'state'. Given the fragmentation of the country into fiefs controlled by different armed groups, a remarkable recentralization of authority under the most powerful warlord, Charles Taylor, took place. It is the dynamics of erosion and re-establishment of central authority that this chapter seeks to explain. Some of these dynamics are obvious. In particular, the Liberian civil war was not about how Liberia should develop in the future, i.e. it was not a national project on governance for the benefit of all Liberians. The war was, essentially, an elite struggle for political-military power and associated opportunities for personal enrichment (cf. Ellis 2007a). As evident and widespread this feature of internal wars is, it seems to have puzzled many observers and led to a number of questionable conclusions, as I pointed out in the introduction. Yet the question remains as to what extent these objectives were compatible with a continuous state of war. It remains to be answered why Charles Taylor eventually emerged victorious, and why his rivals lost out. Finally, it has to be analyzed why Liberia descended into war again some three years after Taylor took over the presidency, and to what extent this development calls into question the prospects for Liberia's re-establishment of a central political authority. As I will argue, the decay of the Liberian state had little to do with the economic strategies of war actors and their exploitation and marketing of resources on the world market. In contrast, the state's decay was largely a political phenomenon, sustained by the deliberate and strategic (if often confused and contradictory) involvement of external state actors.

This chapter lays down the argument in four sections. The first section shows the continuity of elimination contests in Liberia. I argue that despite considerable collusion between mutually hostile armed actors, competition remained dominant. A long-term equilibrium between actors did not develop, preventing a settlement and mutual respect between areas of influence. Stronger actors faced incentives to militarily challenge weaker ones and appropriate their power resources. Less powerful actors tried to overcome their weaknesses by establishing alliances with other actors and appropriating the resources of rivals. The weaker actors were thus able to prolong their own existence and consequently continue to fight the war, but in the end had to succumb to an actor more powerful.

Explaining the strengths and weaknesses of armed actors requires taking a closer look at the actors themselves, i.e. their patterns of internal organization of authority and legitimacy, as well as the economic bases of military power. Section 2 takes a detailed look at the most powerful rebel group, Charles Taylor's NPFL. The section is based on a comprehensive review of data on the Liberian war economy and contradicts findings of previous research. In particular, I argue that Charles Taylor's wartime revenue has been significantly overestimated. Much of the furor about the Liberian-Sierra Leonean war economy was based on faulty interpretations of Belgian diamond import statistics. Section 3 provides an analysis of Taylor's rivals, explaining why they could not impose themselves. By way of comparison, it becomes clear their defeat was due to a relative lack of legitimacy, relatively weak economic bases dependent on politically motivated support from *Economic Community of West African States* (ECOWAS) members, and weak systems of authority incapable of ensuring the domination of civilians and the discipline of military staff.

Finally, section 4 analyzes Charles Taylor's attempt to extend his domination within the framework of the sovereign state and explains how a remarkable re-centralization of domination took place. The section is testimony to the resilience of the "sovereign state" as a model of domination. Taylor eventually failed in his attempt. That failure and its reasons, however, will be explained in the next chapter.

3.1. Collusion, Competition and Military Combat

3.1.1. The Actors

A key feature of the First Liberian Civil War was the large number of armed actors. Eight of these were relatively stable and of military importance at some point of time during the conflict. Additional ones were of an ephemeral nature or had a minor impact on the military situation only. In order to provide the reader with a clear impression of lines of conflict and also to give an overview of the structure of violent competition, the following section will shortly introduce the eight most important groups. At the end of this subsection, a few of the smaller, less important armed groups will also be mentioned in order to further clarify the situation. Subsequently, I describe the course of violent competition between these actors.

3.1.1.1. The Armed Forces of Liberia (AFL)

The AFL were remnants of the regular army of Liberia under Samuel Doe. It consisted of some 2,000 troops, mostly ethnic Krahn (Montclos 1999, 227). Soldiers from other groups, in particular those from Nimba, had been driven out. A substantial part was made up of so-called "1990–soldiers", mostly Krahn and Mandingo civilians hastily recruited and widely considered to be even less disciplined and professional than the trained soldiers. The AFL controlled central Monrovia and in particular the Executive Mansion grounds until the regional intervention force, the *ECOWAS Cease-Fire Monitoring Group* (ECOMOG), took over effective control after the death of Doe. The troops continued to consider themselves the legitimate state army, but did not follow the orders of any of the interim governments and effectively constituted an irregular force. Yet ECOMOG exercised significant control, temporarily encamped the army, restricted their movement, and took over command when AFL forces served as auxiliary troops. The AFL entertained strong links, which included transferring weapons, with the other factions emanating from the Doe regime, i.e. the *United Liberation Movement for Democracy in Liberia* (ULIMO) and the *Liberia Peace Council* (LPC). All of these groups rhetorically defended "constitutional government" and refused to be labeled rebels.

3.1.1.2. The ECOWAS Cease-Fire Monitoring Group (ECOMOG)

The regional intervention force was deployed by the ECOWAS on the initiative of Nigeria and prevented Taylor from conquering Monrovia in 1990. The intervention enjoyed support notably from Anglophone states and Guinea, while ECOWAS members Burkina Faso and Côte d'Ivoire supported its adversary Taylor. In military terms, it was the strongest actor in the war. It employed advanced military hardware, including Alpha fighter jets and, most importantly, was the sole force capable of continuously securing a core territory, i.e. the capital. ECOMOG's mandate had been the impossible task of securing a non-existent cease-fire, while Nigeria's primary objective as the most influential contributor was to prevent Charles Taylor from taking over the presidency. ECOMOG entertained strong links with factions opposed to Taylor and to a large extent pursued a deliberate strategy of fighting Taylor by proxy. As part of that strategy, the Nigerian contingent supported the formation of ULIMO and LPC and provided them and others with weaponry.

3.1.1.3. The Independent National Patriotic Front of Liberia (INPFL)

The INPFL split from the NPFL in January 1990, yet its leader made public its autonomous existence in June only. The faction emanated from a segment of the NPFL under the command of former AFL officer and aide-de-camp of Thomas Quiwonkpa, Prince Yormie Johnson, and assembled a sizable number of former AFL soldiers originating from Nimba.[25] With a core of 300 professional fighters and a total fighting strength of probably 2,000, it was one of the smallest factions. It exerted significant control over Monrovia's Bushrod Island from 1990 to 1992, though it was progressively contained by ECOMOG and partly encamped at its base near the Freeport. Its greatest success was the capture and killing of Samuel Doe in September 1990. However, as the result of a heavy battle, the INPFL ceased to exist in late 1992.

25 By his own account, Prince Johnson was a Major when he deserted the army in 1983 and assumed the rank of Brigadier General in 1990 only, i.e. when he was leader of the INPFL (Konrad Adenauer Foundation 2006, 90; cf. Ellis 2007a, 2).

3.1.1.4. The Interim Government of National Unity (IGNU)

The IGNU was established on the initiative of Nigeria within the framework of ECOMOG after President Samuel Doe was killed in September 1990. It was an attempt to assemble civilian Liberian elites—the bulk of which had their background in the "progressive" movements of the 1970s—to provide an alternative to warlord rule. Recognized by the UN General Assembly, it became the sovereign government though it did not effectively control any territory or militarily relevant armed forces. IGNU exerted control over a few sources of revenue, including the ship registry and a share of imports and exports. Internally, the IGNU was essentially a set of personal networks appropriating revenues they had access as representatives of the sovereign state. The IGNU redistributed these resources between the more powerful members of Liberian society. It was portrayed as the civilian, legitimate alternative to the NPFL and on the international stage, defending the IGNU became a prominent justification for ECOMOG. The IGNU was eventually dissolved in March 1994 to make way for a *Liberian National Transitional Government* (LNTG) integrating the major armed factions. Distinguished by its chairpersons, these interim governments will subsequently be referred to as LNTG I to III. When the first LNTG was established, "state decay" can be considered to have reached its zenith as no more was there any government authority independent of the non-sovereign warlords.

3.1.1.5. The Liberia Peace Council (LPC)

Initially, the LPC had been created as a civil society movement by a former Minister of State and businessman, Dr George Boley. The LPC had then been a founding though little important member of ULIMO. It emerged as an independent faction in early 1993 and in its early days drew Krahn recruits from ULIMO and the AFL. It quickly became dominated by ethnic Sarpo, who are related to Krahn and who were targeted in NPFL attacks. The LPC massively gained strength after a peace agreement had, inter alia, been signed by ULIMO and IGNU, the latter formally representing the AFL, in July 1993. In the attempt to violate the peace agreement without being identified, former government forces and the Nigerian contingent of ECOMOG redirected resources to the LPC. The emergence and rise of the LPC was not so much an expression of factional tendencies within the former government camp than the result of a tactical proliferation of factions.

3.1.1.6. The Lofa Defense Force

The *Lofa Defense Force* (LDF), totaling some 400 fighters, was the smallest and shortest-lived of the politically relevant armed factions. Little is known about it, and it will not be dealt with in detail in this chapter. The faction emerged in response to ULIMO-Kromah attacks on "native" Liberians and, in particular, the desecration and looting of holy shrines in Lofa. Reportedly on the initiative of religious Poro authorities, the organization was established in refugee camps in Guinea. It recruited its members in particular from the Kissi and Loma ethnic groups, and appears to have been the faction most deeply integrated with the civilian population of its territory. First reports of its activities emerged in late 1993 (cf. Inquirer Dec. 2, 1993). The LDF gained strength through the support of Charles Taylor, who copied the Doe regime forces' strategy of fighting by proxy. Nevertheless, it appeared to have quickly found ECOMOG and the former government forces more promising partners. A few months after its creation, it allied with the LPC and a breakaway NPFL faction to form the *Coalition Forces*. These cooperated with the LDF's former enemy ULIMO-K to attack Taylor in September 1994. In the fighting, the LDF effectively lost the tiny territory in Northern Liberia it had controlled. It was subsequently occupied by ULIMO-K and NPFL forces. As a member of the *Coalition Forces*, LDF elites were integrated into the LNTG II and LNTG III interim governments. These developments entailed dissociation between the LDF leadership and its popular base.

3.1.1.7. The National Patriotic Front of Liberia (NPFL)

The NPFL was the most important irregular faction in the war, and its attack on the small town of Butuo in Nimba County on December 24, 1989 marked the beginning of the war. It initially drew particular support from Nimba, which remained a stronghold, but in ethnic terms was the most representative of the factions. At an estimated combatant strength of 8,000 to 25,000, it was the largest of the factions. While there were close links between the adversaries of the NPFL, Taylor's force entertained hostile relations with virtually every other faction and so it can be considered one side of its own in the Liberian imbroglio. The NPFL gained notoriety early on in the war for committing atrocities against civilians, notably Krahn, Mandingo and other suspected beneficiaries of the Doe regime, but was also considered a relatively orderly and disciplined force. I was as well the economically best organized faction.

3.1.1.8. The United Liberation Movement for Democracy in Liberia (ULIMO)

The ULIMO was an alliance made up of three groups that emanated from the Doe regime. Most important among these were a Sierra Leone-based group of Krahn soldiers and a Guinea-based group of Mandingo, all of whom had fled Liberia. The ULIMO was created in 1991 when NPFL and *Revolutionary United Front* (RUF) activities rendered Sierra Leone less safe for Liberian exiles. It then occupied territories in Western and North-Western Liberia as well as eastern Sierra Leone, and at times collaborated closely with ECOMOG contingents, notably Nigerian and Sierra Leonean ones. Effectively, at least two chains of command existed. As a consequence of competition for access to state resources offered by a peace agreement, the 3,000–strong Krahn faction officially split from the Mandingo faction in 1994. It became known as ULIMO-J (in reference to its leader Roosevelt Johnson), while the larger Mandingo faction headed by Alhadji Kromah became called ULIMO-K. Kromah's group became the second most important irregular faction, numbering some 5,000 to 6,000 combatants towards the end of the war.

3.1.1.9. Local Militias

There were a host of other, ephemeral armed groups during the war in Liberia, such as the *Nimba Redemption Council of Liberia,* the *Royceville* or *Congo Defense Force* and the *Bong Defense Force*. The latter two were groups sponsored by the ULIMO-K as a proxy to fight the NPFL, while the former most likely had been organized by ECOMOG. By and large, forces other than the major ones named above were irrelevant in that they had no impact on the configuration of actors or on the cleavages between them. None were able to become institutionally stable. When the groups were dissolved, many of their fighters switched to other groups.

3.1.2. Elimination Contests

The Liberian civil war started when Charles Taylor's NPFL crossed over from Côte d'Ivoire into Liberia's Nimba County and attacked the small border town of Butuo on December 24, 1989. The attacking unit was some 100 to 150 persons strong, while additional units had infiltrated into Liberia and awaited weapons deliveries at designated points. At that time, the NPFL was still poorly organized and consisted of several groups assembled by different members of the Liberian political and military elite. Loyalties were heterogeneous and no person had yet been clearly established as the rebels' leader (Ellis 2007a, 70–76; Huband 1999, 52–53).

Already in January 1990 the chief military commander, former AFL Major Prince Yormie Johnson, ran into a dispute with Taylor, split from the NPFL and formed the INPLF (Ellis 2007a, 77). Despite the split and inter-factional fighting (Johnson 2003, 62), the two rebel movements advanced quickly on the capital Monrovia. The INPFL took a western route, arrived first and occupied northern Monrovia's Bushrod Island, which is the location of the country's most important sea port. Government troops, meanwhile, still held the city center. The INPFL established its base in the Caldwell neighborhood on Bushrod Island from where it controlled the vicinity.

The NPFL advanced through central Liberia and occupied Monrovia's eastern suburbs of Paynesville and Congo Town as well as parts of Sinkor. In August 1990, while the group was laying siege to the city center, the ECOMOG intervened. The regional intervention force had been deployed on the initiative of Nigeria; it was dominated by Nigerian troops and aimed first of all at preventing a rebel takeover of Liberia. Partly because of his connections to Nigeria's regional rival Côte d'Ivoire and partly because of his immediately displayed hostility towards ECOMOG, Charles Taylor quickly became the prime adversary of the intervention force. The Freeport, where ECOMOG arrived and set up its headquarters, was INPFL-controlled. Prince Johnson initially considered the intervention force a support in his rivalry with Charles Taylor, and the weak and extremely poorly equipped ECOMOG was in desperate need of access to local resources and intelligence.[26] Consequently, a cooperative though not

26 ECOMOG Lieutenant Colonel Aboagye even called allying with the INPFL a matter of "common sense" (Aboagye 1999, 157–158).

harmonious relationship between ECOMOG and the INPFL developed (Aboagye 1999, 157–158; Ellis 2007a, 3).

Front lines were fluid and changed quickly. Under pressure from the NPFL, the Doe government and the INPFL started negotiations which eventually concluded in an alliance. Amid mutual mistrust, the agreement was not effectively implemented but did result in a lull in confrontations between the INPFL and the army (Youboty 2004, 241). ECOMOG by then had paid conspicuously little attention to the government, and within about a month had not even had an official or unofficial meeting with the president. Doe eventually moved out of the AFL-controlled Executive Mansion to Bushrod Island to meet the ECOMOG Field Commander. Before entering the ECOMOG base, his escort was obliged to hand over its arms. Under not fully clarified circumstances, Prince Johnson and his men then stormed the ECOMOG headquarters, killed several of Doe's bodyguards and abducted the president. He was tortured to death the same day, September 9, 1990.[27] The death of Samuel Doe did not, however, mean the end of his political-military faction.

Already before the internationally recognized president was killed, ECOWAS member states had sought to establish an interim government as the nationally isolated and internationally discredited Samuel Doe was considered untenable. ECOWAS invited Liberian civil society and political party stakeholders to a conference in Banjul, where they established the IGNU. *University of Liberia* political science professor Amos Sawyer, a founding member of MOJA and prominent critic of both the TWP and the military governments, was agreed on as interim president. Yet Samuel Doe refused to step down despite pressure from ECOWAS and the US. His death thus enabled Sawyer to take over.

The IGNU was mainly composed of members of the different "progressive" movements, many of whom had served in the Doe government. After Samuel Doe was killed, the AFL effectively turned into another irregular armed faction. The AFL, however, continued to consider itself the legitimate state army, and its self-legitimation was largely built on representing the state. Given its lack of legitimacy and weak domestic power base, its goal of maintaining power was most likely to be achieved by international recognition of the AFL as an institution representing the sovereign state. The AFL consequently formally recognized the IGNU but

27 Samuel Doe's ordeal was filmed on camera. Later, the video became widely available in Liberia and West Africa.

did not follow its orders. Interim president Amos Sawyer took office in a "roach-and-rat infested" (Berkeley 1992) city center hotel, as the AFL refused to vacate the Executive Mansion grounds and threatened the interim government. Throughout the war, the AFL's territory was downtown Monrovia, their headquarters being the *Barclay Training Center* (BTC) just behind the Executive Mansion. The IGNU early on had a contingent of 450 AFL soldiers trained in Nigeria and Guinea for its security. These *Black Berets* earned a reputation of being relatively reliable, professional forces and occasionally fought for ECOMOG but were dissolved following the installation of the LNTG I in March 1994.[28]

Being blocked by foreign troops from conquering the capital, Charles Taylor attacked Sierra Leone, one of the weakest members of the intervention force. Taylor and Foday Sankoh, leader of the so far inactive Sierra Leonean rebel group *Revolutionary United Front* (RUF), had met when Taylor was shortly incarcerated in Freetown.[29] The connection was maintained: both allegedly pledged mutual support and later met again in Libya where they received military training (Johnson 2003, 46–47). The RUF was provided weapons by Taylor and reinforced by NPFL combatants and regular Burkinabé soldiers sent to support Taylor. The RUF entered Sierra Leone on March 23, 1991 from its base in Taylor-held territory in Liberia. Foreign mercenaries constituted the majority of combatants (Richards 1996, 5).

There have been speculations as to what extent economic interests in diamond smuggling have been a motive for Taylor's support for the RUF from the very beginning (cf. Reno 1998, 123). While economic considerations are likely to have been a factor, involvement of the RUF in the diamond business appears to have been "on a sporadic and individual basis" (Panel of Experts 12/2000, 16) during the first years of its existence and did not appear to have been a strategic priority. Rather, Taylor aimed at extending his network of political influence by helping allies to achieve positions of power. Yet positions of power always promise opportunities

28 The creation of the Black Berets was heavily criticized by Doe's and Taylor's supporters. Both camps considered the Black Berets to be another irregular faction personally controlled by Amos Sawyer, promoting his political ambitions and complicating the security situation. A perspective close to the NPFL's is provided in the New African (March 1995) and the AFL position is argued by Youboty (2004).

29 Sankoh had been serving a prison sentence for his involvement in a coup attempt while Taylor was shortly arrested on a recruitment mission in Sierra Leone (Ellis 2007a, 70; cf. Johnson 2003, 46–47).

for economic accumulation. Taylor's strategy was successful; the dysfunctional army and government representatives quickly fled areas attacked by the rebels and thus ceded control (Richards 1995, 149). However, lines of conflict became blurred and fluid, alliances between army soldiers and rebels developed, and territories changed hands several times in the years to come.

While extending his influence into Sierra Leone, Charles Taylor also assumed control over the Liberian hinterland. His power reached its zenith when the NPFL conquered Ziah Town in Grand Gedeh in July 1991. Ziah and its surroundings had been held by the *Gedeh Defense Force*, a local self-defense group largely made up of ethnic Krahn soldiers who had returned to and protected their home area (Youboty 2004, 210f+336). Then, Charles Taylor "controlled" more than 95% of the country, if control essentially meant there was no other armed force contesting his power. Yet that situation was soon to change.

In response to the RUF attack, ECOMOG and the Sierra Leonean government systematically supported the creation of a fighting force of Liberian Krahn soldiers who had fled into Sierra Leone (Ellis 2007a, 156; Montclos 1999, 227). Using a proxy fighting force was part of a "sophisticated strategy on the part of at least some elements in ECOMOG" (Ellis 2007a, 98). The soldiers had already been organized into the *Liberia United Defense Force* (LUDF) by General Albert Karpeh, Doe's ambassador to Sierra Leone. The LUDF combined with the purportedly "civil society" movement *Liberia Peace Council* (LPC) headed by the Krahn George Boley, Doe's Minister of State, and Guinea-based refugees of Mandingo ethnicity led by the former Deputy Minister of Information, Alhadji Kromah (Youboty 2004, 334). The three organizations merged to form the *United Liberation Movement for Democracy in Liberia* (ULIMO) around autumn 1991. Soon, Guinea joined the list of supporters of ULIMO. The faction rapidly gained strength and progressively conquered the Sierra Leonean-Liberian border area, thus complicating transactions between Taylor and the RUF. Furthermore, the areas under its control in what are now Gbarpolu, Lofa and Bomi Counties contain the few gem-stone quality diamond deposits Liberia has and their occupation thus deprived the NPFL of valuable resources.

Throughout the war there were three instances of major fighting in Monrovia. The first of these took place when ECOMOG intervened and fought back advancing troops of the NPFL. The second occurred when the NPFL launched a major offensive against the capital in autumn 1992, which became referred to under its code name *Operation Octopus*. Beforehand, Charles Taylor and Prince Johnson had formed an alliance, and about 20,000 NPFL fighters infiltrated into the Caldwell base. A further 6,000 NPFL combatants attacked from other positions around the city (Aboagye 1999, 105). However, the NPFL quickly turned against Prince Johnson, forcing him to flee into the US embassy. ECOMOG, upset about Johnson's betrayal, forced the warlord into exile in Nigeria. Most of his combatants then joined the NPFL (West Africa Nov. 16, 1992). The INPFL thus ended in a classical elimination contest fashion, enabling the winning party to accumulate combat capacities.

The *Operation Octopus* offensive was repelled by ECOMOG, with considerable support from the AFL, ULIMO and *Black Berets*. From then on, Taylor's "Greater Liberia" territory shrank almost continuously. Taylor's forces were first pushed out of Monrovia's suburbs, and ECOMOG and its support troops then established a much larger triangular zone nominally under its control. In early 1993, ULIMO conquered Kakata, the provincial capital of Margibi County some 50 km north of Monrovia, and formally handed it over to ECOMOG in March 1993 (Nass 2000, 100). In fact, Kakata remained jointly controlled by ULIMO and ECOMOG, with both forces jointly manning checkpoints. This pattern of joint control became typical for officially ECOMOG-held areas. ECOMOG further took over the office complex and processing facilities of the *Firestone* plantation close by, leading to a halt of official production and payment of protection money to Taylor by the company. Most importantly, the ECOMOG took Buchanan some 100 km to the east in early April 1993, completing the triangle. This deprived Taylor of his major harbor, used to export logs and iron ore. However, the Monrovia-Kakata-Buchanan triangle remained vulnerable to infiltration and the highways were prone to ambushes.

In late May 1993, first reports of activities of the LPC in the Southeast emerged. AFL elite units featured prominently in its ranks (ibid., 108). Generally, the war's Krahn and Sarpo factions—AFL, ULIMO(-J) and LPC—cooperated well. In particular, AFL and LPC collaborated openly (Amnesty International 1995, 6–10).[30] Yet at that time, neither ECOMOG

30 The Sarpo, who came to dominate in the LPC, are officially considered a Kru-subgroup but most feel more closely related to the Krahn, including in terms of language. As Youboty, himself Krahn, writes in his apologia of the Doe regime and the armed factions it produced: "Sarpo considered themselves non-Krahns because they are from

nor the AFL or ULIMO were interested in being identified with a large-scale offensive against the NPFL. Within one year, the LPC took almost all of the eastern counties of Grand Bassa, Sinoe, River Cess, Grand Gedeh and Grand Kru from the NPFL. Parts of Maryland and its port of Harper in the extreme southeast of Liberia, however, remained NPFL-controlled.

Notwithstanding, Taylor lost his "most productive territory" (Ellis 2007a, 100), and insecure access as well as temporary ECOMOG blockades restricted use of the port of Harper. Log exports then took place by road through NPFL-controlled Nimba County into Côte d'Ivoire and reached the world market via the Ivorian port of San Pedro. A few direct exports were made possible by striking deals with ECOMOG commanders (cf. ibid., 104) or the LPC (Montclos 1999, 242). Yet Taylor lost access to important natural resources. "NPFL control of Liberian territory had shrunk from 95 percent in 1990 to 50 percent in [mid-1993], and it faced continued challenges" (Adebayo 2002b, 56–57). In addition, transaction costs of marketing resources still under NPFL control increased significantly. The need to secure revenue thus acted as an incentive to regain military control. Yet, in the wake of the failure of *Operation Octopus*, Charles Taylor started attributing greater importance to peace negotiations as a means to achieve control over Liberia (Ellis 2007a, 100–101).

Before, numerous cease-fires had been signed but only intended by the parties, particularly the NPFL, to provide opportunities for a military reorganization. In July 1993, an agreement was signed in Cotonou that was meant to dissolve the IGNU and stipulated the creation of a *Liberian National Transitional Government* (LNTG) headed by a civilian representing the IGNU, David Kpomakpor. The LNTG was supposed to be led by a five member Council of State, composed of representatives of IGNU, NPFL and ULIMO. Ministerial posts were to be distributed between these stakeholders. The agreement owed its significance to the fact that it established the principle of giving the main contenders a direct stake in the national government, and thus access to "state" resources while hostilities continued. Yet Charles Taylor did not allow his representatives to assume their posts while negotiations over positions continued, rendering the LNTG dysfunctional. Consequently, Sawyer and the IGNU remained in place until March 1994.

Sinoe and not Grand Gedeh like most of the Krahns in Liberia" (Youboty 2004, 140). The statement illustrates the close link between ethnic identity and state formation in Liberia, i.e. the impact the creation of Counties had on indigenous identities.

Notwithstanding the peace negotiations, the LDF emerged in northern Liberia in November 1993 (Nass 2000, 112; cf. Inquirer Dec. 2, 1993). It was established by Loma and Kpelle refugees in Guinea in response to the destruction of masks and desecration of sacred places by Muslim Mandingo of ULIMO in Lofa County.[31] The LDF had been supported by Charles Taylor in his efforts to weaken the ULIMO while, officially, a cease-fire was in place (Ellis 2007a, 105). It controlled a small territory in Lofa and acted largely autonomously of Taylor.

ULIMO's internal coherence had all along been weak since fighters were loyal to their local commanders in the first place and frequently knew little about the supreme leader (Africa Confidential Nov. 6, 1992). As a consequence of rivalries for the internal leadership position its Krahn and Mandingo wings became antagonistic. The formal split finally occurred in March 1994 over the allocation of posts in the LNTG. Roosevelt Johnson from then on led a smaller Krahn-dominated faction called ULIMO-J while Alhadji Kromah presided over the Mandingo-dominated ULIMO-K, which remained the second largest faction. Fighting between the two weakened their control over resources and the split increased the relative military strength of the NPFL.

Similarly in March 1994, the NPFL split. Three senior NPFL executives, Tom Woewiyu, Laveli Supuwood and Samuel Dokie, took their posts against the orders of Taylor, and thus allowed the LNTG I to be established. Taylor maintained that the Justice and Foreign portfolios be allocated to the NPFL before it would partake in the transitional government (Alao 1998, 37). His representatives, estimated they were better off by allying with ECOMOG and formed a breakaway group, the *NPFL-Central Revolutionary Council* (NPFL-CRC). The first transitional government—supposed to unite the factions in a power sharing arrangement—thus effectively excluded Taylor while giving his rivals access to resources of statehood, first of all those generated from the ship registry.

31 Many of the items were highly valued by foreign collectors and sold on the international market by a close ally of Alhadji Kromah (Ellis 2007a, 128).

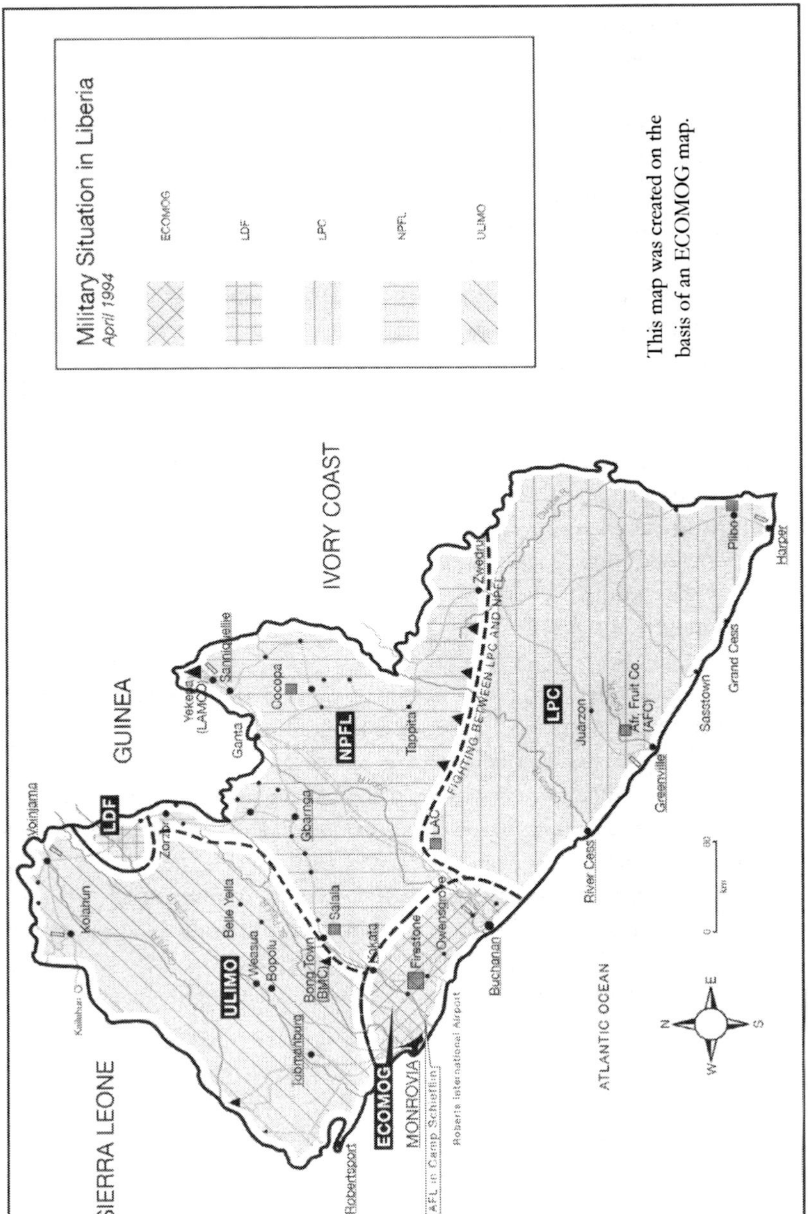

Map 1: Taylor Controls Central Liberia

The mode of competition between Taylor and his rivals remained military in the first place. ECOMOG provided means to bribe NPFL commanders (Nass 2000, 101), enabling the dissident force to recruit some 3,000 fighters (Montclos 1999, 226). In autumn, the LDF and the NPFL-CRC combined with the LPC to form the *Coalition Forces*.[32] From the beginning, there were close links between the *Coalition Forces*, the AFL and ULIMO-J, and the latter two later officially joined the alliance. The ULIMO-K cooperated with the *Coalition* and both attacked the NPFL in various locations. In September 1994, the headquarters of Taylor in Gbarnga fell to the ULIMO-K, but Taylor managed to relocate further north, to Saclepea in Nimba County.

As for Taylor, in addition to suffering the loss and depletion of war materials, a high number of combatants had defected or been killed. NPFL patterns of domination and discipline took a lasting blow; in the following years, indiscipline, violence against civilians and switching between factions became much more common (cf. Ellis 2007a). More importantly, Taylor only narrowly escaped defeat. General Nixon "Striker" Gaye, then commander of the elite NPFL *Marine Strike Force*, had joined the NPFL-CRC. Yet, apparently information had been leaked to Taylor, and Gaye was tricked into a meeting at Gbarnga. He died during interrogation (West Africa Sept. 5, 1994) and it was probably on the basis of information he surrendered before that a further 80 NPFL fighters, several of whom were important commanders, were killed on the orders of Taylor (cf. Amnesty International 1995, 27). Preventing the *Marine Strike Force* from joining the *Coalition* quite likely saved Taylor. Internal control mechanisms were partly functional and superior internal organization accounted for this, although the fact that the NPFL-CRC succeeded to mobilize some 3,000 fighters indicates there were severe deficits in control and command.

After having reasserted control over the remaining combatants, Taylor went on the offensive again and managed to retake Gbarnga in December 1994. The ULIMO-K fighters charged with defending Gbarnga hardly offered resistance due to Taylor's successful bribing of senior ULIMO-K and *Coalition Forces* commanders (Nass 2000, 101). The end of 1994 and early 1995 were marked by significant military advances of the NPFL.

32 The NPFL-CRC leaders were likely to have been instrumental in turning the LDF against Taylor. Laveli Supuwood, himself of Loma ethnicity, had extensive links to Lofa elites.

Large parts of Eastern Liberia were taken from the LPC, and both ULIMOs suffered losses of territory in the West and Northwest of Liberia.

In order to explain the events, we have to consider that Taylor emerged weakened from the confrontation, but that the battles had as well consumed important resources of the *Coalition Forces*. The *Coalition* could only appropriate few resources of immediate use from Taylor as a result of victory but faced the task of quickly securing a vast territory. Accumulating capacities for war requires time-consuming exploitation of the occupied territory. Consequently, victory pays off with a delay only. Yet, "diseconomies of scale in command and control" (Tilly 1985, 177) make themselves felt immediately. A lack of material and organizational resources meant that the attackers' capacities were overstretched in trying to secure Taylor's fief.[33]

The fighting effectively furthered the recentralization of authority both because the NPFL could significantly extend control, and because the LDF ceased to exist as a militarily autonomous force. LDF territory was partly occupied by the NPFL and partly by the ULIMO-K. At the same time, LDF-leader François Massaquoi remained integrated into the LNTG.

Despite extensive territorial gains, the NPFL was less in control of the hinterland of Liberia than had been the case from 1990 to 1992 when it was not challenged by other armed actors. Frequently, fighting occurred in areas it was considered to control. Despite its recent military successes, war weariness developed even within the elite *Marine Strike Force* unit (New Democrat May 11, 1995a).[34] Taking into account that the unit had almost joined the *Coalition* assault against Taylor, these developments had the potential to undermine Taylor's military power. Taylor realized that he

---

33 The ULIMO-K fighters who vacated Gbarnga to be taken over by the NPFL without putting up any serious resistance had issued a protest note to Kromah before, complaining about a "lack of ammunition, maltreatment of their wounded fighters and lack of welfare for their families" (West Africa Dec. 26, 1994). The weakness of the ULIMO-K in Gbarnga thus was linked to its poor internal organization, which included disposal over few economic resources and the insufficient provision of material incentives to senior commanders.

34 Increasing war weariness on the part of combatants may also indicate a decreasing attraction to loot. Although "there is always loot, no matter how small" (Pepper Bird Newspaper 2 (1996), quoted in Ellis 2007a, 125) as goods were imported by humanitarian actors and many items were looted repeatedly, fighters apparently became disillusioned about the material benefits of war. Most humanitarian goods are consumed quickly, and valuable items wore down or frequently were exported, thus depleting the pool of potential loot.

could not take power without Nigeria's consent, and started attributing greater priority to a negotiated settlement granting Nigeria the opportunity to save face. The major impediment to a peaceful settlement before had been Taylor's refusal to stand in elections that he would not be able to fully control, fearing that he would lose or Nigeria would manipulate them to his detriment.[35] Eventually, Taylor became willing to take that risk.

The shifts in the distribution of military power sparked renewed fighting between the two ULIMOS (cf. Monrovia Daily News Mar. 30, 1995). This prompted an ECOMOG offensive in May 1995, as a consequence of which the intervention force occupied several towns hitherto held by the ULIMOs (cf. West Africa May 29, 1995). The events indicated a decline in support of the ULIMOs by Nigeria and entailed a recentralization of military power at the ECOMOG command. As a consequence of developments from late 1994 and 1995, the circle of contenders tended to narrow down to the NPFL and ECOMOG.

At the same time, however, the NPFL maintained its military pressure against the ECOMOG-controlled zone. The NPFL infiltrated Monrovia and other towns held by ECOMOG, and insecurity at the *Firestone* plantation area mounted.

The Nigerian President Sani Abacha openly expressed that his administration's interest in maintaining the regional intervention was decreasing and that Liberian actors would need to find a solution involving the ECOMOG as long as that opportunity still existed (Inquirer Jan. 25, 1995). In as much as ECOMOG would organize disarmament of the factions, ECOMOG could be helpful to Taylor's consolidation of power by allowing him to monopolize means of military coercion.

Taylor and the Nigerian military dictator Sani Abacha met personally in May 1995, after which the NPFL stopped all anti-Nigerian propaganda while Nigeria "started appreciating Charles Taylor's popularity in Liberia" (Nass 2000, 120). In retrospect, the meeting marked a turning point at which the recentralization of domination in Liberia in the hands of Charles Taylor became definitive. On August 19, 1995, the 13th peace agreement (Ellis 2007a, 105) was signed in Abuja. The so-called Abuja Agreement is generally considered the contractual basis for the eventual ending of the war though it was amended subsequently.

35 Liberty (1998, 140) affirmed that "anyone who had seriously reviewed the Liberian scene of the '90s could have predicted that [Taylor] would win" in elections.

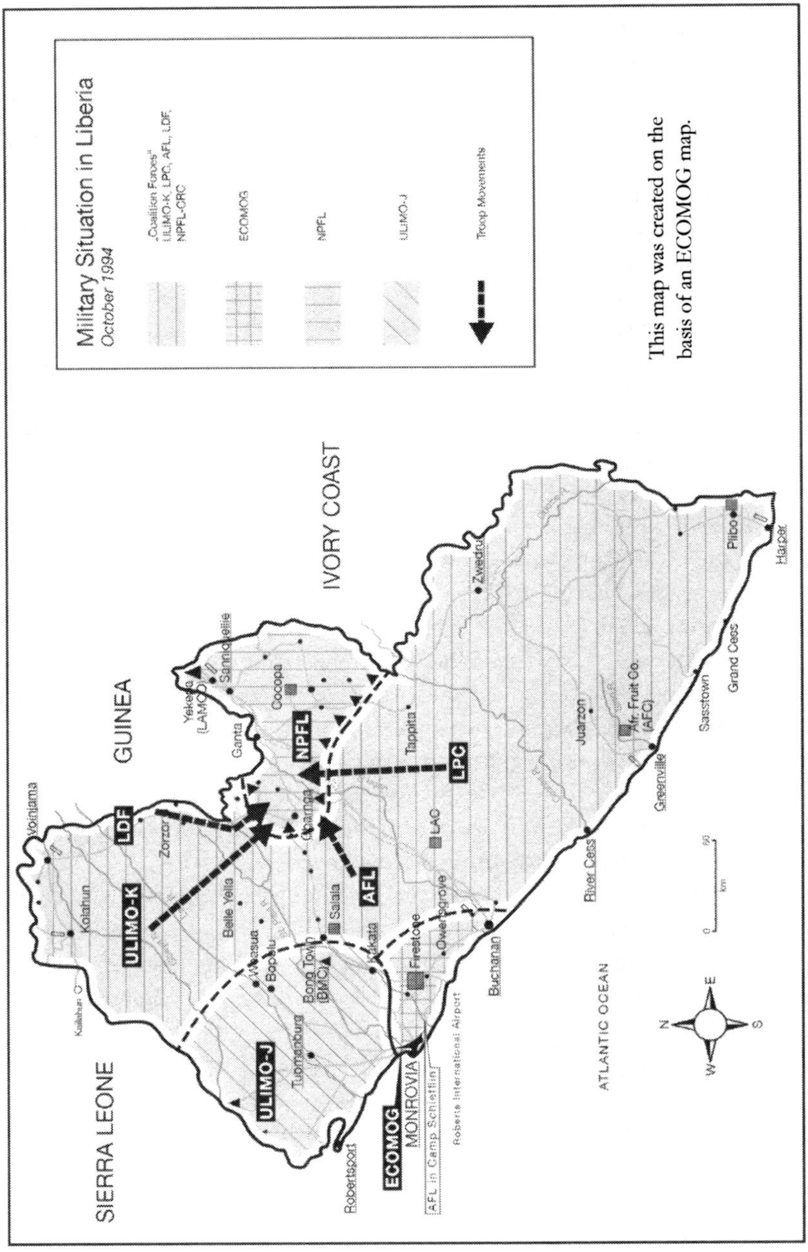

Map 2: Taylor Loses Territory to Coalition Forces Attack

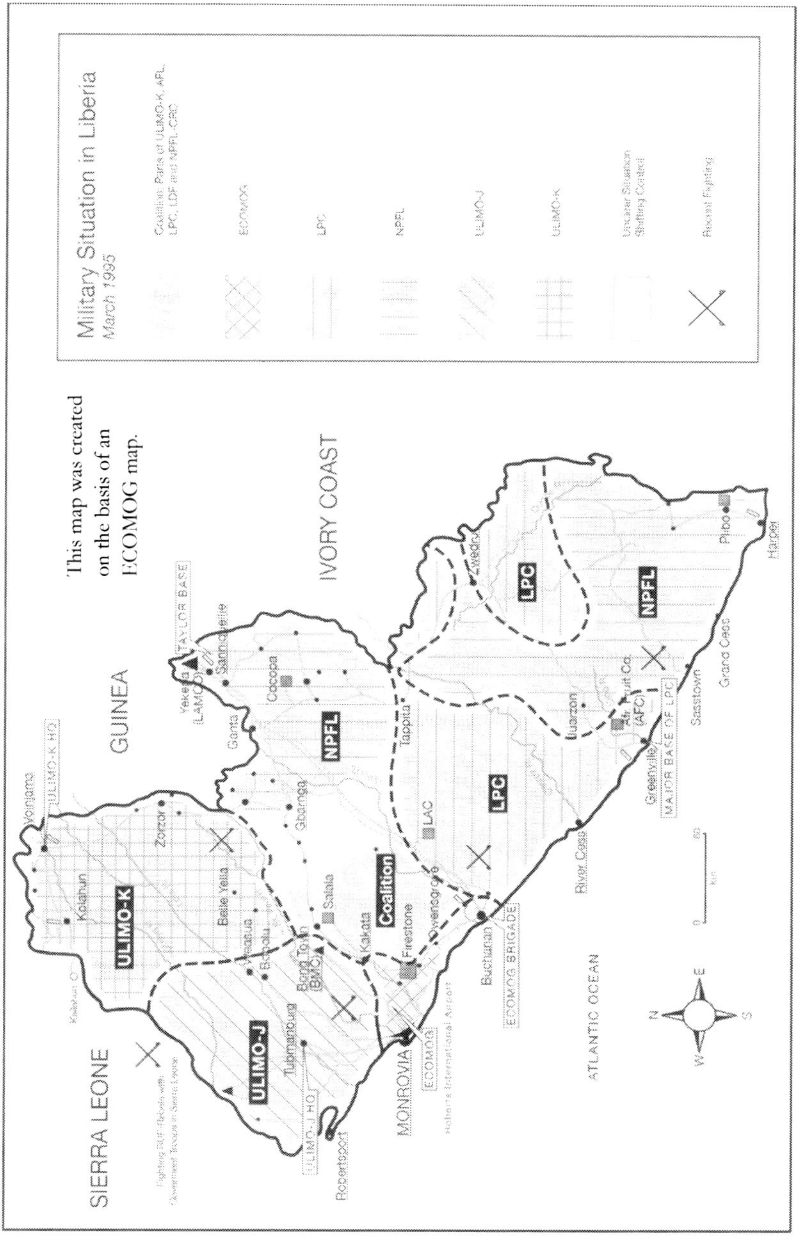

Map 3: Taylor Regains Territory

The agreement constituted a new transitional government subsequently referred to as LNTG II that was eventually inaugurated on September 1, 1995. Its highest organ was a Council of State presided over by a civilian Chairman, Wilton Sankawulo, seconded by five Vice-Chairpersons.[36] As part of the agreement, faction leaders personally occupied the posts, thus symbolically attributing greater importance to the central government relative to their regional fiefs. George Boley, Alhadji Kromah and Charles Taylor eventually took their seats as Vice-Chairmen, with Boley representing the *Coalition Forces*. Tamba Taylor, a respected but old, weak and illiterate paramount chief, and the former "progressive" and Minister of Internal Affairs under Samuel Doe, Oscar Quiah, were supposed to represent civilian forces. Oscar Quiah obtained the post as representative of the *Liberia National Conference* (LNC), a body uniting diverse civil society organizations. Yet Quiah, a Sarpo from Sinoe County, was considered close to the *Coalition Forces* (West Africa Feb. 13, 1995) while Tamba Taylor lacked fitness and was systematically excluded from proceedings due to his poor English skills. Ministries, state-owned enterprises and government agencies were distributed among the warring parties. ULIMO-J's Roosevelt Johnson, the AFL leader General Hezekiah Bowen, the NPFL-CRC executives Tom Woewiyu and Samuel Dokie, and the LDF leader François Massaquoi, received ministerial posts from the *Coalition's* share. In essence, the situation was one in which the warring parties jointly enjoyed the material prerogatives of sovereign statehood, while able to simultaneously exploit the territories they controlled as non-sovereign armed entities. Yet violent competition between the parties persisted. In the east, fighting between the NPFL and the LPC went on, albeit sporadically. In the west, the two wings of ULIMO occasionally clashed.

Meanwhile, the LNTG II apparatus could be used by Taylor to extend his network. Significantly more than his rivals, Taylor strove to appoint individuals with diverse regional backgrounds to government positions, integrating even a key Doe loyalist (West Africa Feb. 19, 1996). Importantly, the LNTG II prepared the ground for a recentralization of domi-

36 Sankawulo was well respected because of his professional background as a professor of literature. He was, however, proposed to become Chairman by the leaders of armed factions essentially because he did not have a political base that could make him a potent leader (West Africa Feb. 19, 1996). He was acceptable because of his professional status and because, originating from Bong County, he served to strike a regional balance on the Council (Inquirer Aug. 23, 1995).

nation by Charles Taylor. Owing to his intransigence, Taylor had succeeded to be allocated certain key Ministries: Foreign Affairs, Agriculture (overseeing and regulating the rubber industry), Information (historically essentially a "Ministry of Propaganda"), Justice (controlling the police as well as the judiciary) and Internal Affairs (the Ministry controlling the hinterland administration). Taylor thus focused on ministries important for the exercise of political power, rather than the extraction of revenues, which he was well prepared to effectively control without official responsibility.[37] From then on, the police was essentially a paramilitary NPFL force (cf. International Herald Tribune Aug. 30, 1996), making the NPFL an important armed actor in the capital, second only to ECOMOG. A (temporarily) cooperative relationship between Councilmen Taylor and Kromah further allowed marginalizing less important rivals.

In late 1995, ECOMOG started to deploy to Tubmanburg, the ULIMO-J headquarters, to prepare disarmament. Roosevelt Johnson then attacked the ECOMOG forces, apparently tricked by Charles Taylor into believing that the Liberian factions would ultimately make a concerted effort to challenge the ECOMOG (Ellis 2007a, 107). After fierce fighting, the ECOMOG forces finally withdrew from the area after negotiating a face-saving settlement with the ULIMO-J, but took a much less supportive attitude towards Roosevelt Johnson from then on. The battle had severely weakened the faction and ULIMO-K used the occasion to attack and take territories between Monrovia and Tubmanburg. Yet fighting consumed military equipment of both groups, giving the NPFL the chance to take over the territories almost instantly (Nass 2000, 144). The NPFL then took Bong Mines, and ULIMO-J forces were pushed out of Kakata almost without a fight. Once Kakata was cleared and the civilian administration there staffed with NPFL personnel (Daily Observer Mar. 22, 1996), the town was handed over to the ECOMOG (Inquirer Mar. 22, 1996), demonstrating that the force had become integrated into Taylor's strategy to control Liberia. In early 1996, the ULIMO-J was in "total disarray" (West Africa Mar. 18, 1996). Yet, as the NPFL concentrated resources on territories close to Monrovia, the LPC was able to advance in the east, albeit temporarily.

37 Taylor was little interested in the Ministry of National Defense. As a matter of fact, a post as Minister of Defense would have meant presiding over a hardly effective military force that would have been anything but prepared to follow the orders of an NPFL representative.

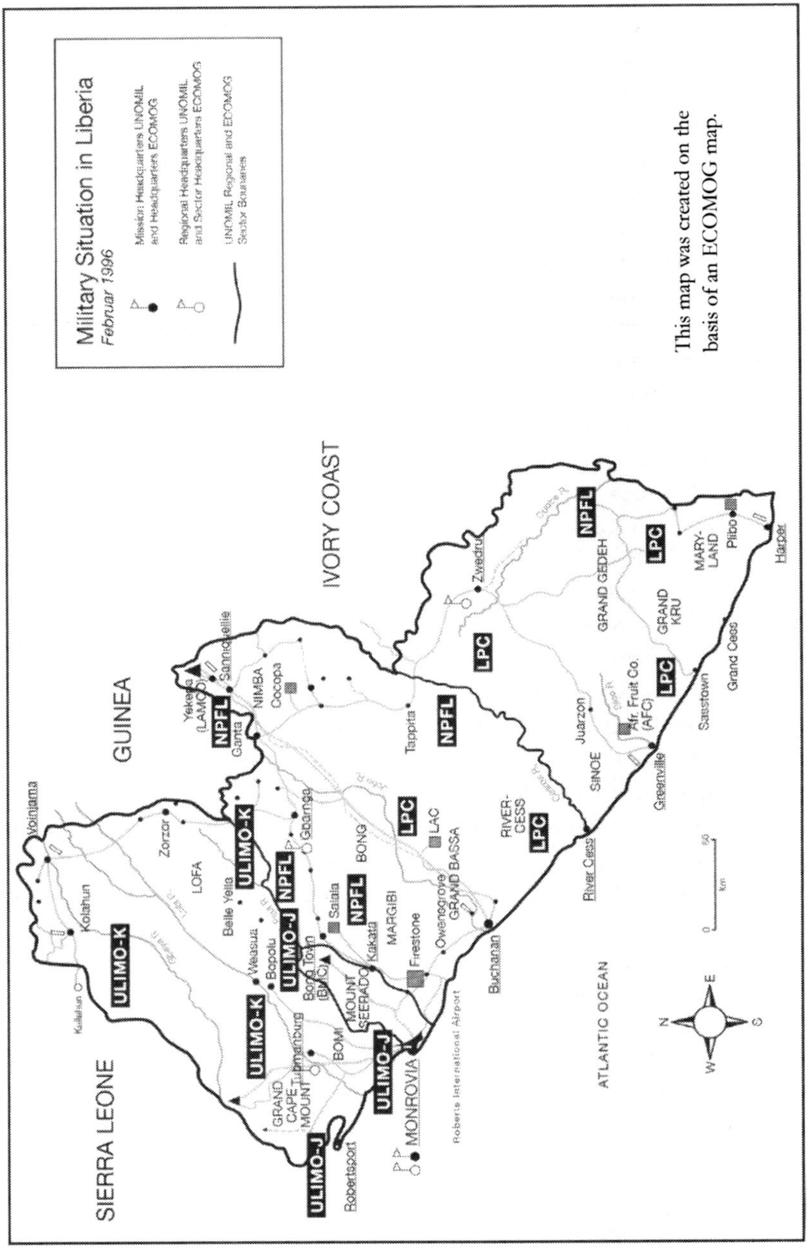

Map 4: *LPC Gains Territory in Eastern Liberia*

Enticed by what appeared to be a weakening of the ULIMO-J leader, a faction around the founding member Armah Youlo tried to replace Roosevelt Johnson and declared him deposed. In the context of these rivalries, a member of the Youlo faction was allegedly killed by Johnson. Charles Taylor and Alhadji Kromah, who developed a "relatively cordial" (Alao 1998, 29) relationship while on the Council of State, joined forces and declared Roosevelt Johnson wanted for murder. In April 1996 their forces tried to arrest Johnson in his Monrovia residence. In the build-up of tensions, combatants of all factions streamed in from hinterland positions into the city. Johnson's forces were reinforced by those of the AFL and the LPC. When fighting started they retreated into the inner city BTC barracks, where they held out with about 2,000 Krahn civilians.

The fighting represented the third major instance of combat in Monrovia. The April 1996 fighting largely was a looting spree; combatants were reported to have preferred opportunities for looting to fighting with rival factions. The fighting constituted an opportunity for Kromah and Taylor to reward their combatants before the ending of the war would dampen opportunities for looting but appeared politically motivated. Strategically, it was rational to try removing a weakened rival militarily. ECOMOG this time refrained from intervening directly, but provided weapons to Roosevelt Johnson's forces to maintain a balance, as did the US (Ellis 2007a, 108). The ULIMO-J, AFL and LPC forces under siege in the BTC suffered heavy losses—400 people are estimated to have died in the barracks as a result of shelling (Nass 2000, 152)—but were not subdued. Following a cease-fire, ECOMOG started to redeploy throughout Monrovia on June 2, 1996.

The battle in the capital sparked fighting in the hinterland as factions sought loot to strengthen capacities in preparation for a new round of fighting (Weissmann 1996, 108). The ULIMO-J/AFL/LPC forces, however, lost territories and were considerably weakened. The NPFL conquered areas containing gold deposits and forest resources in the east so far held by the LPC (Ellis 2007a, 108). Buchanan had for the last few years effectively been jointly administered by ECOMOG and the LPC. Yet when an LPC unit tried to take control over the city in order to loot, it was fought back by the ECOMOG and the city was then peacefully handed over to the NPFL. The ECOMOG further allowed the NPFL to clear Buchanan of LPC fighters (Nass 2000, 159–161). Within a short space of time, the NPFL regained most of the territories lost to the LPC in Grand

Bassa, Grand Gedeh, Maryland, River Cess and Sinoe Counties (Adebayo 2002b, 205). Thus, due to decreasing support of the LPC by ECOMOG and more systematic cooperation between NPFL and ECOMOG, Charles Taylor once again militarily controlled almost the whole of Liberia.

Given the loss of hinterland territories, a weakened position of the ULIMO-J/AFL/LPC forces in Monrovia, and a pronounced tendency of re-centralizing relations of domination in the capital, the LPC decided to switch to a strategy of obtaining power through sort of a coup d'état. On October 31, 1996, a few weeks before the start of the disarmament process, heavily armed LPC fighters attacked Charles Taylor and his mixed NPFL and ECOMOG security detail inside the Executive Mansion, which housed the Council of State. The assault had been well prepared: at least three remotely controlled bombs were exploded and numerous RPGs as well as automatic rifles fired. The attack failed, if just because the squad believed Taylor had already been killed while he hid defenselessly in a bathroom a few meters away. ECOMOG eventually secured the area after the attackers had left the scene. Although chances of success of the coup were in doubt given ECOMOG control of the capital, some observers indeed considered the coup strategy the most promising one for Boley. West Africa (Nov. 18, 1996) thus opined that it was

> "clear to everyone […] that had the assassination attempt against Councilman Taylor succeeded, nothing would have stood in the way of other non-Krahn council members being also eliminated thus ushering a return to a Krahn-dominated government in Liberia, resembling the ousted Doe regime."

The attack first of all resulted in substantial weaponry being removed from Boley's office (ibid.). Further, as Nigerian soldiers had been killed in the confrontation, LPC relations to ECOMOG suffered severely.

3.1.3. Winning a War by Way of Elections

Amid the loss of power of the LPC and the ULIMO-J, the disarmament process eventually started on November 22, 1996. ECOMOG troops under a new and assertive Field Commander, General Victor Malu, were deployed to disarmament sites throughout the country. Within the first four days, 2,000 fighters disarmed, but subsequently the process slowed down (West Africa Dec. 9, 1996). At that time, estimates of combatants were around 60,000 but the figure was reduced to 33,000 later. When the process was finally concluded in early February 1997, ECOMOG officially estimated the proportion of disarmed fighters at 62 percent (Alao 1998, 148). The process was clearly an important step in the recentralization of domination although official figures overestimated its success. The situation was calm from January 12 to March 19, 1997, and only a few, minor confrontations were reported thereafter (Adebayo 2002b, 208).

Much as the LPC, the ULIMO-K devised a strategy of obtaining power through a coup once relations of domination were sufficiently recentralized, rather than further pursuing the conquest of territory. In March 1997, less than two months after disarmament had been completed, ECOMOG searched the residence of Alhadji Kromah on a tip-off and discovered some three truckloads of weapons there (West Africa Mar. 17, 1997). According to the testimony of a senior ULIMO-K commander at the *Truth and Reconciliation Commission* established after the Second War, the weaponry had been stored to prepare an attack on Taylor in Monrovia (cf. Inquirer Nov. 12, 2008). The arms were confiscated by ECOMOG and Kromah was shortly arrested. Given the importance the mission had for Kromah, most likely substantial resources had been invested and the confiscation should thus have seriously weakened the ULIMO-K. All in all, the success of Taylor was massively furthered by the failure of the coups of ULIMO-K and LPC. The peace process then unfolded a dynamic unforeseen by Taylor's rivals, who lacked the resources to sabotage.

Table 1: State of Disarmament after Deadline February 9, 1997

Faction	Strength as Estimated Nov. 1996	Strength as Revised During Disarmament	Disarmed Combatants	Percent
NPFL	25,000	12,500	11,553	92.42
ULIMO-K	12,460	6,800	5,622	82.68
AFL	8,734	7,000	571	8.15
ULIMO-J	7,776	3,800	1,114	29.32
LPC	4,650	2,500	1,223	48.92
LDF	750	400	249	62.25
Total	59,370	33,000	20,332	61.61

Source: Alao (1998, 148)

The warring parties were partly transformed into political parties and, in line with the amended Abuja Agreement, the faction leaders who wanted to run in the elections stepped down to be replaced by hand-picked successors. Charles Taylor was presidential candidate of the *National Patriotic Party* (NPP), George Boley headed the *National Democratic Party of Liberia* (NDPL) once founded by Samuel Doe, and Alhadji Kromah ran for the *All Liberia Coalition Party* (ALCOP) he created. Although the factions maintained their organizational structures and continued to occupy their fiefs, the election campaign went ahead with only minor incidents. Protected by ECOMOG, political parties were able to campaign nation-wide despite a few reported disturbances (Adebayo 2002b, 221).

The NPP was able to translate its sizeable organizational and economic war resources into political campaign resources. Charles Taylor, using a helicopter and a flotilla of vehicles, could travel most widely, and his radio station constituted a valuable advantage given that many Liberian voters had few other chances to access information. Relative economic wealth allowed Taylor to distribute patronage more generously than his rivals, most importantly campaign t-shirts and rice for people attending rallies. The NPP organizational network was employed to mobilize potential supporters country-wide, and Charles Taylor's campaign clearly stood out, frequently overshadowing opponents (Pham 2004, 133; cf. Harris 1999).

On the initiative of Amos Sawyer, five opposition parties headed by the most prominent civilian politicians plus Boley's NDPL and the *Liberia Unification Party* (LUP) headed by NPFL-CRC executive Laveli Supuwood tried to establish an alliance and present a common candidate against Taylor (Adebayo 2002b, 219). However, the alliance broke up when Cletus Wotorson, an official of the Ministry of Lands and Mines[38] and leader of the *Liberia Action Party* (LAP), was elected presidential candidate. PAL-founder Gabriel Bacchus Matthews and Togba Nah Tipoteh withdrew their support amongst allegations of vote buying against Wotorson, and ran as candidates of their parties, the *United People's Party* (UPP) and the *Liberia People's Party* (LPP) respectively. Ellen Johnson Sirleaf, who had earlier tried to become presidential candidate of the LAP but had been outmaneuvered, then ran as candidate of the *Unity Party* (UP). To the Liberian public, the developments indicated the self-serving orientation of Liberia's political elite, and the split considerably reinforced the widespread

38 The official appellation is Ministry of Lands, Mines and Energy but it is most often referred to in this shortened form.

perception of a mediocre civilian political class (cf. Harris 1999; Pham 2004, 173).[39]

The election on July 19, 1997 was won by Taylor in a landslide victory with 75.3 percent. The process was endorsed as essentially free and fair by foreign observers (cf. Harris 1999). Taylor's closest competitor Johnson Sirleaf obtained 9.6 percent, while Kromah came third, scoring 4.2 percent. George Boley obtained 1.3 percent, rendering him 7th out of thirteen candidates. Even in Grand Gedeh, were the NPP obtained its second- lowest score of 55.0 percent, Boley won only 35 percent. About 85 percent of registered voters went to the ballot. Furthermore, the NPP won 21 of the 26 seats in the Senate as well as 49 of the 64 House of Representatives seats (Adebayo 2002b, 222). In these "Special Elections", the legislature had not been elected separately as the constitution would have required. Instead a "single ballot system" was adopted that distributed assembly seats to parties proportionally to the votes obtained by their presidential candidate. This effectively gave Taylor huge leverage to allocate legislative posts in a patrimonial fashion and exert significant control over the legislature.

3.1.4. Summary: Civil War as State-Building

This section demonstrated how competition for power forced actors into military confrontation aimed at victory. The background was the zero-sum nature of competition: one's gain was another's loss, and losses posed a potential threat to the existence of an armed group as rivals got proportionally stronger. Control of violence and economic strength are closely related. Particularly for the NPFL, the need to exploit natural resources and thus control territory to sustain itself was a major motive to attack. Other factions enjoyed substantial politically motivated support from Nigeria, Guinea and Sierra Leone, were less dependent on military conquest and could sustain themselves despite a weak economic base. Over time, patterns of domination changed and so did forms of violence. As power became re-centralized, losing elites planned taking power in a

39 As Liberty (1998, 180–181) noted, Taylor was a polarizing personality, and any civilian candidate reaching the second round in presidential elections could expect to be a de-facto consensus candidate of Taylor's opponents. As most observers expected a second round of elections, running on their own was rational for those not chosen to represent the alliance.

coup. In the end, peace was achieved temporarily because a relatively clear hierarchy of armed actors emerged, and the weaker ones estimated they would be eliminated if they continued to fight. A major factor in this was ECOMOG's withdrawal of support to them.

3.2. Political Economy of the NPFL

This section explains why Taylor was able to outperform his rivals. It argues that he established a system of domination far more comprehensive and effective than any of his rivals. Key features of this system were revenue extraction, legitimacy and internal control. The section argues that Taylor better controlled his subordinates, enjoyed a relatively superior degree of legitimacy, and that the NPFL was better organized economically than other factions. It is the combination of these factors that accounted for Taylor's success.

The NPFL was dominated by Charles Taylor to the extent that it could be considered his personal endeavor; the faction and its leader were inextricably linked. The imposition of Charles Taylor as leader had little to do with structural characteristics but his personal strategy and tactics. Actions and events leading to Charles Taylor assuming the leadership are thus described in an introductory section. I then turn to structural patterns and analyze the NPFL system of domination as relating to revenue extraction, legitimacy and discipline.

3.2.1. Creation of the NPFL and Imposition of Taylor

Charles Taylor's leadership was anything but self-evident in the early days of the NPFL, and his rise from civil society organization leader to most successful warlord needs to be explained. Key advantages over his rivals were features that also underlay his success in the long run: charismatic talent, international connections and ruthlessness.

When Samuel Doe undertook his coup and became president, Charles Taylor was residing in the United States where he had studied and obtained a BSc in economics. In 1980 he was chairman of the board of the *Union of Liberian Associations in the Americas* (ULAA), an umbrella organization of some 35,000 members (Adebayo 2002b, 58).[40] Shortly after the coup, Taylor returned to Liberia to pursue a career in the public sector. Through his long-time girlfriend Enid Tupee Boakai, a relative of Quiwonkpa, he had access to the military high command (Waugh 2011, 77) and was made Director of the government procurement body *General Services Agency* (GSA). Accused of embezzlement, Taylor fled Liberia in 1983 and eventually resurfaced in West Africa.

A significant share of Liberia's elites and civilians from Nimba left Liberia as the Doe government's popular base became smaller and the regime more oppressive. Since the mid-1980s, several of Liberia's military and intellectual elites engaged in establishing an oppositional military force abroad and partly collaborated, yet no single person was poised to become the insurgents' leader (cf. Ellis 2007a, 68–70). Taylor was arrested several times in Ghana and Sierra Leone during his recruitment drive. In Sierra Leone, he met the dissident Foday Sankoh in jail and both maintained their relationship. Among Taylor's dissidents was Moses Duopu, formerly Minister of Labor under Doe and "probably the most successful recruiter of Liberian military exiles" (ibid., 70). Duopu established contacts with the Minister of State and de-facto number two of Burkina Faso, Captain Blaise Compaoré, and was promised military training for his rebel group. Many of the trainees were remnants of Quiwonkpa's force and Nimbaian soldiers who had fled in the wake of Quiwonkpa's attack of 1985.

Of particular importance among those who went to Burkina Faso for training were Prince Johnson and Elmer Johnson (no relation). Prince Johnson had joined the AFL in 1971 and became aide-de-camp to Thomas Quiwonkpa. Prince Johnson later took part in Quiwonkpa's coup attempt (ibid., 317–318) and fled to Côte d'Ivoire after its failure. By his own account, Prince Johnson played a key role in reorganizing the dissident forces (Johnson 2003). Elmer Johnson was from a leading "Americo-Liberian" family, a career soldier who had served the Liberian and the US armies, the latter as a marine, and was widely respected by rank-and-file combatants.

Once more out of prison, Taylor headed for Burkina Faso. Reportedly, the Liberian exile Tonia King, a former Immigration Commissioner and

40 After Taylor, Tom Woewiyu became Chairman of the ULAA. Woewiyu was later made Minister of Internal Affairs in Taylor's 'Greater Liberia' but led the splinter group that was to seriously confront the NPFL in 1994. Taylor and Woewiyu demonstrate the extent to which the rebellion was rooted in the intellectual Liberian diaspora in the US.

relative of President William Tolbert, had introduced Taylor to Blaise Compaoré who was initially the key backer of the dissidents (Johnson 2003, 42).[41] Compaoré in turn introduced Taylor to Gaddafi, who invited the rebels for training (Ellis 2007a, 69). At that time, there was no sole leader of the group, and several of the organizers appeared likely to assume the position (ibid., 74).

Charles Taylor's major advantage vis-à-vis the other leading dissidents were his regional contacts. In particular, he gained the trust and personal support of Gaddafi. While training in Libya, Taylor became the key intermediary between the dissident trainees and their sponsor. In addition, he had succeeded to establish high-level contacts in Côte d'Ivoire and Burkina Faso, which the rebels-to-be needed (ibid., 70–74). Despite this elite-level collusion, the rank-and-file trainees remained loyal to their immediate commanders, such as Prince Johnson and Elmer Johnson.

The regional connections supporting the formation of Charles Taylor's rebel NPFL were of utmost importance to Liberia's internal war. Côte d'Ivoire's attitude of tolerating Liberian dissident activities on its soil was initially motivated by personal factors, particularly Doe's killing of Adolphus Tolbert, married to a god-daughter of Ivorian President Félix Houphouët-Boigny. Blaise Compaoré's prime interest was to establish regional connections that would further his goal of assuming and holding the presidency. While Minister of State, he had already established secret contacts to the conservative Houphouët-Boigny, whose relation with Burkina's revolutionary president, Captain Thomas Sankara, was strained to the point of being hostile. Compaoré later approached the professional soldiers around Prince Yormie Johnson (but apparently not Taylor) to assist him in his coup d'état against Sankara of 1987, which they did (ibid., 68–70; cf. Johnson 2003, 52). As Sankara had substantial support both within the army and the populace, it was strategically prudent to organize a foreign support group. This support group would be even more valuable if it took over power in Liberia. Finally, Libya sought to extend its influence into Sub-Saharan Africa and counter US-American interests. Liberia was a

41 Concerning Taylor's connection to Burkina Faso, Ellis attributes more importance to a meeting between President Sankara and Taylor, brokered by the Burkinabé ambassador in Ghana (Ellis 2007a, 68). Despite several inconsistencies in Prince Johnson's autobiography, his account of these events is plausible and better explains subsequent developments, i.e. the role of the Liberian exiles in the later coup of Compaoré against Sankara (cf. Johnson 2003, 52).

particularly attractive target as the country symbolized American influence in the region like no other.

Taylor imposed himself on the NPFL after the war had begun. His career was significantly furthered by him becoming the internationally recognized voice of the NPFL. Taylor had announced the NPFL rebellion on the BBC, secured a satellite telephone link, and maintained contact with international media (Ellis 2007a, 83). Yet more important than this was his elimination of real and potential challengers.

Immediately after the war started, splits in the NPFL became visible as the two principal commanders began to distance themselves from Taylor. Prince Johnson advanced on Monrovia on his own from January 1990, and there were indications that Elmer Johnson was about to do the same. At that time, Taylor had effective control over newly recruited Gio youths sensitive to his charismatic talent and a contingent of some 400 regular Burkinabé soldiers put at his disposal (ibid., 80–82).[42] Gio youths had joined the rebels *en masse* when they entered Nimba. Early on, Taylor had shown his determination to tightly control the rebel group and become president of Liberia. Whilst Prince Johnson would probably have handed power to a Nimba politician like Jackson F. Doe (ibid., 80–81), Duopu opined that the NPFL Executive Council should chose the new president and made his intention to run for the post clear (ibid., 84). In a series of assassinations and ambushes between June and August 1990, about 80 individuals posing a potential challenge to Taylor were killed behind NPFL lines,[43] among them Jackson F. Doe, Elmer Johnson, Prince Johnson's mother,[44] and Moses Duopu. Although Taylor's responsibility is not clearly established, he appeared to have masterminded most of the killings (ibid., 85, cf. West Africa Mar. 1, 1993).

42 It was somewhat later, after extensive discussions with Mano elders, that youths of the other major ethnic group of Nimba joined the rebels in large numbers (Ellis 2007a, 78). As the NPFL started being considered a movement with a narrow regional base, Taylor deliberately embarked on a recruitment strategy broadening the faction's constituency, thereby strengthening his claim for national power (Liberty 1998).

43 The figure includes an NPFL unit of 64 Libyan-trained Special Forces under the command of former AFL officer Cooper Teah that remained independent of Taylor (cf. Ellis 2007a, 72).

44 Prince Johnson's mother was rumored to possess supernatural powers.

3.2.2. Politics of the NPFL: Administration and Legitimacy

Domination in its most trivial, daily form is administration. In Weber's understanding, legitimacy is essentially conferred on a ruler by his administrative staff which coerces subjects into obedience. A ruler first of all has to assure his legitimacy vis-à-vis his staff.[45] As such, administration and legitimacy are closely linked, and principles for the generation of legitimacy are expressed in the organization of the administration. Thus both dimensions of rule are jointly discussed here.

Key categories applied in this analysis are Weber's ideal-typical notions of legal-rational, traditional and charismatic domination—and the associated forms of legitimacy—as well as modes of administration, as laid down in chapter 2. As such, I describe domination as established by Liberia's wartime rulers on the heuristic basis of ideal-types, taking into account that in reality different logics work at the same time, partly reinforcing and partly contradicting each other. The analysis presents a nuanced picture of domination, emphasizing differences in neo-patrimonialism and variance in the relative importance of Weber's ideal-types in empirical forms of authority.

The formal institutions representing the modern Liberian state served as the model through which Charles Taylor formally organized his system of domination in the NPFL's "Greater Liberia" territory. One of Taylor's first steps was to establish a *National Patriotic Reconstruction Assembly Government* (NPRAG) featuring symbols of conventional statehood. Among these were the legislative body *National Patriotic Reconstruction Assembly* consisting of 24 hand-picked county "representatives" (two for each of Liberia's then twelve counties) and functionally specified ministries. By and large, the structures of formal Liberian administration were maintained, i.e. Superintendents were installed as highest provincial authorities and oversaw district commissioners, mayors, etc. Under a "dual-command system", the civilian authorities formally answered to the political NPRAG authority, i.e. its Minister of Internal Affairs. The military chain of command existed separately, preventing a merger of political and military powers at the local level (Liberty 1998, 163).

45 Tilly's definition of legitimacy as "the probability that other authorities will act to confirm the decisions of a given authority" (Tilly 1985, 171) is thus essentially synonymous with Weber's, in as much as Weber would consider the "other authorities" part of the administrative staff of a higher authority.

The formal offices—including the Ministries—had some importance for administration of the territory, though administrative practice was riddled with the personal and frequently patrimonial features of Liberian administration. State-owned corporations active in "Greater Liberia" were maintained but taken over by the NPFL and executive positions were filled with NPFL loyalists. For instance, the post of Managing Director of the state-owned *Liberian Mining Corporation* (LIMINCO), which held the government's share in an important Nimba iron ore project (see below), was given to the brother of one of Taylor's most trusted confidantes. "Greater Liberia's" LIMINCO then served as the body through which the foreign shareholders interested in maintaining the project dealt with Taylor (Prkic 2005, 118–119). The public corporation *Forestry Development Authority* (FDA) was put under the lead of Taylor confidantes and played a leading role in the exploitation of timber (cf. Africa Confidential May 17, 1991). These symbols of modern statehood served the purpose of generating internal and external legitimacy as they were intended to assimilate Taylor's position to that of the regular president of a sovereign state.

More reminiscent of bureaucratic principles than the functioning of the Ministries, senior commanders and senior officials often were paid regular salaries in addition to handouts allocated according to Taylor's discretion (cf. Ellis 2007a, 91). Taylor's personal security reportedly received some 75 to 200 dollars a month (West Africa July 22, 1991), several times the official salary of regular government employees in similar positions. Regular pay was largely restricted to the center of power and Taylor's core territory. Commandos manning checkpoints were remarkably more disciplined and better clothed and fed the closer they were stationed to Gbarnga (New Democrat Jan. 13, 1994).

"Greater Liberia" essentially was not organized according to legal-rational principles, and Taylor's system of domination prominently featured principles of traditional-patrimonial administration. Similar to conventional neo-patrimonial states, personal considerations determined the staffing of supposedly formal institutions. As a general principle, key positions in the political-military and economic institutions were filled with persons who could be expected to be particularly loyal. A significant proportion of NPFL elites belonged to the "Americo-Liberian" segment of society in which Taylor had been socialized. Several senior executives were members of Taylor's family, for instance his brothers Gbatu, Bob and Nelson as well as his then-wife Agnes Reeves-Taylor, a senior military commander. Others, such as military commander Benjamin Yeaten, had won the confidence of Taylor during the years when the NPFL was built up.[46] A third group of loyalists consisted of foreigners, in particular Burkinabé and Sierra Leoneans, who could be expected to remain loyal because they lacked alternative patrons in Liberia. A substantial number of Taylor's personal bodyguards were foreign nationals. "Beyond this commercial and military core, he distributed jobs and largesse to maintain an ethnic and regional balance of support, in the usual fashion of West African politicians" (Ellis 2007a, 92–93).

The formal bureaucratic structure was little important in structuring personal relations of domination. Taylor's system of rule was centered on himself; subordinates held little authority over their designated remits, and the formal hierarchy was frequently bypassed to the benefit of personal connections.[47] Further indicating the extent to which Taylor dominated the NPFL and dealt directly with subaltern staff, NPRAG ministers complained on several occasions that they were harassed, e.g. beaten, at checkpoints (West Africa July 26, 1993) as they were either not known or not respected by combatants. Even long-term close allies of Taylor such as John T. Richardson and Cyril Allen were not exempt (New Democrat Jan. 13, 1994a; Ellis 2007a, 145). Rowland Befell, temporarily Acting Minster of Finance of "Greater Liberia", defected in December 1991, complaining about deficiencies in the civil administration and a general frustration of technocrats in the NPFL with Taylor's personal style of rule (West Africa Dec. 16, 1991).

Ties of patrimonial character in part structured relations between Taylor and ordinary combatants. This was reflected in semantics of domination and deference referring to kinship, i.e. the naming of Taylor as "Papay" by his mostly youthful combatants. Generally, the analogy

46 Benjamin Yeaten, native to Nimba County, attracted Taylor's interest as a particularly brave and loyal recruit in Libya. Throughout the war and Taylor's presidency, Yeaten held the most important security positions.

47 For instance, Tom Woewiyu complained: "And even after I came on the ground [i.e. into 'Greater Liberia'] as Minister of Defense, I really didn't have any military power which way men went or didn't go. I can see a man like Isaac Musa, who was chairman of the Chiefs of Staff. He never had military power to decide which way men went and didn't go. These were [sic] all done by Charles Taylor himself and people [sic] and those people who know Charles Taylor would know that in the NPFL, and even in the NPRAG, one gallon of gasoline coming into the organization, he issues the gasoline and rice, and everything. He was everything in himself" (New Democrat Aug. 18, 1994).

between father and ruler implies a specific ideal of domination; a fatherly ruler assumes responsibility for the upkeep of his subjects. At the same time, he has the right and duty to punish. "The 'father of the people' (*Landesvater*) is the ideal of the patrimonial states" (Weber 1978b, 1107). There was no clear formal hierarchy and Taylor frequently bypassed his staff (cf. Africa Confidential Nov. 6, 1992).

A special case of "military patrimonialism" (Murphy 2003) were the ties connecting Taylor, commanders and child soldiers in a narrow sense, i.e. those serving in *Small Boys Units* (SBUs) typically aged nine to thirteen (cf. ibid., 74).[48] SBUs were established early on in the war and were considered exceptionally loyal to "Papay" Taylor (Ellis 2007a, 79) and their commanders (Murphy 2003). Structural similarities between patriarchal households and patrimonial states were particularly pronounced concerning patterns of authority over child soldiers. Many SBU combatants were war orphans, and the Unit replaced the family, with commanders assuming the position of a head of family. The lower levels of the military hierarchy were characterized by patrimonial relations of the exchange of (frequently unconditional) loyalty for basic protection and items of basic need.[49]

Rural subjects were patrimonially integrated through the intermediation of locally influential persons. "Taylor was shrewd enough to seek the support of clan chiefs and other local leaders where possible, so that daily life continued with some degree of normality in much of his territory after the disruption caused by the first months of the war" (Ellis 2007a, 91). Throughout its territory, the NPFL "encouraged traditional rulers to administer justice and adjudicate minor civic affairs" (ibid., 143). Taylor thus co-opted traditional parts of the existing state administration, i.e. the Chieftaincies, as well as locally powerful personalities of different backgrounds.

---

48 As Utas noted, Western media and agencies frequently use the term "child soldier" to refer to the same age group designated "youths" in Western contexts, thereby denying agency of young Africans (Utas 2003, 8–9).

49 The lack of opportunities for children to enter into alternative relationships and the high levels of violence characterizing relations between commanders and child soldiers have been put forward as arguments against the patrimonial character of these ties. Murphy, discussing the former point at length, concludes however that patrimonial relations of exchange were at the core of SBUs (Murphy 2003). Utas further equates SBUs and families by pointing out similarities in the use of violence and the extent to which harsh corporal punishment is considered part of a good education, particularly by the modernized segment of Liberian society (Utas 2003, 136).

Bureaucratic and, more importantly, patrimonial patterns of administration engendered a relatively high degree of order within "Greater Liberia" (cf. West Africa July 22, 1991). The NPFL was "conceivably better disciplined than ULIMO or LPC" (Harris 1999, 447), and many of those with the experience of being occupied by different factions considered the NPFL as the "least destructive" force in the war (Ellis 2007a, 129). Two factors impacted on the degree of order: proximity to the center of "Greater Liberia" and the duration of war. The core territory was much more orderly than the periphery, both because of closer supervision of commanders and traditional moral bonds between combatants and civilians. Patrimonial domination is more regular were it is embedded in a wider traditional order. Thus, a woman from Nimba explained: "With the rebel soldiers, we don't have much problem because we are from the same group. If you know how to live among them, you'll get along" (ibid., 143). Even people in peripheral areas of "Greater Liberia" could enjoy a significant degree of security. Thus, a Kissi chief, most likely originating from Lofa County, compared the NPFL favorably to the ULIMO-K, which had occupied the area before: "Taylor is our son[;] when his men came, they left us alone. We were doing our farming. They did not take our belongings" (ibid.,).

Most combatants went unpaid, and had to assure their subsistence on their own, which may have meant begging civilians for food in the core territory. The opportunity to loot enticed combatants to take on frontline assignments (cf. Utas 2003) and granting the opportunity to loot was part of a military strategy. Yet this strategy entailed accelerated individualization. Looting for personal enrichment became a way of life, as the

> "sense of moral righteousness which characterised the NPFL in 1990, rooted in the traditional values of the village, was to diminish as the war went on. [...] Fighters were becoming ever more materialistic over time as war became a way of life. [...] The war seems to have been instrumental in creating a category of young men and women who are avid consumers of imported goods which they want to keep as personal possessions." (Ellis 2007a, 123)

Particularly since the NPFL suffered severe defeats in 1994, looting and violence against civilians in the core territory increased (ibid. 91–92; cf. Utas 2003). Yet even before, units behaved more arbitrarily in the periphery of "Greater Liberia", which was directly related to weaknesses of central personal rule over wider territories.

"NPFL control of Cape Mount, Bomi, parts of Lofa and Grand Geddah [sic] counties [in the periphery of 'Greater Liberia'] takes two forms: either soldiers living in the villages while the civilians live out in the forests, afraid to return, or else civilians living in their villages but are [sic] constantly subjected to soldiers demanding food and money. Communications between Taylor and his far-flung 'Generals' are poor: although he would like to keep them disciplined, they operate a fiefdom system for self-protection and revenue." (Africa Confidential Nov. 6 1992)

In as much as patrimonial domination means private appropriation of power, these arrangements conform to patrimonial principles. Military staff appropriated powers of the ruler, i.e. Taylor, and increased their private discretion. Though this fiefdom system made possible NPFL control over an extended territory at little cost, this decentralized patrimonialism indicated limits of legitimacy and implied weak central control of domination. It thus was a factor promoting NPFL instability. For instance, the appropriation of powers by combatants and their private material motives help to explain the switching of sides in the war, which was a "relatively common occurrence" (Ellis 2007a, 130).

"Where political alliances revolve almost exclusively around economic gain, enterprising associates shift allegiances at any sign of superior opportunity in some other alliance. They may seize opportunities for themselves during momentary weakness or inattention on the part of the leader. Taylor's brand of [...] patrimonialism, imperfectly enforced, may prove especially vulnerable to further fragmentation." (Reno 1995, 116–117)

Fragmentation was indeed a significant problem for the NPFL. Patrimonial relations of reciprocal exchange may turn into relations maintained by the staff because of material interests rather than personal bonds. Material interests, however, are an unstable foundation for domination (Weber 1978a, 213). Yet Taylor always managed to reassert control, and the NPFL remained the dominant faction. Taylor's resilience points to a source of legitimacy that was not traditional and not dependent on patrimonial patterns.

A clue to that legitimacy is Taylor's popularity in Liberia. Foreign and Liberian opponents of Taylor frequently point to the atrocities committed against civilians by his fighters, insinuating that he was unpopular and survived through brutality. Yet, "[it appears] that Liberians' view of Taylor was not quite that of most of the international press" (Harris 1999, 447). Western perceptions may have been strongly informed by a typical bias in selecting informants, i.e. choosing these among the educated segment of society. Yet while "most Liberians preferred the [1997 election] candidacy of Charles Taylor, […] the intelligentsia and opinion leaders hated him" (Nass 2000, 177).[50]

During my research in Liberia between 2005 and 2012, people frequently expressed their support for Taylor, though his popularity seemed on the decrease during the period. Blair (2009) similarly noticed widespread support for the former president. Partly explaining the minor impact of atrocities on Taylor's reputation, "Taylor's fighters […] aimed much of their violence in the early days against Krahns, Mandingos and suspected Doe supporters, groups that had not endeared themselves in recent times to the rest of the population" (Harris 1999, 447).[51] "All factions retained close links with Liberian society" (Ellis 2007a, 134), and the NPFL was the largest one.

Several scholars and observers at least hinted at Taylor's popularity (cf. Nass 2000, 120; cf. Aboagye 1999, 137–139, 207). Baffour Ankomah, writing for the *New African* and occasionally for *West Africa,* continuously reported sympathetically about Taylor. By his own account, his views were informed by the "depth of the affections Taylor had from the 'country people'" Ankomah experienced when he first travelled to "Greater Liberia" in 1992 (New African Sept. 1997). In similar vein, former US President Jimmy Carter, whose NGO Carter Center was deeply involved in mediating between the parties, later stated that Taylor had the "strong support of people whom he had dominated in the rural areas" (quoted in Pham 2004, 173). Taylor seems to have appealed especially to the new, youthful recruits (who initially mostly came from Nimba) rather than the professional soldiers loyal to Prince Johnson (Ellis 2007a, 82).

Yet few observers indeed explained that popularity. Several authors vaguely refer to "charisma" as one of the reasons for Taylor's success (Kulah 1999, 42; Aboagye 1999, 138; Nass 2000, 177), though "charisma" would need to be specified. Harris (1999, 447) provided a more thorough explanation, arguing that "far from being a brutal warlord, [Taylor] was

50 A notable exception is Clarence E. Z. Liberty. For an intriguing critique of the Liberian intelligentsia and the international community see Liberty (1998).

51 Similarly, the Krahn Youboty describes AFL Sergeant Tailey Yonbu as a "hero" for leading a massacre of some 600 civilians from Nimba in the St. Peter Lutheran Church (Youboty 2004, 190–192). It appears that the killing of civilians ethnically associated with enemy factions was often considered legitimate in Liberia.

seen by many Liberians as the liberator of Liberia from the undoubtedly violent, predatory and deeply unpopular regime of Samuel Doe. It is certainly true that Taylor initiated a multiethnic rebellion against the despised Doe regime" (Harris 1999, 447). Ellis reported a personality cult in Gbarnga centering on Taylor's chosen name "Ghankay", translated as "the stubborn" or "strong one" (Ellis 2007a, 92). Personal strength is strongly appreciated in Liberia. Under the circumstances of the 1997 elections, his strength and determination meant that "voting for him [Taylor] meant voting for an end to the crisis" (Nass 2000, 177). While the Western press tended to interpret Taylor's election victory as informed by fear of him returning to war, ECOMOG Major Nass contended that "Liberian voters often go to great lengths in order to have the chance to exercise their voting rights once assured of secret ballot. They are fiercely independently minded and not tied to any candidate they may have been coerced to support during the campaign" (ibid.).

These observations conform to what I identified during numerous individual and focus group interviews as ascribed qualities of Taylor.[52] Taylor was considered a liberator or rather a "revolutionary" representing in particular the youths, an objectively and subjectively marginalized segment of society. As fuzzy as his nationalist ideology may have been, to his youthful country supporters he represented a new, more inclusive Liberia (cf. Liberty 1998, 150–151, 185–192).[53] Generally, breaking established norms is characteristic of revolutions and may be considered necessary for their success. In Liberia, there is furthermore a pronounced tendency to consider ends to justify means (cf. Utas 2003, 167).

As a revolutionary leader, a key quality of Taylor was being "stubborn", i.e. strong and determined, and being a "trickster" (cf. Chabal/Daloz 1999). Taylor's dictatorial style of leadership (Africa Confidential Nov. 6, 1992) is likely to have furthered the aura of strength, rather than having impacted negatively on his popularity. The notion of trickster refers to his ability to remain at the top of his rebel faction, despite an environment of disloyalty, deceit and manipulation, and his ability to outsmart his

52 Results of my research do but provide a hint of attitudes towards Taylor in the 1990s, as the time when he was president is likely to have altered public perceptions.

53 Indeed, Taylor stressed the "National" in NPFL, NPRAG and NPP. Amongst others, he led rallies dressed in the national flag and mounted vociferous speeches denouncing international and regional "interference" in Liberia's affairs. A widely propagated motto of his regime was "Above All Else, the People", and the NPP's 2005 election slogan was "Giving Liberia Back to Liberians".

competitors, apparently being in the know about rivalries and intrigues being played out. Hinting at specific cultural roots of Taylor's charisma, Paul Richards (1995, 136) referred to the "violent, amoral, forest-going trickster of Mende tradition, Musa Wo", as a "hero figure" and role model for youths in the region. Taylor's mere ability to survive at the top of his rebel faction in an extremely dangerous environment is likely to have been considered to prove his charisma in both a secular as well as transcendental interpretation. In a perspective stressing the transcendental, his trajectory appeared "to prove that he himself is indeed the master willed by God" (Weber 1978b, 1114),[54] and an individual well connected to the spiritual world. Towards the end of the war, Taylor was initiated into the Poro society and adopted a title of traditional religious experts (*zoes*), *Dahkpanah* (Ellis 2007a, 251). From the secular perspective, Taylor embodied a Liberian version of the American Dream. As Liberty (1998, 148–149) explains:

"Without endeavoring to be an *aficionado*, I must confess to having a certain fascination with and grudging admiration for Charles Dahkpana Ghankay Taylor… the odd-breaker, the long-distance runner, the high risk-taker, the uncrushable rubber ball, the rampaging iconoclast, the man with little in his favor at the time of his bid for power (pedigree, wealth, ethnicity, military background) but with everything breaking his way (particularly stamina and good fortune or "luck", the potency of which Machiavelli ingeniously wrote), [sic] 'Fascination' and 'admiration' are not indicators of personal friendship because men of his predisposition are usually loners whose ultimate friend is power itself."

The clue to Taylor's legitimacy was his charismatic talent. The essence of that talent was his ability to talk to people, to entertain, to persuade and to convince (ibid., 143). Taylor's "command of words and smooth talking ability convinced even the most serious antagonist" (Kulah 1999, 42). Given that Taylor preferred a distant style of leadership, radio broadcasts, including a phone-in program, were the most important means to communicate with the populace. His legendary oratory skills enabled

54 While "President" of "Greater Liberia", Taylor presented himself, for instance, as a "non-drinking, non-smoking Baptist" (cf. Financial Times July 22, 1997) to increase his spiritual credentials. The topic of Taylor being God's choice for the President of Liberia became particularly prominent during and after the election campaign of 1997 (see e.g. West Africa Aug. 4, 1997). Ellis' account implies that Taylor's mere ability to maintain his position was considered proof of supernatural support already when he ruled "Greater Liberia" (cf. Ellis 2007a, 280). In general, Liberian Christianity tends to promote authoritarian concepts of domination (Gifford 1993).

Taylor to continuously recreate, or in Weber's terms "prove", his charisma. In the process of continuous recreation, Taylor combined seemingly disparate personae, from saint to trickster to "cold-blooded capitalist" (cf. Ellis 2007a, 84) in his personality. As Ellis (2007a) has pointed out, Liberian spiritual thought does not distinguish "good" and "evil" power. Thus one of Taylor's legendary sermons in his Baptist church, in which he evoked saint-like qualities and told the audience "how bad I am" (Kamara n.d; cf. Reno 2007, 73) may appear as a perfectly coherent display of power.

Charismatic domination as a concept helps to make sense of the arbitrary, unpredictable and little ordered character of significant segments of Taylor's military-administrative administration. It further helps to explain why violence against civilians by his combatants hardly damaged his reputation. The charismatic leader is not judged by the actions of his staff, and legitimacy is not conferred through mediation by subaltern legitimate elites. Charisma is perceived as the extraordinary personal quality of a particular individual and directly legitimates his rule. Charismatic domination as well explains the extreme extent to which Taylor maintained direct relations with his staff and abdicated patrimonial, clientelist pyramids as administrative tools, much to the detriment of administrative efficiency and regularity.

3.2.3. Discipline, Repression and Material Interests

This section explores features of Taylor's rule of non-legitimate character, where respect for authority is not based on a belief in its righteousness. Two objects of non-legitimate domination, targeted with different intentions, need to be differentiated: administrative staff and subjects. The administrative staff are subject to discipline, i.e. measures intended to make the staff implement the ruler's wishes. Subjects are, firstly, targets of repression, i.e. measures intended to deter or prevent them from actively challenging the authority in place. Secondly, they are subject to enforcement, i.e. the coercive implementation of the ruler's wishes by the staff.

At the same time, disciplinary action, repression and enforcement make use of similar techniques. In all cases, efficiency is supported by a control system able to detect contraventions of the ruler's wishes. A control system is part of a disciplinary apparatus, as the subjective feeling of being controlled increases the propensity to act in a conformist way (cf. Foucault

1994). One category of techniques makes use of force. Such techniques include punishments intended to align an individual's actions with the interests of the ruler, and the killing of persons accused of gross misconduct in order to deter others from engaging in similar activities. Another category of techniques includes creating rational interests, in particular material interests, in submitting to the ruler. While there is always a need to underpin rule by creating interests in it, Weber explicitly differentiates between interests in domination and beliefs in its righteousness, as only the latter can provide an enduring basis for domination. Payment of incentives and more subtle ways of increasing material interests amongst parts of the population are techniques of non-legitimate domination.

Physical violence was a key resource employed by Taylor in order to both rise to the top of the NPFL and maintain this position of leadership. As has been mentioned above, rivals within the NPFL were systematically eliminated, and popular Nimba elites who could have rallied support and jeopardized Taylor's position were similarly killed. The latter form of repression mirrors techniques employed in totalitarian states, as the aim was to destroy nuclei of alternative social organizations that could potentially challenge Taylor, rather than punish disloyal behavior.

Domination requires making the staff execute the ruler's wishes. In patrimonial systems that allow considerable appropriation of powers by subaltern staff for their personal benefit, this is notoriously difficult. Private considerations largely drive staff behavior and often conflict with interests of the paramount ruler. Disciplinary action against staff is therefore of major importance to ensure obedience. In "Greater Liberia", disciplinary action essentially consisted of violent corporal punishment. In at least some cases, suspected violators were detained and some form of court martial was held before punishment. Cutting off the ears of combatants and beatings were the most common forms of punishment (cf. Amnesty International 1995, 9). Serious violations were punished by executing the offender. A few instances are known in which looting by NPFL combatants was punished by the death penalty (cf. Dolo 1996, 78), although in many cases looting was tolerated or encouraged. Generally, in "Greater Liberia", there were no universal rights, but there were privileges; the privilege, for example, not to be looted was imposed. Taylor by and large succeeded in providing effective security to businesspeople who were paying fees to the NPFL (cf. Ellis 2007a, 91). The principle of awarding privileges rather than rights had important implications for the general security situation.

A central element in Reno's (1998; 2000) warlord politics concept is general insecurity. General insecurity is deemed instrumental to a warlord ruler because it serves to prevent alternative social organizations from coming into being, and provides room for rewarding loyal individuals with special protection. As no major economic activities are possible without reliable protection, "free riding" of disloyal individuals is prevented, and the ruler adopts a position as monopolistic provider of patronage (Reno 2000, 48–56). Yet the coexistence of some degree of public order and arbitrary violence in "Greater Liberia" calls into question the appropriateness of the concept. Apart from instances of actual battle, arbitrary violence and resulting general insecurity was most pronounced in the periphery of "Greater Liberia". In the core territory, general insecurity was not characteristic of the first years of the war; it took combatants several years to become less constrained by traditional norms, less disciplined and more materialistically motivated. General insecurity became a central feature of the NPFL core territory only after 1994, when the faction had been considerably weakened due to the defection of the NPFL-CRC and battle losses. I will later analyze the impact of these developments on the micro-level of political control. As a start, I briefly describe systemic issues affecting the emergence and control of elites.

What became known in Liberia as the "gate system" was a key institution of control. It effectively meant that there were checkpoints every few kilometers on Liberia's few roads. These checkpoints were severe hindrances to movement. Many were scenes of horrific targeted as well as arbitrary violence (cf. Ellis 2007a, 89, 116–118) that impeded travel. Further, travelling was restricted; passers at checkpoints were "screened". Men of fighting age were likely to be considered either defectors or enemy spies if they did not have written travel permissions signed by senior commanders. An important function of the "gates" was to prevent combatants from leaving their assigned posts (ibid., 116). Furthermore, the checkpoints were sites of extortion that rendered any business unprofitable, lest the businessperson enjoyed special protection. In "Greater Liberia", the "few travellers who could move freely were Gio and Mano people, overwhelmingly supporters of the NPFL, who soon acquired control of local trade" (ibid.,). To these people, and provided that charges due to Taylor had been paid, roads in NPFL territory were safer than before the war up until late 1994, and transport of large amounts of cash was possible (ibid.,). The "gate system" thus provided a means for far-reaching and effective control over the movement of people and trade. Under these circumstances, it is indeed hardly conceivable that independent social organizations with a sound material basis or independent strongmen could emerge.

Yet Taylor was not unchallenged in his territory. Of particular importance is the rebellion of the *Nimba Redemption Council of Liberia* (NRCL) because it broke out in Taylor's heartland. It started in January 1993 and in the following month the NRCL captured Butuo in Nimba County, which had been the first town to be conquered by the NPFL and was symbolically as well as strategically important. As a consequence of NRCL advances and ECOMOG air raids, Taylor relocated the NPFL headquarters from Gbarnga to Saclepea further north. The NRCL, however, was a short-lived movement that was militarily defeated by the NPFL and quickly fell into oblivion (cf. West Africa Mar. 1, 1993). Much as the LPC and ULIMO, the NRCL was likely to have been supported by the Nigerian ECOMOG contingent. External provision of resources remains a key challenge to rulers operating a warlord politics system.

Yet in patrimonial systems, the greatest challenges to rulers typically arise from their staff. Staff members exploiting fiefs may be able to privately accumulate resources (in terms of material means and social connections) that can be employed to overthrow the ruler. Taylor consequently tried to directly control resource flows, as is illustrated by Woewiyu's and Bedell's complaints quoted above. However, NPFL commanders to a large extent worked on their own account, particularly in the periphery (cf. Africa Confidential Nov. 6, 1992). "NPFL" was frequently a kind of a "brand name" used by combatant units in order to profit from a myth of strength, rather than indicating Taylor's leadership (ibid., 104). Numerous defections demonstrate that even at the leadership level the NPFL was not a stable, coherent force.

The NPFL-CRC rebellion provides an interesting example of the extent of Taylor's capacities of control. The three NPFL executives are estimated to have made some 3,000 combatants break away (Montclos 1999, 226). This is a sizeable force, demonstrating the limits of Taylor's control and the extent to which the three executives had been able to accumulate social connections. It is likely that the NPFL-CRC assault would have meant the end of Taylor if General Nixon "Striker" Gaye's willingness to join the renegade force had not become known. Taylor established a comprehensive intelligence apparatus inter alia responsible for preventing defection. At the center of the apparatus was the military intelligence unit G-2. The G-2 was the first unit that disposed of an effective command structure, underlining its status as a key security institution (ibid., 113). It was made up of individuals considered particularly loyal to Taylor, and was employed to secure some of the most important strategic locations, among them Taylor's radio station. The death of Gaye and the killing of a further 80 NPFL fighters associated with the NPFL-CRC rebellion further demonstrates the importance of intelligence and disciplinary action for Taylor's control of the NPFL.

Generally, Taylor was reported to have been extremely concerned about threats emanating from his own combatants, and he adopted a reclusive style of governance (cf. Africa Confidential Nov. 6, 1992). As the war went on and the NPFL became less stable, he became increasingly concerned about his personal safety. Taylor was reported to spend most of his time in his fortified Gbarnga Executive Mansion, where access was tightly controlled (New Democrat June 23, 1994).[55]

An important strategy of Taylor to guarantee his personal security and maintain disciplinary power over combatant units was to put a mix of persons expected to be particularly loyal into key security positions. Generally, foreigners, child soldiers and combatants in their early youth, and a few individuals trusted for special reasons, were charged with the most delicate tasks. However, Taylor was betrayed even by some of his most trusted commanders, e.g. "Striker" Gaye and General Cassius Jacobs. The latter was in charge of the defense of Gbarnga and thus occupied one of the most important security positions but accepted a bribe from ECOMOG, allowing the *Coalition* to take the NPFL capital in 1994 (cf. Ellis 2007a, 142). Much as several African heads of state, Taylor created competing security outfits intended to protect him and control each other. Most important as a final safeguard were foreign troops, i.e. units made up of Sierra Leoneans and Burkinabé. Up to 700 regular Burkinabé soldiers were put at Taylor's disposal by President Compaoré (ibid., 163), some of whom were detailed to provide security to his Gbarnga Executive Mansion. Similarly, RUF units featured prominently in NPFL ranks.

55 In 2002, a paranoid-looking Taylor refused to take part in a dinner which was attended by most ECOWAS presidents and took place under tight security, apparently fearing an assault (BBC July 28, 2009). The scene was probably indicative of concerns Taylor had already had much earlier.

Employing strangers for security has historically been associated with patrimonial polities in which the ruler enjoys little traditional legitimacy, and has been widespread in the case of sultanistic domination (Weber 1978b, 1017–1018). As has been noted above, child soldiers were considered particularly loyal, and some were reported to guard Taylor's Mansion. John T. Richardson, a senior NPFL executive,[56] even argued that "SBU" in fact did not mean *Small Boys Unit* but *Special Bodyguard Unit* (West Africa Oct. 10, 1994).

The impact of widespread physical and material insecurity on patterns of domination was particularly pronounced at the micro-level. As has been mentioned, the security situation in areas controlled by Taylor worsened over the course of the war and, particularly from 1994 on, looting by NPFL troops in their territory increased markedly (Ellis 2007a, 91,123). Even in Nimba, women were in constant danger of being raped by Nimbaian combatants (ibid., 143; cf. Utas 2003, 169–221).[57] Civilians' strategies to establish personal security included building personal links to the NPFL or its commandos, respectively.

> "Having a relationship with at least one fighter was crucial for the survival not only of the woman herself, but of her entire family. Looted goods for example would be delivered by boyfriends returning from the war front and would help to support the family network. Furthermore, it was important for the family to have a 'big man' in the rebel movement around so that their estate and property would not be looted and ravaged. It was therefore good to have at least one son join the military, or at least to be related to people with important posts in a particular rebel movement. It was even better if one of the daughters was having a relationship with a local commando." (Utas 2003, 176–177)

General insecurity had the effect of creating a closely knit network linking combatants and civilians. The relationships established involved a fair degree of control by combatants over civilians on the one hand, and provision of means of livelihood for civilians by combatants on the other. Because of these exchanges, relations appear to follow a patrimonial,

---

56 Richardson's war name was General Octopus. He allegedly masterminded the 1992 assault on Monrovia.

57 The association between gender and security was complex. Ellis held that women were more free to move, as civilian men were in constant danger of being accused of siding with the enemy, e.g. at checkpoints, and being killed. As a consequence, women's economic and social station was strengthened during the war (Ellis 2007a, 143). Utas (2003) emphasized that men could move more freely within towns, while women not protected through association with a commando were in constant risk of rape.

clientelist logic. As I said, patrimonial, charismatic and warlord politics patterns share the character of personal relations. Yet if we consider the "claim to legitimacy" (Weber 1978a, 215) to distinguish between different types of domination (and associated patterns of administration), and the traditional symbolism of reciprocal exchange to constitute a core element constituting the belief in the righteousness of the ruler (cf. Jung 1995, 135–136; cf. Kilson 1966), there is a fundamental difference between warlord politics and other patterns of domination. For patrimonial personal exchanges need to embody, actualize and symbolize much wider personal relations of piety and mutual obligations. Warlord politics exchanges, in contrast, are direct transactions essentially based on short-term material interests (cf. Utas 2003, 169–221). They thus provide a weak, unstable basis for domination.

The recourse to warlord politics tactics as well highlights the limits of a patrimonial extension of domination. There are parallels in Liberia's history of state-building, which to a significant extent relied on coercion, repression, and material interests. Factionalism has been a long-running feature of Liberian politics. Socio-political groupings are instable and alliances are quickly established and dissolved. There is precious little trust and solidarity in society. Historically, political settings were small-scale, in-groups tended to be restricted, and nationalism has been particularly weak. Norms of reciprocity are little binding outside a narrowly defined in-group. Cultural dispositions thus historically challenged a patrimonial extension of domination, including the one undertaken by Charles Taylor. Modernization reinforced these challenges rather than mitigated them. Modernization implies a more rational organization of society, and thus a greater role for cost-benefit analysis in personal relations, thereby rendering personal relations more instable.

3.2.4. Economics of the NPFL

Economic motives played a central role in the war in Liberia, and the NPFL was no exception. Opportunities to make a profit motivated combatants of all ranks and military strength of the NPFL is frequently explained with reference to large war economy profits (cf. US Department of State 1996). This section first aims to document characteristics, such as goods, volumes and value of the NPFL economy in order to enable the reader to get an idea of the magnitude of its business dealings. Second, it aims at identifying trends. I argue that profits of the NPFL were significant but nevertheless frequently overestimated. The most important impact of relatively high profits was their translation into military and organizational strength. Further, I argue that profits were declining. Although "self-enrichment […] with a ruthlessly short-term perspective" (Ellis 2007a, xxvii) is and was a well-established factor in Liberian politics, this secular decline meant that profits became an increasingly unlikely war motive. More importantly, a fall in revenues translates into difficulties to maintain a given standard of military and organizational strength, and exerts pressures on elites to adapt strategies accordingly. A "long war" strategy became increasingly risky for war elites, including those of the NPFL.

Data on NPFL trade as reported by various authors and based on multiple sources—NPFL insiders, international business associations, international organizations and import statistics of destination countries, to name the most important ones—vary widely. For example, Stephen Rapp, erstwhile chief prosecutor of the *Special Court for Sierra Leone*, once remarked that he had evidence of five billion dollars held in private bank accounts of Taylor (BBC May 2, 2008).[58] Frequently quoted, a US ambassador in Liberia once estimated that an amount "upwards of $75 million a year [was] passing through his [Taylor's] hands" (US Department of State 1996). Investigative journalist Farah (2005, 22), an expert on West Africa's arms trade, estimated that Taylor had managed to transfer 150 to 210 million dollars abroad during his six years as president. This figure may also give clues about opportunities for profit during the war. Contradictions become even more apparent when we look at different commodities. For instance, data from the intergovernmental *International Tropical Timber Organization* (ITTO) as quoted by Atkinson (1997, 11) show log exports from Liberia of 197 m^3 in 1992. For the same year, the *Economist Intelligence Unit* as quoted in Montclos (1999, 230) reported exports of 143,000 m^3. William Reno reported that foreign stakeholders in the Nimba iron ore project paid Charles Taylor "$10 million a month"

58 That would imply Taylor would have had to transfer little more than US$357 million abroad annually on average in the fourteen years he held power either as a warlord or a president. The whole administration of Samuel Doe was estimated to have embezzled US$300 million in ten years. Under Samuel Doe, the Liberian economy offered many more opportunities for personal enrichment than during the war while the state invested equally little in public infrastructure. If the money can indeed be traced to Taylor, this would indicate war economy profits had been invested quite successfully in business outside Liberia.

since late 1990 in order to be allowed to export stockpiled iron ore (Reno 1998, 100).[59] Prkic' (2005, 119) meticulously researched paper puts royalties paid by the same interests to the NPFL at 10,000 dollars a month between 1990 and 1992.

In this section, I take a closer look at value and amount of the various commodities traded by the NPFL. The section is based on third party research results, but for the first time compares all publicly available data on the Liberian war economy. By cross-checking data and taking into account differences in data quality, I hope to provide a convincing estimate of NPFL revenues.

3.2.4.1. Iron Ore

In the early days of the First War, iron ore was an important source of income for the NPFL. Iron ore extraction is capital intensive, and because of the lack of juridical standing of rebels and the inability of irregular armed actors to guarantee long-term security, iron ore extraction is unlikely to be undertaken during war. Yet in Liberia, iron ore production did take place under rebel authority. As will be shown, exceptional circumstances account for this.

In 1989, just before the war started, the *Liberian-American-Swedish Minerals Company* (LAMCO) finally ceased extracting iron ore in Nimba County, as reserves viable at the then-prevailing world market prices had been exploited, and handed the facilities over to the Liberian government. On the Guinean side of the border, however, there were still huge untouched reserves of high grade iron ore. A new project, the *Nimba International Mining Company* (NIMCO), was concluded to exploit these reserves and transport the ore via the LAMCO railway line to the port of Buchanan. Export through Guinea would have required the construction of some 350 km of new railway line through difficult terrain and the upgrading of a further 650 km of existing railway connections, implying tremendous costs and jeopardizing the commercial viability of the Guinean mines. Initial stakeholders in the NIMCO project were the states of Guinea and Liberia, which created the two public corporations *Mines de Fer de Guinée* (MIFERGUI) and the *Liberian Mining Corporation* (LIMINCO). Private investors who joined the project included the Swedish group

59 Information is not consistent and a reference table puts the total value of iron ore trade at US$40 million in 1990 and US$30 million in 1992 only (Reno 1998, 99).

Wallenberg (which had been a LAMCO stakeholder) and the London-based *African Mining Consortium Limited* (AMCL), which brought together rich Liberian exiles in the US with ties to Taylor and Japanese, British and US-American investors (Körner 1996, 167).

"While waiting for the first Guinean ore to come, it was then crucial for the Liberians to keep railways and port facilities in a good state since they were the only justification for their participation in the project. For this purpose, they decided that mining activities should go on a little longer in Yekepa in order to keep using the facilities and to sell enough iron ore to cover the wages of the remaining staff as well as the cost of all necessary minor repairs. The 'Liberian Mining Corporation' (LIMINCO) was thus created specifically for this linking project." (Prkic 2005, 118)

Taylor's invasion threatened the project, but as he appeared to be poised to win quickly, stakeholders considered the threat manageable. In April 1990 iron ore extraction was stopped in Nimba, yet "by October some partners in the project started negotiations with the NPFL leadership and it was agreed that the whole linking project should go on" (Prkic 2005, 118). As has been mentioned, by then LIMINCO had become a "public corporation" of "Greater Liberia" under the control of, and staffed by, Taylor.

Mining facilities had suffered damages of about 6.3 million dollars in the fighting and needed to be repaired. The AMCL granted the NPFL-led LIMINCO 800,000 dollar, and three foreign banks, *Sifida Investment Company Ltd., Credit Suisse*, and *Société Générale* awarded loans of 3.2 million dollars a little later. Awarding these loans was a high-risk business as the Taylor-led LIMINCO had at best no legal standing and could, at worst, be considered an organized crime outfit. It has been suspected that the loans indeed represented covert French government support for the NPFL (Reno 1998, 101). Initially, it was exclusively stockpiled iron ore that was exported, incurring minimal costs. "In 1991, one million tons of iron ore was sold abroad, for a total amount of 16 million dollars, three quarters of which were bought by the French firm Sollac on behalf of the state-owned company USINOR for 11.2 million dollars" (Prkic 2005, 119). Some of the money may have been diverted to the benefit of the NPFL, although it was essentially "used to pay wages, to buy small spare parts, and to pay back part of LIMINCO's debt. The new funds were not enough to finance the linking project" (Prkic 2005, 119).

Thus "by the end of 1991, it became necessary to start exploiting the mines again" (ibid.). The activities were relatively small scale, as there was little iron ore left and the project was cash-strapped. Several shipments were sent to Europe in 1992, among them at least three to Sollac and additional ones to Eurofer. When ECOMOG captured Buchanan in early 1993, iron ore exports had to cease.

Table 2: Estimates of Value of Iron Ore Exports from Liberia, in US$ Million

	1988	1989	1990	1991	1992	1993	1994
Iron ore exports	*119	n/a	40	30	25	0	0

*Sources: Reno (1998, 99); *Atkinson (1997, 9)*

Charles Taylor may have received 80,000 dollars per shipment of iron ore (cf. Reno 1998, 100) or per month (Ellis 2007a, 164). Prkic considers a royalty of 10,000 dollars a month paid by LIMINCO to the NPFL to be the main, direct financial benefit of the ore (Prkic 2005, 119). All this indicates rather small profits for the NPFL of less than one million dollars a year, compared to both capital investment in mining and the costs of waging a war. The NPFL may have profited in additional ways, i.e. embezzling LIMINCO monies, charging additional fees when opportunities presented themselves, and using the railway for military purposes. What is important is that costs of production were rising during war and profit margins were falling; eventually iron ore mining was not compatible with a state of war. From the start, the mining activities of NIMCO stakeholders took place under unusual circumstances and were dependent on these: LIMINCO was not intended to be profitable but should merely continue to exist. Investments of both banks and NIMCO stakeholders in mining activities represented a special case of "booty futures" (cf. Ross 2005) predicated on the assumption that Taylor would win the war, and business could start once he was president. Generally, "Taylor's ties to larger, more bureaucratized firms were predicated on those firm's (sic) assumption that he would win the war and become ruler of a sovereign state" (Reno 1998, 102). When peace failed to materialize, private investors abandoned the project. Generally, Taylor had to deal with small and middle-sized firms with limited capital and human capital endowments. This was particularly evident concerning timber exploitation.

3.2.4.2. Timber

Available data suggests timber was more important a source of revenue for the NPFL than iron ore, although sources differ concerning the volumes involved. Generally, the more reliable estimates of trade volumes are based on import statistics of receiving countries. However, few authors take the pains to distinguish between value in cif prices, value in fob prices, and profits. For example, in what is the most detailed analysis of war economy commodities, Prkic states that "the NPFL should [...] have received around 40 million dollars in the sole two years 1991 and 1992" according to data from diverse sources suggesting exports of some 142,900m³ of timber from NPFL territory to Europe in 1991 and 200,000m³ in 1992 (Prkic 2005, 120).[60]

Table 3: Figures on Timber Trade, in US$ Million

<table>
<tr><th>Source</th><th>Specifications</th><th>1990</th><th>1991</th><th>1992</th><th>1993</th></tr>
<tr><td>Reno (1998, 99)</td><td>Value of NPFL Timber Trade</td><td>15.0</td><td>21.3</td><td>30.3</td><td>25.0</td></tr>
<tr><td>US Department of State (1996)</td><td>Liberian Timber Exports, All Factions, annual average 1990–94</td><td>53.0</td><td>53.0</td><td>53.0</td><td>53.0</td></tr>
<tr><td>Prkic (2005, 120)</td><td>Payments to NPFL</td><td>n/a</td><td colspan="2">40.0</td><td>n/a</td></tr>
</table>

Table 4: Post-War Timber Exports, FOB, in US$ Million

Source	1997	1998	1999	2000
IMF (2000a); (2003a)	5	12	23	61
Global Witness (2001, 3)	n/a	n/a	n/a	130

Tables 3 and 4 present available figures on the timber trade. Estimates for the value of trade post-1993 are in extremely short supply. While Twaddell's estimate of 53 million per year (US Department of State 1996) appears overstated, records of the *International Tropical Timber Organization*

60 An important impediment to obtaining figures on NPFL timber trade is that a substantial part of production was exported through Côte d'Ivoire and is likely to have been recorded as Ivorian in destination countries. Yet in 1992 Taylor still had two important harbors used for log exports under control, and exports through Côte d'Ivoire are likely to have been rather few.

(ITTO) showing, for instance, exports of 40 m^3 in 1996 (quoted in Atkinson 1997, 11) are implausible. Official post-war figures as used by the IMF (Table 4) are limited in reliability, and were doubted both by IMF staff (2003b, 27) and Global Witness (2002, 11). Yet clearly, post war exports of Liberian timber increased drastically from a rather low base as larger firms entered the market (cf. Consortium Agrifor Consult 2004). Timber exports thus appear not to have been particularly high during the war, and may have been particularly low towards the end of the first war.

Assuming that Prkic's figure more appropriately describes the value of trade than NPFL revenue, it implies a price of some 116 dollars per m^3, roughly corresponding to a price of 117.70 paid for Liberian timber in 1991 according to governmental data (Prkic 2005, 120). Generally, fob prices for Liberian logs oscillate between 100 and 150 dollars per m^3, and due to "creaming out" of the forests, prices approached the higher range of the extremes at least from 1996 to 1998 (Consortium Agrifor Consult 2004, 95), giving us more of an idea of the domestic turnover of the trade during the war.[61] A price of 150 dollars paid for the volumes identified by Prkic would imply a fob value of 21.4 million in 1991 and 30 million dollars in 1992, bringing us closer to Reno's estimate of the value of trade, which I therefore take as the basis for further calculations.

Given the situation of military control, NPFL timber trade is likely to have peaked in 1992, have fallen drastically until mid-1995, and then have slightly increased again since, although in the final war years timber "production [was] greatly reduced by the continuous insecurity in the [south-eastern] Buchanan and Greenville port areas" (Atkinson 1997, 11). Assuming that Reno's figures for the value of timber trade in the early 1990s were roughly correct and the timber sector developed roughly in parallel to rubber (see below), while taking into account that due to the loss of sea ports and greater depletion of reserves in easily accessible areas the rebound in times of extended military control should have been weaker, I estimate the African fob value of the Liberian timber trade at some ten million dollars in 1994, 13 million in 1995, and 15–20 million in 1996.

But how much of this trade was profit for the NPFL? Generally, the timber war economy was privately organized, i.e. small firms not directly

61 Most likely, "creaming out" of the forests took place throughout the war, as instability promotes short-term time horizons. As the Liberian fob price of US$150 per m^3 of high quality timber is extremely cheap by international standards, it should have been possible to find buyers even under circumstances of war.

associated with a particular faction (indeed, many of them operated under different factions) organized logging and export, while the political-military power in place taxed the business (Montclos 1999; Prkic 2005).[62] Taylor reportedly charged 300,000 dollars for a license allowing log exports (Africa Confidential May 17, 1991), but as there is insufficient information on the number of log exporters in "Greater Liberia", we can only guess that these fees amounted to a few million dollars throughout the period of the first war. According to Rowland Bedell, the NPRAG Deputy Minister of Finance who defected in late 1991, log exports were taxed at 10 percent (West Africa Dec. 16, 1991). This appears to be quite low and may have been intended to attract loggers when the NPFL's economic basis was still weak, and license fees would have to be added. Taxed at 10 percent, Taylor should have made some 3.03 million dollars from timber in 1992. Other sources allege that Taylor taxed exports at about a third of the value (Farah 2005, 18). In order to get an idea of profits accrued to the NPFL, taxes and fees officially collected by the regular Liberian government under Taylor's presidency provide another reference. If Taylor had charged fees and taxes at the same terms as the "state", roughly amounting to 26 percent of the fob value (cf. Consortium Agrifor Consult 2004, 95),[63] the NPFL should have made some 8 million from timber in 1992.[64] It should be noted that under Taylor's control, too, timber companies had to shoulder considerable costs for (access) road construction, maintenance of port facilities, provision of electricity, logging and transport equipment, and personnel, decreasing potential NPFL revenue. Based on the above, we may tentatively estimate Taylor's income from timber at 26 percent of the estimated fob value, as stated in the preceding paragraph (for detailed figures see Table 9 at the end of this section).

62 Generally, Taylor personally dealt with the more important businesspeople in his fief (Ellis 2007a, 90). Yet the arrangements imply that only part of the fob value can be considered NPFL income, casting doubts on Prkic's (2005, 120) estimate of NPFL timber revenue.

63 Calculation is somewhat more complicated than a flat 10 percent. The Taylor government charged US$26.50 per m^3 plus 8.9 percent taxes on the fob value (consisting of 5 percent export tax, 2,5 percent turnover tax, and 1,4 percent BIVAC inspection taxes). The above estimate is based on Prkic's (2005) figure of 200,000 m^3 log exports and an estimated fob value of US$150 per m^3 (cf. Consortium Agrifor Consult 2004, 95).

64 This is broken down in US$5.3 million in fees and US$2.67 million in taxes.

3.2.4.3. Rubber

Another important war economy resource in Liberia was rubber. Charles Taylor quickly entered an agreement with *Firestone* and the *Liberian Agricultural Company* (LAC) after the NPFL had conquered the plantation areas. Already in July 1990, LAC recommenced rubber production at its plantation near Buchanan, Grand Bassa County. A Memorandum of Understanding with *Firestone* was concluded in January 1992 (Ellis 2007a, 167) and provided that the company paid its taxes in rice to feed NPFL combatants (Montclos 1999, 231). Goods needed for the subsistence of fighters are considered the main benefit to the NPFL and it is unclear which direct financial benefits it received from either LAC or *Firestone*.[65] According to Reno (1998, 99), rubber valued at some 27 million dollars was exported annually 1990–1992 from Taylor-held territory, well below the official 120 million dollars fob value of the trade in 1989 (EIU 7/1996, 33).[66]

Management-controlled production on the two largest, foreign-held plantations ceased after ECOMOG and its allies captured Kakata and Buchanan in early 1993. From then on, *Firestone* was ECOMOG-patrolled and LAC plantation areas were alternately controlled by LPC and NPFL forces. In the years to come, extensive "illicit tapping" took place on all plantations, including *Firestone* and LAC. It is estimated that some 40,000 tons of rubber were "stolen" from the *Firestone* plantation in four years (Montclos 1999, 231–232). Prkic estimated that throughout the war, 20,000 to 30,000 tons of rubber were exported every year (Prkic 2005, 122). He argued that official data should underestimate exports, as significant volumes were considered to have been "smuggled" into Côte d'Ivoire and exported as Ivorian.

---

65 The TRC (2009, 178) reported that *Firestone* was alleged to have paid US$ 2 million a year to Taylor. The figure roughly corresponds to my estimate of Taylor's rubber profits (see below).

66 Data quality is poor, and the official value of rubber exports can neither be reconciled with the New York cif value of Liberian exports nor the IMF estimate (see Table 4). Another problem is that official export figures were given in Liberian dollars. In 1989, the L$ and the US$ were officially still on a par, and many international statistics consider the L$ to represent the US$ value. On the Liberian black market, however, Liberian dollars traded at a significant discount (cf. EIU 7/1996, 33).

Table 5: Data on Liberian Rubber Exports and Prices

	1989	1990	1991	1992	1993	1994	1995	1996	1997
Recorded Exports, In Thousand Metric Tones	106.0	19.0	32.0	30.0	45.0	10.0	13.0	30.0	67.2
New York Cif Value of Exports in US$ Million, Based on TSR 20 Prices	96.0	16.2	27.9	27.9	39.9	12.5	21.9	42.6	74.3
Reno Estimate of Exports, in US$ Million**	–	27.0	27.0	27	–	–	–	–	–
IMF-Estimate of Rubber Exports, in US$ Million***	55.1	27.6	17.2	13.8	10.3	3.9	2.4	8.1	19.4
Fob Value at US$300/Ton, in US$ Million*	31.8	5.7	9.6	9.0	13.5	3.0	3.9	9.0	20.2

The drastic increase in recorded exports in 1993 is surprising, if not implausible, as large-scale fighting and displacement had particularly negative effects on the Firestone and LAC plantations. Last-minute clearance, looting of stocks of large producers, and increased "slaughter tapping" as factions assumed partial control may be an explanation.

*Sources: International Rubber Study Group (2002, 10, 56); * Ellis (2007a, 167); **Reno (1998, 99); ***IMF (2000a, 29)*

Yet the most authoritative international statistics (International Rubber Study Group 2002) suggests Liberian exports were significantly higher during most of the war and approached the lower end of the range in 1994 and 1995 (Table 5). Statistics of Ivorian rubber exports do not show any conspicuous developments, and given wide spread collusion between ECOMOG officers and the NPFL, it is quite likely that a large proportion of Liberian rubber was exported through Liberian ports, in particular Monrovia.[67] While the statistics should underestimate exports, the sketchy data we have on war time rubber exports broadly appear to support it (see as well the analysis of the INPFL and the LPC in the subsequent section). I suggest it comes quite close to depicting actual exports and quite reliably indicates trends.

Much as the timber business, the rubber economy was organized on a private enterprise basis in "Greater Liberia". Rubber was sold by producers and looters to brokers who organized exports. This trade was then taxed by the NPFL (cf. Prkic 2005, 122). In some cases, NPFL commanders were known to have personally established business contacts with foreign buyers and sold rubber (cf. Prkic 2005, 121). NPFL fighters and business-people closely associated with the NPFL are likely to have taken over a large proportion of the internal rubber trade (cf. Ellis 2007a, 89, 97). Information on volumes, quality, destination and taxing of rubber exports is deficient, and Prkic holds that it was "impossible to get any idea, even an approximation, of the revenues generated by rubber export" (Prkic 2005, 122).

I will nevertheless try to give a reasoned, if very rough, approximation of the NPFL's rubber revenue. According to Ellis (2007a, 167), Monrovia-based exporters paid some 300 dollars per ton of rubber during the war. A plausibility test can be made on the basis of international prices. Liberia produces various qualities and types of rubber. One of the few of these types for which international prices for the period concerned are available is the New York price for *Technically Specified Rubbers 20* (TSR 20). According to the amended 2008 agreement between Liberia and *Firestone* of (cf.

67 Both rubber production and exports of Côte d'Ivoire were volatile, but fluctuations were similar to those experienced by other producers, and no clear pattern of exports shifting from Liberia to its neighbor is discernible (cf. International Rubber Study Group 2002, 9–10). In 1989, Côte d'Ivoire's rubber exports approached some 63 percent of Liberia's, and if substantial amounts of Liberian rubber had been exported via Côte d'Ivoire and recorded as Ivorian, the statistics should have given conspicuous evidence.

Government of Liberia 2008), the TSR 20 Singapore price determines *Firestone's* export prices,[68] suggesting the use of TSR 20 prices as proxies for the international value of trade.[69] A price of 300 dollars per ton amounts to some 27 percent of the New York TSR 20 cif price (a 1990 to 1996 average), which appears plausible.[70]

I assume that exports recorded by the International Rubber Study Group (2002) indeed accurately represent Liberian exports. Given military control, Taylor is likely to have administered almost all (95%) of this trade until late 1992, about half (50%) of it from 1993 to mid-1995, and significantly more (75%) in the years thereafter. I further assume that the Monrovian price represents prices at points of export. Rubber was valued at 300 dollars per ton (fob), and rubber exports were taxed at levels similar to the situation in 2008, i.e. at roughly 25 percent (cf. Government of Liberia 2008). On the one hand, prices are likely to have been lower in Greenville and Harper, Taylor's international ports, but on the other, unrecorded exports may have offset foregone revenue. Based on the above, I estimate NPFL rubber revenue to have oscillated between 0.4 and 3.8 million dollars per year (for details see Table 9 at the end of this section).

These profits were not particularly high given the cost of war, but extremely volatile and anything but a sustainable basis for warfare. In the long run, rubber could not have financed the war as it cannot be sustainably produced under conditions of war. Important characteristics of rubber are that plantations frequently cover large areas difficult to control, that plantations require long-term planning and that tapping needs to be regulated in order to prevent damages to trees caused by overexploitation. Rubber trees become productive about seven years after planting and need to be replaced after some 27 years. No investment into replanting took place during the war. Furthermore, illicit tappers have incentives to overexploit trees by cutting deep and long trenches into the cortex. This practice initially allows high yields, but quickly leads to diminishing pro-

68 TSR 20 Singapore prices are only available since 1996 when the commodity started being traded regularly on the Singapore Commodity Exchange (SICOM).

69 TSR 20 prices may also serve as a point of reference for the value of trade as the variety is of average quality, situated between excellent quality TSR 5 and fair quality TSR 50.

70 During my research in rubber areas in Liberia in 2006, New York TSR 20 cif prices stood at around US$2,100 per ton. In Liberia, prices for raw rubber reached US$800 in the vicinity of Monrovia and close to processing facilities, and US$535 in Greenville, some 120 km sea transport distance to the LAC buying station in Buchanan. This amounts to 38% and 25% respectively of the international price.

ductivity and finally death of the trees. In addition, plantations were damaged by charcoal production (cf. Montclos 1999, 232). The Liberian wars have almost totally destroyed the once thriving rubber industry (US Embassy in Monrovia n.d. [2006]: 26). However, even if at a rather low level, rubber continued to finance war efforts (Weissmann 1996, 98). Taxing of exports enabled the leadership to strategically dispose of resources, while conduct of business by combatants and NPFL sympathizers enabled rebels on different levels of the hierarchy to acquire part of the profits.

3.2.4.4. Diamonds

While the role of rubber in the Liberian war economy has hardly been discussed, the role of diamonds has generated a heated debate. Largely due to NGO campaigns denouncing profits made in the wars in Liberia and Sierra Leone, the term "blood diamond" has become common usage. Furthermore, the phenomenon of diamonds funding war has triggered a global political initiative for stricter supervision of the diamond industry, the Kimberley Process. Yet despite much international uproar, rather little was known about the role of diamonds in the Liberian and Sierra Leonean wars, and they appear to have been of minor significance for the NPFL for most of the war.

Liberia has very few gem-stone quality diamond deposits, mainly along the Lofa River in Lofa and Gbarpolu Counties. The NPFL undertook some small-scale mining there and in Bong County until the areas were progressively occupied by ULIMO, starting in 1991 (cf. Prkic 2005, 123). In contrast, eastern Sierra Leone features alluvial fields renowned for the quality of the diamonds they contain. Cross border trade between the RUF and the NPFL, in which the RUF is considered to have mostly bartered diamonds against weapons (Panel of Experts 12/2000, 16), and re-export of gems by the NPFL thus was at the center of the debate about Liberian "Blood Diamonds".

Estimates of the Liberian diamond trade vary widely. For instance, Atkinson quotes estimates of the value of the trade of some 300 to 500 million dollars (Antwerp cif) in 1995 (Atkinson 1997, 9–10). IMF statistics gave figures of Liberian diamond imports into Belgium of 309 million in 1994 and 317 million in 1995 (quoted in: ibid.). Reno quoted figures suggesting diamond exports of 391 million dollars value in 1994 and 217 million in the first half of 1995 (Reno 1998, 103). Official figures showed diamond export earnings to be between 8.4 (Atkinson 1997, 9) and 8.8 million (Smillie 2007, 9) for Liberia in 1988, suggesting immense growth of the trade to the benefit of rebels. However, interpretation of these figures is complicated. Firstly, Belgian import statistics are anything but reliable. Secondly, data quality on the pre-war diamond trade is extremely poor. Official Sierra Leonean exports fell strongly over the last decades, as political elites and businesspeople increasingly resorted to smuggling (cf. Gberie 2002). There was no consensus which past official statistics could serve as the most accurate indicator of contemporary production.

A most influential voice in the debate on conflict diamonds has been Ian Smillie, a specialist on the international diamond industry. Smillie was a co-author of probably the most influential early publication on Sierra Leonean "blood diamonds" (cf. Smillie/Gberie/Hazleton 2000). Shortly after its publication, Smillie was recruited as diamond expert into the newly constituted Panel of Experts on Sierra Leone, which dealt specifically with the gem trade of the RUF, and later served in the Panel of Experts team on Liberia. The UN reports and other publications by Smillie have become the most authoritative sources on diamonds in the war economies of Sierra Leone and Liberia.

Readily available data on the diamond trade (see Table 6) is implausible. Variations in trade volumes are massive and unrelated to productive capacity, and per carat value fluctuates widely. The most plausible explanation is that "almost none of the huge volume of diamonds entering Belgium [...] as Liberian (1990–1999) were of Liberian origin" (Smillie 2007, 10). Some surely were mined in Sierra Leone. Yet it is widely believed that a significant amount originated from other countries, particularly Russia, and were declared Liberian in order to obscure the violation of contracts that had been concluded with diamond giant De Beers (ibid., 11). De Beers used to have a quasi-monopoly over the worldwide diamond trade and still controls the majority of the business e.g. through contracts with producers and traders intended to limit supply of the commodity.

Table 6: Liberian Diamond Exports and Belgian Imports (Weight in Thousands of Carats; Value in US$ Thousand

Year	Liberian exports (Liberian Government)			Belgian Diamond Imports from Liberia (Diamond High Council)		
	Carats	Value	US$/carat	Carats	Value	US$/carat
1985	138.0	–	–	–	–	–
1986	252.0	–	–	–	–	–
1987	295.0	10,944	37.09	–	–	–
1988	267.0	8,838	52.92	–	–	–
1989	150.0	8,633	57.55	–	–	–
1990	No official exports because of war			5,530	365,510	66.09
1991				684	134,710	196.94
1992				1,909	313,800	164.37
1993				5,006	283,930	56.71
1994				3,269	392,380	120.03
1994 (sic)				10,678	358,800	33.60
1996				12,629	616,200	48.79
1997				5,862	329,180	56.15
1998	8.0	800	100.00	2,558	269,950	105.53
1999	8.5	900	105.88	1,876	298,820	158.28

Source: Smillie (2007, 9)

Within a few weeks of the war in Sierra Leone, the RUF rebels (who at that time were still largely composed of NPFL combatants) occupied alluvial mining areas in the east of the country (Prkic 2005, 123). However, "until 1995, RUF diamond mining and digging was probably done on a sporadic and individual basis" (Panel of Experts 12/2000, 16). While the quoted Panel of Experts report estimated diamond exports of the RUF at 25 to 125 million dollars annually during the second half of the 1990s, production appeared to have been much less before 1995. Furthermore, while diamonds surely contributed to the subsistence of combatants and thus to the continuation of war, the industry seems to have been hardly controlled by the rebel leadership, and accordingly was of limited use strategically. During the first half of the 1990s, Taylor's main interest in the diamond fields of Sierra Leone may have been to deny the Sierra Leonean government revenue, as the country served as a staging base for ECOMOG (Smillie 2007, 11–12). Logistical difficulties may have partly accounted for this, as ULIMO occupied western Liberia and was active in eastern Sierra Leone

Of particular importance to the Sierra Leonean diamond economy were Tongo Field in Kenema District and Koidu Field in Kono District. Kono was Sierra Leone's most important gem mining province and had historically produced some 65–70 percent of the country's diamonds (cf. Gberie 2002, 6). Kono was conquered by the RUF in September 1992 for the first time, and was held for a total of almost six years in the nine years to come. Control over Tongo Field was only assumed in 1997, though the site had frequently been attacked before. Between 1997 and 2001, the RUF controlled Tongo for about two-and-a-half years between then and 2001 (cf. Smillie 2007, 28).

Mining by individual RUF commanders for the upkeep of troops and personal purposes seems to have aroused the interest of the Sierra Leonean rebel leadership as well as its Liberian sponsor, Charles Taylor. "By 1995 [...] the RUF and its patrons were clearly taking a much greater interest in the diamond fields of Kono District", and profits soared (Panel of Experts 12/2000, 16). Yet from December 1995 to May 1997, the RUF was prevented from mining in Kono by the private South African military security firm Executive Outcomes, which had been hired by the government.[71] After Executive Outcomes had left, "the diamond areas of Kono and Tongo Field became a prime military focus of the RUF, and diamond mining became a major fund-raising exercise" (ibid., 16). A lower estimate of annual productive capacity of both diamond fields is 25 million dollars, and analysts of the war economy assume that RUF diamond production grew from a low level to substantial volumes once the rebels put emphasis on the business (cf. ibid; cf. Farah 2005, 17). Meanwhile, post-war diamond production in Sierra Leone has generated new data, allowing a more accurate estimate of productive capacity. Based on this, the value of the RUF diamond trade at its peak post-1997, i.e. when the RUF controlled both Kono and Tongo Field, is now estimated to have been 60 to 80 million dollars a year (Smillie 2007, 11).[72]

71 Executive Outcomes actually had to leave Sierra Leone in February 1997 as part of a peace deal between the government and the rebels, but it took the latter some two more months to team up with renegade army soldiers, topple the government and subsequently occupy Kono.

72 The value, based on Sierra Leonean government figures, reflects African export prices (i.e. prices Charles Taylor would have tried to negotiate when selling the diamonds to international dealers), rather than money received by the RUF.

Given that the RUF controlled only Kono, accounting for roughly 75 percent of the capacity of both fields, for some eleven months of 1995, I estimate the value of the trade at some 17 million dollars for that year. I further assume that Taylor marketed some 80 percent of the RUF diamond production and cashed in two thirds of the proceeds as profits (cf. Farah 2005, 17). This implies Taylor made a little over nine million dollars from Sierra Leonean diamonds in 1995. A similar calculation for 1997, taking into account that the RUF controlled both fields for about seven months, suggests Taylor made a profit of less than eight million dollars that year.

Several points are worth emphasizing concerning the NPFL's diamond deals. For the first three-and-a-half years of the Sierra Leonean war, the diamond business seems to have been organized by mid-level commanders at a low level of sophistication. There is no serious estimate of the value of the business before 1997. Given that it may have been worth around 20 million dollars by then, the trade is likely to have been a multi-million dollars business already by the early 1990s. Yet a rather small fraction of this seems to have been at the disposal of either the RUF leadership or Charles Taylor, and the business hardly had any impact on military strategy, either in terms of enabling acquisition of weapons or in terms of control of the mines being a primary military objective. This changed in 1995 when, domestically, the NPFL was getting stronger and gaining territory again. During that year, Sierra Leonean diamonds may already have been a major income source for Taylor.

Important in terms of strategy, Taylor's diamond profits were dependent on the war in Sierra Leone. If the RUF had secured a position in government and the ability to sell diamonds legally, it would likely have bypassed Taylor and monopolized profits. There are clear indications that Taylor tried to sabotage the Sierra Leone peace process, urging RUF commanders close to him not to disarm and to maintain control over the diamond fields (cf. Smillie 2007, 16–17). Alluvial diamonds are considered particularly suited to war economies, as extraction requires little capital while the stones can easily be concealed and transported. Yet while diamonds indeed had a strong impact on the continuation of war in Sierra Leone, the trade only assumed major political importance in Liberia when Charles Taylor was the sovereign president of Liberia. This will be dealt with in the section on Charles Taylor's presidency at the end of this chapter. My estimates of the war-time diamond trade can be found in Table 9 at the end of this section.

3.2.4.5. Miscellaneous

There were further war economy resources of lesser importance, in particular gold, coffee, cocoa, and marihuana. Liberia's gold reserves are concentrated in the east of the country, in areas over which the NPFL lost control in 1993 and only regained partially from 1995 to 1996. Generally, NPFL involvement in gold mining and trade was limited in significance,[73] and the "little production of gold at their disposal [...] seems to have [been] used [...] as a way to keep up its networks of influence, especially among Ivorian officials", rather than directly financing the war effort (Prkic 2005, 123).

Coffee and cocoa seem to have been somewhat more important, though figures are limited in reliability, as a significant proportion of the pre-war production was smuggled into Côte d'Ivoire and never entered any statistics. Taylor also sold virtually the whole production of his territory to Côte d'Ivoire. However, coffee and cocoa historically were not major export goods of Liberia, and volumes were small from the beginning. Production was estimated to have fallen by some 50 percent between 1989 and 1991, and was almost extinct by 1995. Post-war export figures only show a very modest recovery, indicating that production had indeed massively fallen during the war. Although the figures should be treated with care, this trend does make sense, as coffee and cocoa are sensitive crops that need regular care, e.g. under-brushing, as well as steady harvesting and are thus severely affected by (temporary) displacement. Furthermore, much as rubber, the stock should become depleted naturally during war.[74] While the war is likely to have pushed down producer prices and thus temporarily increased the profit margins of NPFL trade, within a few years it had almost totally destroyed production.

Coffee and cocoa were exclusively produced by smallholders, notably in Nimba, Lofa and central Liberia. The coffee and cocoa trade during the war appears to have largely been controlled by the NPFL rather than any

73 Gold exports from Liberia of all factions combined may have averaged one US$ Million annually 1990–1994 (US Department of State 1996).

74 For instance, coffee trees are usually replaced after about 30 years lifetime, the first six of which are needed to reach commercially viable productivity levels (cf. http://www.coffeedetective.com/what-is-the-full-life-cycle-of-coffee.html (10.02.2008)). Cocoa reaches full productivity after about ten years and produces on a high level for some 13 years, although plants may be harvested for up to 30 years. (cf. http://www.worldcocoafoundation.org/learn-about-cocoa/tree-to-table/growing.asp (10.02.2008)). Replanting is unlikely to have taken place during the war.

other faction, and much in the tradition of African marketing boards, Taylor bought the whole production in his territory at a price he fixed himself. The proceeds seem to have been used to buy goods in Côte d'Ivoire needed for the upkeep of the NPFL administration (Prkic 2005, 122–123).

Table 7: Coffee and Cocoa Production, FOB Prices, in US$ Million

	1989	1990	1991	1992	1993	1994
Coffee	1.0	0.7	0.5	0.4	0.3	0.1
Cocoa	8.1	3.7	2.5	2.1	1.6	0.8

	1994	1995	1996	1997	1998	1999
Coffee	0.1	0.0	0.1	0.1	0.3	0.4
Cocoa	8.1	3.7	2.5	2.1	1.6	0.8

Source: IMF (2000a, 28)

Another prominent war economy resource was cannabis. The NPFL induced farmers to grow the drug, which appears to have been destined primarily for the faction's combatants. There were "no indications that this production was taxed" (Prkic 2005, 129). The NPFL probably even imported the drug from the Casamance region of Senegal, in exchange for weapons for the *Movement des Forces Démocratiques de la Casamance* (MFDC). Yet significant volumes were traded by the NPFL itself, much of it into Côte d'Ivoire (ibid.) Exports may have reached Europe, as in 1997 Dutch police "revealed the existence of a large-scale racket said to be operating under the protection of the NPFL" (Ellis 2007a, 170). Although marihuana clearly contributed to the NPFL economy, profits should not be overestimated. African prices are low, with transport costs (to Abidjan and places of export) constituting a major price component. The Dutch and European markets in the 1990s were characterized by intense competition and rather low demand for African-grown "natural" cannabis, as new Dutch breeds dominated the market.

3.2.4.6. Looting, extortion, and racketeering

Finally, a major form of economic activity, and probably the economic activity most suited to war, was looting. Looting had a significant impact on war actors on different levels of the hierarchy. Of greatest importance, of course, was looting that benefited strategic designs of the rebel leadership. Reportedly the greatest strategic looting took place when the NPFL occupied the *Bong Mining Company* (BMC) complex. Charles Taylor's brother Gbatu succeeded to sell part of the company's heavy machinery on the international market (Montclos 1999, 229). The BMC was just about to close its operations because the low grade reserves in Bong County had been exploited when the war started. However, at least until late 1994, Charles Taylor generally tried to protect facilities and infrastructures that could generate important revenue once he became president, such as the LIMINCO facilities in Nimba and the port of Buchanan (cf. Ellis 2007a, 143). As revenue generation through productive activities decreased and future production became increasingly unlikely due to war damages, more infrastructures were dismantled, though this seemed to be organized by lower levels of the hierarchy. The sales of BMC equipment was most likely a major element in transforming the NPFL from a poorly organized force into the most important armed faction. Yet by and large, looting as part of a centrally organized military strategy aimed at acquiring goods needed to undertake revenue generating activities or increase military capacity, or else provided incentives to combatants.

The NPFL directly targeted locally active businesspeople. "NPFL attacks on Liberian Mandingo [... constituted an] ambitious attempt to replace a vulnerable minority group and foreign traders as intermediaries and directly conduct commerce for the benefit of NPFL fighters" (Reno 1998, 98). By late 1990, trade in several Lofa County towns was in the hands of NPFL combatants (ibid., 97). Generally, supporters of the NPFL, many of them civilians, "soon acquired control of local trade" (Ellis 2007a, 89). Though many of these appear to have retired to civilian life after having "plundered something of substantial value to set themselves up in business" (ibid., 124), the NPFL is likely to have benefited by way of taxes and contributions.

Of particular importance to the NPFL business were means of transport. As has been shown, the value of NPFL trade in most cases was rather low. The profit margin is crucially affected by costs of capital goods, e.g. trucks and spare parts. In the beginning of the war, these goods could be sourced from different actors: government, domestic businesspeople, foreign companies, development assistance agencies. Yet the pool of lootable capital goods quickly diminishes, and those appropriated wear down. Profits based on externalizing investment costs thus should be temporary and unsustainable. Yet humanitarian actors continue to bring in means of transport, spare parts and other capital goods when other actors have abandoned the scene. Major looting of humanitarian agencies took place during and after "Operation Octopus" (end 1992/early 1993), during the battles for Gbarnga September to December 1994, and April/May 1996. During the fighting for Gbarnga, humanitarian organizations lost 27 trucks and 74 light vehicles (Prkic 2005, 128), and in the two months of 1996, about 500 of its vehicles were stolen. Including other goods looted, the humanitarian community lost some 25 million dollars in these two instances alone (Weissman 1996, 102–103). Furthermore, since late 1991, "chaque offensive s'est accompagnée du pillage quasi integral des organismes d'aide dans les regions concernées" (ibid., 102), leading to substantial losses over time. Even relative to other sources of armed faction income, the humanitarian community provided substantial amounts. More importantly, humanitarian resources were apparently used to exploit the productive branches of the Liberian war economy and are likely to have increased profit margins of trade in war economy goods.

Looting mostly took place during military battles (though some battles were feigned in order to create opportunities for looting). "In their core territories, most factions attempted to reach some sort of *modus vivendi* with the civilian population, if only because the fighters required them to provide food from their farms" (Ellis 2007a, 143). The same held true for relations between humanitarian actors and the NPFL. Compared to the other factions, the NPFL appeared to have established a relatively high degree of order in territories under its control (ibid., 129). Yet that involved regular taxation of humanitarian agencies. "In September 1994, the NPFL created an office that used to require a fee of 15 percent of the budget of every mission undertaken in NPFL territory and on the use of all equipment needed for the mission after it was completed" (Prkic 2005, 127). The NPFL further charged some 5,000 Liberian dollars for humanitarian ships using the port of Greenville (ibid.). In 1992, Charles Taylor forbade humanitarian assistance entering from Monrovia and decreed it should be delivered via the NPFL-controlled ports (Africa Confidential Nov. 6, 1992). Furthermore, humanitarian agencies were required to pay for a security detachment accompanying convoys, and they faced further charges at the numerous checkpoints throughout "Greater Liberia" as well as at distribution centers (cf. Prkic 2005, 127).

Humanitarian actors thus appear to have provided valuable income, often in the particularly attractive form of cash, to NPFL leaders at different levels of the hierarchy. This income is of particular importance because the humanitarian sector is one of the two economic branches that typically grow during war and quickly constitutes a large part of the economy, while most other sources of income typically dry up. It probably is not a coincidence that the NPFL office for the taxation of humanitarian agencies was established in 1994, when income from other sources had fallen considerably. Yet the overall value of fees extorted from humanitarians was probably not too high. For much of the war, all regular humanitarian activities were confined to the ECOMOG-controlled zone, and humanitarian activities in "Greater Liberia" took place on a "sporadic" basis only (cf. UN Secretary General 02/1995, 8–9). Not least, during some periods ECOMOG imposed an economic embargo against "Greater Liberia", and even attacked a *Mèdecins Sans Frontières* convoy delivering humanitarian goods from Côte d'Ivoire (Ellis 2007a, 100).[75] ODA levels for the whole of Liberia, which largely represent humanitarian aid including overhead costs, give an idea of amounts involved, though much of the value undoubtedly remained in Monrovia or even outside Liberia.[76]

75 Given its assessment that humanitarian aid contributed substantially to Taylor's war economy, the "*United Nations Observer Mission in Liberia*" (UNOMIL) officially backed the embargo (cf. Atkinson 1997, 21).

76 The contribution of humanitarian assistance to the war is extremely difficult to assess, not least because the humanitarian community is tight-lipped on the issue. While humanitarians readily admit that they were allowed into faction territories because the fighters would succeed to divert some supplies, no one I have spoken to would admit directly paying the NPFL, although the existence of the respective office was widely known. David Bryer, head of the British NGO Oxfam, considered humanitarian agencies in Liberia to have furthered rather than alleviated the suffering of civilians. The comments were made when Oxfam withdrew from Liberia following the April/May 1996 looting (cf. Weissmann 1996, 103).

Table 8: Bi- and Multilateral Official Development Assistance to Liberia

	1990	1991	1992	1993	1994	1995	1996	1997
$m	112.1	158.0	118.9	122.9	128.5	123.1	206.1	95.4

Source: Economist Intelligence Unit (EIU 1996; 1999)

"For much of the time, aid agencies were relatively immune from workaday looting by factions" (Ellis 2007a, 139). Humanitarian actors were mostly targeted during battles, often as part of faction strategies. As in many other places on the world, looted pickups with mounted AK 47s were the combat vehicles of choice. Taylor and his brother Nelson reportedly rode in cars looted from relief agencies (Africa Confidential Nov. 6, 1992). Importantly, opportunities for extortion were a major incentive for combatants to guard checkpoints, and granting opportunities to loot frequently substituted for regular pay. "Loot is also the motivation for the young fighters to take on front-line assignments. When assigned to their bases in the hinterland they get little or no pay, and may even have to beg for food. To them any kind of loot, be it big or small, is the only way to find any money" (Pepper Bird Newspaper 2/1996, quoted in Ellis 2007a, 125).

Even though many items were looted multiple times and thus continued to feed the cycle, a depletion of the pool of lootable goods did arise from exporting, wearing down, war-related destruction and consumption. As incentives to produce are eroded, the pool is not refilled and looting becomes an unsustainable economic activity. For instance, rice production in Liberia was estimated to have fallen to 23 percent of its pre-war level by 1995 (Weissmann 1996, 102). In order to increase incentives for fighters and logistically prepare for the invasion of Sierra Leone in 1991, the NPFL alerted humanitarian agencies about the plight of civilians in the border area and urged them to provide assistance. Nevertheless, frontline looting most often appeared not to have been centrally organized (Prkic 2005, 128).

By substituting for pay and motivating combatants,[77] looting positively contributed to the combat capacities of the NPFL. Yet on an organizational level, looting appears to have been a destabilizing influence. Only

77 Utas provides some intriguing accounts as to what extent looting was necessary for combatants to maintain their social status, including the ability to entertain multiple girlfriends (Utas 2003, 169–221).

a few combatants managed to acquire significant riches, and many combatants became disillusioned with the promises of war partly because major assets were stolen early on and partly because commanders confiscated looted goods from their commandos. Selling loot before it was confiscated by commanders was an important motive for defection (Ellis 2007a, 127). The attraction of loot suffered when prices for goods fell drastically as purchasing power of civilians deteriorated (cf. Utas 2003, 197–199), a development which was only partly countered by the increasing relative value of goods as general poverty increased. Generally, to the extent that looting was based on the initiative of lower ranking combatants and means of subsistence were not controlled by the rebel leadership, it contributed to defections, switching of sides and instability of factions.

3.2.4.7. The NPFL Business

As should have become clear, the NPFL indeed was an economically well organized and diversified venture. Yet it does not appear to have been a money-making machine. Rather, the NPFL depended on trade in several goods, while the value of each trade was limited, and so were associated profits. Table 9 lists profits the NPFL leadership, i.e. Taylor, may have had direct access to and that could thus be strategically employed. Only by adding up profits realized in several sectors do we arrive at substantial amounts. Yet while the proceeds go a long way in explaining the military and organizational strength of the NPFL, Table 9 also serves as a reminder on the limits of war-as-business. There is a downward trend concerning profits of commerce of internally produced goods, although this is partially obscured by territorial gains of the NPFL from mid-1995 to 1997. Second, profits were volatile and neither reliable nor predictable, which decreases interests in war. Third, looting, the unsustainable income generating activity *par excellence*, had a major impact on profits (though it is only partly accounted for in the table). Fourth, diamonds were a post-war rather than a war economy resource. Yet then, profits were high and quickly assumed major importance for the financing of Taylor's apparatus of power.

Table 9: Profits Controlled by Taylor, in US$ Million

	1990	1991	1992	1993	1994	1995	1996	1997
Iron ore[78]	0.5	0.5	0.5	-	-	-	-	-
Timber	3.9	5.5	7.9	6.5	2.6	3.4	5.2	6.5
Rubber	1.4	2.3 (rice)	2.1 (rice)	1.7	0.4	0.7	1.7	3.8
Diamond (SLeone)	n/a	n/a	n/a	n/a	n/a	9.2	?	7.8
Coffee & Cocoa[79]	1.5	1.0	0.8	0.6	0.3	0	0.2	0.2
Looting[80]	10.0	-	5	-	2,5	-	15.0	-
Profits	17.3	9.3	16.3	8.8	5.8	13.3	22.1	18.3

Author's estimate

Clearly, this estimate is subject to considerable uncertainties. Diamonds may have contributed a few million dollars annually to Charles Taylor's profits already in the early 1990s. The value of loot as a whole and the share controlled by the rebel leadership has proven particularly hard to estimate, and the true value to the NPFL leadership may differ substantially. Most looted items of some value were confiscated by commanders, and the higher the value, the more senior the leaders to profit. Yet the "pay yourself" mode of rewarding fighters increased the instability of factions, decreasing substantially the overall value of looting to the leadership. All estimates are rough approximations, and actual figures may deviate substantially. Furthermore, I have decided to omit a column "miscellaneous", as it would have to be based on guesses. Taken as

78 For convenience, the US$120,000 to US$960,000 reported by different sources as annual taxes paid by iron ore stakeholders are counted as 0.5 million.

79 Rather roughly, I estimate that about a third (33%) of the fob value of trade was Taylor's profit. By buying the whole production, Taylor was well placed to maximize profits on the trade, yet costs of transport and relatively low world market prices for both commodities in the 1990s limited opportunities for profit.

80 Only major instances of looting were included, i.e. looting while advancing on and attacking Monrovia in 1990, during Operation Octopus 1992/1993, during the battles for Gbarnga 1994, and during the April/May 1996 assault against Roosevelt Johnson. The 1990 figure is an informed guess of mine, based on diverse reports of the situation.

a whole, further sources of income such as "incorporation fees", the cannabis trade, the gold trade, the taxing of humanitarian actors, and the taxing of other trades may have provided revenue worth mentioning. Yet, my assumption that Taylor traded 80 percent of the RUF diamond production, cashed in two thirds as profits, and imposed similarly high taxes on timber exports as the state may overestimate profits from these sectors.

On the positive side, however, this estimate is based on a comprehensive review of most recent, publicly available data on the Liberian war economy. It implies that war economy profits have widely been overestimated. Many analyses are invalidated by erroneously taking Belgian diamond import statistics at face value (cf. Atkinson 1997; cf. Reno 1998) and mistaking value of trade for NPFL profits (cf. US Department of State 1996; cf. Reno 1998; cf. Prkic 2005). The literature is fraught with other evident mistakes, such as accepting implausible figures on royalties paid by foreign firms in NPFL territory and equating pre-war production of goods with wartime production. In view of this, as deficient as the data quoted above is, Table 9 still represents the most reasoned estimate of NPFL war economy profits.

A somewhat surprising result is the salient role looted humanitarian resources played in the war economy. Local prices for worn-down humanitarian equipment may be substantially less than acquisition costs claimed by humanitarian agencies, and the value of looted humanitarian resources may have been less. Yet it is important to note that Liberian war actors could invest little in capital goods given the small overall value of the war economy. The most valuable humanitarian resources, trucks and pick-up vehicles, are likely to have significantly contributed to rendering other segments of the war economy profitable.

3.3. Taylor's Adversaries and their Weaknesses

This section analyses the interlinked systems of authority established by Taylor's adversaries. I thereby seek an answer to the question of what political relevance the respective configurations had, what their power was based on, and why, ultimately, they could not impose themselves against the NPFL. This section thus constitutes an important step in drawing up a procedural analysis of the evolution of patterns of domination in Liberia. I proceed by conceptualizing Taylor's opponents as systems of domination, using similar categories like those applied to the analysis of the NPFL. I thus compare comprehensive social systems of domination to explain a specific outcome, i.e. Charles Taylor taking the presidency after a prolonged war. The approach further allows describing the evolution of patterns of authority in Liberia in more general, theoretically relevant terms.

The actors considered jointly here exhibited considerable autonomy, and it may appear odd to group them together. Many observers understood the Liberian war as anarchy pitting "all against all" or nihilistic factions preying on defenseless civilians (cf. Ellis 2007a, 132–134). Yet, although the war indeed triggered multiple cleavages, the initial master cleavage continued to exert strong influences structuring the war. The initially dominant cleavage opposed beneficiaries of the Doe regime against the NPFL's multi-ethnic oppositional mass movement (that drew strong support from ethnic groups marginalized during the later years of the military regime). That cleavage was reshaped following the entry of actors not directly emanating from either side of the divide, i.e. ECOMOG and IGNU. Subsequently, the major cleavage opposed pro- and anti-Taylor forces. In the process of formation of that cleavage, (informal) institutional links between the anti-Taylor forces were established. These actors were united by pertinent features, notably by opposition to Charles Taylor's NPFL. Furthermore, by and large, they avoided fighting among themselves and considered the NPFL the primary rival. Yet all actors did possess considerable autonomy and first of all pursued their proper interests, which caused severe conflicts between Taylor's adversaries.[81]

81 For instance, the INPFL initially fought against the AFL, but switched sides several times and essentially was an anti-NPFL force. Dynamics that entailed ULIMO's disintegration resulted in sustained fights between the two splinter groups. The LDF started out as a pro-Taylor, anti-ULIMO-K force, but quickly allied with the latter to attack the former. In late 1995/early 1996, heavy fighting pitted ECOMOG and ULIMO-J against each other. There were numerous further instances in which organizational autonomy entailed conflicts between Taylor's adversaries that by and large remained secondary to the master cleavage.

3.3.1. The Doe Government

The bases of rule of the Doe regime have already been described and do not need to be repeated here. Suffice it to say here that the foundations of domination had eroded to such an extent that Doe's authority crumbled once it was challenged by a poorly organized armed force whose major advantage vis-à-vis its adversary was its legitimacy. "AFL countermeasures were ineffective since the army was receiving no support from any part of the population of Nimba County other than its Mandingo residents" (Ellis 2007a, 78). The government thus essentially responded to the insurgency by arbitrarily targeting Gio civilians (cf. Huband 1999, 116–117). The killings were widespread as they were financially rewarded through the highly personalized patrimonial system Doe based his authority on.

> "Soldiers would come back to the [Executive] mansion [and] say they had killed some rebels dead. Doe would give money to ministers to give to the soldiers who had killed the rebels. The ministers would give a small amount to the soldiers and keep the rest for themselves." (Vice-President Harry Moniba, quoted in Huband 1999, 117)

Nevertheless, Doe's patrimonial network eroded. Both central control over troops and strategy were weak; substantial numbers of non-Krahn AFL deserted and within the first six months of the war, Doe replaced the field commander five times (Ellis 2007a, 78). Since early January 1990, violence characterized Monrovia too, as the AFL started eliminating suspected NPFL supporters. Steadily, beheaded bodies of individuals arrested by soldiers were found around Monrovia in the morning (ibid; cf. Huband 1999), while remaining Gio and Mano troops were put under "protective custody" (Youboty 2004, 173). Hundreds of people originating from Nimba were thus rounded up. Many more fled into the United Nations compound but were nevertheless attacked by AFL soldiers there (Ellis 2007a, 76–77).

As its weakness became evident, the government enlisted Mandingo and Krahn civilians, themselves fearing for their lives, and handed them weapons. The new soldiers gained a particular reputation for indiscipline. By early July 1990, Prince Johnson's forces entered Monrovia from the north-west. The NPFL advanced from the north and east, instilling fear of annihilation in Krahn and Mandingo and catalyzing the erosion of the army. While chains of command had partly broken down earlier, indiscipline increased and many soldiers who had not yet defected changed for civilian clothing and deserted the front. AFL troops freely looted the city (cf. Blunt 1990). In what was the worst known single atrocity in the war, a band of some thirty troops led by a "1990–soldier" massacred some 600 civilians from Nimba in Monrovia's main Lutheran Church.[82] Prince Johnson's forces by then controlled parts of central Monrovia, and Samuel Doe's territory was for considerable periods restricted to the Executive Mansion grounds, defended by some 300–500 remaining AFL troops. By then, central authority had largely crumbled, and Doe was as much hostage to his own troops, which refused to let him leave without their security being guaranteed, as he needed his troops to defend himself. On August 24, ECOMOG finally landed at the Freeport of Monrovia and was immediately attacked by the NPFL. On September 5, Doe and Prince Johnson signed a two-week cease-fire agreement to jointly fight back Taylor. Though quickly broken, the agreement signaled a rapprochement of the anti-Taylor forces. Furthermore, it is likely to have played a role in Samuel Doe's decision to venture into Johnson's territory to meet the ECOMOG Field Commander. After Doe was killed on September 9, troops turned desperate, and started marauding through central Monrovia chanting "No Doe, no Liberia", looting and burning down parts of the city. Doe's apparatus of domination appeared to have completely disintegrated. First, the deputy commander of the army, General David Nimely, declared himself president, and little later, Vice-President Harry Moniba did the same.

After ECOMOG had deployed, a stalemate accompanied by relative calm developed. In the former government faction as a whole, Moniba and former presidential advisor Bai Gbala adopted informal leading roles. Former Minister of State and businessman George Boley contributed substantially to the Doe loyalists' finances. General Albert Karpeh, who had been ambassador to Sierra Leone and refused to vacate the post, assumed authority over many of the soldiers who had fled to the neighboring state. However, amid internal rivalries former Chief of Staff Colonel Hezekiah Bowen emerged as its leader. Bowen had not been part of Doe's inner circle, had had a difficult relationship with the president and indeed was

82 It is hardly surprising that the commander, Tailey Yonbu, was killed by military police little later. When the latter tried to arrest him on charges unrelated to the massacre, he shot two of his comrades before being hit himself. The massacre may have been carried out without Doe's approval, but the president did not take any steps to subject Yonbu to disciplinary measures (cf. Youboty 2004, 190–192).

quite "disillusioned" with the AFL (Huband 1999, 116–117). As "one of the few remaining senior military officers of the military establishment who cannot be accused of advocating state-sponsored genocide against selected tribal groups during the civil crisis" (West Africa Oct. 5, 1992), Bowen enjoyed relative international acceptability, which was a major asset in power struggles within the AFL.

Bowen, quickly promoted to General, gained recognition as a key political figure not subject to any civilian interim government authority when he signed the ineffectual Akosombo Agreement as representative of the AFL in September 1994, the other sole two signatories being Charles Taylor and Alhadji Kromah. The agreement would have made the three interim heads of government.[83] Bowen then reduced in stature. As part of the Abuja agreement of August 1995, he became defense minister but had to accept George Boley taking the Council of State post for the forces of the Doe regime. Indicative of Bowen's weak position, General Charles Julu attempted a coup in September 1995 that was supported by a substantial proportion of AFL soldiers.[84] The attempt was, however, quickly put down by ECOMOG and Julu was arrested.

ECOMOG ordered the soldiers into the barracks and prevented them from carrying arms in public, though they were not disarmed (West Africa Oct. 5, 1992). The AFL then became auxiliary troops for ECOMOG in Nov. 1992 to assist the ECOMOG in repelling Operation Octopus (Amnesty International 1995, 5). The AFL thus became institutionally

83 The Akosombo Agreement was initiated by Ghana, which had tried to assume a leading role in the peace process. However, the agreement sparked virulent opposition from Liberian civil society, as it appeared to endorse a "military government" and appeared to equate the AFL with the "legitimate" government. In previous agreements, the interim governments were considered to represent the AFL. As a consequence of Bowen having opted for the AFL "to be considered a faction" (Amos Sawyer, quoted in Brewer/Pajibo 1995, 128) when signing the agreement itself, the LNTG demanded that the army chief resign, which was rejected by Bowen and the AFL. The plan faced opposition from Nigeria, too. Allegedly, the September 1994 offensive against Taylor was organized by the Nigerian ECOMOG contingent partly in order to sabotage the peace treaty (Ellis 2007a, 103).

84 Julu had been the security chief of the LAMCO mine complex in 1983 and had lost his family in the Nimba County raid that took place then. As military commander, he became notorious for massive human rights abuses in Nimba after 1985 and in the early 1990s. He had later fled abroad and sneaked into Liberia to undertake the coup, probably believing he could take the presidency. Julu was liberated during the April 1996 fighting and has not been subjected to any disciplinary or judicial measures related to the coup or absconding from prison.

linked to the force who re-defined as its prime task to secure the interim governments. It further became institutionally linked to the interim governments. All of them had continued to pay the army, including benefits and pensions (Burrowes 1995, 122; cf. Human Rights Watch 1993, 19), although the AFL did not submit to any other than the internal authorities. Militarily, it was a force of little significance without any real pretension to assume power. Not least, it virtually controlled no revenue sources except those constituted by petty bribery and crime.

3.3.2. The Interim Government of National Unity

The *Interim Government of National Unity* (IGNU) was established on the initiative of ECOWAS as a political counterpart to its military intervention. Six Liberian political parties, ten interest groups and a few individuals had accepted an invitation by the intervention force, sent representatives and selected the interim government at a conference held in Banjul in December 1990 (Barr 1993, 75). Amos Sawyer, professor at the *University of Liberia* and leading member of the "progressive" movement, was chosen to b-ecome interim president. He was also Nigeria's preferred choice for the Liberian Presidency (Ellis 2007a, 15). The IGNU integrated an important segment of Liberia's long-standing "progressives", as these dominated the groups participating at the Banjul conference.

The IGNU as a whole and Amos Sawyer as its head faced two core structural problems preventing effective governance. Firstly, as a unity government it integrated individuals from diverse backgrounds. Generally, Liberia's politics have been characterized by factionalism, lack of trust between elites, and competition rather than cooperation, and those constituting the IGNU had not gone through any common politically socializing institution. Its inclusive character meant that Sawyer had few possibilities to use allocation of offices to reward loyal followers and discipline others.

Second, the IGNU inherited a dilapidated administration that had ceased to be able to provide services conventionally expected of states years ago. The IGNU thus gained a reputation for ineffectiveness, opportunism, corruption and, at best, patronage. "No members [sic] of the interim government is in high reckoning among Monrovians. [...] Craze for patronage, junketing and epicurean tendencies permeate the entire governmental machinery in Monrovia" (Midweek Concord Dec. 2, 1991).[85] For instance, in the first half of 1992, the government spent some 1.3 million dollars on travel and per diem allowances, "creating numerous possibilities for personal enrichment" (Ellis 2007a, 136). Private appropriation of offices is likely to have had a particularly negative impact on IGNU's legitimacy despite wide-spread acceptance of "the cultural thing" in Liberian society (Ellis/Haar 2004, 157) because its representatives had in the past vocally denounced personal enrichment of political elites. IGNU practices of rule thus directly contravened the strategy of legitimization its officials had pursued.

To his credit, Amos Sawyer succeeded to represent a government that was little more than a loosely connected set of offices employed for private financial gain for some four years whilst keeping his personal reputation hardly tarnished. While in office, he protected relative freedom of speech and allowed almost daily exposure of corruption scandals (cf. Berkeley 1992). Yet in the absence of political or judicial consequences, such subtle "naming-and-shaming" means proved ineffective in disciplining subaltern elites. Sawyer's ability to lead was severely compromised by him not disposing of meaningful power resources. The resources he disposed of–intimate knowledge of Liberian politics and intellectual charisma–were inadequate for the challenges he was facing, as were the means to discipline his staff.

Consequently, those integrated strove to establish their personal patronage networks, thereby undermining capacities for effective governance. "IGNU became a virtual employment agency, putting persons on the payroll who had no desks, chairs, or papers to work with and whose salaries it could not finance" (Barr 1993, 78). As has been mentioned, the

85 The question of legitimacy of the diverse interim governments cannot be definitely answered. However, there are significant doubts over the IGNU's claim to represent legitimate authority. IGNU proponents claimed people "had voted with their feet" (cf. Fahnbulleh 2002) and flocked to Monrovia and into refugee camps. A relatively high level of security rather than generalized acceptance of the authority in place attracted people to Monrovia. All the armed factions, including the NPFL, had considerable numbers of supporters in Monrovia (cf. Youboty 2004). As late as 1995, when just 300,000 people were estimated to have remained in the hinterland while the population of Monrovia stood at around 1.2 million (Frankfurter Rundschau Aug. 9, 1995), "NPFL men roam[ed] the streets and bars freely" in the capital, as did followers of other factions (New Democrat May 11, 1995a). When Taylor eventually entered Monrovia on August 30, 1995 to take his seat in the interim government to be installed the next day, he was given a hero's welcome by the population (Neue Zürcher Zeitung Sept. 2, 1995).

AFL were the only "government body" that regularly received its pay. Yet Sawyer had no meaningful coercive apparatus at his disposal. During the first year of the IGNU, civil servants were not paid at all (West Africa June 24, 1991) and they generally were not paid on time. Consequently, employees invented new schemes to derive income from their positions.

Yet the IGNU controlled large revenue income, even relative to the NPFL, although it had no control over the revenue-generating economy of the hinterland. About 60 percent of its internally generated revenues came from fisheries. These were, however, little important compared to the resources derived from the prerogatives of internationally recognized sovereignty. The IGNU owed its financial survival to being the internationally recognized legitimate government of Liberia.[86] By far the most important source of revenue was the ship registry, managed off-shore by the US-based company *International Trust Company* (ITC) owned by *International Registry Incorporated* (IRI), which provided some 16 to 20 million dollars annually to the IGNU (US Department of State 1996). The IGNU further, officially, received up to ten million dollars a year from immigration, import and export duties (Atkinson 1997, 9). Significant parts of state income were generated by charging fees for imports and residence permits needed by non-profit humanitarian actors (cf. Montclos 1999, 234). While armed factions similarly taxed humanitarian activities, the collection of duties in "government" territory, in particular the Freeport of Monrovia and the Spriggs Payne Airport, was considered legitimate and could thus be considered a prerogative of sovereignty. The ship registry even grew during the war, as ITC reacted to increased international competition in the business by offering extremely competitive prices. Another important yet not transparent source of finance for the IGNU were grants from Nigeria, as well as small contributions from different international sources.

The IGNU and its civil servants further generated substantial unofficial revenues. For instance, informal customs had to be paid, and more or less voluntary contributions from importers and exporters represented a significant source of income for officials on all levels of government. Per-

86 The IGNU was recognized as the sovereign government of Liberia by the UN General Assembly and, amongst others, Nigeria. Notwithstanding, there was hardly any material "sovereignty". The US did not officially recognize the IGNU, but crucially US courts did accept the IGNU as the state's representative in litigation against US-based corporations active in Liberia.

sonal links between IGNU executives and ECOMOG were quite effective when it came to opening and securing new sources of revenue. "The amount of bureaucracy involved in exporting goods has markedly increased, with the RPAL calculating 31 paid signatures required to export a shipment of rubber, 26 of which are illegal" (Rubber Planters Association of Liberia, 1996, quoted in Atkinson 1997, 12).

What is interesting about the quotation is not so much the (erroneous) equation of "red tape" administration and bureaucracy, but the stability and reliability of an arrangement making sure that the collection of 26 legally unnecessary signatures was enforced. The scam however did not need elaborate organization. It was just necessary to make sure that the signatures were demanded at the location of the final, ECOMOG-controlled export proceedings.

Another prerogative of sovereignty that could be marketed was the right to award concessions and the right to define other armed actors as illegal. Most concession companies had declared *force majeure* and ceased to provide revenue to the IGNU, although several of them entered into agreements with Taylor in order to continue economic activities. The government consequently issued several writs of arrest in respect of several managers that it charged with economic sabotage for supporting Taylor (West Africa Apr. 12, 1993). Fines and arrears could thus be collected. For instance, *Firestone* had entered into an agreement with Charles Taylor, who controlled the area, and continued to produce.[87] The IGNU charged *Firestone* with supporting the insurgents, and the out-of-court settlement reached in March 1993 (cf. Reno 1998, 100) is likely to have increased both the IGNU budget and the private wealth of IGNU elites.

Another classic prerogative of sovereignty is the right to issue an official currency and have bills printed when the need arises. In early 1992, the IGNU tried to undermine Taylor's economy by taking the old "JJ dollar" (named after the first president) out of circulation and introducing the "Liberty" dollar. The IGNU, however, failed to translate its power over the official currency into an advantage, as it tried to improve its financial situation by printing new bills. Money supply was estimated to have doubled between 1989 and 1994 while production plummeted, and

87 According to Lindsay Barrett, a videotape was found after ECOMOG conquered the plantation showing former US President Jimmy Carter, then US Ambassador to Monrovia Bill Twaddell, a *Firestone* Manager, and Charles Taylor negotiating terms of an agreement that would allow *Firestone* to continue production (West Africa Apr. 5, 1993).

inflation rose accordingly. Meanwhile, Taylor forbade the use of the "Liberty" in his territory, continued to use the "JJ" and consequently disposed of a relatively stable currency. Taylor himself tried to have new JJ bills printed, but was refused his request by the British company Delarue which had historically printed most of Liberia's money (Montclos 1999, 233).

Though differentiated from warring factions in terms of sources of revenue, the IGNU was partly integrated into the faction's economies. As Sawyer hardly controlled the administration, profits could be appropriated by civil servants and executives in different positions of authority. For example, while the export of scrap metal was officially banned because of the damage caused to Liberian infrastructures, a

"businessman arranged with one of the armed factions to loot material from the Bong Mines, which he then bought from the faction and exported as scrap metal. The transaction required licenses from the Liberian Electricity Corporation, Liberia Telecommunications Corporation, the Ministry of Justice, the Ministry of Finance, the Liberia National Police, the National Security Agency and an export permit from the Ministry of Commerce, all of which could be obtained through bribery, thus keeping civil servants and their political masters on funds and no doubt Ecomog too, since it controlled the port of Monrovia." (Ellis 2007a, 137)

As a protection force under control of the government, the *Black Beret* militia, initially known as *Medusa 'Secret Army'* (West Africa Nov. 16, 1992) was created in 1992. It largely consisted of former AFL soldiers who had been trained in Nigeria and Guinea in order to enhance chances for loyalty to the Sawyer government. Some three years after the war had been started Sawyer again adopted the AFL as the national army and formally became its supreme commander (New African Apr. 1993). This, however, was irrelevant on the ground. The ECOMOG provided security to the interim government, but was not controlled by it and thus could not be strategically used to extend its domination. The IGNU was supposed to be dissolved as a consequence of the Cotonou Agreement of August 1993. Taylor's intransigence, however, allowed its successor to take over in March 1994 only. The *Liberian National Transitional Government* (LNTG) then included the IGNU as one of its constituent parties, the others being NPFL and ULIMO. From then on, the purportedly sovereign governments became closely linked to the non-sovereign armed factions. It could be argued that only then the "state" decayed, as the Monrovia polity ceased to be organizationally distinct from the non-sovereign factions controlling portions of Liberia's territory.

Given the steady stream of some 16 to 20 million dollars maritime revenue that was topped up by income from other sources, it is doubtful whether the IGNU as a whole generated substantially less revenue than the NPFL. Further, it should have been to its advantage that revenue, in particular ship registry revenue but to a lesser extent fishery and import duties too, could well be centrally controlled. In contrast, the burden of sovereignty, i.e. the obligation to repay sovereign debts, had a minor impact. Already, the Doe government had defaulted on repaying loans, and the IGNU did not resume servicing state debt. This was internationally largely accepted, yet the IGNU could not obtain new multilateral loans (which may have been a blessing rather than a curse). IGNU's inability to evolve into a serious challenger to the NPFL was caused by features of the system of domination, in particular a lack of legitimacy (cf. Brewer/Pajibo 1995) and absence of central control of staff.

The lack of internal leadership was related to the inclusive and heterogeneous structure of the IGNU. The lack of legitimacy was owed to its character as an ECOMOG "puppet government" (Ellis 2007a, 87) elected by "a few dozen people who were invited [to Banjul] and could afford to attend" (Burrowes 1995, 117). It essentially represented a small but factionalized political party and civil society establishment. Importantly, it had failed to build legitimacy through effective governance in the aftermath of its induction.

By contrast, revenues were reasonably high, and the IGNU hardly had to shoulder any military costs, which should have made up for the larger population in its territory. Yet the IGNU provided virtually no public services,[88] which enabled other institutions (in addition to communal ones) to fill a politically relevant void. Of particular interest in that respect was the *Special Emergency and Life Food Program* (SELF). SELF was a non-governmental organization headed by a leading member of the "progressive" movement, Blame Nelson. It implemented the greater part of the distribution of humanitarian goods provided by the international community. In the process, it built up a rudimentary administrative order. Specifically, it organized administrative structures at the neighborhood level in Monrovia, including democratic elections of quarter leaders (cf. Frank-

88 Popular appellations for IGNU were "Imported Government of No Use" and "I Got Nothing for U" (cf. Montclos 1999, 236).

furter Rundschau Mar. 1, 1993; New Democrat Jan. 13, 1994b). Structurally important is that SELF was essentially internationally financed and thus relatively independent from the national political and economic power holders. It is, however, indicative of the stature gained through community work and coordinating with key international and national power holders that Blamoh Nelson was made Director of Cabinet by Charles Taylor in 1997. In a wider perspective, SELF was an example of how the IGNU failed to control relations of authority, or, respectively, how Taylor later succeeded to recentralize control.[89]

3.3.3. The Independent National Patriotic Front of Liberia

The INPFL had from its inception been based on personal connections Prince Johnson had acquired as a career soldier and on the authority he commanded as former aide-de-camp of Quiwonkpa. His force was constituted of a core of 300 former AFL soldiers, in particular Gio like Johnson himself (Ellis 2007a, 3). The troops were nevertheless relatively effective compared to Taylor's hardly trained forces. At the time, the maximum strength of the INPFL was estimated at 2,000 combatants (Daniels 1991). His base was the Caldwell quarter of Bushrod Island, though his area of authority was significantly larger for considerable periods, extended into the port area and temporarily included parts of central Monrovia.

Prince Johnson controlled his combatants through maximum personal supervision and draconian physical disciplinary measures. He was widely considered an "alcoholic psychopath" (Berkeley 1992) characterized by unpredictability and a propensity for casual killings (cf. Ellis 2007a, 14–15; cf. West Africa Oct. 14, 1991). He used to undertake extensive night-time patrols through his territory, during which combatants judged to have looted or otherwise violated orders were shot by him personally on the spot.[90] While the Truth and Reconciliation Commission considered the INPFL one of two factions that had instituted minimum measures to

89 Nelson had been Charles Taylor's deputy in the General Services Agency in the early 1980s, giving rise to speculations that he had supported Taylor already during the war.

90 US American journalist Bill Berkeley accompanied Johnson on one of these tours and provides an intriguing account (Berkeley 1992). Generally, Johnson did not hesitate to kill people in front of journalists (cf. Gunston Dec. 2, 1990), and his indifference to public attention clearly contributed to his reputation.

protect civilians (TRC 2009, 166), it noted that "Prince Y. Johnson [was] recorded as having the highest number of violations ever recorded for individual perpetrators" (ibid., 266). Combatants considered to have committed (frequently minor) acts of indiscipline or who aroused his anger generally faced immediate deadly justice. Fear of Johnson appears to have been a central factor for even his bodyguard force not to desert, several of whom were women forcefully conscripted (cf. Gunston Dec. 2, 1990, 46–47). Johnson's legendarily unstable character instilled fear in many who had to deal with him.

Prince Johnson's forces had captured substantial material from the AFL and thus disposed initially of significant military resources. Yet it was economically weak. Johnson collected taxes from marketers and business-people in his territory, though this appears to have taken the form of unsystematic extortions. However, as the port area is a major industrial area, there were ample opportunities for extortion. Further, he constructed a market within the perimeters of the Caldwell base at an alleged cost of 350,000 Liberian dollars, for the use of which he collected fees (Eye Oct. 15, 1992). Further opportunities to obtain revenue were related to the integration of the INPFL into the IGNU.

The INPFL was initially allocated the Vice Interim Presidency, the Ministry of Lands, Mines and Energy and the posts of Police Director and City Mayor. Yet after he had once again publicly killed several of his own combatants on allegations of supporting the NPFL, senior IGNU executives called for his arrest. Johnson consequently withdrew his representatives from the IGNU in August 1991 (West Africa Oct. 5, 1992).

When ECOMOG landed, it disposed of hardly any resources, came under immediate attack by the NPFL, and had no intelligence on the situation on the ground. As Johnson controlled the immediate vicinity of the port and welcomed the intervention, close links developed between him and the ECOMOG. In the initial effort to secure the capital, ECOMOG and INPFL forces jointly fought the NPFL. Yet Johnson's power eroded as the ECOMOG established a stronger position. His fighters were effectively encamped and were forbidden by the ECOMOG to leave Caldwell bearing arms (West Africa Oct. 5, 1992). By 1992, the INPFL had lost most of its political-military importance. In order to turn the tide, Johnson allied with the NPFL in preparation for Operation Octopus, and some 20,000 NPFL fighters were infiltrated into the Caldwell base to attack the ECOMOG headquarters nearby (Aboagye 1999,

105). Yet the NPFL attacked the INPFL when the offensive started, quickly forcing Johnson to flee. Prince Johnson was rescued by ECOMOG and later evacuated to Nigeria, where he pursued a career as an evangelical reverend. Many INPFL combatants were likely to have switched to the NPFL. The faction thus ceased to exist in a classical elimination contest fashion.

Tracing the demise of the INPFL, several factors appear pertinent. Johnson's force was quite small from the onset and appealed essentially to ethnic Gio socialized in the AFL. To that segment, his military career as well as his particular display of strength may have been qualities legitimizing leadership. Yet Johnson's rule was largely built on fear and his personal capacities to control, rather than legitimacy. Economically, the INPFL was poorly organized and continuously lost relevance once its initial weapons reservoir had worn out and weaponry generally became an insufficient means to assume a position of power in Monrovia's politics. In a situation of weakness, a strategic error of Johnson resulted in defeat of his faction.

3.3.4. The ECOWAS Cease-Fire Monitoring Group

The ECOMOG differed structurally from other armed actors because of its character as a multilateral intervention force and the impact of regional state policies on its activities. It had been created on the initiative of Nigeria, who contributed the bulk of forces and shouldered most of its budget.[91] Unlike the Liberian factions, maximization of political-military power as a means to appropriate resources cannot be considered to constitute its overarching goal. Put differently, the factors driving ECOMOG action were comparatively complex, and ranged from regional political strategies to the personal motives of military officers.

From the beginning, ECOMOG's mission was confused. In the very document founding the intervention force, it is variously referred to as "*ECOWAS Cease-Fire Monitoring Group*" and as "*ECOWAS Monitoring Group*". The relevant document further defined the task of ECOMOG as "assisting the ECOWAS Standing Mediation Committee in supervising the

91 Other regional states contributing troops were Gambia, Ghana, Sierra Leone and, temporarily, Senegal (Körner 1996, 59–60) and Mali (Barr 1993, 77). East African Tanzania also provided troops during the final phase of the war. Apart from Nigeria, Ghana and Guinea were the most important actors in ECOMOG.

implementation and in ensuring the strict compliance by the parties with the provisions of the cease-fire throughout the territory of Liberia" (ECOWAS 1990, Art. 2). As there was nothing remotely resembling a cease-fire by then, the purported objective of the intervention was testimony to considerable political creativity.

Nigerian President General Ibrahim B. Babangida was reported to have rallied support for the intervention by arguing to regional heads of state that

> "what happens in Liberia would set an unfortunate precedent for the region's many military rulers, since Taylor was a civilian arming ordinary civilians to march on the capital and overthrow a military government. Such behaviour could spread throughout the region. Sierra Leone, Ghana, Nigeria, Guinea, Togo, Burkina Faso, Mali and others all at that time had heads of state who had come to power through the army." (Africa Confidential May 17, 1991)

However, preventing Taylor from taking over power was the overarching goal, rather than maintaining the military regime in Liberia. Taylor was considered a threat to regime security interest by Nigeria (and partly Guinea, too) because of his association with the francophone governments of Burkina Faso and Côte d'Ivoire as well as (at least tacit) French support for the NPFL. The Nigerian perception ~~of~~ security threats was related to its history of rivalry with francophone states, particularly Côte d'Ivoire, for regional hegemony and French support for the Biafra secessionists (1967–1970).[92] Despite a "special relationship" between Doe and Babangida, the Liberian president, "fading into his own alcohol- and drug-induced fantasyland" (Cohen 2000, 133) had lately become an embarrassment to Babangida (Alao 1998, 48–49). "Democratically conducted elections" (ECOWAS 1990, 67) were defined as the appropriate way to install a new regular government in Liberia.

The ECOMOG thus arrived at the port of Monrovia hardly prepared, poorly equipped and with an ill-defined mission. As mentioned above, the force came immediately under fire from the NPFL. Links with the INPFL controlling the port of Monrovia were established within days of landing. The intervention force even had to borrow boots and uniforms from Prince Johnson (Adebayo 2002b, 78). The INPFL manned checkpoints together with ECOMOG, and ECOMOG frequently relied on INPFL intelligence in order to receive information about the NPFL (ibid).

92 Cf. Inegbedion (1994, 222–225); cf. Körner (1996, 100–113)

ECOMOG became closely linked to several anti-Taylor factions. During Operation Octopus, ECOMOG fought together with the AFL, INPFL and ULIMO against Taylor, and the LPC established in 1993 was an important auxiliary force in the eastern territories. Coordination with the LPC appears to have been strongest (cf. Amnesty International 1995, 10) but, generally, ECOMOG had little control over the irregular factions. Only the INPFL's and the AFL's use of weapons was controlled for some time by effectively encamping the factions.

An analysis of relations of authority over ECOMOG meant to explain its actions needs to take into account three different levels.[93] The highest one was constituted by the Nigerian presidents, i.e. General Ibrahim Babangida and, after 1993, General Sani Abacha. The second yet often most influential level was that of the ECOMOG High Command on the ground, embodied in the Field Commander. Formally, the Nigerian and other contingents were under his command. The Field Commanders had considerable autonomy in defining short-term objectives and devising strategies, and the performance of ECOMOG was strongly dependent on the person of the supreme Field Commander (Alao 1998, 72). This was due to a lack of intelligence and incoherence of strategies formulated in Lagos and Abuja, respectively. The third level was that of subaltern commanding officers, who frequently devised private (commercial) strategies. Despite difficulties to maintain effective control as rivalries and different military cultures hampered smooth coordination between contingents, relations of authority basically corresponded to the military hierarchy. Levels of discipline of the contingents varied. While a leaked report of the US Department of State described the Senegalese contingent as professional, many others were considered "worse than useless, repeatedly abandoning positions without a fight and leaving to others the task of recovering terrain" (West Africa Nov. 16, 1992).[94]

A Nigerian strategy emerged only slowly after it became clear that the NPFL posed a serious challenge. Initially, planners had reportedly assumed

93 A comprehensive analysis would need to include at least another level, that of governments other than Nigeria providing troops. For purposes of this analysis, we do not need to explicitly investigate that level. For an analysis of Guinea's interests and strategies, see Gerdes (2006; 2010).

94 The only other contingent talked about in favorable terms in the report was the Guinean one. However, the reputation of the Guinean contingent deteriorated during its presence in Liberia (cf. Adebayo 2002b, 76; Ellis 2007a, 174) while that of the Ghanaian one improved (cf. Montclos 1999, 237).

that Taylor's ragged, youthful combatants would disperse when facing a "professional" army (cf. Ellis 2007a, 3). The first (Ghanaian) Field Commander thus found himself in an unexpected situation, and during his roughly two months in office he improvised to consolidate ECOMOG's position, in particular by teaming up with the INPFL. The second Field Commander, the Nigerian Major-General Joshua Dogonyaro, was considered effective as he restored relative stability to Monrovia, but he was replaced in mid-1991. The replacement was widely attributed to his successes, as he became considered a potential rival to Babangida (Tuck 2000). Rivalries for national leadership in Nigeria impacted negatively on ECOMOG performance. Under pressure from many corners, Babangida eventually pursued a compromise solution aimed at weakening Taylor in the long run. Facing resistance from other regional states, including ECOMOG-supporting ones, and probably estimating it a costly option with limited chances of success during the early 1990s, Babangida was unwilling to order a major military offensive against Taylor. Yet he was not interested in a negotiated settlement either, as it would have been "most likely to result in confirmation of his enemy [Taylor] as president of Liberia" (ibid., 88).

The Field Commanders were decisive in formulating unofficial policies towards armed factions. As is abundantly clear, the Nigerian ECOMOG contingent actively supported the formation of ULIMO and LPC, and helped most other anti-Taylor groups with weapons and logistics at one instance or another during the war.[95] The policy had its roots in the predicament faced by the first Field Commander Arnold Quainoo, but was systematically developed by Dogonyaro and evolved into a "sophisticated strategy" (ibid., 95) apparently sanctioned at the highest level of Nigerian and Guinean political authority (cf. Gerdes 2006; cf. Gerdes 2010). Initially, contacts between ECOMOG officers and the NPFL were of a sporadic, financially motivated nature (cf. Ellis 2007a, 172). Under Field Commander Major-General John Mark Inienger (November 1993 to mid-1996), communications between the ECOMOG High Command and the NPFL became intense. Indicating close ties, Inienger was reported to be dating a sister of Charles Taylor (Frankfurter Rundschau Sept. 23, 1996). These contacts prepared the May 1995 rapprochement between Nigerian

95 See Nass (2000, 108); Montclos (1999, 227); TRC (2009, 127).

President General Sani Abacha, a close friend of Inienger, and Charles Taylor (cf. Ellis 2007a, 177).

The financing of ECOMOG was not transparent. Formally, funding should have been channeled through a *Special Emergency Fund* of the *ECOWAS Standing Mediation Committee* (ECOWAS 1990, Art. 3). Yet that never materialized, and contingents were generally financed by their governments (Alao 1998, 73). Nigeria is considered to have contributed most to ECOMOG as a whole, yet information about the costs of the intervention varies widely. According to data provided by ECOMOG to the UN Observer Mission Office in Liberia, the ECOMOG budget for an unspecified year was around 91 million dollars (ibid., 74), suggesting costs of 728 million dollars for the period of eight years in which the force was in Liberia. In 1996, Nigerian Foreign Minister Tom Ikimi claimed expenses of four billion dollars by Nigeria alone, though the figure was widely considered exaggerated in order to attract more western funding (Africa Confidential May 10, 1996). A year later, Nigerian President Sani Abacha declared the state had spent some three billion on ECOMOG (Alao 1998, 73), and in 1999, his successor Olusegun Obasanjo stated that the intervention had cost his country about eight billion dollars (BBC Oct. 25, 1999).

Given that ECOMOG soldiers frequently were "unpaid or underpaid" (Tuck 2000), not getting the basic package of 15 dollars a day they were supposed to receive it appears doubtful whether ECOMOG spent the 91 million dollars budget, in which military personnel costs were by far the most important component. However, there is a consensus that Nigeria budgeted considerable financial means for ECOMOG though up to 3/4 of the amount may have been embezzled in Lagos and Abuja, respectively (Ellis 2007a, 173). Limited support was given to ECOMOG by third parties and mostly channeled through the *UN Trust Fund for Liberia*. By 1995, the US had made available some 30.8 million dollars to ECOMOG (ibid.). At one instance in 1994, the US refused to sanction fuel purchases supposed to be paid from the trust fund in reaction to "rackets operated by some Nigerian officials in the last two years" (Africa Confidential Mar. 4, 1994).

Within a short space of time ECOMOG commanders developed material interests in their presence (cf. ibid., 88). Foreign firms operating in "Greater Liberia", in particular *Firestone* and the AMCL, were reported to be paying "taxes" not only to the NPFL but ECOMOG, too, in order to be able to operate (Montclos 1999, 240). Yet the major opportunities to generate revenue appear related to the forces' control over points of export in Liberia.[96] ECOMOG traded with all factions in the war or, respectively, taxed trade linked to the factions, as the quotation above on scrap metal exports illustrates. Much of the trade would qualify as fencing. ECOMOG became notorious for trade in looted cars that earned it the appellation "Every Car or Moving Object Gone" by ordinary Liberians (Tuck 2000). From 1993 on, ECOMOG (together with the LPC) controlled the eastern port of Buchanan, and for some time rendered the port of Harper dangerous and largely inoperative through blockades and weekly bombings (cf. Africa Confidential Mar. 4, 1994). However, factions were able to export or import through Monrovia or other ports by paying "taxes" to ECOMOG (cf. Ellis 2007a, 168). Even parts of the NPFL trade with private weapons dealers appear to have been protected by ECOMOG commanders in return for payments (cf. ibid., 172). Though these practices allowed factions to remain active, the need to generate revenue to pay "taxes" to several authorities reduced the overall profitability of the Liberian war economy.

Additionally, ECOMOG officers sold fuel, weapons and other goods embezzled from its stocks to factions, though little is known about how systematic these deals were. ECOMOG units, in particular the Nigerian and Guinean ones, regularly supplied anti-Taylor factions with needed equipment, and at least sometimes received war economy goods in return. To what extent the trade with allied forces was profitable is in doubt as it was largely politically motivated (on Guinea see Gerdes 2006; 2010).

Other sources of income were constituted by directly engaging in criminal activities, rather than taxing these. Probably most important for soldiers needing to sustain themselves in the absence of regular pay, extortion of passage money was common at checkpoints. The higher ranks profited particularly from looting and organizing export of loot. At least one impounded weapons smuggling ship was sold under questionable circumstances. The major instance of looting took place after Buchanan had been taken in early 1993. The LIMINCO facilities in Buchanan, among them a pellet plant, were completely dismantled. Industrial equipment ori-

96 It is further widely assumed that Nigerian ECOMOG used control over ports for drug trafficking though there is no evidence. Nigeria is a global hub for narcotics trafficking, and the wife of President Babangida was alleged to be involved in the business (cf. Ellis 2007a, 170–172).

ginally worth some 50 million dollars was exported, much of it as scrap metal. Furthermore, ECOMOG soldiers, particularly from the Guinean contingent, participated in looting during the April 1996 fighting (Ellis 2007a, 173–174). Yet unlike the irregular factions looting was not part of a comprehensive war strategy.

On the whole, the failure of ECOMOG to achieve its goal of preventing Charles Taylor from acceding to power was first of all due to a lack of regional political cohesion and a corresponding lack of political will to allocate the resources necessary for effective military action. The whole intervention had been based on a flawed analysis of the situation in Liberia and the Nigerian assumption that the untrained NPFL forces would back down when confronted by an army more professional than the Liberian one. When on the offensive, ECOMOG achieved remarkable military successes. Yet it remains in doubt whether a foreign regular military force could have defeated the NPFL. Guerrilla tactics are notoriously hard to counter for regular troops, and foreign actors face particular difficulties in creating a legitimate public order that could have weakened Taylor politically. Establishing a legitimate public order is hardly possible if the political Liberian counterpart intended to generate legitimacy lacks credibility and backing in society.[97]

3.3.5. The United Liberation Movements

The roots of ULIMO lay in the former Doe regime. When created in 1991, it started out as an alliance of three separate groups. One was the Liberian-based *Liberia Peace Council* (LPC), which was headed by former Minister of State George Boley and grouped an important part of Doe's political and military cadres. The second was the Guinean-based *Movement for the Redemption of Muslims* (MRM) lead by former Minister of Information Alhadji Kromah, which organized Mandingo refugees who had fled the NPFL and faced an insecure environment in south-eastern Guinea's Forest Region (cf. Gerdes 2010). Initially the most important constituent party was the Sierra Leone-based *Liberian United Defense Force* (LUDF) under the lead of General Albert Karpeh. Karpeh had been Doe's ambassador to Sierra Leone, refused to follow Amos Sawyer's order to vacate the post,

97 In several respects, the ISAF Mission in Afghanistan appears to face problems similar to ECOMOG.

and reorganized former AFL soldiers who had fled to Liberia's western neighbor. The LUDF formation was catalyzed by the RUF war, which had begun in March 1991 and rendered the situation for Doe loyalists in Sierra Leone considerably more dangerous. In order to dispose of an auxiliary force against the RUF, the Sierra Leone government provided support to the LUDF, which incited Kromah to propose a merger to Karpeh (Ellis 2007a, 95).

When the three organizations formally merged to form ULIMO, the banker and businessman Raleigh Seekie, an ethnic Kru close to Karpeh, was given the post of Chairman, reportedly in return for his financial contributions to ULIMO. Senior military positions were held by Karpeh and Armah Youlo. The latter had a background as agent in Doe's *National Security Agency* and had been close to the president while Kromah was only given the post of spokesman. However, ULIMO's formal structure was of minor relevance for relations of authority within the faction. Essentially informally organized and based on personal connections, Karpeh controlled a force based in the Waterloo refugee camp near Freetown that included many Mandingo, Youlo commanded units on the frontline at the Leonean-Liberian border, and Kromah led the Mandingo-dominated segment based in Guinea. From the very beginning there were frictions in ULIMO (cf. ibid.).

A rivalry between Karpeh and Youlo entailed non-cooperation and mutual obstruction of activities by their two groups (cf. Perspective Oct. 25, 2000). Alhadji Kromah for his part used his privileged access to media to present himself as the real ULIMO leader and gained increasing control over Mandingo that belonged to Karpeh's group, which led to confrontations with Seekie and Karpeh. Eventually in June 1992, Kromah organized the murder of Karpeh in his home in Sierra Leone, and the attackers almost killed ULIMO's Deputy Field Commander Roosevelt Johnson the same day (Ellis 2007a, 96).[98] Johnson then emerged as leader of the ULIMO's Krahn faction. The increasing rivalry finally entailed the official split of ULIMO into a Kromah- and a Johnson-faction in 1994.

All along there had thus been separate chains of command within ULIMO that were later identified with ULIMO-K and ULIMO-J. Legitimacy of central leaders was weak. ULIMO combatants in several

98 Roosevelt Johnson had a civilian background as official in the Ministry of Finance but emerged as ULIMO's main military commander in Sierra Leone between 1991 and 1992 (cf. Ellis 2007a, 318).

locations in Liberia were not able to name any supreme leader and considered their local commanders their leaders (Africa Confidential Nov. 6, 1992; Anderson 1993). ULIMO was thus subject to feudalization in the sense of the predominance of local relations of authority and a wide-ranging appropriation of powers on the part of commanders. Even to a larger extent than was the case with the NPFL, ULIMO was a "brand name" meant to instill fear and deference rather than an institutionalized organization. By and large, ULIMO was considered more brutal and less disciplined than the NPFL (cf. Ellis 2007a, 102–104). Yet the central leaders had a discernible degree of control over the troops. For instance, ambushes on ECOMOG by ULIMO units bribed by the NPFL ceased after ECOMOG lodged complaints to the ULIMO High Command (Nass 2000, 100).

Discipline of fighters largely depended on local commanders and varied widely. There are indications that ethnicity had a significant impact on personal security and insecurity. Lindsay Barrett quoted a man married into a Krahn household who had been helped when sick by ULIMO fighters and was positive about public order supplied by ULIMO (New Democrat Jan. 27, 1994). I myself was told by Mandingo peasants in Lofa, who had fled during the war that they would have stayed in the area if it had been reliably controlled by ULIMO.[99] However, these features were far from ubiquitous, as, for instance, starving civilians in ULIMO-J territory told journalists it were their "own people" who had looted them (West Africa Oct. 14, 1996).

ULIMO and, in particular, the forces under control of Kromah gained strength during the war. While the strength of the whole organization was estimated at about 850 combatants in late 1991 (Aboagye 1999, 51), ULIMO-K's strength alone was estimated at 5,000 to 6,000 fighters by late 1996 (Ellis 2007a, 134), rendering it clearly the second most important faction. ULIMO-J was about 3,000 combatants strong in the mid-1990s (cf. Montclos 1999, 227).

Such a force needs to mobilize considerable revenue. Start-up finance and some regular support were provided by the governments of Sierra Leone and Guinea. Additional support came from the Nigerian ECOMOG contingent (cf. Nass 2000, 315). These revenues were controlled by the supreme leadership and enhanced its control over troops.

---

99 Interviews in Lofa County, March 2007.

Yet by and large, ULIMO was considered weakly organized economically. When Kromah's faction invaded Lofa County from bases in Sierra Leone in 1992/93, it took massive revenge for massacres committed by the NPFL, which it considered to have been supported by the local Loma and Kissi population of Lofa County. Revenge involved destruction of holy shrines of these peoples and looting of sacred objects, in particular masks. These objects were sold on international arts markets by a Conakry-based key associate of Kromah (Ellis 2007a, 128).

Yet the ULIMO-factions occupied territories on both sides of the Sierra Leonean-Liberian border containing gem-quality diamond deposits, and diamond trade was considered their main source of income (cf. Montclos 1999, 235; Prkic 2005, 117). The ULIMO-K was closely linked to diamond traders in Guinea, many of whom belong to the Mandingo ethnic group (Richards 1995, 156). The links between the Sierra Leone army and the ULIMOs make it likely that diamonds mined under control of the army were traded by the ULIMOs, in particular Kromah's wing. There is no plausible source on the value of this trade, but it is likely to have been worth several million dollars a year. These revenues partly explain the military strength of the ULIMO but they also contributed to instability and rivalry within factions. A substantial share of mining was controlled by local commanders who developed interests different from those of the supreme command (cf. ICG 2002a, 7; Lidow 2011, 184–193).[100]

Another source of revenue was rubber from the Guthrie plantation stretching over Bomi and Grand Cape Mount Counties, the third largest plantation in Liberia. For the latter part of the war, Guthrie was controlled by the Johnson faction. In 2005, production of Guthrie was estimated at 4,500 (UNMIL 2006, 79) to 10,000 tons a year (Panel of Experts 06/2005, 33). If we assume an average production of 10,000 tons per year during the 1990s,[101] the Monrovia-value of trade at 300 dollars a ton (see above) was around three million dollars. A substantial part of rubber was sold by ULIMO factions to ECOMOG and then traded to Monrovia (cf. Ellis 2007a, 104), reducing profits available to the factions. Taking into account

100 Interview with Joe Wylie, LURD Spokesman and former ULIMO executive, Jan. 12, 2006, Monrovia.

101 Productive capacity should have been higher in the 1990s than the 2000s as trees degraded during the period. On the other hand, more frequent fighting in the 1990s should have reduced production.

that rubber tapping and transport need to be financed, profits are likely to have been less than a million dollars a year, and much of this was appropriated by subaltern commanders.

As a consequence of the Cotonou Agreement of July 1993, ULIMO became integrated into the LNTG established in March 1994 and had thus access to "state" resources. The agreement itself had been signed by "Major-General Alhadji Kromah" as "leader" of ULIMO who thus had become accepted as head of the movement by foreign actors. Internally, competition for posts made evident further splits within the organization. ULIMO had obtained two seats on the five-man Council of State, one each to represent the Krahn and the Mandingo-faction. However, Roosevelt Johnson's de-facto representative at the Council refused to support Kromah's efforts to determine the LNTG Chairman, and was replaced immediately by the latter. As a consequence, Johnson declared Kromah sacked as ULIMO leader less than two weeks after the inauguration of the LNTG. Kromah's ability to withstand calls for his removal, however, reinforced him in his position.

Yet, 1994 was marked by heavy fighting between the two factions in eastern and northern Liberia. Subsequent negotiations were complicated by ULIMO-J's increasing autonomy, with mediators urging its leaders to join either ULIMO-K or the *Coalition Forces* (then made up of LPC, LDF and NPFL-CRC) (Adebajo 2002b, 161–162). The Abuja Agreement of August 1995 explicitly recognized Roosevelt Johnson as leader of ULIMO-J and allocated four ministerial posts to the faction but did not give it official representation at the Council of State. Johnson became Minister for Rural Development while Kromah kept a Vice-Chairman post on the Council. A final major stand-off related to the spoils of integration into the purportedly sovereign government occurred after ULIMO-J was pressurized to return weapons looted from ECOMOG during the fighting between the faction and the intervention force in late 1995 and early 1996. A ULIMO-J faction around Armah Youlo declared Johnson sacked and replaced by the little-known student William Karyee, and found support for the coup among Councilmen Charles Taylor and Alhadji Kromah. In the process, the ULIMO-J nominee to the Central Bank and an important source of income for Johnson was sacked and replaced by Raleigh Seekie. Eventually, the events should lead to the fighting of April 1996 that confirmed Roosevelt Johnson in a position of military power.

Given this weak structure, the strength of ULIMO-K appears surprising. Most likely, three factors allowed the force to become the second most important faction. One is the relative coherence of Liberian Mandingo and the legitimacy they bestowed on the organization, considering it as defending their corporate interests. Mandingo, making up some 20 percent of the Liberian population, are one of the largest groups in Liberia and carry considerably more weight than Krahn, estimated at 5 percent. They are characterized by their status as outsiders in Liberia and a correspondingly strong subjective sense of group identity. Second, Kromah's good connections to the Guinean leadership and the desire of that leadership to prevent Taylor from acceding to power brought with it valuable logistical, military and financial support that Kromah as central leader could strategically dispose of. Third, the existence of a regional Mandingo trading network may have offered opportunities for profitable marketing, and Kromah's connections in that community, coupled with support from the Guinean president, may have enabled him to exert some control over ULIMO-K's diamond trade. Yet in the final analysis, the ULIMO-K was strong in numbers rather than in command (Lidow 2011, 184–193). However, Kromah's lead over the ULIMO in the long run increased his reputation, and in post-war Liberia he is the key political figure representing Mandingo.

3.3.6. The Liberia Peace Council

Reports of activities of a new group by the name of *Liberia Peace Council* emerged in March 1993 (Nass 2000, 108). The LPC massively gained strength after the signing of the Cotonou Agreement in mid-1993 to number about 2,000 troops (cf. Montclos 1999, 227). The emergence of the LPC indeed did not represent a further factionalization of ULIMO but the tactical creation of a new proxy force under the lead of George Boley. Cotonou had made accessible state resources to the factions in return for committing to a cease-fire. Yet a purely peaceful strategy was dangerous to the forces that had emanated from the Doe government in view of Taylor's military strength and repeated violations of cease-fires by the NPFL.

The LPC earned a reputation for both military effectiveness and weak discipline. The latter can be explained with reference to the background of its leadership. Both George Boley and the second most important leader,

Doe's Minister of Justice Chea Cheapoo, had their roots in Liberia's "progressive" movements. At home in Liberia's intellectual milieu but without military background, control over both professional soldiers and country youths was difficult to maintain. Strategic interests of the leadership were secured by having sensitive issues dealt with by a few personally loyal commanders. Thus, Ruth "Attila" Milton, a former AFL Major, considered Boley's most trusted commander, was charged with supervising the rubber business. Milton was popular among rank-and-file LPC combatants, and was appreciated for "mothering" her youthful combatants (cf. Prkic 2005, 122; Ellis 2007a, 130–131). Initially, the vast majority of LPC combatants had been former AFL soldiers. Later, youthful Sarpo recruits made up the bulk of the fighting force. Members of the ethnic group, considered to originate from Sinoe County, faced particular incentives to fight, as they were linguistically closely related to Krahn and had been a prime target of NPFL violence (cf. Youboty 2004, 140).

The LPC essentially relied on warlord politics techniques to control the civilian population. Its offensive of 1993–1994, as a consequence of which the group occupied large parts of eastern Liberia, was marked by strategic violence and atrocities against the civilian population. LPC strategy essentially consisted of emptying the countryside of civilians that could support the NPFL and force these into designated areas held by ECOMOG (Ellis 2007a, 102), thus assuring control. Inside these secured areas, such as the cities of Greenville and Buchanan, ECOMOG and LPC jointly held authority. LPC members routinely killed and harassed civilians even within these "safe havens" (cf. Nass 2000, 160). Even in Greenville, capital city of Sinoe and dominated by Sarpo, levels of violence against civilians were too high for humanitarians to organize relief, in contrast to the time the NPFL had occupied the area (Weissmann 1996, 108–109).

The formation of the LPC as well as its operations were supported by the Nigerian contingent of ECOMOG (Nass 2000, 108), and the force received considerable support in terms of weaponry and manpower from the AFL under Bowen (Africa Confidential Mar. 4, 1994). This central support, and the relatively weak military effort of the NPFL in much of eastern Liberia (cf. Weissmann 1996, 108), were decisive for the strength of the LPC. The LPC's economic basis was weak and very few revenues were controlled by the central leadership, although weapon transfers from ECOMOG and AFL to the LPC through George Boley allowed maintaining some control. Yet commanders were much more engaged in doing business than building military strength and essentially pursued private objectives. ECOMOG officers reportedly found it difficult to get LPC warlord entrepreneurs to move to the front to fight. In doing their business, LPC were hardly concerned with economic sustainability. Industrial infrastructures in their territory were comprehensively looted and exported as scrap. Due to insecurity, only one logging company remained active in the Buchanan area, diminishing the LPC tax base (cf. Montclos 1999, 236). Prkic documented two timber shipments from LPC-held Greenville and Buchanan within four months, with a total fob value of some 270,000 to 350,000 dollars (Prkic 2005, 120–121).[102] The LPC further exploited the small gold reserves in eastern Liberia, and made a business of providing protection to humanitarians. The *Sampson-Philipp International Agency* of LPC Generals Sampson and Philipp thus charged some 1,500 Liberian dollars a month for guards to protect vehicles travelling the road to Monrovia (Prkic 2005, 127). Assuming we can extrapolate from Prkic' findings on volumes of log exports, and applying my estimate of Taylor's level of taxation on the LPC case (see above), the LPC should have made some 240,000 dollars a year from timber.

Yet probably the most important income earner was rubber from the LAC plantation. As the LPC had driven away most civilians, reports that tapping was done by about 6,000 forced laborers held captive appear credible (Amnesty International 1995, 24; cf. TRC 2009, 176). The LPC exported some 4,660 tons of rubber onboard five vessels in about half a year (Prkic 2005, 122). According to another source, ECOMOG taxed up to 1,700 tons of rubber to be exported from Buchanan every month (Ellis 2007a, 168). The latter figure is designated as a maximum and should not be treated as an average. The LPC may thus have roughly exported about 10–15,000 tons of rubber a year. A Monrovia price of 300 dollars a ton implied a fob value of three to six million dollars a year, yet value in Buchanan was certainly much less, and ECOMOG surely took a significant cut. As for 1994, the value of LPC rubber trade was estimated at 1.5 million dollars only (Pham 2004, 121). Assuming that the LPC succeeded to reap some 25 percent of the higher Monrovia value as profit (see above), it gained some 750,000 to 1.25 million dollars a year from the

102 Prkic documented exports of some 2,321 m^3 of timber. The fob value is calculated on the basis of a minimum price of US$118 /$m^3$ (Liberian government data, cf. Prkic 2005, 121) and a maximum price of US$150/$m^3$ (cf. Consortium Agrifor Consult 2004, 95).

trade.[103] All in all, LPC revenue appears to have been little above one million dollars a year.

The LPC was the latest of the armed groups to emerge from the ruins of the Doe regime. Despite impressive territorial gains, it could not reverse the long-term trajectory of the forces of the Doe regime into political irrelevance. Essentially being an economically weak, poorly organized and undisciplined auxiliary force of ECOMOG, it had few chances to do so from the beginning. The LPC's close links to ECOMOG were a major factor for George Boley becoming the prime representative of the Krahn forces in the Council of State. Despite attempts to cling to the territory they occupied, the LPC lost military and consequently political relevance once ECOMOG withdrew its support.

3.4. Summary: Taylor and his Rivals

Looking at Taylor's opponents, common features of patterns of domination are apparent. First of all, domination was based on a very weak basis of legitimacy. The AFL, ULIMO-J and LPC based their claim to power on small ethnic groups, while the IGNU was the political representative of Liberia's small and divided intelligentsia. The leaders of the anti-Taylor groups, including the ULIMO-K, hardly succeeded to control their staff, though there were important differences, with Bowen instilling relative discipline, while Boley and Sawyer appeared least successful. Legitimacy of ECOMOG was strongly dependent on the Field Commander, with ostentatious display of strength by "no-nonsense" Generals like Joshua Dogonyaro and Victor Malu being strongly appreciated. The factions were characterized by pertinent extremely *decentralized patrimonialism*, i.e. far-reaching appropriation of powers by the staff, in particular those powers related to generating revenue. In general, the economic basis of Taylor's opponents was rather weak, too, although the IGNU disposed of substantial sums. The creation of the most important irregular armed factions was sponsored by ECOMOG, and ECOMOG support

103 Direct organization of the trade by the LPC and use of slave labor may have increased profits, justifying the assumption that the LPC could appropriate a relatively high share of the value of the trade.

during the war seems decisive for them having been able to continue to exist.

While the NPFL was better organized economically, revenues have frequently been overestimated. NPFL revenues were significant, but so were the costs of war, and claims that their fight was about the material spoils of war are unconvincing. The decisive advantage of Taylor vis-à-vis his opponents was his legitimacy, or more specifically, his charismatic legitimacy, allowing him to maintain significant control over combatants, civilians, and sources of revenue. Taylor's legitimacy among "country" youths has either not been understood and or been ignored by the International Community. Essentially for cultural reasons, it chose to support a government framing its claim to power in more familiar terms of human rights, civilian democratic government, and development. In hindsight, it seems bizarre how the International Community accepted as interpretation of events in Liberia a narrative that essentially was a justification for Nigeria's strategic response to the crisis.

As should be clear, the Liberian internal war was a matter of politics. More importantly, the decay of the state in Liberia essentially was a consequence of politically motivated international interventions, rather than a particular economic organization of warfare. Nigerian and Guinean support for irregular armed factions was only one of these interventions. Further, the power sharing solutions the International Community devised for Liberia resulted in the remnants of a coherent state apparatus being destroyed, as factions autonomously controlling territories used it to operate their respective patronage systems. By contrast, internal elimination contests entailed a concentration of power.

3.5 From Warlord to Statesman: Charles Taylor as President

This section analyzes how Charles Taylor converted his position of power as a warlord into that of the head of state of a sovereign country. It is intended to show to what extent there were structural changes and continuities in the exercise of political power when a warlord system was transformed to fit principles of sovereign statehood. An analysis of these changes also shows how power resources underpinning warlord rule could be employed to secure power in a more democratic dispensation, i.e. one that required the winning of elections. As we know, Taylor's attempt to maintain power eventually failed. This section, however, focuses on the ascent of Taylor and his accumulation of power until reaching its peak around 2000. The subsequent breakdown of his regime is dealt with in the following chapter.

The first section densely describes patterns of rule in Liberia under Charles Taylor. It is structured into two parts. The first deals with the properly civilian dimension of the state, excluding its military component. It emphasizes the increasing importance of conventional, neo-patrimonial patterns of rule, i.e. the co-optation of influential personalities into the "civilian" state administration, and briefly portrays developments concerning legitimacy and repression. The second analyzes the structure of the security sector, which served both the purposes of generating patrimonial legitimacy and compensating for a lack of legitimacy through repression. Similar to its civilian counterpart, patterns in the security sector show characteristics of patrimonial and charismatic domination, yet while the civilian dimension of the state was to a significant extent employed to buy support in certain segments of Liberian society, the security sector can be considered the core of Taylor's system in that considerations of loyalty determined the staffing of key positions. Both the civilian and the security-related government institutions occupied a central position in the political economy, and impacted on collection and allocation of revenues.

The political economy of Charles Taylor's Liberia is thus a cross-cutting issue recurring throughout the section. Yet revenue generation and the associated political arrangements are described in detail in the following sections. It serves to show how Charles Taylor personally controlled a significant proportion of the profits generated in the national economy. Further, it is intended to demonstrate that peace and sovereign rule were of benefit to Taylor, as he could not only increase turnover and profits of existing economic sectors, but exploit newly arising business opportunities too. An important feature of Taylor's rule was that it was politically and economically essentially informally organized. Informal relations transcended national boundaries, giving rise to a quite particular political system.

3.5.1. Transplanting a System of Domination

A pertinent pattern of Taylor's transformation from warlord to sovereign president was the transfer of his "Greater Liberia" administration into the formal institutions of the state of Liberia. This concerned in particular the core institutions of his regime, the leading positions of which were staffed with individuals who were considered particularly loyal, either because they had proven themselves in positions of authority of "Greater Liberia" or because they belonged to Taylor's immediate family. For instance, the post of Commissioner of the *Bureau of Maritime Affairs* (BMA) was allocated to Benoni Urey, a long-term associate of Taylor who had served as his representative at high-level negotiations and had been responsible for taxing the NPFL-controlled rubber production. The BMA was of major importance for state finances as it collected the fees generated by the ship registry. Similarly, Roland Massaquoi became Minister of Agriculture, an office he had already occupied in the NPRAG. The ministry is of particular importance because it controls the rubber industry, which is not only a major source of revenue. Rubber corporations assume state-like authority in significant parts of Liberia by policing vast plantation areas and providing the few public services and goods available to tappers. Probably the financially most important position in Charles Taylor's Liberia was that of the Managing Director of the FDA, which was given to a brother of the president, Robert Taylor, illustrating the importance of personal bonds. Control over core state institutions was organized according to principles of charismatic legitimacy and "pure patrimonialism", with Charles Taylor exercising significant personal control over revenue intake and allocation.

A key characteristic of Taylor's transformation from warlord to president was an increase in patrimonial practices to generate legitimacy and a corresponding weakening of—nevertheless important—charismatic principles. The Liberian polity included a greater number of elites who could challenge Taylor than "Greater Liberia", and the president partly reacted by accommodating potential opponents. As president, Taylor was "generous with the money he (stole), doling out huge amounts and expensive cars to secure support, silence or at least limit opposition. He typically [tried] to buy off or befriend opponents before using harsher measures" (ICG 2002a, 21).

Practices of co-optation were reflected in Taylor's first cabinet. NPFL-CRC leader Tom Woewiyu was made Minister of Labor, ULIMO-J's Roosevelt Johnson and Raleigh Seekie were made Ministers of Rural Development and Transport, respectively, AFL General Philip Kamah received the post of Minister of National Security, and the head of the LDF, François Massaquoi, became Minister of Youth and Sports. Similarly, prominent "progressive" activists were integrated, most evidently SELF's Blamoh Nelson as Director of Cabinet. Private economy enterprises apparently contributed to Taylor's patronage portfolio. The former leader of the 1970s PAL Gabriel Bacchus Matthews was eventually employed as public relations officer of the *Oriental Timber Company* (OTC).[104] Probably the most important patrimonial intermediaries for the populace were religious personalities. Both Poro officials and leaders of independent churches were freely handed money and provided other forms of patronage (Ellis 2007a, xxxii).

The interplay of democratic institutions is of particular interest in the context of this study. A general trend was the informal remodeling of democratic institutions into institutions of patronage. Due to the difficult circumstances of the elections and contrary to conventional procedures, a "single ballot system" had been adopted in the 1997 elections. As Charles Taylor won about 75 percent, he could distribute a corresponding number of legislative posts, i.e. 70 of 90 seats. The parliamentarians in turn were subject to informal influences and pressure from the executive.

Relations between the Senate President Charles Walker Brumskine and Charles Taylor illustrate important aspects of the workings of the legislature. Brumskine is a prominent Liberian lawyer who served as intermediary between the state and the most important foreign corporations in the country. He was a candidate in the 2005 presidential elections and came third, demonstrating both his intra-elite connections as well as the size of his political constituency. Brumskine had joined the NPP only shortly before the 1997 elections but was quickly made Senate candidate for populous Grand Bassa County. Demonstrating the continued prevalence of factional politics and Taylor's difficulties in controlling his parliamentary clients, the Senate refused to confirm the executive's choice for the office of Foreign Minister. Brumskine then, almost surely on the instruction of Taylor, announced that the president's office would from now

---

104 OTC (see below) was the largest logging firm active in Liberia during Taylor's presidency. Given that Taylor had publicly declared OTC his "pepper bush", i.e. something dear and private, one does not need to refer to his alleged stakeholder role in OTC to consider the appointment political. Matthews had once been a very prominent opponent of Taylor.

on be responsible for declaring the results of confirmation hearings, effectively lifting an important legislative right to control executive appointments (cf. EIU 10/1997, 32). Yet, as will be explained later, Brumskine also exemplifies the limits of executive control over the legislature. In general, the administration was dealt with in an almost purely patrimonial manner. Civil servants received their salaries irregularly only, and the state budget was of a virtual character.

"Although the official national budget of Liberia fluctuated between $80 million and $87 million a year from 1997 to 2003, the public budget figures were essentially meaningless. They reflected neither real government revenues nor real expenditures. Most years, virtually none of the money budgeted for infrastructure, health, education or rebuilding was spent on the designated activities" (Farah 2005, 16).

Compensating for regular salaries, "Taylor regularly made U.S.$100,000 'personal gifts' to government agencies and ministries to be shared among staff. [...] In the time-honored manner of the patronage state, Taylor accumulated all resources and then generously distributed them back among various recipients, all the while taking care to obtain their gratitude" (ICG 2002a, 17).

There were thus strong tendencies of patrimonialization when Taylor accommodated a larger circle of beneficiaries in the process of extending his rule. This could be expected, as charisma tends to be transient and rule tends to be based on more conventional forms of legitimacy in the medium run. Charismatic legitimacy is notoriously difficult to maintain for rebels-turned-presidents: an important feature of charismatic rule is that it tends to project satisfaction of needs into the future; once the war has come to an end, the charismatic rulers is expected to deliver on expectations and is likely to fail (cf. Schlichte 2009, 85–115). Yet while patrimonial practices of reciprocal exchange served to accommodate elites and absorb the shatters of Liberia's state administration, the circle of beneficiaries effectively was small. Charles Taylor's domination considerably deviated from the arrangements of broad-based patronage politics sustaining power elsewhere, and patronage is insufficient to explain Taylor's legitimacy. Taylor's popularity appeared to be informed by interpretations of his rule, justifying a brief look at the evolution of Taylor's symbolic representation of power.

As has been explained, the key charismatic quality ascribed to "Ghankay" Taylor during war had been strength, and the same quality was useful in a post-war context. Formulating Taylor's election in more rational terms than the concept of charisma implies, Taylor's election victory could be interpreted as a vote for peace (Harris 1999). To a significant extent, Taylor later was considered to deliver on the expectation of stabilizing Liberia. For the better part of his time in office, his former foes fell into political-military irrelevance. The first police chief, whose draconian approach in law enforcement alarmed foreign human rights organizations, quickly became popular. A key quality appreciated by Liberians was that Taylor "did not like those who do not respect the law",[105] and was considered to have effectively re-introduced order. Yet there were notable deficits in security provision. The ULIMO-J was not fully demobilized, resulting in a shootout in 1998 and other breaches of security. Crime was a significant problem in many communities and, furthermore, the security forces themselves often caused insecurity, although residents of the heavily patrolled area around Taylor's White Flower residence in Monrovia enjoyed a high degree of coincidental security. Yet security forces enjoyed relative impunity and frequently harassed civilians, in particular in hinterland areas and logging concessions (Global Witness 2003a). In some rural areas, loot continued to substitute for the pay of government paramilitaries (cf. Malan 2008, 9).

Taylor's particular strength was the continuous fostering of charisma by way of public performances. Taylor regularly attended a phone-in radio program that included him being called on by more or less prominent critics. The radio program allowed the president to make use of his key quality, the "gift of the gab–if ever anyone had it, that was Charles Taylor" (BBC July 28, 2009). Eloquently, Taylor refuted criticism, frequently ridiculing rather than threatening opponents and thus displaying a relaxed and self-assured attitude in the face of adversity. Further, as had been the case in the past, Taylor tapped diverse sources of transcendental power. He frequently held sermons in churches that equally pronounced his saint-like characteristics as well as his preparedness to meet out violence (cf. Kamara n.d.) and left a strong impression with Liberians.[106] Drawing on more local religious semantics of power, his Poro title *Dahkpanah* became part of his official appellation as president.[107]

The darker side of Taylor, establishing a peculiar Liberian version of "law and order", was repression. Generally, repression was geared towards

105 Focus Group Interview in Ganta, Nimba County, Mar., 19 2007.

106 Various interviews in Monrovia, 2005–2007.

107 For official purposes, Taylor had to be addressed as His Excellency Dahkpanah Dr Charles Ghankay Taylor, President of the Republic of Liberia.

ensuring Taylor's victory in future, purportedly democratic, elections. Its main aims were to stifle uncontrolled criticism (as different from controlled criticism in Taylor's phone-in show) and prevent oppositional activities from gaining organizational power.

Already in November 1997, Taylor ordered the closure of two radio stations that had been part of externally funded projects to recreate a vibrant and professional media sector, and Liberia's most important newspaper, the *New Democrat*, was refused registration. In December, a journalist was arrested for covering the funeral of the recently murdered former NPFL-CRC leader Samuel Dokie. In January 1998, the editor of *The National* newspaper was beaten up by police after criticizing Taylor's harsh attitude towards ECOMOG, and the same month the only private printing press in Liberia was ordered not to print the *Heritage* newspaper (West Africa Feb. 23, 1998). Amos Sawyer, now leading the civil society organization *Center for Democratic Empowerment* (CEDE) remained one of the most outspoken critics of Taylor and was severely manhandled. Numerous similar violations of civil liberties marked Taylor's rule. His son Charles "Chuckie Taylor" became notorious for both privately and politically motivated murders, rape and torture as head of the most important paramilitary group, the *Anti-Terrorist Unit* (ATU).[108] Rather than averting any imminent and evident menace to the government, the main benefit of such actions was to intimidate oppositional activists that could later, probably in elections, become serious rivals.

In a number of cases, Taylor threatened patrimonially co-opted strongmen who failed to conform to his expectations. He dealt most brutally with (former) members of the inner NPFL and NPP circles who were considered to have accumulated too much power or to have betrayed him. Yet in retrospect, much of the violence of Taylor's regime has contributed to the fragmentation of relations of authority rather than a stabilization of domination. This, however, is the subject of the following chapter.

108 "Chuckie", son of an American-Trinadian girlfriend of Taylor, combined the features of being a family member and a stranger to Liberia without moral or social bonds in the country and was thus particularly suited for a role in the security sector. Being a US-American citizen, "Chuckie", whose real name is Charles McArthur Emmanuel, was sentenced to 97 years in prison in the US for torture in 2009.

3.5.2. The Security Sector

Two major concerns informed the reconstruction of a "state" security sector under Taylor. One was the desire to maintain control over security forces without foreign interference. The other, immediately more important one was his mistrust of the Krahn-dominated army. Charles Taylor thus built his security apparatus on a number of paramilitary units which were frequently based on NPFL command structures. Most were organized separate from the army's command structures and responded more or less directly to Taylor. The security sector was characterized by fragmentation of chains of command and personal control by Taylor.

At the core of Taylor's personal security system was the ATU which assumed functions of a presidential guard and an elite combat force. It was estimated to be comprised of up to 90 percent RUF fighters. The paramilitary *Special Security Services* (SSS) were officially responsible for the security of the Executive Mansion but only partially employed for that purpose. The SSS was headed by Benyamin Yeaten, who was as well informal supreme commander of all paramilitary units.

A large share of other government paramilitaries was employed to provide security for logging companies and assure state oversight over export. For instance, when Taylor became president, the *Bush Marines* were renamed *Navy Rangers* and charged with providing security to Liberia's sea ports. Outside Monrovia, logging corporations were the main users of port facilities and required to pay for the security outfits which, however, would be employed for both company and regime security. Roland Duo, former commander of the *Bush Marines*, was made head of the *Navy Rangers* as well as Managing Director of the *National Port Authority* (NPA), traditionally one of the economically most important positions in Liberia (Global Witness 2003a, 15).

The timber industry became dominated by a few large, partly foreign-held corporations, the *Inland Logging Company* (ILC) of NPFL "Captain Marvel" Oscar Cooper being the only major Liberian-held logging firm. In all cases, paramilitary groups directly linked to the government acted as company security guards in the countryside. The largest logging company, OTC, had a militia of some 2,500 troops while the *Maryland Wood Processing Industries'* (MWPI) security force mustered some 500 combatants. In some cases, former NPFL officials personally controlled paramilitary groups employed on their logging concessions. NPFL General Cucoo Dennis, who had already run a logging operation in "Greater Liberia", commanded security forces for his own as well as other logging concessions (ibid., 14).

Being considered far less reliable than these paramilitary groups, the AFL were situated at the margins of Taylor's security apparatus.[109] By the end of the war, the AFL officially numbered about 7,000 troops (Adebayo 2002b, 209), yet the figure may have included a sizable number of inactive and "ghost" soldiers. Some 2,600 AFL troops were "demobilized" on the orders of Taylor in 1998 (Adebayo 2002a, 70). The AFL then grew; after the second Liberian war, 12,240 regular soldiers were officially demobilized. Although this figure was likely to have been inflated,[110] too, Charles Taylor clearly had embarked on a significant recruitment exercise for the AFL aimed at controlling and diluting the weight of beneficiaries of the Doe regime.

At the center of the new recruitment drive was the military intelligence unit G-2, which was effectively replaced with the NPFL's G-2 unit. The NPFL G-2 had been central to Taylor's coercive apparatus in "Greater Liberia". Under Taylor's rule it was as well employed to provide personal security to individuals of prime importance for the regime. For instance, some executives of logging corporations as well as a group of foreign diamond dealers suspected to have been associated with *Al Quaid* (cf. Global Witness 2003b) had G-2 detachments posted to their residences.

3.5.3. Revenue Generation in Charles Taylor's Liberia

The major sources of revenue for the Charles Taylor government were timber exports, diamond exports and the ship registry. In this section, I firstly describe major developments in each of these sectors. I then explain general characteristics of the political economy of Taylor's Liberia.

---

109 For instance, Taylor's then-Minister of Defense stated that "because of his own suspicion of the army, he [Taylor] decided to transfer most of the responsibility of the army into militia groups" (Frontline World May 2005). See Global Witness (2003a, 15) for an (incomplete) list of paramilitary groups.

110 Much as the other factions, the AFL did not submit a roster of its staff. The identification of soldiers to be included in the demobilization process was partly based on marks typically left by the shoestrings of soldier boots. Interview with Othello Warwick, Deputy Minister of Defense, Nov. 16, 2006. Family members of soldiers and other civilians with the right connections were likely to have been presented as soldiers in order to benefit from the demobilization package.

3.5.3.1. The Sierra Leone Diamond Connection

A most important feature of Taylor's rule with a tremendous negative impact on Liberia's international relations was the maintenance and extension of the diamond trade with the RUF. Investigating Taylor's involvement in the diamond trade, two issues need to be explored. The first one is the military situation, i.e. periods of RUF control over the Kono and Tongo Fields producing the bulk of Sierra Leones diamonds. The second one is constituted by the patterns of the network(s) organizing diamond production and trade, in particular concerning major intermediaries.

In this respect, three events that took place before the takeover of sovereign power by Charles Taylor in July 1997 need to be kept in mind. Firstly, as has been mentioned, the private security company *Executive Outcomes* had to withdraw from the Kono diamond field in February 1997. Second, in March 1997, RUF leader Foday Sankoh was arrested in Nigeria on charges of illegal possession of firearms. General Issa Sesay, strongly loyal to the incarcerated leader, formally took his position. While Sankoh was in detention, an alliance of army soldiers under the army Major Johnny Paul Koroma and RUF rebels toppled the civilian government in May 1997 and took over, ruling as self-proclaimed *Armed Forces Revolutionary Council* (AFRC). The RUF then controlled the major diamond fields again.

In the context of the coup, fighting between bilaterally deployed Nigerian troops stationed in Freetown and the AFRC/RUF began. In August 1997, these troops, as well as Ghanaian and Guinean contingents in Sierra Leone, were put under an ECOWAS mandate and integrated into ECOMOG command structures. The mission itself became informally known as ECOMOG II. Eventually in February 1998, an offensive by Nigerian troops pushed the AFRC/RUF out of Freetown, and the RUF lost Tongo Field in the process (Smillie 2007, 28).

Charles Taylor's provision of military equipment to the RUF in return for diamonds was a major reason for the rebels' military successes. ECOMOG II's Nigerian commander, Brigadier-General Maxwell Khobe, in turn organized Liberian dissidents in Sierra Leone and supported the building of alliances between these and Sierra Leonean *Civil Defence Forces* (CDF) (ICG 2002a, 3).[111] Supported by its auxiliary troops, ECOMOG

111 At the time, Khobe was also officially supreme commander of the CDF (EIU 07/1998, 27).

advanced in the countryside, conquered the eastern border region, and forced the RUF out of Kono by mid-1998 (ibid; Smillie 2007, 28). The RUF then regrouped, received new supplies and put major emphasis on control of the diamond producing enclaves. They succeeded to re-occupy Kono in late 1998 and Tongo in January 1999, and held both areas until disarmament at the end of 2001.

Despite Taylor's aggressive policy towards Sierra Leone, Nigeria was eager to withdraw from the country in the wake of its disengagement from Liberia. In the context of Nigeria preparing to withdraw, a peace agreement between the government and the RUF was hastily concluded in Lomé in July 1999. The Lomé Agreement made important concessions to the RUF: it included an amnesty for human rights violations committed during the war and declared all natural resource concessions null and void, bringing resource exploitation under direct political control. The rebel group was transformed into a political party and obtained four ministerial posts for a transitional period of two years. Most importantly, a new *Commission for the Management of Strategic Resources, National Reconstruction and Development* was established and headed by RUF leader Foday Sankoh.[112] In addition, Sankoh became vice-president. Thus, the RUF-Taylor connection was about to control sovereign power and natural resource exploitation in both Sierra Leone and Liberia. By early 2000, Charles Taylor was at the peak of his power and "poised to win the Mano River War" (ICG 2002a, 3).

Taylor had personally dealt with a number of senior RUF cadres handling the rebels' diamond and weapons transactions. While Sankoh was in detention, a split between units associated with the military chief Sam "Mosquito" Bockarie and those close to the political leader, Issa Sesay, had developed within the RUF. The rift deepened after Sankoh returned to the head of the movement and in December 1999, the tensions led to fighting between forces under the command of Bockarie and units loyal to Sankoh (ibid., 14). Taylor's links at least partially bridged these divisions though Bockarie was considered most closely associated with the Liberian president (cf. ICG 2002a, i). Bockarie and his troops subsequently went into exile in Liberia where they became one of Taylor's key military backup forces, partly integrated into the ATU.

---

112 Sankoh had been released by Nigeria and handed over to Sierra Leonean authorities in August 1998. He remained in detention until April 1999 and was freed in order to participate in the negotiations leading to the Lomé Agreement.

Table 10: RUF Diamond Exports (Liberia FOB Prices) and Taylor's Profits; in US$ Million

	1997	1998	1999	2000	2001
RUF Exports	15	10–20	40–60	50–70	60–80
Taylor's Profit[113]	8	5–11	21–30	27–37	30–43

Author's estimate

An analysis of events allows us to make informed guesses about volumes and profits of the RUF diamond trade (Table 10). Several assumptions underlie these estimates. Firstly, I assume that Kono contributed some 75 percent and Tongo some 25 percent to the RUF's diamond income (cf. Gberie 2002, 6). Secondly, I assume that the RUF exported diamonds worth some 60–80 million dollars (Liberia fob) at the peak of its mining activities (Smillie 2007). Third, I consider the military situation the major factor determining whether the RUF tapped the full potential. Fourth, I assume that RUF mining activities "increased steadily in volume and sophistication" until the RUF was disarmed towards the end of 2001 (Farah 2005, 17).[114] Further, for purposes of calculating Taylor's revenue, I assume that he marketed 80 percent of the RUF production. It is widely considered evident that part of the RUF production was not exported through Liberia but either directly from Sierra Leone[115] or through Gambia, Guinea and Côte d'Ivoire (Smillie 2007). Yet Liberia appears to have been the main transit country (Farah 2005). Finally, I accept Farah's finding that Taylor took 2/3 of the fob value as profit (ibid., 16), although this is a very high share.[116]

---

113 An alternative estimate is provided by the Farah (2005, 16). As the report uses the outdated figure of a US$125 million export value of RUF diamonds at the peak of production (cf. Panel of Experts 12/2000) and assumes Taylor to have handled 100 percent of the RUF's diamond trade, the estimates are significantly higher than mine.

114 There is no data available on the impact of the diamond embargo against Liberia of May 2001 and its effects are not included in the estimate. The embargo, however, is likely to have significantly reduced trade and profits, and I may significantly overestimate revenue for 2001.

115 Government-licensed diamond dealers played an important role in RUF diamond exports (cf. Panel of Experts 10/2002, 80).

116 For instance, Sierra Leone's post-war export taxes for diamonds stand at 3 percent of the fob value, and these taxes are considered the main state income from diamonds (cf.

All evidence thus points to the fact that the trade in illegally sourced Sierra Leonean diamonds increased massively during Taylor's rule as president, and assumed particular importance only after the Liberian war had ended. The revenue derived was a major source of finance for Taylor's sovereign system of domination.

3.5.3.2. The Timber Industry

As a consequence of the UN diamond embargo against Liberia of May 2001 and, more importantly, disarmament of the RUF, the trade in Sierra Leonean diamonds ceased to be a significant source of revenue for Taylor by the end of 2001. Yet increased timber exports compensated for lost diamond revenue.

Table 11: Post-War Timber Exports, FOB, in US$ Million

	1997	1998	1999	2000	2001	2002	2003
Govt. Data*	7.5	12.3	23.4	67.5	79.9	**59.0 –146.5	**44.0
Importing Countries' Records	8.5	25.2	31.6	94.0	88.4	183.2	n/a
Other estimates	n/a	n/a	n/a	*** 130.0	**** 105.5	**** 126.6	n/a

*Sources: * Schwidrowski/Thomas (2005, 4); ** IMF (2006, 11)117; *** Global Witness (2001, 3); **** Author's estimate, based on Table 12 and Consortium Agrifor Consult (2004, 95)*

Pugh et al. 2004, 118). Liberia later decided a 3 percent export tax on diamonds, too, although the figure was criticized as too low by some (cf. Panel of Experts 12/2008, 15).

117 The first two sources are IMF publications. Schwidrowski/Thomas (2005, 4) explicitly refer to the data in the second row as "official data", i.e. government data. IMF (2006, 11) names "Liberian authorities; and Fund staff estimates" as sources, and the data differs extremely, as can be seen in the column for the year 2002. It is, however, implausible that an IMF revision of government data would result in reduced figures for volumes of exports, as international statistics rather suggest an upward correction. A possible explanation is the provision of divergent data by different government agencies. For instance, in its 2001 annual report, the FDA reported timber exports of "approximately US$ 80 million [as quoted in Schwidrowski/Thomas (2005)]. The MoF [Ministry of Finance], in contrast, quoted only US$ 60 Million" (Global Witness 2004,

Charles Taylor was personally involved in all major business operations to such an extent that critics called the country "Liberia Inc." (cf. ICG 2002a). Logging concessions were personally awarded by Taylor, with little concern for existing legal titles of other corporations. Several concessions were given to companies or individuals suspected of links to the international illegal arms trade. The OTC, of which Charles Taylor was a 50 percent stakeholder, was allocated some 70 percent of Liberia's concessionable area. The investor behind the joint venture appeared to be the mainland China and Taiwan-based *Global Timber Corporation* (GTC) (Global Witness 2003a, 23–24).[118] Gus Kouwenhoven, a Dutch businessman who once ran Liberia's most prestigious hotel and later managed logging concessions in "Greater Liberia" (cf. Panel of Experts 10/2001, 71), thus possessing long-term business experience in Liberia as well as intimate knowledge of the country's elite, became its Managing Director. OTC was alleged to pay half of its dues in money and half in weapons, and was blamed for a spate of Chinese-manufactured weapons in Liberia (Global Witness 2003a).

Similarly, two other major timber firms, the MWPI and the *Mohammed Group of Companies* (MGC), owned by the Lebanese businessmen Abbas Fawaz and Mohammed Salame,[119] respectively, were suspected to be involved in timber-against-arms deals. Further illustrating the link between logging companies and private security sector financing, Robert Taylor, in his position as head of the FDA, ordered the MWPI to effect monthly payments to a paramilitary General (Panel of Experts 06/2004, 28; cf. Global Witness 2003a). While many observers have stressed the foreign character of the companies (cf. Johnston 2004), it is worth noting that leading management personnel had generally been in contact with Liberia's elite circles for decades. While Taylor needed foreign capital, access to Liberia's markets for foreigners depended to a significant extent on personal intra-elite connections. Recruiting individuals who were defined as foreigners into the management of firms exploiting natural resources served to econ-

27). IMF (2006, 11) indicates exports of US$69 million for 2001. There are massive uncertainties concerning export volumes.

118 Indonesian, Malaysian and Hong Kong-based corporations also appeared to have major interests in OTC (cf. Panel of Experts 10/2001, 72; Global Witness 2003a, 23–24).

119 Mohamed Salame was additionally Taylor's ambassador to Côte d'Ivoire (Global Witness 2003b, 40).

omically empower elites that could not aspire to positions of political authority, as has been long-running practice in Liberia.

Most likely, timber overtook Sierra Leonean diamonds as the major source of revenues around 2000. Though a lot of figures on the volumes of timber exports are available, all lack reliability.

Table 12: Export Volumes in Thousand m³ and State Timber Revenue in US$ Million

	1997	1998	1999	2000	2001	2002
Exports	*57.0	*168.0	**190.0	***934.0	1,000.0 ****	1,200.0 *****
Corresponding State Revenue[120]	2.9	8.5	9.9	46.6	46.9	56.3

**Author's estimate, based on "Exports" row in Table 11) and prices of US$150/m³ (Consortium Agrifor Consult 2004, 95); **Liberian Government, cf. Global Witness (2001, 16); ***Global Witness estimate (2001, 3); ****Author's estimate, based on Consortium Agrifor Consult (2004, 80) data; *****Author's estimate, based on Global Witness (2003a, 19) data*

Despite widely diverging data, we can make a few claims about trends. Though certainly higher than recorded, exports of timber towards the end of the first Liberian war were relatively small in volume. Exports rose strongly then, as is partly reflected in official data, and jumped in 2000 when OTC started production. The most authoritative study on Liberian timber puts exports for 2000 at 130 million dollars (fob), noting that the figure represents a minimum as exports could not be comprehensively monitored (Global Witness 2001, 3). In following years, monitoring was even less comprehensive, yet activities of logging companies suggested an increase in timber exports until 2002 (Global Witness 2003a), as is reflected in data from timber importing countries. Timber is thus appears to have replaced diamonds as the prime source of income around 2000.

---

120 Author's estimate. The calculation is based on average rates of taxation as used in Consortium Agrifor Consult (2004, 95). Details of taxation can be found in Schwidrowski/Thomas (2005). Government taxes and fees are partly calculated on the basis of volume and partly on the basis of the fob value. Fob Values were taken from Table 10 (row "Other Estimates" if available and "Exports […]" if not. For an estimate of Liberian state income from logging based on official government figures see Panel of Experts (10/2001, 70–71).

Based on available export data and information from Liberian insiders, Farah (2005, 17–18) estimated Taylor's cut of the profits at an average annual 23 million dollar, most of it during the last three years of his presidency. To calculate the money available to Taylor to finance his system of domination, a few million dollars, probably 6.5 million (Global Witness 2003a, 18) that went into the state budget should be added (cf. Farah 2005, 17–18). However, in view of the military situation, it is unlikely that significant timber exports took place in 2003, and there are significant uncertainties in the latter estimate. My own estimates (Table 12), based on the assumption that exports were "taxed" by Taylor at levels corresponding to the legal situation, suggests an average of 24.5 million a year was available from timber to Taylor. Yet while revenues were hardly significant during 1997–1999, they averaged some 50 million dollars annually from 2000–2002.

3.5.3.3. The Ship Registry and the Rubber Industry

The large corporations managing the ship registry and rubber plantations could not be directly controlled by Taylor. For instance, headquarters of major companies were based in the US and had to submit to relatively stringent accounting standards, barring, e.g. direct rubber-against-arms deals. Yet evidently, significant though not quantifiable sums stemming from these sectors were diverted after having been paid into the Liberian treasury and could be used by Taylor to finance patronage and weapons.

For about 40 years, Liberia's ship registry had been managed off-shore by the US-based firm *International Trust Company* (ITC). Shortly after Taylor acceded to the presidency, his government complained about a lack of control over the company and announced a renegotiation of the contract. Relations between the ITC's mother company *International Registry Incorporated* (IRI) and the Liberian government turned bad as the latter sued IRI for allegedly having diverted 40 million dollar. IRI countersued for 100 million dollar, accusing Lester Hyman, a lawyer and US-based public relations officer of Taylor representing the Liberian government in the case, of "conspiracy, falsification and defamation" (EIU 08/1999, 45).[121] The case was finally settled through a substantial payment by the Liberian government to IRI (ibid.). Eventually, the contract with IRI was cancelled

121 By coincidence, Hyman (2003) wrote a methodologically weak apologia of the Taylor regime.

and an agreement concluded with a newly established firm, the US-owned and -based *Liberian International Ship and Corporate Registry* (LISCR). Lester Hyman became LISCR's first Chairman. He was seconded by Vice-Chairman Yoram Cohen, equally a lawyer and former public relations officer for Taylor (cf. EIU 01/1999, 44).[122] Although details of the settlement with IRI are not public, it is very likely that Taylor's attempt to increase personal control over the registry was financially extremely costly.

Taylor's Commissioner of the *Bureau of Maritime Affairs* (BMA), the Liberian government agency liaising with LISCR, later successfully put pressure on the registry management to make payments directly to companies associated with foreign arms merchants instead of remitting the funds into government accounts, thus obscuring illegal international arms transfers (cf. Panel of Experts 11/2003; Panel of Experts 10/2001, 17). The ship registry officially generated some 25.7 million dollar, 18 million of which were due to the government (ibid.). Yet witnesses reported that the government additionally received some five million dollars not accounted for and that appeared to be diverted, "as is the entire income of the corporate registry" (Panel of Experts 10/2003, 22). Taylor thus probably received well above 20 million dollars a year from the registries.

Table 13: Rubber Exports, in US$ Million

1997	1998	1999	2000	2001	2002	2003
19.4	37.6	61.7	*57.0	*50.3	55.4	46.0

*Source: IMF (2000a, 29); *IMF (2006, 4)*

As for rubber, the well-established corporations *Firestone* and LAC continued to dominate the market. As has been said, all plantations suffered severe damages during the war, substantially reducing productive capacity. During Taylor's presidency, some replanting took place, yet it was limited as investors judged the political situation too unstable to make investments that would start generating revenue about seven years later only (cf. Panel of Experts 04/2002, 32). In any case, Taylor did not rule long enough to profit from rehabilitation of plantations.

Nevertheless, the rubber sector grew strongly after the war due to increasing formalization and improved security: from 49,000 tons in 1998

122 More details on the change in management of the register can be found in Panel of Experts (10/2001, 85–86).

to 63,000 tons in 1999 and 102,000 in 2000. From 2000 to 2001, production grew by 11 percent only, indicating the sector had reached a plateau (Panel of Experts 10/2001, 70; Panel of Experts 04/2002, 32). Declining world market prices meant that in terms of generating income, the rubber industry had already reached its zenith in 1999. Although performance of the sector was rather disappointing as a whole, the value of the rubber trade multiplied compared to the war years (cf. Table 13), indicating that Taylor should have been able to reap a "peace dividend" and increase his income from rubber when he became sovereign president.

3.5.3.4. The Services Sector

Under Charles Taylor, Liberia's market was structured monopolistically and oligopolistically. This pattern allowed relatively easy direct, personal control of opportunities for accumulation. Owing to historical developments and reinforced by political intervention under Charles Taylor, some ten families of Lebanese descent controlled almost the whole import trade in consumer goods. Most important among these imported goods were rice and fuel.

The pattern of political control was simple. *Bridgeway Corporation* was awarded a sole license for rice imports, while *West Oil Corporation* got a contract to exclusively supply the monopolistic state-owned fuel storing body *Liberia Petroleum Refining Company* (LPRC). The companies and their bank accounts were part of an elaborate network of non-government accounts and intermediaries through which the personal transfer of finances was organized (cf. Panel of Experts 4/2003, 38–39), and the cases mentioned here are meant to be exemplary. For instance, *Bridgeway* supplied rice directly to Taylor's paramilitaries, indicating that a substantial part of defense expenditures was not accounted for in the state budget (Panel of Experts 10/2003, 19–20).

In the case of *West Oil*, in 1998 the company had made available a loan of ten million dollars to Taylor used apparently at the president's discretion (cf. IMF 2000b, 9). The loan was recorded as prepaid taxes and thus to be repaid by the Liberian state (Panel of Experts 10/2003, 19).[123] In addition, both the rice and the fuel importer enjoyed large exemptions and waivers

123 Effectively, the interim government succeeding Taylor repaid the final installments while numerous other creditors with less dubious claims were put off. International observers suspected a ruse intended to make funds available to Taylor's network.

without any "economic justification" (Panel of Experts 04/2003, 40–41), leading observers to believe that taxes were privately levied on the companies. According to calculations by the Panel of Experts, exemptions and waivers cost the state some seven million dollars import taxes on rice and some eleven million on fuel every year (ibid., 40). Yet when Taylor left the presidency, the loan to *West Oil* officially had not yet been repaid.

Another case indicating substantial direct involvement of the president into economic ventures is that of the mobile phone company *LoneStar Communications Corporation* (LCC). *LoneStar* held a monopoly on mobile communication, and as there was no land-based telephone system to speak of, it controlled virtually all telephone communication under Taylor's rule, allowing it to charge exorbitant rates. For instance, a local call cost 50 US cents a minute and a SIM card 65 US dollars. *LoneStar's* SIM card price dropped to 5 dollars when the market was opened. A Liberian company by the name of PLC Investment held a 20 to 40 percent share in *LoneStar*, and received at least 10 percent of the company's profits plus substantial dividends.[124] Two of Taylor's most trusted confidantes, generally considered his most important economic advisors, Emanuel Shaw and the Commissioner of the BMA Benoni Urey, represented PLC on the board of *LoneStar*.[125] PLC was suspected of being a front company for Taylor.

From a national economy perspective, control of the services sector allowed appropriation of surplus value in the sectors generating revenue in dollar. Profit in the services sector was thus dependent on performance of the export sectors (if we consider the ship registry a case of export of services), and thus a secondary chance of appropriating profits that could not be captured during prior economic activities.

3.5.4. Key Features of Liberia Inc.

As sovereign president, Charles Taylor ruled in a way that was marked by his centrality in terms of both personal control of relations of political domination and appropriation of national economy profits. Politically, his realm was organized in an almost totally informal manner. Political domination featured charismatic and patrimonial principles concerning both

124 The main investor was *Investcom Global Ltd.*, a Lebanese-owned company registered on the British Virgin Islands (New Democrat July 1, 2007).

125 Cf. Panel of Experts (06/2005, 49); Panel of Experts (12/2006, 36), TRC (2009, 343).

administration and legitimacy. While there were significant continuities in the organization of the system of domination when Taylor underwent the transformation from warlord to sovereign president, there were as well significant changes. In particular, Taylor faced the challenge of extending domination over additional segments of the population, and reacted by establishing conventional patrimonial patterns of rule. Yet violence remained a key characteristic of his domination. This was illustrated by the key role accorded to security agencies in Taylor's political-military apparatus. There was continuity in that Taylor's most important power resource had been the control of means of violence, and he continued to rely on that control. Repressing dissent and preventing credible oppositional forces from organizing was a central concern of his regime. Coupled with a patrimonial bending of democratic institutions, this meant that democratic quality of the Liberian polity quickly eroded.

Economically, the organization of power conforms to a particular version of African nationalism. More specifically, Charles Taylor's rule was economically based on regional resources, most importantly Liberian timber, Liberian rubber, Liberian sovereignty (i.e. the ship registry) and Sierra Leonean diamonds. In combination with Taylor's central political role, his central role in the control of surplus value justifies to speak of Liberia under Taylor as Liberia Inc., or a personally controlled economic venture. Still, Taylor's interest in power should not be reduced to seeking opportunities for profit. Charles Taylor was able to significantly increase his revenues once the country stabilized, yet the potential of the country had suffered drastically during the war, limiting overall opportunities for appropriation.

International support played virtually no role in Taylor's system of domination. Relations with Western donors were difficult from the start, and turned sourer as internal repression and regional destabilization reinforced concern over Taylor. At Liberia's first international donor conference in April 1998, western donors had pledged over 200 million dollars, the full amount requested by the Liberian authorities, but had made disbursement conditional on "continued progress on security and human-rights issues" (EIU 04/1998, 39). Virtually none of the funds were disbursed. ECOMOG surely helped Taylor to extend his domination but its political role was restricted. Despite his comprehensive control over sources of revenue, Taylor essentially ran a low-cost system of domination.

The financial turnover of his system of domination can hardly be specified. As has been said, the official but largely virtual budget fluctuated around a paltry 85 million dollars a year. Farah (2005, 19) estimated Charles Taylor's informal income, which can be considered part of his budget for exercising domination, at 105 million dollars a year. As my estimate of diamond revenue is significantly smaller, my study suggests informal revenue to have been some 25 million dollars less a year. Yet even a budget of 190 million dollar, i.e. 85 million official plus 105 million dollars unofficial revenue, would be far from exorbitant for a post-war country like Liberia. There is significant evidence that the amounts available to Taylor were much smaller, and a considerable share of available funds may have been transferred abroad and not been used for consolidating authority.

3.6. Summary: The Rise of Charles Taylor

This chapter spanned a number of issues related to dynamics of domination during the first Liberian war and the subsequent peace process. The first analytical section demonstrated the continuous prevalence of competition as mode of relations between the major camps in the war, i.e. the NPFL and the factions emanating from the Doe regime. Needless to say, for all factions a state of war was preferable to a state of peace that would effectively have meant their marginalization. Yet a comfortable stalemate could not develop, and factions had to accumulate power or perish. Classic features of armed "elimination contests" persisted, namely winners accumulated powers at the expense of losers, but importantly, contests were framed by the prior formation of the Liberian state and the war was about obtaining state power. Repeated fighting produced a winner, and once the NPFL had accumulated power above a certain threshold, weaker factions had to change strategies. Continued fighting meant risking annihilation, and co-optation into a position of inferior authority or subjugation became preferable options.

A detailed analysis of the internal order of the war's most important actors helped to explain why the NPFL prevailed and others could not impose themselves. Of major importance was the superior basis of legitimacy of Charles Taylor. This has to be understood against the background of the almost complete erosion of the Doe Regime's legitimacy, the inability of Liberia's intelligentsia to organize an appealing alternative, and considerable charismatic talent of Taylor. Legitimacy was the basis on which Taylor could build a system of strong political-military and economic control. In contrast, Taylor's rivals were weakly organized both politically and economically. The fact that they survived the first year of combat is best explained with foreign support for weak internal actors. This means that "state decay" in Liberia had little to do with the war economy but was first of all a political phenomenon.

When Taylor became sovereign president, core features of his political system remained unchanged. In particular, Taylor maintained patterns of informal control over security forces, and the use of violence remained a key tactic to hold on to power. Further, there was significant continuity in patterns of administration, though there was discernible change in response to having to govern a more sizeable and socially diverse population. Economically, Taylor could massively increase revenue when he became president, demonstrating that peace and sovereign statehood were more attractive than war. Nevertheless, chances to appropriate profits were limited due to Liberia's post-war situation.

Finally I would like to highlight two features of domination in Liberia under Charles Taylor. Firstly, the system of domination was organized informally to an exceptional degree, and informal relations of power, partly related to revenue generation, stretched national boundaries. Second, Taylor's domination was financed autonomously and did not depend on donor assistance, i.e. it was economically based on the appropriation of profits generated by activities in Liberia and Sierra Leone over which Taylor could exercise political control. However, as I will show in the next chapter, these unconventional patterns of exercising domination were vulnerable and hardly successful as a political innovation.

4. Taylor's Fall and the Dawn of a Neo-patrimonial Democracy

4.1. The Government: Cracks in the System

The Second Liberian War in Liberia was the expression of the disintegration of Charles Taylor's system of domination. It was due to a dilemma in a dialectical sense, i.e. it arose from the same source as his successes in accumulating power. Eventually, the balance turned negative and his strategy failed.

Four major issues form the background to Taylor's demise. The first one was his failure to monopolize means of military violence. Second, his patronage system disintegrated as clients did not respect the implicit accord of exchange of posts against political loyalty. This refers to the limits of principles of traditional rule in Liberia as patrimonial exchange is often not the material expression of complex personal bonds but a modern and rational cost-benefit affair. Taylor increasingly resorted to violence to enforce loyalty but this further undermined personal trust as a foundation of patterns of authority. Third, Taylor's relations with relevant states in the region were strained to the point of hostility, essentially caused by the Liberian president's strategy of securing sources of funding for his apparatus of domination abroad. Fourth, the economic basis of his regime was vulnerable and eventually collapsed when pressures related to the three issues above became too much.

4.1.1. Disintegration of the Security Sector

The International Community had hoped for Liberia to begin re-establishing conventional statehood structures, in particular those of a coherent, bureaucratized army subject to civilian authorities. However, Charles Taylor had won the war based on his personal control over competing armed units, and sought to maintain similar patterns. Security sector reform became the first major issue of contention between the new Liberian government and the International Community. General Victor Malu was ECOMOG Field Commander when Taylor was elected president and was renowned for his energetic, sometimes aggressive approach towards Liberian factions. Based on a contingent interpretation of a provision of the Akosombo Peace Agreement of September 1994 confirmed in later agreements, Malu insisted that ECOMOG assume a leading role in restructuring the AFL.[126] Malu was replaced with a more pliant General in January 1998 in response to pressure from Taylor, and the intervention force was withdrawn by the end of the year (Adebayo 2002b, 234; cf. Pham 2004, 177). Foreign troops thus played a very limited role for a short period of time in organizing security in post-war Liberia while Taylor made control over security outfits a centerpiece of his politics, maintaining wartime patterns while attempting to co-opt rival forces.

When Taylor became president, ULIMO-J's Roosevelt Johnson was one of the first ministers nominated, and he quickly accepted the post as Minister of Rural Development. In some ways similar to Taylor, Johnson nevertheless maintained his personally controlled militia as a power resource in Liberian politics. Having been based in suburban Sinkor until the fighting of April 1996, he had then moved into the city of Monrovia and occupied a residence in Camp Johnson Road, a few hundred meters from the Executive Mansion and other major government installations. His fighters controlled access to the neighborhood, closed it to motor traffic and constituted a potential threat to the president. In February 1998, Charles Taylor for the first time publicly expressed his concern over the arming "of certain elements around" Johnson, and demanded explanations for a number of issues from the former rebel leader (Inquirer Feb. 16, 1998). The next month, Taylor demanded that Johnson relocate to a less sensitive location but the ULIMO-J leader refused. Taylor then relieved him of his ministerial posts and named him Ambassador to India but Roosevelt Johnson declined to take up the post. Trying to compensate for the loss of a senior Krahn patron, Taylor gave the post of Minister of Rural Development to AFL General Hezekiah Bowen. ECOMOG units were posted to the residence to prevent a new round of fighting, Johnson reinforced his position, and the stand-off continued.

---

126 None of the peace agreements explicitly attributed authority to ECOMOG on questions of security sector reform nor did any stipulate a role for the intervention force after the seating of a regular government.

Eventually in September 1998, the paramilitary police force *Special Operations Division* (SOD) was ordered to arrest Johnson. Short of weaponry in the wake of disarmament and no longer supported by ECOMOG, Roosevelt Johnson's forces were overpowered after 17 hours of fighting. A high number of combatants and civilians were killed but Johnson and significant parts of the ULIMO-J elite managed to escape into the US embassy and were subsequently evacuated. In the wake of the incident, Taylor's forces pursued and arbitrarily killed suspected members of Johnson's force.[127] A number of prominent individuals associated with the former *Coalition Forces* were arrested and sentenced to ten years in prison (cf. Youboty 2004, 359–360). Fleeing the crackdown, between 600 (ICG 2002a, 8) and 4,000 former *Coalition Forces* fighters of Krahn ethnicity (Adebayo 2002b, 232) left Monrovia, most of them for Côte d'Ivoire. A substantial number of fighters went to Sierra Leone.

Taylor's attempt to co-opt Alhadji Kromah was even less successful. Alhadji Kromah had been offered the post as Chairman of the *National Commission on Reconciliation* but only about half a year after Taylor was elected. In an atmosphere of mistrust reinforced by the murder of NPFL-CRC executive Samuel Dokie in late November 1997, Kromah declined to accept the post and went into exile in Guinea. He later claimed that Taylor had planned to eliminate him (Perspective Oct. 25, 2000). Concerning Kromah's constituency, reintegration of Liberian Mandingo was much more delicate a task than was the case with Krahn. A disproportionate share of Mandingo had been active in trade and had owned valuable real estate in the market areas of towns and cities, particularly in Nimba County. During the war their properties had been appropriated by NPFL combatants and the NPFL elite grabbed the most valuable possessions. Returning means of subsistence to Mandingo would have meant alienating an important segment of elites close to the NPFL, and would have met fierce resistance in Taylor's heartland of Nimba. While Mandingo peasants frequently were able to reclaim their land, there was hardly any attempt to reintegrate the more important segment of Mandingo traders (cf. Gerdes 2010). Given their insecure political and economic situation in Liberia, a

127 Figures on victims vary widely. 50 to 100 persons died during the fighting and 300 to 1,500 Krahn civilians and ULIMO-J fighters were executed during the following crackdown (cf. Africa Confidential Feb. 19, 1999; July 21, 2000; cf. Utas 2003, 59; TRC 2009, 185).

substantial number of Mandingo refugees remained in Guinea, among them about 2,800 former ULIMO-K combatants (Brabazon 2003, 7).

Taylor's strategy of aggressively securing sources of revenue in a neighboring state resulted in the foreign-sponsored mobilization of dissident forces. As stated in the previous chapter, former *Coalition Forces* combatants and others in Sierra Leone were reorganized by ECOMOG II General Maxwell Khobe in order to fight back the RUF. Khobe sponsored an incursion into Lofa County by a small dissident group baptized *Justice Coalition of Liberia* (JCL) in August 1998. The group's leader, former senior NPFL General Liberty, had reportedly decided to fight the government after his mother was murdered because he planned leaving the NPFL (cf. ICG 2002a, 8), which would demonstrate the dysfunctional dynamics of repression.

The September 1998 fighting in Monrovia constituted a key event as the number of former combatants in Sierra Leone prepared to take up weapons increased significantly. Liberian refugees in Guinea and former ULIMO-K cadres based in the US then created an *Organization of Displaced Liberians* (ODL), which made a brief raid into Lofa County in April 1999. Due to Sierra Leonean resistance against foreign rebel bases in their country the JCL relocated to Guinea in the meantime (Reno 2007, 76). The two groups eventually constituted the core of the *Liberians United for Reconciliation and Democracy* (LURD) founded at a meeting of various dissidents in Freetown in April 2000. The LURD command structure was about 90 percent former ULIMO, and about 60 percent of its combatants had fought with one of its two factions (Brabazon 2003, 7). It was reinforced by a substantial number of Sierra Leonean combatants, mostly CDF, and a significant share of the AFL soldiers demobilized by Taylor (ICG 2002a, 3–9). The LURD later tried to extend their base of recruitment and attracted a significant number of combatants deserting Taylor's paramilitaries, as well as other groups (Brabazon 2003, 2; Pham 2004; ICG 2002a).

While the rebel groups were relatively stable, there were numerous defections on the government side by combatants choosing to join the rebels. This indicates decreasing charismatic legitimacy of Taylor and cash constraints. Patterns of charismatic domination remained dominant in the organization of the security sector. There was very limited institutional continuity due to frequent paramilitary leadership reshuffles and a systematic pattern of suppression and re-creation of paramilitaries. From a theoretical perspective, an erosion of charismatic legitimacy was to be expected in more regular times (cf. Schlichte 2009). As combatants expected more from Taylor once he was president than most ordinary Liberians would, Taylor's charismatic legitimacy was compromised among military staff. This concerned in particular demobilized ex-combatants, who were quickly marginalized and felt betrayed (Utas 2003, 223–250; cf. Bøås/Hatløy 2008). Furthermore, as Taylor's charisma was to a large extent based on his ability to be in control, commandeer resources and subdue his adversaries, charismatic legitimacy further eroded as the rebels advanced. Taylor's legitimacy and, consequently, control over troops suffered even more because of his inability to pay combatants.

During the first year of his rule, ATU and SSS still received relatively high salaries of about 150 to 200 dollar, while the army and most militias not employed with natural resource exploiting companies went unpaid (ICG 2002a, 13–14). Annual costs for the elite troops, weapons and ammunition not included, were estimated at some 30 million dollars (Farah 2005, 21). In 2002, in the midst of war, pay for the elite troops was cut by 75 percent,[128] most likely because of economic difficulties. The pay cuts had a significant negative impact on moral and combat readiness of Taylor's troops. For instance, in "the struggle over Tubmanburg in July 2002, no more than five hundred government troops were or could be deployed in the field; at one point the government's total strength in the Bomi sector [...] numbered only 34 men, with a desertion rate of over 10%" (Brabazon 2003, 7). Inability to pay compromises all three Weberian types of legitimacy: it indicates weaknesses in control and thus compromises charisma, it violates the reciprocal nature of patrimonial arrangements, and renders ineffectual any bureaucratic salary structure. The rebels, in turn, adapted their strategy towards the dissatisfaction of government troops, treating prisoners of war humanely and thus succeeding to integrate an important share into their ranks (ICG 2002a, 10).

4.1.2. Repression and the Erosion of a Patrimonial System

Most important for Taylor's demise was the failure to integrate or control combatants of enemy factions. Much wider patterns of violent repression

128 On this issue cf. Brabazon (2003, 7); Global Witness (2003, 41); ICG (2002b, 5); ICG (2003b, 6–7).

and the consequent disintegration of a patrimonial system underlay this failure. Taylor did not succeed to create the complex bonds between ruler and clients that render patrimonial arrangements stable, and actively prevented the evolution of alternative, more democratic patterns of power. A key feature of complex personal bonds is trust, yet that hardly developed. Charles Taylor and Alhadji Kromah had cooperated well in the LNTG II and III, but relations turned cold once Taylor was elected president, as is evident in the fact that Kromah was offered a minor post about half a year after the new government was inaugurated. A single event then had a major impact on the psychology of subaltern elites. In late November 1997 former NPFL-CRC executive Samuel Dokie and two of his family members were found dead shortly after having been arrested by well-known *Special Security Service* (SSS) officers. The SSS officers were put to trial but acquitted of all charges a little later. The murder strongly reinforced latent doubts over Taylor's willingness to engage rivals in a spirit of reconciliation. The NPFL-CRC's Laveli Supuwood fled the country in January 1998. He became a key figure in the creation of the LURD and, being a well-connected ethnic Loma from Lofa County, successfully persuaded former LDF combatants to join his rebel group in 2002 (Pham 2004, 183). About a year earlier, former LDF leader François Massaquoi, by then Minister of Youth and Sports, had been assassinated on the orders of Taylor (cf. TRC 2009, 186), facilitating Supuwood's task.

Generally, the most violent acts of repression were directed against those members of the Taylor regime who became considered unreliable. Among the high-profile personalities who died under conspicuous circumstances were the widely popular police chief Joe Tate, the Deputy Director of the National Security Agency, and the vice-president (cf. Reno 2002, 66). All of these had been among Taylor's closest allies in the NPFL and the NPP. As Taylor became increasingly paranoid (cf. BBC July 28, 2009; cf. ICG 2002b, 5), even his closest allies faced a latent threat. Elites whose loyalty may have been doubted faced incentives to switch sides. Taylor's "carrot and bullet" approach to patrimonial rule prevented the creation of stable personal bonds among regime elites.[129] Murders of senior NPFL

129 An interesting example is the case of Taylor's last Vice-President Moses Blah. Since the early days of the NPFL in Libya, Blah had been considered one of Taylor's most reliable confidantes. When Taylor was shortly arrested in Ghana in 2003, he assumed the Presidency in line with constitutional provisions, in the process alienating other ambitious elites, notably SSS Director Benjamin Yeaten. When Taylor returned, Blah

officers further impacted negatively on control over combatants as influential military elites were eliminated while Taylor's charisma suffered due to relative stability.

Similar patterns were also evident concerning relations between Taylor and co-opted civilian elites, e.g. Grand Bassa Big Man Charles Walker Brumskine. In 1999, Brumskine got into a row with Taylor over the timber industry and the smuggling of Sierra Leonean diamonds. He fled Liberia in 1999 for the United States, claiming to fear for his life, and prepared to contest in the aborted 2003 elections (cf. Washington Post June 5, 2005). While temporarily Taylor had prevented a political heavyweight from using his position to threaten the president's sources of income and enlarge his own constituency, he had at the same time alienated a significant segment of Liberian society.

Similarly, Milton Teahjay, a formerly leading "progressive" of MOJA and a *United People's Party* opposition politician, was co-opted into the government as Deputy Information Minister. Teahjay has a significant constituency in his native Sinoe County and was important for the political integration of the region. At the beginning of his tenure, Taylor was widely popular amongst youths in the regional capital Greenville.[130] Responding to local grievances, Teahjay organized a town hall meeting in Greenville and criticized the *Inland Logging Company* (ILC) and its militia, mobilizing citizens against the company.[131] He fled the country a little later in early 2000 under turbulent circumstances, after Charles Taylor had already publicly announced his arrest for "destabilizing Liberia" (Perspective Apr. 9, 2000). The exclusion of Teahjay entailed a significant drop in support for the Taylor government in Sinoe, and when the *Movement for Democracy in Liberia* (MODEL) rebel group entered the city in 2003, youths volunteered *en masse* to join the insurgents.[132]

---

was arrested and tortured but reinstated a little later. He later testified against Taylor in the *Special Court for Sierra Leone*, using the occasion to complain about the way he had been treated.

130 Interviews in Greenville, Sinoe County, Feb. 2007.

131 Focus Group Interviews in Greenville, Sinoe County, Feb. 2007. Teahjay was appointed Superintendent of Sinoe County by Johnson Sirleaf in 2009. He was one of the very few politicians allocated a post by Johnson Sirleaf despite having supported her rival George Weah in the 2005 elections and having vocally criticized her, demonstrating his importance for legitimizing domination in the region.

132 Interviews and Focus Group Interviews in Greenville, Sinoe County, Feb. 2007

4.1.3. An Aggressive Regional Policy

A key feature of Taylor's presidency was an aggressive policy towards unsympathetic states in the region, in particular supporting foreign rebels with the aim of toppling the governments of neighboring states. Already in early 1999, Africa Confidential (Jan. 22, 1999) opined that it "seems Taylor and his key ally, Burkina Faso's President Blaise Compaoré, envisage a string of military-style states from Niger through to Guinea, Guinea-Bissau and Gambia. They would be led by younger, authoritarian leaders, happy to build a network of informal (often criminal) business operations". This perception became shared by a number of regional states as well as the United States, who increasingly resorted to supporting Taylor's armed enemies (ibid; ICG 2003a, 22).

As has been said, the RUF occupied important locations of diamond extraction until late 2001, yet its demise had started much earlier. The weakening of Taylor's regional network directly impacted on his domination at home. In response to the Lomé Peace Agreement of July 1999 and Nigeria's intention to withdraw its ECOMOG troops, a *United Nations Mission in Sierra Leone* (UNAMSIL) peacekeeping force was established in October of the same year. Eventually in April 2000, the ECOMOG II mission was officially ended. Two Nigerian battalions and one tank company, adding up to some 4,000 troops, were integrated into UNAMSIL. Nevertheless, the peace process quickly unraveled.

Starting May 1, 2000, RUF troops launched a major offensive despite being integrated into the government and both factually and legally controlling the country's natural resources. The background of the offensive is not fully clear. Before, there had hardly been any sign that the peace process would falter before. Later, evidence pointed to Liberia as the location where the attack was designed. Quite likely, Taylor's access to Sierra Leonean diamonds was jeopardized since Bockarie went into exile, and he chose to pursue his interests militarily (cf. ICG 2002a, 3).[133] British

133 For the RUF, the offensive made sense only in the long run, taking into account that the group was deeply unpopular and stood few chances to successfully convert its military power resources into civilian ones, which would have allowed them to continue to occupy a position of political power. Taylor had more immediate interests, as the RUF would not have needed his expensive intermediary services if it had not needed weapons and been able to sell diamonds legally. Africa Confidential (June 23, 2000) reported that "Taylor took a substantial slice of the [diamond] profit" and "Sankoh's attempts to find new trading partners in Europe suggest a dissatisfaction with Taylor's terms of business."

military intelligence officers monitoring radio communications between Taylor and Bockarie claimed to have recorded Taylor giving orders to Bockarie during the fighting. Victor Bout, then the world's most important illegal arms merchant and temporarily residing in Liberia, may have pre-financed the operation in order to seize control over rutile mines (Farah/Braun 2007, 149–169; cf. Smillie 2007). Yet the RUF offensive eventually turned into a failure.

During the first days of fighting, 500 UNAMSIL peacekeepers were taken hostage. The action drew major international condemnation and sparked the intervention of British Ghurkhas, as a "rebel takeover of the capital would [have been] an irreversible defeat for UN peacekeeping and British policy" (Africa Confidential May 12, 2000). These bilaterally deployed elite troops not restricted by any UN mandate were eventually given "carte blanche to use whatever means necessary to keep the RUF at bay" (Farah/Braun 2007, 167) and, under minimal international media coverage, inflicted heavy losses on the RUF. A political backlash in the wake of a demonstration held on May 8 in front of Foday Sankoh's residence further weakened the RUF. Feeling threatened by the crowds, RUF bodyguards opened fire and killed more than 20 people. The mansion was then attacked by militias loyal to the president yet Sankoh managed to escape. However, as a consequence of the RUF offensive, the president declared the Lomé Agreement lapsed. Some ten days after the shooting, Foday Sankoh was found, arrested and incarcerated, as were other senior Freetown-based RUF officials.

Already by June 2000, the situation stabilized and the offensive had failed. In response to the events of May, the UN Security Council imposed a diamond embargo against Sierra Leone in July 2000 that, however, was unlikely to have any positive effect. Probably, it instead served to reinforce existing illegal export connections, i.e. links between RUF officers and Taylor. In contrast, a diamond embargo against Liberia of May 2001 was likely to have seriously complicated the trade in Sierra Leonean diamonds for both the RUF and Taylor as legal exports were not possible anymore and expensive new connections had to be established.

Meanwhile, the LURD had been formed and started to attack Taylor from Guinea. Guinea had stopped providing support to ULIMO forces in the refugee-populated areas after 1997 yet considerable mistrust between both heads of state persisted, which was not helped by Taylor's aggressive attitude towards Sierra Leone. Furthermore, at latest since 1998 there had been specific information on Taylor training Guinean dissidents in order to overthrow President Lansana Conté's military government (Africa Confidential Jan. 22, 1999). Essentially for reasons of internal and border security, the presence of the ODL and somewhat later the LURD was tolerated in Guinea (Gerdes 2006, 83–84).

Starting in September 2000, Taylor went on the offensive again, attacking Guinea in an apparent attempt to install a friendly government there. Liberian paramilitaries attacked the Guinean Forest Region on its Liberian border, aiming to destroy the LURD bases there and occupy the region for its natural resources. Simultaneously, RUF units loyal to Taylor attacked Guinea on two fronts. One was at Sierra Leone's border with the Forest Region, strategically well located to both attack LURD bases and block government reinforcements coming into the Forest Region. The RUF further attacked from Kambia several hundred kilometers to the west, targeting the Guinean capital about 100 kilometers away (ICG 2002a, 4). A third force by the name of *Union des Forces Démocratiques de la Guinea* (UFDG) claimed to be responsible for the attack but appeared to have been the smallest of the groups involved. It seemed to be led by a dissident Guinean army General involved in a coup attempt of 1996 and exiled in Liberia (ibid.). In many ways, the attack appeared to be modeled on that of the RUF and NPFL in 1991 that started the Sierra Leonean war. Given illegitimate rule, pronounced conflicts within the Guinean elite as well as segments of the population, and an undisciplined and criminally oriented army (Gerdes 2009), there were reasons to believe that an attack would be similarly successful.

However, in contrast to the experience in Sierra Leone, the invading forces were repelled by the LURD,[134] Sierra Leonean CDF militias, Guinean "Volontaires" militias hastily recruited by the Guinean army, and the army itself. The Guinean armed forces pursued the attackers deep into Sierra Leone and inflicted further losses.[135] These military setbacks formed the background to a cease-fire agreement between the Sierra Leonean government and the RUF signed in November 2000 (cf. AKUF 2003, 104). The pact led to the final peace agreement of May 2001, which constituted

134 "The over 500 LURD fighters in Guinea played a key role in repulsing the Taylor-backed forces" (ICG 2002a, 5).

135 The Guinean army did not differentiate between civilians and enemy combatants, which facilitated their advance but caused massive civilian casualties (Africa Confidential June 29, 2001; ICG 2002a, 24).

the basis for ending the Sierra Leonean war. In mid-2001, the last battles pitching CDF and Guinean troops against RUF units were fought. The RUF subsequently lost any political influence, and, much in contrast to Taylor, featured exceptionally badly in presidential and parliamentary elections in 2002, scoring just 1.7 and 2.2 percent, respectively.

Taylor's attempt to militarily extend his regional influence and resource control thus precipitated the demise of the RUF. Furthermore, it enticed the Guinean government to systematically strengthen the LURD in terms of military supplies, logistics and training. The Forest Region headquarters of the Guinean army in Macenta henceforth also served as the LURD headquarters (Gerdes 2006). After the Guinean fiasco, relations between Liberia and Côte d'Ivoire turned hostile.

In September 2002, civil war in Côte d'Ivoire began. Initially, a group of former soldiers with supposed ties to Blaise Compaoré and Charles Taylor attacked the government. Two months later, two new rebel groups appeared in the west of the country close to the Liberian border. The two new groups in the west were to a significant degree composed of Liberian and Sierra Leonean fighters commanded by Bockarie and were considered to have gone to Côte d'Ivoire on the orders of Taylor. Their activities were explained with a well-prepared plan of Taylor's to support the sympathetic forces in the Ivorian army in taking over power (ICG 2003b, 15–17), pursuing both medium-term political goals and interests in resource exploitation simultaneously (Global Witness 2003a). In response, the Ivorian government started recruiting Liberian refugees, many of them with a ULIMO-J affiliation, into an auxiliary militia (Panel of Experts 04/2003, 16).[136] The latter became known under the name of Lima Militia, a term initially coined by the French intervention force in Côte d'Ivoire.[137]

Liberian-Ivorian relations thus conformed to the general pattern of an aggressive foreign policy of Taylor and hostile reactions of his neighbors. As rebel forces in Côte d'Ivoire tried to consolidate their positions, the Ivorian government systematically reinforced combat capacities of its Liberian auxiliary forces, which numbered up to 3,000 fighters by spring 2003

136 The two new rebel groups sponsored by Taylor made their existence known on November 28, 2002. The Ivorian government only started to recruit Liberians in December 2002, in response to Taylor's aggression. Before, it had rebuffed several attempts by the LURD to use Ivorian territory (Panel of Experts 04/2003, 16–17).

137 "Lima" is the NATO radio code word for the letter "L", as in "Liberia". LIMA was later considered to stand for "Liberians Mobilized in Action".

(ICG 2003a, 23). These constituted the core of a new Liberian rebel group, the *Movement for Democracy in Liberia* (MODEL), which made its existence officially known in March 2003 and quickly overran eastern Liberia.[138]

4.1.4. The Economics of Taylor's Fall

Taylor's Liberia was characterized by unconventional political economy patterns, featuring aggressive exploitation of resources of neighboring states, unsustainable exploitation of Liberian timber (cf. Consortium Agrifor Consult 2004, 12), and the foregoing of Western donor support.[139] Initially, Taylor's refusal to reform the security sector according to Western expectations and his attempt to entrench authoritarian rule prevented a normalization of its international relations. At the international conference of April 1998 where donors had pledged a conditional 200 million dollars, it was "also made clear that donors view the continued presence of Ecomog as crucial to the maintenance of peace in the short term" (EIU 04/1998, 39).

The continued trade in gems and weapons with the RUF and the associated regional destabilization then became the major point of contention in Liberia's international relations. In May 2001, increasing international dissatisfaction resulted in the diamond embargo against Liberia. Official exports dropped to zero, but the trade in Sierra Leonean and Liberian diamonds most likely was channeled through third countries rather than stopped, nevertheless implying increased transaction costs (cf. Panel of Experts 10/2001, 80). When the RUF was disarmed at the end of 2001, Taylor lost a major source of income. The attempt to get access to alternative resources in Guinea at the end of 2000 had failed, as did the subsequent attempt targeting Côte d'Ivoire at the end of 2002. A UN arms embargo against Liberia in place since 1992 further meant that Taylor did

138 There are contradictory accounts of the formation of MODEL. Initially, many considered it to have split from LURD. Former and actual LURD elites, in particular MODEL leader Thomas Yaya Nimely, played a role in its formation, but its emergence was essentially related to the situation in Côte d'Ivoire. MODEL and LURD cooperated well, and there were ties between members of both organizations (cf. ICG 2003b, 3–5, 20–22; 2003a, 22; cf. Itano 2003, 6; cf. Lidow 2011, 2003–205).

139 Great Britain, concerned about Sierra Leone rather than Liberia, was a major factor in blocking EU assistance to Liberia (cf. Reno 2007, 75).

not have legal access to important military supplies,[140] and the illegal market charged inflated prices. For instance, in a known case of contravention of the embargo, Taylor paid 294 dollars per AK-47 (including delivery), compared to a normal factory price of 129 dollars at the Serbian company that had produced the rifles. The "margin of profit on ammunition [was] even bigger" (Panel of Experts 10/2003, 24).

Until early 2003, the LURD had few significant successes. Although a few isolated battles took place as close as 35 kilometers from Monrovia in 2002, fighting centered on Lofa County. LURD conquered territories there which remained vulnerable to government attacks and major towns changed hands several times (AKUF 2003). Although Lofa was an important logging area and the LURD deliberately tried to undermine Taylor's timber economy (Brabazon 2003, 5), statistics indicate that log exports remained by and large unaffected (see preceding chapter). Diamond mining, concentrated in western Liberia, may have been more seriously affected (Panel of Experts 04/2002, 24). Mining equipment was destroyed by the LURD in order to prevent it being used by the enemy when the rebels had to withdraw (Brabazon 2003, 6), and the LURD strategically displaced migrant laborers.[141]

Beginning with an offensive in January 2003, the LURD steadily gained ground. A new offensive starting in early March brought the rebels close to the capital by the end of the month, allowing them to control three major road axes leading into Monrovia. Taylor's combatants were recalled to defend the capital, while major economically important areas were lost to the LURD (cf. AKUF 2004, 135–140). Meanwhile, the MODEL closed in on Taylor too.

In January 2003, a Liberian town was conquered for the first time by elements crossing over from Côte d'Ivoire. MODEL officially announced its existence in March and quickly made advancements into eastern Liberia that same month. By the end of April, it controlled the major eastern logging areas and the port of Greenville. When sanctions on log exports decided in May (UN Security Council Resolution 1478) became effective on July 7, logging was already severely affected. At the end of July, Buchanan was handed over to MODEL by war-weary government forces, definitely blocking log exports. MODEL control over Buchanan further

140 For instance, Taylor was unable to repair military helicopters (Panel of Experts 04/2003, 21), and often was short of weapons during the war (cf. Pham 2004, 184–188).

141 Interview with Joe Wyllie, LURD Military Spokesman, Jan. 12, 2006, Monrovia,

blocked an arms shipment for Taylor about to arrive. Reportedly, Taylor was preparing to return to the bush and irregular warfare and the weapons had been intended to supply his guerrilla force (TRC 2009, 137). The refusal of NPFL combatants to continue fighting indicates a substantial loss in legitimacy of the leadership. Eventually, Taylor had lost access to all domestic and regional sources of income. MODEL did not advance further on the capital.

4.1.5. The Final Events

In the final months of his presidency, Taylor was thus subject to increasing international and military pressure. Repeating experiences from the first war, he pursued negotiations with the aim of getting an opportunity to reorganize militarily. Yet the rebels were not prepared to have their military advantage compromised by a cease-fire. In early June, the LURD arrived at the outskirts of northern Monrovia but were stopped at St. Paul's Bridge. On June 17, a ceasefire was signed. Five days later, the rebels nevertheless advanced again and entered Bushrod Island, occupying parts of the port area. Fighting subsided and rebels partly withdrew as negotiations went on. Notwithstanding, on July 17 the LURD advanced again and occupied all of Bushrod Island. Taylor thus lost major import and warehousing facilities. In the aftermath, fuel and other supplies became very scarce on the government side, negatively affecting morale and chains of command (Itano 2003).

The LURD then started indiscriminately shelling the city center of Monrovia, causing a high number of civilian casualties.[142] The shelling left a negative impact on the international reputation of LURD, but dealt a severe blow to morale in the government camp. Even Taylor's combatants and his staunchest political supporters increasingly expressed the opinion that he had to leave (Itano 2003, 5), indicating that the prospects of a coup were growing. The shelling also stimulated more urgent calls for international intervention. Based on provisions in the cease-fire agreement of June 17 and under Nigerian leadership, the *ECOWAS Mission in Liberia* (ECOMIL) intervention force mandated to support the cease-fire was established and started being deployed on August 4. Although the

142 Civilian casualties of the battle for Monrovia caused by both sides are estimated at 1,000 people (Pham 2004, 188).

peacekeepers only brought the *Roberts International Airport* under control and prepared for the arrival of more troops, fighting suddenly stopped.

On the night of August 6 to 7, a Boeing 707 arrived from Libya. The arrival was met by Defense Minister Daniel Chea, who initially told ECOMIL troops that he expected a special guest and demanded the troops vacate the airport. The soldiers refused, and it eventually turned out that the flight had a weapons consignment of about 30 tons on board. ECOMIL troops impounded the consignment (Panel of Experts 10/2003, 25), which effectively ended the war. On August 11, an effectively militarily defeated Charles Taylor stepped down and went into exile in Nigeria. Finally, on August 18, Vice-President-turned-President Moses Blah, the leaders of LURD and MODEL, as well as civilian elites representing a "Political Parties" bloc, signed a comprehensive peace agreement. The three warring parties were allocated similarly important state institutions in a power-sharing government expected to rule for two years.

4.2. The Rebels: LURD and MODEL

Why did LURD and MODEL win the Second Liberian War? While the loss of legitimacy of Taylor, reinforced by a lack of financial means, was an important factor, it is insufficient an explanation for the strength of the rebel groups.

A major difference between the forces associated with the Doe regime in the First Liberian War and MODEL and LURD, respectively, was the role of civilians within a broader military strategy. This is not to deny that the rebel groups committed serious human rights violations, and that some of these were part of a military strategy (TRC 2009; Hoffman 2004; Lidow 2011). Yet ULIMO commanders and their Guinean backers had learned from the previous failure, and put much greater emphasis on military discipline and generating legitimacy through the provision of order. In the Second War, violence against civilians was restricted and more targeted than in the First War, and LURD forces were markedly more disciplined and better controlled than those of its ULIMO predecessor. Correspondingly, winning "hearts and minds" figured prominently in the rebels' strategy, although this was not infrequently subordinated to other strategic or even tactical concerns.

Compared to the ULIMOs, a key feature of LURD's organization were its more rational internal structures, oriented towards military victory. On a political level, the former ULIMO commanders who created the LURD decided that the former leaders should not be allowed membership as these were judged to be both internationally discredited and more concerned with their personal success than that of the rebel group (Brabazon 2003, 2). Concerning economic organization, the LURD Executive Council made up of its senior commanders, actively tried to prevent short-term profit motives from dominating commanders' actions in the field.

The highest political body, the *National Executive Council* (NEC), was reportedly elected by all LURD members according to a system of county representation. It is however likely that commander selectorates strongly structure opportunities for an NEC position. The NEC in turn selected the National Chairman. After some leadership changes in the process of establishing LURD,[143] Sekou Damate Conneh, a former mid-level finance ministry official not involved in the First War, was selected National Chairman and Commander-in-Chief. He was the husband of Aicha Conneh, once a humble refugee in Guinea who rose to become an extremely influential spiritual advisor of the Guinean president after she foretold a coup attempt that took place in 1996. Yet, there was little concentration of power in the leader but rather a collective leadership of the NEC. Influential commanders were powerful in LURD as a whole, had interests in its success, and intra-LURD processes of negotiation, coordination and decision-making worked relatively well. Further, Conneh had been made Chairman on insistence of the Guinean president. The channeling of Guinean support through him allowed maintaining central control and coherence of LURD when factional tendencies (cf. ICG 2003b, 3–5) threatened to weaken the group, and Conneh could maintain a core of loyal commanders.[144]

"Realizing his own limitations as a stand-alone player in the Liberian political field, and his vulnerability with respect to his own armed forces should he become isolated from them, Conneh has sought to strengthen his military credentials by

143 LURD's first Chairman, Mohamed Kumandy, was selected because he had promised to provide US$ 1 million for the rebels but was quickly removed when it turned out he was unable to raise the money (Brabazon 2003, 3).

144 Several ambitious commanders, who had tried to depose Conneh, had to flee Liberia (Interviews with senior LURD members, Monrovia, Apr. 2012).

taking direct control of the LURD army, and positioning himself close to those commanders who are most likely to facilitate victory." (Brabazon 2003, 4)

Underlining the relatively rational organization of the LURD, the army was coherently organized according to conventional military structures, i.e. divided into brigades, battalions and companies (ibid., 10). While this was a feature of factions in the First War too (Ellis 2007a, 111), respect of rank and hierarchy among the roughly 3,000 combatants was relatively pronounced in LURD (cf. Brabazon 2003, 10). Discipline was "enforced by a rigorous system of corporal punishment, and the very real threat of execution for mutiny" (ibid., 7). In several cases, combatants were executed for killing civilians (ibid.).

In as much as the LURD engaged in a political campaign targeting civilians with the aim of generating legitimacy, it was little concerned with promoting any individual but rather sought to widen support for the rebel attempt to force Taylor out of office. As part of a strategy designed to attract popular support, a rudimentary civilian administration was established in the controlled territories (cf. ICG 2002a, 9; cf. Reno 2007). This included assembling the civilian population and either refilling local state administration posts, in particular those of the District Commissioner and the Paramount, Clan and Town Chief, or confirming the office holders.[145] This civilian administration existed in parallel to a military one and made possible consultations between the two sides.

A center piece of the policy on civilian-rebel relations was the attempt to have the LURD considered providers of security, rather than a threat. For instance, the rebels escorted some 800 civilians of the Gbandi ethnic group, considered sympathetic to their cause, to safety in Guinea (ICG 2002a, 10). By about mid-2001, the LURD had largely ceased systematic violence against civilians and, to a lesser extent, prisoners of war. Combatants were subject to political education as part of their military training, and strongly warned against maltreating civilians (ibid., 9; Brabazon 2003, 8). Yet in the absence of commanders, "discipline disintegrated rapidly and almost completely" (ibid.; cf. Lidow 2011). In order to counter government propaganda about LURD atrocities, the rebels sporadically forced refugees they equipped with medical and food supplies to undertake fact-finding missions in LURD-controlled territories. As a result of LURD's strategy,

145 Interviews in Bomi, Gbarpolu and Lofa Counties. Many state administration officials had fled when LURD advanced, resulting in the vacancy of most posts.

> "after the temporary loss of Bopolu in July 2002, many civilians volunteered to carry ammunition for LURD in a (successful) bid to retake the town as reports of systematic human rights abuses by the government army filtered through to them. Generally, LURD seem to enjoy a high degree of cooperation and a reasonably strong degree of support from the civilian population. The much-publicized blind community in Tubmanburg, for example, were well treated by LURD, their only casualty resulting from indiscriminate government fire. Over 400 civilians voluntarily followed LURD forces retreating from Tubmanburg in July 2002 fearing government reprisals. Villagers in Bella Mballona, south of Bopolu, described their readiness to accept LURD soldiers in their village after government troops entered it in January 2002 and partially razed it." (Brabazon 2003, 5)

It is likely that Guinean military trainers initiated the change in behavior towards civilians and prisoners of war (Reno 2007, 77), but LURD commanders must have shared the reasoning behind it.[146] Yet members of one of the ethnic groups of Lofa, the Kissi, were systematically targeted because of alleged pro-Taylor inclinations, demonstrating the partially strategic use of repressive violence against civilians. Similarly, a considerable part of LURD logistics depended on the use of forced labor as carriers (cf. Médecins Sans Frontières 2002). Further, a key element in LURD's ultimately successful strategy was to provoke an international military intervention by causing civilian casualties. Well before the rebels laid siege to the capital, military commanders had decided to shell government-held areas in order to cause an international outcry and attract foreign troops (Hoffman 2004).

While LURD's political structure, leaving substantial powers to ambitious commanders, left the movement prone to factional splits, its economic patterns promoted central control. Guinea, likely supported by the US, was the "LURD's primary source of direct military and financial support" (ICG 2002a, 11). Guinean assistance was centrally channeled through Aicha Conneh (ibid.), helping to control the troops once commanders did not have access to alternative sources of income. Guinean support was massively reinforced when the LURD had unexpected successes in 2003.[147] Senior former ULIMO commanders banned diamond mining in LURD territory to prevent factionalization. Although some commanders engaged in diamond mining (Panel of Experts 04/2002, 24), by and large LURD invested little time and energy in natural resource

146 Much as the LURD, the Guinean army was anything but a defender of human rights, demonstrating that the change in policy was of a strategic nature.

147 Interview with senior LURD executive, Monrovia, Nov. 14, 2006.

exploitation (cf. Brabazon 2003; ICG 2002a). However, systematic trade with Guinean soldiers in the low-value goods of coffee and cocoa was observed, and fighters appeared to owe a considerable part of their income to forcing refugees to buy passes allowing them to cross the border (Médecins Sans Frontières 2002; TRC 2009).

Much less is known about MODEL than LURD, but in several respects MODEL mirrored the larger rebel group. Like LURD, MODEL was mostly financed by a neighboring state, in this case Côte d'Ivoire, and hardly needed to generate revenue to persist. MODEL was less disciplined than LURD,[148] but systematically tried to prevent abuses against civilians (cf. TRC 2009, 127). After MODEL had occupied Grand Gedeh's capital of Zwedru, "hundreds of uniformed, well-armed men astonished residents by fixing street lighting for the first time in living memory" (Africa Confidential May 16, 2003). During its advance in the east, youths joined the rebels en masse,[149] enabling the group to occupy large territories and cut off Taylor from important revenue-generating resources as well as a major weapons consignment.

4.3. The National Transitional Government of Liberia

The *Comprehensive Peace Agreement* (CPA) signed in Accra on August 18, 2003 stipulated the installation of an interim government for the duration of two years and specified the power-sharing arrangement (CPA 2003). This provided the framework within which subsequent struggles for power and wealth took place and thus shaped the configuration of power.

The negotiations leading up to it were inclusive. External actors played an important though informal role and pressed for civilian Liberian actors to be included. The latter participated in the negotiations as a fourth bloc of "Political Parties" on similar terms as the three armed actors, i.e. the Government of Liberia (GOL), the LURD and the MODEL. The four parties eventually shared government posts, though the "Political Parties"

148 Lidow (2011) asserts the contrary, but his analysis of displacements does not sufficiently take into account that LURD fought for well over three years and territories in Lofa changed hands many times.

149 Focus Group Interviews in Greenville, Sinoe County and Zwedru, Grand Gedeh County, Feb. and March 2007.

bloc was expanded to include representatives of civil society organizations. Yet posts allocated to the armed actors were financially and politically more attractive. The highest positions of Chairman and Vice-Chairman of the eventual *National Transitional Government of Liberia* (NTGL) were reserved for individuals with a civilian background (cf. Hayner 2007). The inclusive nature of both the CPA and the resulting interim government was due to the role warring actors expected the International Community to play. Following a strategy of extraversion, both government and rebels attempted to attract external resources estimated to further their interests.

As I mentioned, it had early on become central in LURD's military strategy to attract an international intervention. Taking into account that they were widely regarded an illegitimate, foreign force in Liberia, the LURD realized that they would face immense problems when taking over and, more importantly, holding on to power. Well before the end of the war, LURD's official position on a peace agreement was that a transitional power-sharing government integrating the warring parties and civilian forces should be established and be superseded by a democratically elected one. Although several commanders harbored presidential ambitions and were little enthusiastic about democratization (Brabazon 2003, 4; ICG 2002a, 10), LURD's early power-sharing rhetoric decreased the political costs of power sharing and democratization. Moreover, LURD would have had difficulties presenting a presidential candidate. While several commanders were interested in the post, none would have had the support of the whole of LURD in a bid for power, reducing his chances. In return for power sharing and democratization, the International Community could be expected to mobilize resources, allowing the rebels to be safe in a position of power during the transition.

Charles Taylor eventually had welcomed the intervention force, probably because he had expected it to separate both sides, enforce the cease-fire and allow him to reorganize militarily. Yet when the ECOMIL impounded the weapons consignment at the airport, his tactics proved to have failed. In Liberia, it is widely argued that Taylor envisaged a return to the bush to lead a guerrilla war (cf. TRC 2009, 137). Yet to many of his associates, a place in an interim government was much more attractive an option, increasing the likelihood of a coup Taylor feared at least as much as the rebels (Itano 2003). Taylor eventually went into exile before the peace agreement was signed, leaving to his associates the negotiation of the agreement.

Including MODEL into the interim government was meant to deter the group from marching on Monrovia and complicating the security situation, and was attractive to the LURD (and Western states) because it diluted the influence of the GOL. For MODEL, the offer to equitably share important positions with the other two armed actors was quite attractive, given that it had existed for just about half a year.

The most important institutions allocated to the GOL were the Ministry of Internal Affairs, the *Liberia Petroleum Refining Company* (LPRC), and the *Bureau of the Budget*. The LURD's main benefit was the Ministry of Finance, the *National Ports Authority* (NPA), and the *National Investment Commission*. MODEL, remarkably, obtained the Ministries of Commerce, Foreign Affairs and Lands and Mines as well as the *Forestry Development Authority* (FDA) and the *Bureau of Maritime Affairs* (BMA). The Political Parties and Civil Society, by contrast, were given responsibility for neither financially lucrative nor politically powerful and often totally dysfunctional institutions, e.g. the Ministries of Gender and Education and the *Liberia Mining Corporation*. Probably most rewarding was the *Bureau of Immigration*, which provided opportunities for diverting visa and work permit fees.[150]

Generally, if one signatory provided the head of an institution, the other parties provided deputies. Ambitious individuals however were prevented from occupying the top posts and using these to accumulate power resources, as the CPA barred the Chairman, his Deputy and senior cabinet ministers from running for the presidency in the next elections.

A second major issue of the CPA that was to have long-term consequences was security sector reform. It specifically addressed the AFL, statutory (police) security units, irregular (rebel) forces, and special security units, i.e. paramilitary groups. All combatants were supposed to be disarmed as a first step (CPA 2003, Art. VI). An international intervention force was stipulated to provide military security, assist in the maintenance of law and order and monitor an "interim police force". That intervention force eventually was the *United Nations Mission in Liberia* (UNMIL), which integrated the ECOMIL contingent sent earlier, numbering about 15,000 troops and some 1,000 police.

The CPA basically defined two different approaches to the different security institutions. While the rebel "irregular forces" should "disband", the other three categories of security actors should be "restructured" (ibid.:

150 The allocation of institutions is detailed in full in the Annex IV of the CPA (2003).

Art. VII–VIII). Combatants of all sides were assured eligibility for recruitment into the AFL provided they fulfilled further, unspecified criteria. Security sector reform was oriented towards concentrating means of military force in the AFL. This key component of the reform process was explicitly made a responsibility of the US, while the "ECOWAS, the UN, AU, and the [International Contact Group on Liberia] ICGL [were requested to] provide advisory staff, equipment, logistics and experienced trainers" (CPA 2003, Art. VII). Security sector reform was thus essentially made a foreign task.

Despite the slight differences in the approaches towards the different categories of security actors, the external actors steering the reform process adopted a rather uniform approach of disarmament and effective disbandment, i.e. the retiring of active personnel. The AFL and the police force were then rebuilt from scratch.[151] Essential conditions for eligibility for recruitment initially were a clean human rights record and a high school diploma,[152] effectively barring most combatants from both sides from entering.

4.3.1. The Erosion of the Former Regime

Charles Taylor's terms of asylum in Nigeria included that the former president may not communicate with Liberian politicians to influence events. Yet when he left for exile, observers feared he would still yield enough influence to shape political developments in Liberia. Taylor had evidently not given up hopes of returning to the presidency,[153] and was widely considered to be preparing for his political future in Liberia. Both the UN and Nigeria publicly reprimanded Taylor repeatedly for communicating with Liberian politicians in contravention of his terms of asylum (Hoffman 2006, 318).

As has been demonstrated, Charles Taylor was not simply in control of a network he could employ to further his political interests. He had to maintain control over associates in a situation where he was losing access to revenues and was stripped of most of his repressive capacities. Many associates were likely shift to allegiances in pursuit of superior opportunities.

---

151 In order to minimize human rights violations and obstacles to stabilization, the interim police force was armed with batons only.

152 The criterion of holding a high school diploma could not be maintained.

153 One of the closing phrases of Taylor's parting speech was "God willing, I will be back."

In contrast to Hoffman (2006) I argue that Charles Taylor's exile, reinforced by international intervention that included an UN asset freeze and travel ban, eroded his network. Evidently, his extradition from Nigeria to the Special Court for Sierra Leone, initiated by Johnson Sirleaf in March 2006, reinforced that process and supported the consolidation of the president's rule. Taylor was sentenced to a 50–year prison sentence in May 2012.

The support Taylor enjoyed among a large constituency was his most important asset, and his popularity could have allowed him to return to Liberian politics if he had not been found guilty. In the short run, Taylor had to use his personal intra-elite contacts to maintain a position of influence in Liberia. The GOL bargained for the Ministry of Internal Affairs, i.e. a politically rather than financially important one. The Ministry is one of the largest in terms of staff and the most influential one concerning administration of the hinterland. Control over it occupied a central position in the strategy of the GOL.

It is widely alleged that Taylor disposed of significant financial means in exile. Quite likely, he had been able to transfer a significant amount of money abroad while president. Farah (2005, 25) estimated monies hidden in foreign countries at 150 to 210 million dollar, though there are significant uncertainties in the calculations and the figure may significantly overestimate Taylor's wealth.[154] Taylor was reported to have had one million dollars in cash with him when he was eventually arrested in Nigeria in March 2006 (Africa Confidential Apr. 14, 2006). His stakes in firms in Liberia were alleged to continue to generate money for him, and his associates were suspected to use financially lucrative positions in the NTGL to fund political interests of the GOL. In sum, Taylor's chances to maintain a position of political influence was dependent on continued loyalty of his associates and access of these to funds. Yet Taylor's control was challenged on all levels by his rivals, including former associates.

Control over the formal state institutions was weak as formal power was shared and formal political channels were not coherent with informal ones. Firstly, as has been said, senior executives were seconded deputies from the other signatories, who similarly used their positions to build

154 Although this is possible, I consider it less likely that Farah (2005) underestimated Taylor's wealth. As I already mentioned, the estimate of diamond revenues appears too high. Further, there are significant uncertainties in the estimated costs of Taylor's informal security and patronage system.

networks of influence. Successful private appropriation of state powers necessitated collusion between senior executives associated with different factions, leading to the creation of new alliances as well as diminishing control of Taylor's network over the spoils of power. Second, individuals at lower levels of administration, including the Chieftaincies, were likely to seek superior opportunities by establishing alliances with alternative power holders. As Sawyer (2008) has shown, hinterland elites positioned themselves during the transition taking into account multiple imperatives, but they hardly remained loyal to the former president.

Taylor was widely considered to have had stakes in multiple Liberian companies and used bank accounts in different countries under several aliases, implying that sanctions and the asset freeze would at best only be partially effective (cf. Hoffman 2006, 317). On the other hand, Taylor had to use intermediaries to conduct business operations who faced increased incentives to appropriate profits as his capacities for control were weakened. Three factors could compel individuals to remain loyal to Taylor: a belief in Taylor's legitimacy, fear of being marginalized if ties to Taylor's network were cut, and fear of repressive capacities. Taylor was alleged to have established and funded about 36 cells of support groups throughout the sub region (Global Witness 2005, 31). Cells in Liberia were alleged to be made up of ex-combatants and suspected to be organized by the Generals Cucoo Dennis and Adolphus Dolo (Farah 2005, 15). These bands of ex-combatants were suspected of being intended to disrupt the peace process and serve as hit squads.[155] Yet, despite a few disturbances, there was no concerted effort to disrupt the peace process. Given decreasing legitimacy, accommodating tendencies in Liberia's patronage politics, and protection by alternative, foreign actors, Taylor's hold over his former associates was weak. Furthermore, Taylor's loss of power meant he had insufficient capacity to protect his businesses while the economic environment remained extremely competitive.

155 In May 2004 John Auffrey, a security specialist employed with the US Department of State, was murdered in his hotel room in Monrovia. A member of one of Taylor's paramilitary forces was accused to have carried out the murder. It was widely believed that the intended target of the attack had been David Crane, then Chief Prosecutor of the *Special Court for Sierra Leone*, who had resided in the same room a few days earlier, and that Taylor had ordered the assassination (cf. New Democrat May 11, 2005b). Yet there were hardly any rumors of Taylor being responsible for other killings since he went into exile.

Taylor's former financial advisor allegedly accused NTGL Chairman Gyude Bryant of aggressively appropriating the property of *LoneStar Airways*, the small, de-facto national airline alleged to be part-owned by Taylor. Bryant was said to work in concert with his relative Carmina Tolbert, owner of a successor to the *Mesurado Group of Companies* and wife of former Finance Minister Stephen Tolbert, to establish a new cell phone company. The Chairman of Johnson Sirleaf's *Unity Party* (UP), Charles Clarke, as well as Dew Mayson, who made a fortune in Nigeria's oil business and is probably Liberia's most successful non-Lebanese businessman, were reported to have stakes in the company too. The company should allegedly be given preferential political treatment in order to put pressure on *LoneStar Communications*.[156] Indeed, the *Libercell* company established during the interim period offered significantly lower rates than *LoneStar*, causing many customers to switch.

While Taylor thus lost part of his business to competitors, in other sectors profits diminished as formerly excluded forces had to be accommodated. This concerned the LPRC, too, which was by far the most important financial foothold of the GOL network in the transitional state apparatus. The post of Managing Director was allocated to Edwin Snowe, who had held a Deputy Managing Director post in the facility under Taylor. More importantly, Snowe had been personal driver of NPFL elites in "Greater Liberia" and later chairman of the NPP youth wing. He, further, had been married to a step daughter of Taylor. Snowe was internationally considered a close associate of the former president and was subject to the travel ban as well as an assets freeze.

Some incidents suggested that old networks linked to the LPRC continued to function and provide revenues to Taylor. For instance, connections described in the previous chapter involving the company *West Oil* appeared to remain essentially intact. As I mentioned, *West Oil* had provided a ten million dollars loan to Taylor in 1998. The loan continued to be repaid during the NTGL period while most other domestic and foreign creditors of the Liberian state were left without any hint of repayment (Panel of Experts 12/2004, 40–41). At the same time, *West Oil* received a generous reduction in storage fees and paid roughly half the amount other importers were charged by the LPRC. Additionally, huge

156 The allegations were contained in a letter purportedly written by Taylor's financial advisor and PLC representative Emanuel Shaw and addressed to the former president. The letter is reprinted in Farah (2005, Appendix 7).

arrears on fees due and import taxes were tolerated by the LPRC. On top of this, another company belonging to the *West Oil* owners received a twelve million dollars construction contract from the LPRC awarded under "less than fair and transparent tendering" procedures (Panel of Experts 06/2006, 29).[157] Two well-connected sources alleged that Snowe privately received at least 200,000 dollars monthly from *West Oil* in return,[158] part of which may have been transferred to Taylor. The Lebanese *West Oil* owners further assisted in the withdrawal of 141,768 dollars from a supposedly frozen bank account of Edwin Snowe in Lebanon (Panel of Experts 12/2006, 38).

At the same time, the LPRC also illustrates Taylor's loss of control over state revenues. Allegedly in direct relation with business interests of NTGL Chairman Bryant, several new companies competing with *West Oil* were allocated contracts to import fuel (cf. Farah 2005, Annex 7). Accommodating new assertive power holders in the central government required further payments. An EU-financed audit noted, amongst others, donations by the LPRC to Gyude Bryant to the tune of 192,000 dollar, and donations to the *National Transitional Legislative Assembly* (NTLA) to the tune of 12,400 dollar. Donations were generally handed over on oral request and hardly any written documentation existed (Ernst & Young 2005a, 9, 27). The Panel of Experts criticized additional, similar transactions purportedly serving to pay for Bryant's travel expenses. These, amounting to some 400,000 dollars in 2005, were far in excess of budgetary allocation (Panel of Experts 06/2006, 30).[159]

Internal LPRC developments linked to the new institutional set-up further consumed profits. Snowe was seconded by three deputies from the other groups who had signed the CPA. All four directors later ran for legislative seats, ran expensive campaigns, and won their constituencies, indicating the positions were used to establish patron-client networks.[160] Management of the LPRC was patrimonial but appropriation was

---

157 The contract was immediately cancelled by the Johnson Sirleaf government.

158 Interviews in Monrovia, Nov.–Dec. 2006.

159 Generally, travel expenses of politicians are considered expense items particularly prone to corrupt appropriation in Liberia. In one instance alone, Bryant requested and received the implausibly high amount of US$150,000 for travelling to south-eastern Liberia (Panel of Experts 12/2006, Annex IV).

160 LURD's nominee to the post was General Zoe Pennue. MODEL nominated Richard Devine, a businessman not associated with the rebel group. The "Political Parties and Civil Society" bloc sent Mobutu Nyenpan to the post, a former student activist.

decentralized. The actual management structure only roughly corresponded to the formal organizational chart, 90 percent of personnel were not qualified for their jobs, and the "company [...] [did] not have a manual of operational, administrative, accounting and financial procedures" (Ernst & Young 2005b, 11). Auditors refused to express an opinion on the finances of the LPRC due to missing documentation (ibid.). The Panel of Experts estimated missing revenues at 8.48 million dollars at least in 2005 alone. The same year, the LPRC made an official profit of 158,000 dollars only (Panel of Experts 06/2006, 29). At the same time, liabilities of the LPRC grew as the number of employees roughly doubled during the transition (ibid., 28) in consequence of elite tactics of job patronage. There were some 595 regular employees among a total of 750 including interns, casual workers etc. in 2004, while auditors considered some 125 staff sufficient (Ernst & Young 2005b, 10–11).

Developments in the diamond mining sector further illustrate Taylor's loss of power. Dynamics in the sector were strongly shaped by international intervention. Since the early 2000s international efforts of regulation of the industry had increased globally, complicating diamond transactions for Taylor. These dynamics of globalization created pressures to govern in accordance with principles of legal-rational rule domestically.[161] This internationalization of governance thus reinforced bureaucratic state-building on a national level, effectively undermining Taylor's strategy. The two major representations of internationalized diamond governance in Liberia were the UN embargo on the one hand and the monitoring function of the Panel of Experts.

In January 2005, the "Republic of Liberia" concluded a contract with a newly established company represented by a French and a UK citizen, the *West African Mining Corporation* (WAMCO), which effectively granted the firm an exclusive right over Liberia's more valuable diamond deposits. The contract had been negotiated in secret, no bidding process had taken place, and the *Contracts and Monopolies Commission* charged with controlling contract allocation processes was bypassed. The Minister of Lands, Mines and Energy actively tried to conceal the existence of the contract even after it had been signed (Panel of Experts 06/2005, 26–27).

The contract was signed by the Minister of Lands, Mines and Energy, the Chairman of the *National Investment Commission* and a Deputy Finance

161 Taylor's deals with the RUF had violated both international and Sierra Leonean codified law, which was the legal basis for the sanctions regime.

Minister, and was attested to by the Vice-Chairman of the NTGL and the Minister of Justice (ibid., 26–27). Except for the NTGL Vice-Chairman, all these executives had received their posts through MODEL or LURD.[162] Details of the negotiations suggested that the scheme had been designed by Taylor, once again exemplifying his need to accommodate a variety of new stakeholders in pursuit of his interests.

Michel Saint Yrian, one of the representatives of WAMCO, held a Liberian diplomatic passport and was linked to a company accused of trading in "Liberian" diamonds of Sierra Leonean origin when Taylor was president. Yrian also was a director of the *London International Bank*, which held a stake in WAMCO and had agreed to finance the investment. First moves to secure funding for the project had already been made around the time Taylor was overthrown (Africa Confidential Apr. 29, 2005a). Yrian apparently was originally approached by Martin George, who was seeking investors for the diamond project (Panel of Experts 06/2005, 28). George was a close associate of Taylor and Liberia's ambassador to Nigeria, considered to serve as a liaison between the exiled former president and Liberia. However, after the Panel of Experts uncovered the deal and made clear that the contract was a serious obstacle to the lifting of diamond sanctions, the *London International Bank* withdrew its covenant for financing. It is likely that Taylor's network had already considerably invested in getting the necessary support for the deal among Liberian elites.

Taylor's declining control over sources of revenue likely entailed financial difficulties. A letter purportedly written by Taylor's financial advisor indicated the former president was running out of cash. The letter was a response to Taylor, pointing out that making cash available would require dissolving long-term investments, be very expensive and jeopardize future income (cf. Farah 2005, Annex 7). Further indicating financial problems, barely six months after Taylor had left for exile most of the "hundreds of hangers-on", bodyguards and close aides who had accompanied him to Nigeria left as they were no longer taken care of (IRIN Apr. 8, 2004).

Taylor was alleged to have financially contributed to election campaigns of virtually every party that could aspire to muster significant support (Washington Post Apr. 25, 2005), suggesting substantial expenses. Charles

---

162 The minister was a MODEL-nominee who had been working in various positions in the Ministry for most of his career. It was alleged that he had bought the post from the MODEL leader for US$10,000 (Perspective May 7, 2004).

Taylor's former wife Jewel Howard-Taylor,[163] who won the senior senator seat for Bong County in the legislative elections, used the local NPP network to campaign for Ellen Johnson Sirleaf in the run-off presidential elections.[164] Similarly, NPFL General "Peanut Butter" Adolphus Dolo first ran for a senatorial seat of Nimba on the ticket of the *Coalition for the Transformation of Liberia* (COTOL) headed by one of Liberia's most important intermediaries for foreign corporations, the lawyer Varney Sherman. During the campaign, he drew on his connections established under Taylor's rule, too.[165] In the run-off, Dolo backed Ellen Johnson Sirleaf, defying his party's leader. The strong support of NPP elites for Johnson Sirleaf may have had a background in Taylor's strategy, yet Taylor nevertheless eventually lost out while his former associates benefited, illustrating dynamics of fragmentation.

The position of presidential candidate of the NPP was intensely competed for, engendering further rifts. Eventually, former Minister of Agriculture Roland Massaquoi was designated as candidate. His popular rival Francis Garlawolo, widely considered one of Taylor's closest confidantes and a key contact between the exiled leader and Liberian elites (cf. Africa Confidential Apr. 29, 2005b), publicly accused Charles Taylor of having manipulated the election process. Several other elites belonging to Taylor's inner circle succeeded in gaining positions of political power in the post-transition dispensation. Yet that meant establishing new alliances, effectively splintering Taylor's network.

4.3.2. LURD and MODEL: Rebels Falling Apart

Factional rivalries characterized the rebel groups as much as the government. Both groups had hardly been legitimate in the eyes of the Liberian public from their inception, and both were unsuccessful in maintaining internal coherence, accumulating resources during the interim period, and establishing themselves as strong contenders in Liberia's postwar politics.

---

163 Jewel Howard-Taylor divorced Charles Taylor during the transition. It was unclear whether this meant links were severed.

164 NPP election campaigner in Focus Group Interview in Gbarnga, Bong County Feb. 2, 2007

165 Interview with political analyst, Gbarnga, Mar. 19, 2007

These dynamics followed a general pattern of factions organizing themselves around sources of income. Coherence of LURD could not be maintained following exile of the common enemy and decreasing importance of Guinean support. Unity gave way to a decentralized neo-patrimonialism fuelled by individual rebel's access to dispersed and not centrally controlled sources of income. These sources of income were of different kinds; most important were government positions in Monrovia and locally exploited natural resources in the hinterland. The dispersed nature of these sources of income partly explains factional tendencies within the former rebel groups. Competition for access to these sources entailed further splits.

4.3.2.1. The LURD: Marital Conflict and Ethnic Divisions

Sekou Conneh's control over the LURD had always been weak. During the war, his relation with his wife Aicha Conneh, her supposed magical qualities and association with the Guinean president, and funds provided by the latter, constituted the central set of factors allowing Conneh to survive on top without being seriously challenged. However, Guinean funding dried up when Taylor was removed, and internal rivalries for spoils of power entailed internal divisions, notably but not exclusively between Sekou and Aicha Conneh.

Following Guinea's withdrawal, Sekou Conneh's intermediary position vis-à-vis the International Community and Liberian stakeholders allowed him to maintain a central position within the LURD. Foreign actors, well aware of LURD's internal rivalries, were reluctant to recognize nominations for government posts from LURD organs other than the Chairman,[166] as this would have led to multiple claims to positions and exacerbated internal rivalries, rendering containment of the rebel group more difficult. Conneh thus had effective powers to appoint government executives, and LURD commanders had to work through him to be allocated posts.

166 Foreign interference in the staffing of government posts was legitimized by Article XXXVI of the CPA, stipulating that "any dispute within the NTGL, arising out of the application or interpretation of the provisions of this Agreement shall be settled through a process of mediation to be organized by ECOWAS in collaboration with the UN, the AU and the ICGL" (CPA 2003). The ICGL, of which ECOWAS was a member, became more important as a guarantor of the peace agreement than ECOWAS alone.

The major split arose from a rivalry for the position of Finance Minister. Sekou Conneh nominated Luseni Kamara, who was a successful businessman and brother of his first wife but had not played an active role in the LURD. Aicha Conneh objected to the nomination and was supported by a large, apparently majoritarian share of the rebel group. Wrangling for government positions between the two factions sparked several shoot-outs later, notably at the former rebel headquarters in Tubmanburg (Bomi Hills) (cf. UN Security Council 05/2004, 2–3), following which Sekou Conneh was reported to have become more accommodating.[167] A significant number of LURD nominees to government positions belonged to Aicha's faction. Notwithstanding, the dispute continued and Aicha's faction twice declared Sekou Conneh deposed (cf. Analyst Aug. 5, 2004). The rivalry eventually entailed the divorce of the rebel leadership couple.

Rivalries within LURD were reinforced when Sekou Conneh nominated one of his loyalists, the LURD Secretary General Joe Gbalah, for the post of Managing Director of the *National Port Authority* (NPA) after the first incumbent Chayee Doe had died in June 2004 (cf. UN Security Council 09/2004, 3; UN Security Council 12/2004, 2–3).[168] Chayee Doe had been a leading figure of the Aicha Conneh faction, which had nominated him to replace Sekou Conneh. After his death, the NTGL Justice Minister, LURD chief negotiator and former ULIMO-K executive Kabineh Ja'neh was declared LURD Chairman by Aicha's loyalists.

As the nomination of the Krahn Joe Gbalah by the Mandingo Sekou Conneh as well as the selection of the Krahn Chayee Doe as leader of the predominantly Mandingo Aicha Conneh faction illustrate, divisions within LURD did not primarily follow ethnic lines. Yet ethnic identity served as a resource in intra-LURD rivalries and was one of the markers distinguishing competing factions. These factions were primarily shaped in contexts of localized competition for specific economic chances. For instance, in an attempt to gain control over financial transactions, Chayee Doe as Managing Director of the NPA tried to sideline the Comptroller, a Mandingo associated with the Sekou Conneh faction. The incident led to three

167 Interview with Joe Wyllie, once LURD Military Spokesman and NTGL Deputy Minister of Defense, Monrovia, Jan. 12, 2006. Wylie had been a rival of Conneh and been forced to flee LURD territory during the war.

168 Chayee Doe was a brother of the former military President Samuel Doe and both a LURD and MODEL commander.

major shooting incidents in the port premises between LURD-factions primarily structured along the ethnic divide (cf. Ernst & Young 2005d, 5). When Joe Gbalah took over, attempts to control cash flows resulted in further, less violent conflicts over important positions, notably that of Expenditure Manager (cf. Heritage Dec. 28, 2005). The background to these developments was decentralized patrimonialization, a major indicator for which was the extreme weakness of legal-rational principles in managing the NPA.

Auditors "noted instances where the [organizational] chart carried positions and titles which do not exist while there [were] also positions and titles currently unoccupied." The "Port Manager, Financial Controller, the Chief Accountant and the Head of Management Internal Control [lacked] the requisite competencies to hold such positions" (Ernst & Young 2005c, 6). Senior executives treated offices as personal patrimonies and took decisions in a discretionary manner. The "Operations Department blatantly refused to provide [auditors] with shipping manifests which could have enabled [them] to assess the completeness of recorded cargo and container handling fees." "Generally speaking, lots of documentary evidences seem[ed] to be lacking" (ibid. 2005d, 5). Dysfunctional financial administration led to non-payment of wages and port workers went on strike repeatedly.

The difficulties of centrally controlling the NPA resulted in a massive increase in personnel, as different factions and individuals used it to reward clients and loyalists. Disposing of its own police force, the NPA was particularly attractive for former combatants. Colonel Ophorie "Iron Jacket" Diah, former Acting Chief of Staff of LURD, had been allocated the post of Director of Security at the port. Within two years, the number of NPA employees rose from 600 to more than 2,000 (Panel of Experts 06/2006, 31–32). "The Liberia Seaport Police recorded the highest number on the payroll with 533 persons representing about 35% of the total staff strength of the NPA [in 2004]." (Ernst & Young 2005c, 7). Nevertheless, theft at the port drastically increased, illustrating the treatment of security positions as private fiefs. As this had a significantly negative impact on UN and humanitarian imports, UNMIL intervened in mid-2005, took over the port for six weeks, and dismissed 540 Seaport Police, including Ophorie Diah (Inquirer May 16, 2005). This did not mean more rational management of the NPA but nevertheless represented one of the important instances in which UNMIL broke control of organized combatant formations over sources of state revenue.

4.3.2.2. The Irrelevance of MODEL

MODEL had from the very beginning been weak in coherence. Its leader, Thomas Yaya Nimely, ethnic Krahn and a US citizen, had long been in the diaspora and was hardly trusted by his commanders. He had been a LURD NEC member but left the group "with two experienced fighters, Arthur Baygboe and Philip Pardea", and succeeded to become an intermediary for the Ivorian government when it came under attack (Lidow 2011, 203). He owed his position to external backing and had few connections among the refugees recruited into the LIMA militia.

A large share of MODEL's positions in the NTGL were allocated to civilian members of Liberia's elite who did not play a role in MODEL, giving rise to accusations that he favored his "friends from America" (ibid. 208) and sold government posts (cf. Perspective May 07, 2004). Only after commanders ransacked his home did he accord a few positions to senior MODEL leaders. Nimely himself took the position of NTGL Foreign Minister, which meant he could not run in the elections to come. Instead, he focused efforts on rehabilitating his family's 45–hectare plantation in Grand Gedeh (cf. Wikileaks Nov. 30, 2007).

Commanders and executives cut links with combatants quickly in order to free resources and maximize opportunities. Combatants often sought opportunities in hinterland resources on their own, and occupied in particular the *Sinoe Rubber Plantation* and sites in the *Sarpo National Park* (SNP) containing gold deposits. A MODEL ex-combatant and son of the Paramount Chief controlling the main entrance to the SNP sites was reported to be the leader of a large group of miners (Panel of Experts 12/2007, 20).

MODEL Spokesman Eugene Wilson was made FDA Managing Director, yet due to the timber sanctions the position offered only limited economic opportunities arising from small-scale "pit-sawing", which produced planks for the domestic construction industry (cf. Panel of Experts 12/2004, 30). As the SNP is a protected area, the activities symbolized the lack of government control over forests and were an impediment to lifting of the timber sanctions. Alienating those who constituted the social base of MODEL, Eugene Wilson attempted to have the miners evacuated from the protected area. Accompanying a UN team, Wilson directly confronted former combatants, ordered two to be arrested by FDA rangers, and threatened the Paramount Chief as well as the local Superintendent that a "resumption [of mining activities would] suggest the approval of the county authorities", who would be held to account (Inquirer Aug. 23, 2005). Most miners temporarily left the national park amid incentives and pressures from UNMIL and the FDA, only to return a little later.

General Kai Farley had been the head of the MODEL military administration in Buchanan. Similarly, combatants were abandoned when he left for Monrovia to take a job as Inspector General at the Ministry of Commerce and Industry,[169] leading to a violent protest by ex-combatants when MODEL leaders later visited the city (cf. Panel of Experts 06/2004, 30). Farley later ran for a seat in the House of Representatives in the 2005 elections, which he comfortably won. The events suggested that MODEL commanders pursuing a political career had their constituency among people of their places of origin rather than among their ex-combatants, implying disintegration of the group.

4.3.3. Political Parties and Civil Society: Dashed Hopes

A major difference between the 1995 Abuja Agreement and the 2003 CPA was the leading role accorded to civilian political actors. Insistence of foreign actors on the issue was an important reason for the prominent role civilian politicians eventually adopted. Most importantly, both the Chairman and the Vice-Chairman of the NTGL were civilians. Civilian actors were further allocated a large number of government institutions, and they had a majority in the 76–member *National Transitional Legislative Assembly* (NTLA). Each of the warring parties was allocated 12 seats. The remaining civilian slots were filled by three different categories of groups. The "Political Parties" together sent 18 delegates. In addition, each of the 15 Counties named a representative, and "Special Interest Groups" were given a further seven seats.[170] Civilians further occupied several Deputy executive positions in lucrative ministries and agencies.

---

169 Interviews with Esthella Kebeh, Chairperson of *Bassa Concerned Citizens Movement*, in Buchanan, Dec. 14, 2005.

170 Among the "Special Interest Groups" defined in the CPA were the *National Bar Association*, Liberian business associations, refugees, women organizations, youth organizations, unions and the US diaspora (CPA 2003, Art. XXIV)

The civilian bloc was thus particularly heterogeneous and could hardly be expected to act in concert. In addition, civilians' politics was dominated by dynamics generally characterizing the transitional period, i.e. politics evolved around attempts to personally control opportunities for profit, and strategies to achieve that goal featured establishing purpose-driven, mutually beneficial alliances with other office holders.

NTGL Chairman Gyude Bryant and his deputy Wesley Johnson had been elected by the signatories to the peace agreement in Accra. Gyude Bryant for his part was a member of the *Liberia Action Party* (LAP) but not a prominent politician. Neither was he a member of the inner circle of Liberia's historic elite. His background was that of a businessman owning a small company that imported heavy machinery and spare parts. As Cabinet officials were not allowed to stand in the 2005 elections, none of Liberia's political heavyweights were particularly interested in the position, and most of the parties to the agreement were not interested in a strong Chairman. Effectively, the NTGL leadership took responsibility for coordinating the private appropriation of revenues rather than taking on a controlling function, not forgetting its own private interests in the process. Semi-officially, the transition period was defined as a pay-off time for internal forces which in return would allow foreign actors to secure the country and restore stability rather than sabotage the peace process. Thus, ECOWAS investigators criticized a "misconception" on the part of Bryant, his support staff and others "that acts of corruption in the circumstances of present-day Liberia is (sic) understandable, even excusable", and that the formally highest authority was "sacrificing the principles of probity, transparency and accountability" (ECOWAS 2005, 16).

Key associates of Bryant in the organization of patrimonial governance were the LURD-nominated Finance Minister Luseni Kamara and the GOL-nominated LPRC Managing Director Edwin Snowe, illustrating the formation of new alliances transcending factions. ECOWAS investigators uncovered several instances in which money had been provided in cash to Bryant by the Finance Minister on the basis of extralegal requests. The limited investigation found that Bryant alone could not account for more than a million dollars provided to him on his instructions (ibid., 12–17). Amongst others, Bryant claimed to have provided 375,000 dollars to the *National Commission for Disarmament, Demobilization, Rehabilitation and Reintegration* (NCDDRR). The claim was not backed up by documentation, and the NCDDRR Director denied having received the funds. Some

355,255 dollars were paid to the *National Security Advisor's* office directly reporting to Bryant. The advisor's personnel, "with the tacit encouragement of the Chairman of the NTGL, declined to assist in the investigation, [...] on account of 'the sacrosanct nature of matters of national security'" (ibid., 14–15). The payments were all the more questionable as one of the largest elements in the 2004–2005 budget, accounting for 15 percent of expenditures, were allocations to the security sector (although most former government and rebel combatants were demobilized, costs were covered by foreign actors, and UNMIL was largely responsible for providing security). "The Governance Reform Commission noted that the security allocation could have been reduced by at least 50 percent" (Panel of Experts 12/2004, 37).

As has been mentioned, similar extralegal requests for payments were made to Edwin Snowe in his capacity as Managing Director of the LPRC (Ernst & Young 2005a, 9). Bryant was implicated in a number of other dubious transactions. In particular, he initiated the sale of stockpiled iron ore for some 6.5 million dollar, less than a quarter of the world market price, against a stay order of the Supreme Court. The revenue was not deposited in state coffers (cf. Panel of Experts 12/2004, 42–43; 06/2005, 45). Structurally important, there were pertinent accommodating tendencies between NTGL elites from diverse backgrounds, and "corruption" entailed the establishment of new intra-elite connections. These connections evolved around mutual interests in the private appropriation of "state" revenue and engendered the accumulation of social capital useful in other intra-elite conflicts.[171]

An important reason for the international community to insist on a prominent position for civilian actors, and lobbying for them to have a majority in parliament, was the assumption that a civilian-dominated assembly would be more likely to control an executive largely composed of warring party members. However, the workings of parliament followed dynamics characterizing the NTGL in general, i.e. the use of public office for private purposes, most importantly personal enrichment and acquiring funds to build a political constituency. Partly, the overseeing powers of parliament were impeded because circumvented, e.g. large transfers of funds from the Ministries of Health, Public Works, and Education to Presidential (i.e. Chairman's) Affairs, Finance and others were not submitted to parliament

171 As the Chairman could not stand in the 2005 elections there were no short-term incentives to use funds to build a political constituency among ordinary Liberians.

for approval. When given opportunities for control, these were not used as expected. For instance, the Chairman submitted an 80 million dollars budget for 2005–2006 to the NTLA. A budget was eventually passed with considerable delay after the Chairman had paid some 226,000 dollars "petty cash" to the assembly (Panel of Experts 12/2005, 28–29).[172] Even members of parliament publicly voiced that legislative decisions were up for sale (New Democrat Sept. 9, 2005). Notwithstanding, the eventually approved budget was increased to 93 million dollar. No plausible explanation on the source of the missing 13 million dollars was given but on the basis of the budget, an increased number of government elites could present claims to the Finance Minister.

Given an extremely heterogeneous legislative assembly, divisions were marked. However, it is indicative of Liberian political dynamics that some decisions were supported almost unanimously. Symbolic among these was the decision by the NTLA that parliamentarians take possession of their assigned official vehicles, Grand Cherokee Jeeps, purchased during the NTLA period for 37,000 dollars apiece. The decision sparked an international and domestic outcry and the US ambassador threatened not to accord visas to parliamentarians supporting the decision (cf. National Chronicle Nov. 21, 2005). Gyude Bryant initially vetoed the law but was overturned with a 90 percent majority (Africa Confidential Nov. 18, 2005). After the first vote had triggered widespread criticism a single parliamentarian initiated futile moves to have it rescinded.[173] Tellingly, the lawmaker later stood for a Senate seat in the 2005 election but lost, though with a tiny margin of 137 votes (0.4 percent) only. The senior senator seat was won by the Chairman of the LPRC's Board of Directors, who had access to significantly larger funds to build a political constituency and who was alleged to have used his position to allocate an LPRC contract to his own law firm (New Democrat Sept. 5, 2005; Inquirer Sept. 12, 2005). The events demonstrate that Liberian political culture is quite uniform in some respects, i.e. the conception of the state as a tool for privatization of economic resources is widely accepted, provided that clients benefit. Conse-

172 Parliamentarians received further payments facilitated by the executive, such as the US$ 12,400 given by the LPRC to the NTLA on request of Bryant mentioned above (Ernst & Young 2005a, 27)

173 The parliamentarian in question was Conmany Wesseh, Director of the *Centre for Democratic Empowerment* founded by Amos Sawyer and NTLA civil society delegate. Wesseh was a UP member and made Deputy Foreign Affairs Minister by President Johnson Sirleaf.

quently, there are few immediate pressures for legal-rational governance from either elite circles or grass roots.

4.4. Elections and a New Regime

The first post-war elections were a key indicator of major shifts in relations of authority that had taken place during the transitional period. These shifts took place against the background of a relative loss of legitimacy of military actors, the weakening of internal coherence of these actors, and vigorous political competition among and between the dominant political forces of the transition period.[174] Institutionally, these developments were supported by the devaluation of military power, occasioned by UNMIL temporarily taking responsibility for security. The importance of votes as a power resource for political actors correspondingly increased. Attempting to maximize electoral support, political actors negotiated new elite alliances, as a favorable position in elite networks was necessary to attract campaign funds and intermediaries impacting on the opinion of grassroots. As votes became the major power resource, election modalities strongly structured opportunities for political office.

The first round of presidential elections as well as the elections for the House of Representatives and the Senate took place on October 11, 2005, roughly two years after the NTGL had been established. Each of the 15 Counties elected two senators, i.e. citizens had two votes and the two top contenders passed. As for the House, every County was entitled to elect at least two representatives, giving an advantage to the sparsely populated eastern Counties.[175] The president and representatives are elected for a six year term, while senators are regularly elected for staggered nine year terms. However, as constitutional provisions for "first elections" (Art. 46) were applied to the 2005 "Special Elections", the junior senator was elected for six years only (cf. Mihatsch n.d., 9–17). As no presidential can-

174 Indeed, "vigorous political competition" is a major factor provoking the transformation of armed actors from military to civilian political organizations (Manning 2004, 69).

175 Representatives were elected with a simple majority although the constitution required an absolute one, implying a costly second round. In 2011, the simple majority rule was inscribed in the constitution following a government-initiated referendum to the effect.

didate obtained an absolute majority in the first round, a run-off took place on November 8.[176]

This subsection highlights those associated with warring parties and the top contenders in the presidential elections. It aims to explain election results by investigating campaign styles and the formation of political alliances prior to the elections. The run-off finally took place between football star George Manneh Weah and veteran politician Ellen Johnson Sirleaf, who eventually won with 59.4 percent. The analysis below gives special attention to these two top contenders.

4.4.1. Presidential Elections: Warring Parties

MODEL lost political relevance quickly, and it will not be further dealt with in this section. Nimely had maintained a low profile during the transition but shortly tried to establish a *Democratic Movement* party (cf. Inquirer May 25, 2005). Essentially on the basis of common eastern origin, he finally supported the candidacy of George Weah in both rounds of presidential elections.

The breakup of LURD's leading couple Sekou and Aicha Conneh was reflected in later political alliances. Sekou Conneh founded the *Progressive Democratic Party* (PRODEM) and stood as its presidential candidate in the elections. Yet he only obtained 0.6 percent, representing some 5,500 votes. Conneh had hardly been known in Liberia as leader of LURD and he did not raise his profile during the transition period. His campaign was weak and seemed to suffer from a lack of funds. The most widely known personality representing PRODEM was its Chairperson, Ruth "Attila" Milton, the former AFL Major and LPC commander (see Chapter 4) (cf. Daily Observer Aug. 1, 2005).[177] Yet Conneh obtained few votes in Lofa, where Mandingo are concentrated, and even less in the east. After having

176 For more information on election modalities see Mihatsch (n.d.) and Konrad Adenauer Foundation (2006). For election results see NEC (2005a; 2005b) and Harris (2006).

177 The NDPL of Samuel K. Doe could no longer attract the remnants of his regime. While LPC leader George Boley had still run as its presidential candidate in 1997, it fielded a nephew of former President William Tubman as presidential candidate in 2005. Many party militants perceived the nomination of Winston Tubman as a high-jacking of the party by "Americo-Liberians". Despite friction in the party, Tubman came 4th in the election. He, however, scored only 1.8 percent in Grand Gedeh, the traditional stronghold of the party.

been defeated in the first round, Sekou Conneh supported George Weah's bid.

PRODEM competed for essentially the same electoral segment as Alhadji Kromah's ALCOP. Yet while Sekou Conneh came 15th in the elections, Alhadji Kromah managed to secure 8th place, winning 2.8 percent of votes. Kromah had been in exile during most of Taylor's rule, and ALCOP was hardly characterized by greater institutional continuity than PRODEM. Yet in contrast to Conneh, Alhadji Kromah had been an outstanding charismatic leader and a prominent intellectual personality among Mandingo.[178] Kromah attracted 18 percent of votes in Lofa County, while Sekou Conneh only obtained 1 percent there.

Aicha Conneh's faction, in contrast, did not make a bid for power independently but supported Johnson Sirleaf in both rounds. Major personalities in the Aicha Conneh camp were NTGL Minister of Justice Kabineh Ja'neh, mobilizing votes amongst Mandingo and NTGL Minister of State Jackson E. Doe, a close relative of Samuel Doe, representing the Krahn element. The faction overlapped with the *National Mandingo Caucus* (NMC), an umbrella Mandingo organization created by businessman Musa Bility in the run-up to the elections. Bility owned a radio and TV station, the fuel importing and wholesale distributing company *Srimex*, and was Secretary-General of the *Petroleum Importers Association* at the time. He and the NMC vigorously supported Johnson Sirleaf during the campaign.[179] Bility was reported to have been interested in the post of Managing Director of the LPRC but finally was not allocated the position. According to a local newspaper, at least three people had been promised the top job in return for supporting the UP candidate (Liberian Express Jan. 2, 2006; cf. Analyst Mar. 7, 2006; cf. Analyst Mar. 13, 2006).

As has been mentioned above, the NPP was subject to internal divisions impacting negatively on the party's internal coherence. Most important among the internal squabbles was that between the top contenders for the presidential candidacy, Roland Massaquoi, the former Minister of Agriculture, and Francis Garlawolo, Taylor's popular Bong County senator. When Massaquoi eventually won the race, Garlawolo publicly accused him of being hand-picked by Taylor (ICG 2005, 6). At the same

178 In the transition period, he was accorded the title of Adjunct Associate Professor at the *University of Liberia*.

179 Johnson Sirleaf had been married to a Mandingo, entailing connections and some sympathies among Mandingo elites.

time, Garlawolo was considered as close to Taylor as Massaquoi and one of the NPP elites regularly in contact with the former president (cf. Africa Confidential Apr. 29, 2005b). In reaction to his defeat in NPP primaries, Garlawolo supported Johnson Sirleaf in the election campaign. The successor to Taylor, former President Moses Blah, supported George Weah after having been sidelined in the NPP. There was little doubt that Taylor tried to reorganize forces with a view to regaining a position of power (cf. Hoffman 2006), and that his strategy partly relied on placing his supporters in well-positioned political parties or having party stalwarts run as independent candidates, as Edwin Snowe did in parliamentary elections.

It was strategically prudent to maximize the chances of having supporters in high office, and not having popular candidates eliminated through intra-NPP competition. At the same time, those associates of Taylor who had been able to secure a political position by striking the right alliances and appealing successfully to voters were relatively independent of Taylor and simultaneously became integrated into alternative networks, to which they would be socially obliged. Taylor's strategy implied an erosion of institutional coherence, weakening of organizational power and loss of control over political intermediaries. The NPP presidential candidate eventually obtained 4.1 percent in the first round of elections, ranking 6th place.

4.4.2. The Leading Candidates and their Networks

Taken as a whole, the results for places two to five of the first round of the presidential elections indicated a shift of power to a particular stratum of Liberian society, i.e. civilians with a background in the classic elite circles of Liberia and possessing extensive international connections. As such, the results indicate a resurgence of classic *Big (Wo-)Men* patronage politics sustained by funds derived from foreign corporations and sympathetic donors. Theoretically, this suggests two tendencies: Access to foreign-generated rents used to finance domination undermines statehood, as there are few incentives to establish comprehensive bureaucratic systems. However, access to these very rents empowers elites using the state as an apparatus of domination and seeking its extension (cf. Schlichte 2006). Elite interests suggest that the state as a sovereign, centralized apparatus of domination over a defined territory will grow, though this is likely to proceed through an extension of patronage networks defying conventional notions of statehood.

Third in the elections with 13.9 percent came the lawyer Charles Brumskine, the former NPP Senate President pro tempore who had fallen out with Taylor in 1999 and left for exile in the US. Brumskine was well established there already: His family lived in the Washington area, his children went to private elite schools, and he had a law firm in Washington mostly working for companies registered on the Liberian corporate registry. Among his clients in Liberia were important corporations such as *Firestone*, LAC and the Italian *Global Bank* (cf. ICG 2005, 6). His running mate Amelia Ward had been Minister of Commerce and later Minister of Planning and Economic Development under Taylor, but was not part of Taylor's inner circle. Since the Tolbert administration, she had held Deputy Planning Minister positions repeatedly. During the NTGL period she was temporarily General Affairs Coordinator for Gyude Bryant but was most prominent in heading the NGO *Mano River Women Peace Network* (MARWOPNET), one of Liberia's most important women's NGOs and an important interlocutor for foreign and international organizations. Brumskine, himself a born-again member of the evangelical *Bethel World Outreach* church, campaigned on the basis of a fundamentalist but little aggressive Christian political ideology. Brumskine declared himself God's choice for the Presidency, while Amelia Ward stated that she was "led by God to accept his [Brumskine's] request" to become running mate (Liberian Dialogue Aug. 5, 2005).[180] The duo, however, owed its electoral success to votes from the south east and particularly Brumskine's populous home County of Bassa, and hardly succeeded to capitalize on the growth of fundamentalist Christianity in Liberia. Brumskine did not support any candidate in the run-off.

Winston Tubman, a nephew of the longest-serving president in Liberia's history, William Tubman (1944–1971), and running as candidate of the NDPL, ranked 4th place with 9.2 percent of votes. He had joined Samuel Doe's party in 1990 already, in a move that found little sympathy with either Liberia's historic elite or the opposition. Tubman was a lawyer by profession and the Liberian state was a major client of his when his uncle was president, but he has made his career largely within the UN, rising to *Special Representative of the Secretary General* in Somalia. His electoral

180 Less successful candidates Alfred Reeves, George Kiadii and Margaret Tor-Thompson similarly campaigned on a fundamentalist Christian platform (cf. Sawyer 2008, 188–198).

success, however, was largely due to his running mate Jeremiah Sulunteh, who had been Vice-president of Liberia's best tertiary institution, *Cuttington University College* in Bong County. Sulunteh was widely respected in the area and won populous Bong. Tubman further won his much smaller home County of Maryland, and had relevant support in south western and central Liberia, though very little in Montserrado (cf. ICG 2005, 6).

Last among the top contenders was Varney Sherman, who obtained 7.8 percent earning him 5th place. A lawyer who graduated from Harvard in 1982, he made his career during the most lawless of times Liberia had, starting his own law firm in 1990. Sherman was widely considered a central figure of Liberia's historic establishment although he stressed his indigenous roots in the campaign. Among his clients were most of the major foreign corporations in Liberia, inter alia *Mittal Steel* and *Firestone*, and he is considered a major advisor and intermediary for the richest members of Liberia's Lebanese business community. Sherman shared membership in the LAP with Gyude Bryant (whose business affairs he handled) and was considered the NTGL Chairman's preferred candidate (cf. ibid.). He was further perceived to be using state resources for his campaign (cf. Africa Confidential Oct. 21, 2005). Sherman's campaign was expensive (cf. Johnson Sirleaf 2009, 258), and running as the standard bearer of a party alliance he had crafted, the *Coalition for the Transformation of Liberia* (COTOL), he mobilized an extensive network of supporters among Liberia's political class.[181] Eventually, however, Sherman's elite connections gained him significantly fewer voters than expected. He won his small home County of Grand Cape Mount with some 62.8 percent, but actually obtained more votes in Montserrado and most in Nimba, where the former government paramilitary General Adolphus "Peanut Butter" Dolo campaigned for him.

The two candidates who emerged as final contenders for the presidency, George Weah with 28.3 percent and Ellen Johnson Sirleaf with 19.8 percent, were opposites in many respects. Both had strikingly different personal backgrounds, different political styles and appealed to different social and regional constituencies. I subsequently shortly portray both candidates before describing how the political spectrum eventually gravitated toward the two top contenders.

---

181 COTOL was composed of LAP, TWP, the People's Democratic Party of Liberia (PDPL) and the Liberian Unification Party (LUP).

Ellen Johnson Sirleaf was a veteran Liberian politician, an internationally successful banker and UN official. She campaigned on the image of a professional and technocrat. She was raised in the circles of Liberia's "civilized" establishment and used to be considered an ethnic "Americo-Liberian" but has parental Gola and Kru roots, which she stressed in the election campaign.[182] As member of the *True Whig Party* (TWP), Johnson Sirleaf rose to be appointed Secretary of State for Finance in 1972, but she earned a reputation for being independently minded and severely clashed with Stephen Tolbert, the Minister of Finance, owner of the *Mesurado Group of Companies* and brother of the president (Porte 1974, 2). She nevertheless remained integrated into the government and took over the post of Finance Minister when Tolbert died in a plane crash in 1979, and remained in the position until the coup of 1980. During the period of military rule, Johnson Sirleaf was prominent as a critic of the government, was incarcerated twice and narrowly escaped being killed (Johnson Sirleaf 2009, 93–112). As Liberia appeared set to democratize in the mid-1980s, she was one of the founding members of the LAP, whose presidential candidate was widely considered to have won the 1985 elections. Like all other opposition candidates except Ruth Perry, she refused to take the Montserrado Senate seat she won in 1985 in protest over electoral fraud.

Under circumstances of widespread repression, Johnson Sirleaf spent a considerable time during the military dictatorship in exile, foremost in the US. There, she was a prominent member of the *Association for Constitutional Democracy in Liberia* (ACDL), a civil society body opposing the military regime. As the First Liberian War began, the ACDL split into two groups, one identified with Ellen Johnson Sirleaf and supporting the NPFL and another one led by Amos Sawyer opposing it (TRC 2009, 118). The issue of Johnson Sirleaf's support for the NPFL has generated heated debate in Liberia and beyond. She maintained to have been part of an ACDL faction that only once sent 10,000 dollars to "provide food for Taylor's troops and for the citizens of Nimba County" (Johnson Sirleaf 2009, 173), while others accuse her of having occupied a leadership position in the NPFL (cf. Liberian Dialogue Sept. 15, 2005).[183]

182 For a profile of Johnson Sirleaf, detailing her social background and conservative as well as progressive attitudes see Gerdes (2011).

183 A major controversy surrounded a statement by Johnson Sirleaf on the BBC, in which she stated that "if they [NPFL] burn the [Executive] mansion down, we will rebuild it" (Johnson Sirleaf 2009, 179; cf. Liberian Dialogue Sept. 15, 2005).

The *Truth and Reconciliation Commission of Liberia* (TRC) considered Johnson Sirleaf's statements unconvincing and recommended she be barred from holding public office for 30 years (TRC 2009, 125, 271), but her involvement in the NPFL appeared limited. The TRC's work was characterized by severe infighting and a lack of professionalism, and it produced a deeply flawed report (Steinberg 2010; Taz.de July 7, 2009). Most plausibly, Johnson Sirleaf ceased supporting the NPFL in the early period of the war, when Taylor eliminated (potential) rivals and monopolized power. However, Johnson Sirleaf had extensive connections to NPFL and NPP circles, particularly to individuals emanating from the "progressive", "professional" and "Americo-Liberian" milieus of Liberian society, like Harry Yuan, Benoni Urey, Toga MacIntosh, Grace Minor, and others.

Ellen Johnson Sirleaf was one of Liberia's internationally best connected personalities (cf. Ellis 2007a, 67) and represented particular strata and qualities. Socio-politically, she was the face of a modernized, formerly "Americo-Liberian" establishment, embodying its virtues of education and Western orientation but being much higher educated and professional than Liberia's historic elite. Her careers in both the private sector and the UN appeared to prove professionalism, integrity and enlightenment, as she imposed herself and gained respect in a highly competitive but relatively rule-bound, bureaucratic environment. Further, for a considerable time she had striven not to be associated with exploitative practices of "Americo-Liberian" rule, although Liberians were not fully convinced. Elements of her pro-poor credentials were her UNDP position, her indigenous parental roots and her NGO *Measuagoon*. *Measuagoon* started working shortly after Johnson Sirleaf had been defeated in the 1997 elections. It essentially was a poorly funded publicity stunt with a very limited scope of operations.[184]

With a declared value of some two million dollars obtained mostly from Liberian Diaspora members (Johnson Sirleaf 2009, 258), costs of Ellen Johnson Sirleaf's campaign appeared roughly in the mean of the top five contenders. Yet her campaign was particularly sophisticated and included frequently tracking voter preferences and attitudes by means of polls and adapting the campaign according to intelligence thus obtained. Education, a professional attitude and connections to experienced techno-

184 Johnson Sirleaf (2009, 261) provided US$1,400 to the NGO, which supported rebuilding efforts in her ancestral village of Kormah. Her loyalist Harry Greaves used the occasion to write a newspaper article showering praise on its founder (Perspective n.d.).

crats thus made themselves felt as a power resource. Her campaign stressed personal qualities rather than abstract political concepts, focusing on her level of education, her international connections promising external assistance, and her compassionate iron lady image. As her background in Liberia's establishment was her greatest disadvantage, Johnson Sirleaf travelled widely through Liberia, visiting remote villages in order to appear closer to the people (cf. Johnson Sirleaf 2009, 247–273).

In order to run an effective campaign, a maximum number of influential supporters needed to be mobilized. Convincing voters is not only a question of the message of a candidate but also of the person conveying the message. Voters need to be convinced, but trusted, influential personalities are of great help to convince grassroots. A predominance of locally rooted networks and a dearth of party loyalty characterized the campaign. Personalized politics correspondingly meant that voting patterns hardly reflected party lines.[185] "The real strength of [Johnson Sirleaf's] campaign was the collection of individuals from other parties, civil society organizations, and elsewhere in Liberian society" (Sawyer 2008, 190).

A key group of supporters of Johnson Sirleaf was made up of important figures of Liberia's erstwhile "progressive" movements and included personalities such as H. Boima Fahnbulleh, Amos Sawyer, Conmany Wesseh, Francis Karpeh, Dusty Wollokollie, Dew Mayson and Edward Spencer.[186] She, further, was supported by renowned human rights activists Kofi Samuel Woods and Tiawon Gongloe. Another group was more closely identified with Liberia's historic "Americo-Liberian" elite, as for instance Harry Greaves and Willis Knuckles. Balancing this group were successful indigenous business elites, most notably running mate and Lofa County businessman Joseph Boakai. The Kissi Boakai was important for Johnson Sirleaf's victory in medium-sized Lofa, as were Aicha Conneh and Musa Bility. Francis Garlawolo was likely to have significantly contributed to Johnson Sirleaf's 10.1 percent in populous Bong County, placing her close to second-placed George Weah, who obtained 10.7 percent. Another senior NPP official, former Minister of Information Reginald Goodridge,

185 Although Johnson Sirleaf won the presidential elections, her UP only won four of 30 Senate seats and eight of the 64 seats in the House of Representatives. The CDC won three senatorial and 15 House seats.

186 By 2005, several of these were characterized by their political, civil society and/or business success and thus elite status. In particular, MOJA's Dew Mayson had become one of Liberia's richest businessmen, having made a career in the Nigerian oil industry.

as well supported her. However, Johnson Sirleaf ranked 6th in the important Nimba County only, obtaining 5.8 percent. Yet she had significant electoral support in the smaller Counties of Gbarpolu and her native Bomi, as well as the important Margibi County, site of the *Firestone* plantation.

A major reconfiguration of alliances took place after the first round, as candidates and supporters sought new opportunities and the two successful candidates sought to strengthen their networks. A number of intellectual professionals supported Johnson Sirleaf on the basis of shared social position. Among them was Joseph Korto, presidential candidate of the 7th placed *Liberia Equal Rights Party* (LERP). Korto had been responsible for educational facilities in Nimba in the 1980s and was popular there. He won 21.9 percent of local votes in the first round, less than 2 percentage points behind first-placed Weah. Former *Cuttington University College* president and NDPL vice-presidential candidate Jeremiah Sulunteh, influential in populous Bong County, decided to support Johnson Sirleaf in defiance of his party's standard bearer Tubman.

Further, Johnson Sirleaf attracted significant support from former NPP officials. Most important among these were Charles Taylor's wife Jewel Howard-Taylor, who had won a Senate seat in Bong County, and General Adolphus "Peanut Butter" Dolo, who had won one in Nimba. NPP presidential candidate Roland Massaquoi also declared support for Johnson Sirleaf. Both Dolo and Massaquoi had significant support in Nimba.

As this line-up of forces suggested, Johnson Sirleaf's run-off campaign focused on the densely populated central corridor leading from Montserrado over Margibi and Bong to Nimba, where more than half of the electorate was registered. Final resources were employed and, for instance, a helicopter reportedly financed by Dew Mayson (Africa Confidential Jan. 20, 2006) was leased to facilitate movement. Influence and resources of key supporters reinforced the campaign. For instance, Jewel Howard-Taylor employed the well-developed NPP machinery in Bong County to campaign for Johnson Sirleaf.[187] In the end, Ellen Johnson Sirleaf won western and central Liberia as well as small Maryland County in the east,[188] leaving only sparsely populated eastern Counties to Weah. A particularly important turnaround was represented by a 77.1 percent victory in Nimba. The

187 Focus Group Interview, Gbarnga, Bong County, Feb. 2, 2007.

188 Both of Maryland's senators were from the Unity Party, indicating that Johnson Sirleaf's network was well-positioned there. One of these senators was Gloria Musu-Scott, Chief Justice under Charles Taylor.

County had been won by George Weah in the first round with 23.8 percent while Johnson Sirleaf had been left far behind.

Nimba was won by newly introducing the ethno-political factor into the campaign. When campaigning in Samuel Doe's home village, Weah "announced he was a son of Doe, emphasized his debt to Doe for starting him on his career, and said he would do his best for Grand Gedeh" (Harris 2006, 389). Samuel Doe was still detested in Nimba, which bore the brunt of his repression. Weah's remark was exploited to represent him as heir to Doe. The remarks were made in a remote village, but several of Monrovia's newspapers quickly seized on the story,[189] expanding it to Weah having promised cabinet positions to the LURD General George Dweh and the former AFL General Charles Julu, notorious for massacres in Nimba. Joseph Korto was one of the campaigners warning of Weah because of his alleged closeness to Samuel Doe (cf. ibid.). Others from the NPP camp, for instance Adolphus Dolo, campaigned for Johnson Sirleaf by promising that formerly Mandingo-owned real estate occupied by others in a context of war and flight would not be returned.[190] In the end, Johnson Sirleaf's campaign proved superior.

Although politically inexperienced, George Weah was a serious challenger. This was possible because the distinction between Johnson Sirleaf and Weah represented a major cleavage in Liberian society. Apart from having proven himself in an extremely competitive international environment, George Weah was the opposite of Johnson Sirleaf. Being of Kru ethnicity and thus considered a native of eastern Liberia, he grew up in Monrovia's Clara Town slum. Having a low educational background not surpassing high-school level,[191] his talent for football and ambition took him to play for several African clubs and, from 1988 to 2001, for Europe's most prestigious ones. In 1995, he was voted FIFA World Footballer of the Year, European Footballer of the Year and African Footballer of the Year.

His international success entailed an appointment to the position of UNICEF Goodwill Ambassador, a task he fulfilled from 1997 to 2005. He

189 Many if not most partisan articles in Liberia's newspapers are "sponsored advertisements" though they are frequently not marked as such.

190 Focus Group Interviews in Ganta, Nimba County, Mar. 19–20, 2007.

191 A great embarrassment to Weah came when it was revealed that the university from which he claimed to have obtained a BA in Sports Administration had been selling fake UK university degrees (ICG 2005, 8).

had occasionally supported humanitarian activities in Liberia before. Yet most widely known and praised were his efforts for the Liberian national football team. George Weah was considered to have enabled the team to persist when state funding ceased and to have led the team to qualify for the *African Cup of Nations* in 1996 and 2002. He was reported to have spent considerable sums of money on the team, amongst others covering the cost of participating in an *African Cup of Nations* contest (cf. Liberian Soccer.com n.d.).

George Weah's appeal was populist and resonated particularly among urban youths. The 2005 and 2011 elections showed he had strong support in Monrovia and the eastern Counties. As was the case with Johnson Sirleaf, the campaign focused on the personal qualities of the leader rather than abstract political concepts. Among these personal qualities, strength, leadership capabilities, success despite humble origins and philanthropy—as evidenced in support for the national football team—were the most important ones. His poor background and relative isolation from Liberia's established elite meant that he symbolized indigenous success and the end of "Americo-Liberian" dominance. However, emphasizing the riches Weah had earned was an important element in his campaign. Wealth is widely considered not only proving patronage capacities but intelligence and aptitude.[192] An important share of campaign rhetoric aimed at delegitimizing education as an elite credential, pointing out that, formerly, well-educated leaders had either been ineffectual or merely self-serving.[193]

Weah created a new party, the *Congress for Democratic Change* (CDC) as a vehicle for the election bid. Weah employed considerable means to undertake his campaign and, despite not making use of a helicopter, travelled

192 According to the declarations of assets as requested from candidates by the National Elections Commission, George Weah was the second-richest candidate after the irrelevant David Farhat, owning about three US$ Million (cf. Sawyer 2008, 185). According to campaign rally observers, Weah exaggerated his wealth in his speeches.

193 A pro-Weah newspaper article that appeared to be a "sponsored advertisement" used rather unconventional comparisons but summarized main themes of the campaign pointedly. The article, entitled "Academic Standards vs. Real Issues" held that "the academically smart kids normally usually sit in the background" while "it has been established that great leaders [...] are people who barely scraped through formal academic walls" (National Chronicle Sept. 14, 2005). The article went on to explain that Sékou Touré and Adolf Hitler had lacked formal education but had been great leaders and left marks on history. Weah's campaign and post-election statements often were authoritarian in character.

widely throughout Liberia to convince voters. His radio station Kings FM, of course, supported his campaign.

Considered the most promising candidate early on, Weah attracted a disparate group of supporters. Yet he had particular support among elites from eastern Liberia. These included MODEL's Thomas Yaya Nimely and the LURD NTLA Speaker George Dweh; CDC Chairman Orishall Gould, considered associated with MODEL; the party's Secretary-General, Lenn Eugene Nagbe, a former senior NPP executive and assistant to Moses Blah; and Sinoe's Milton Teahjay. Along with "progressive" "Americo-Liberian" Gabriel Bacchus Matthews, Teahjay was a leading organizer of the election campaign. Both individuals became key CDC spokespersons.

As his running mate, George Weah chose little known J. Rudolph Johnson from Lofa County, who had served as Foreign Minister under Samuel Doe (1987–1990). Yet individuals like former NPFL General Roland Cooper Kaine campaigned (and won) a Senate seat on a CDC platform too. Representing a different segment of Liberian society, Rufus Neufville, nominee of civil society youth organizations to the NTLA, stood as CDC representative and won.

After the first round of elections, two strong candidates joined Weah's campaign, i.e. Winston Tubman and Varney Sherman. The less successful aspirants Alhadji Kromah (2.8 percent), Togba Nah Tipoteh (2.3 percent), a veteran MOJA "progressive" politician from eastern Sinoe, Sekou Conneh and George Woah-Tee (both 0.6 percent) also supported George Weah, as did NPP vice-presidential candidate Somah Paygai and Moses Blah. The independent, newly elected legislators Zoe Pennue from LURD and Prince Johnson as well reinforced Weah's campaign.[194] All in all, Weah received support from markedly heterogeneous elites.

Yet George Weah's campaign lagged between the two rounds, which was epitomized by Weah arguing that he had already won the elections and could only lose through fraud. Creating the impression that people did not in fact need to vote for him may have been a severe campaign mistake.[195] To the surprise of many observers, Weah hardly succeeded to enlarge his constituency, and he notably lost the important Nimba County. Weah and

194 Prince Johnson had attempted to be nominated as candidate of the UP but was defeated in primaries. He then ran as an independent candidate and, suspecting that Johnson Sirleaf had a hand in his defeat, supported George Weah in 2005.

195 Most Counties experienced a significant drop in voter turnout between 9 and more than 20 percent. Montserrado and Grand Gedeh were notable exceptions.

many of his backers initially refused to accept the results, alleging fraud.[196] As concern for Liberian peace and stability mounted, Sekou Conneh was the first among Weah's prominent backers to call on him to accept his defeat. Eventually, Weah withdrew his complaint.

Both Johnson Sirleaf's and George Weah's campaign teams were decidedly heterogeneous. In some ways, both campaigns indicated that a "psychology of inclusive ownership" (Sawyer 2008, 186) developed in Liberian politics. In both cases, formation of campaign alliances was informed by personal ambitions, rather than collective party, class, ethnic or warring faction loyalties. Yet a degree of difference between the two campaign teams may have held the difference between success and defeat. Ellen Johnson Sirleaf's campaign team was strategically inclusive and relatively more coherent. Eminent and sometimes controversial personalities were strategically included to obtain votes in important areas and were centrally briefed on how to proceed. Johnson Sirleaf's campaign was significantly more strategic, professional and coherent.

Table 14: Presidential Election Results 2005: Top Contenders

Pos.	Pres. Candidate; VP Candidate	Party	Result Oct. 11, in %	Result Nov. 8, in %
1	E. Johnson Sirleaf; Joseph Boakai	Unity Party (UP)	19.8	60.2
2	George Weah, Rudolph Johnson	Congress for Democratic Change (CDC)	28.3	39.8
3	Ch. Brumskine; Amelia Ward	Liberty Party (LP)	13.9	n/appl.
4	Winston Tubman; Jeremiah Sulunteh,	National Democratic Party of Liberia (NDPL)	9.2	n/appl.
5	Varney Sherman; John Fania	Coalition for the Transformation of Liberia (COTOL)	7.8	n/appl.
6	Roland Massaquoi; Somah Paygai	National Patriotic Party (NPP)	4.1	n/appl.

Source: NEC (2005a; b)

196 The elections were judged free and fair by all observer missions and evidence of tampering in the Liberian 2005 elections was very weak (cf. Harris 2006).

4.4.3. The Legislature

This section analyzes the post-war evolution of the legislature between late 2005 and early 2012, focusing on the role of elites-of-war in parliament on the one hand and the governing Unity Party (UP) on the other. It empirically describes the relative strength of elites directly associated with the actors of Liberia's wars, investigates the reasons for their political trajectory and analyzes pertinent trends. Key among the latter is the relative loss of influence of warring party elites, the rise of professionals, and the growth of the presidential network of power.

As detailed in Table 17, 21 members of the 52nd legislature (elected in 2005) had been directly associated with a party to the conflict,[197] and 16 of these lawmakers had been associated with the former regime or the NPFL. This indicates that support for the Taylor regime was limited though not insignificant. Relative to the 94 seats in both Houses, conflict party elites assumed a relevant but far from dominant position. As Harris noted, compared to other African post-war countries Liberia's elections were characterized by a marked weakening of military actors (Harris 2006). In the 53rd legislature, the number of conflict party elites dropped to 16 and a sizeable share of these possessed significant civilian credentials. We can thus firstly observe a trend of decreasing importance of military credentials for political success. Further, many conflict party elites integrated into essentially civilian parties, rather than those that emerged out of armed factions. This indicates the second trend of fragmentation of former warring parties and the concomitant extension of the presidential network of power, although this needs to be qualified as the NPP remained remarkably strong. The NPP moderately increased its share of seats from seven to nine between the 2005 and 2011 elections and may remain a significant political force. Yet the ALCOP and NDPL obtained two seats each in 2005 but none in 2011, as did the PRODEM in both elections.

---

197 I define those having held positions in the Ex-GOL, the NPP, a rebel group or having done business requiring close cooperation with combatant units as associated. As Liberian elites often try to obscure their links to warring factions, this list might not be exhaustive despite extensive research. We can further assume that many more were indirectly linked. For instance, the 53rd Senate's president pro-tempore is the husband of a Special Advisor and key confidante of Charles Taylor. The advisor unsuccessfully ran as NPP candidate for a House seat in 2011. As her husband ran as an independent and did not hold office under Taylor, I counted him as not associated, although he is considered well-connected in NPP circles.

However a significant share of the post-war NPP parliamentarians were subaltern elites during Taylor's reign, indicating that the party may not fully subscribe to defending vested interests of the old guard. A number of reasons explain the loss of status of established elites and the parallel rise of younger ones. For one, the longer a government stays in power, the more important is social capital in the form of intra-elite connections to maintain status.[198] When the regime crumbles and the president is removed, this form of social capital is devalued. Further, due to the exclusive character of Taylor's clientelism, large parts of the population were not patrimonially integrated at the end of the Second War. Under these circumstances, lower level elites face little competition from more resourceful patrons, are likely to have better connections to prospective voters and can build their own networks. Further, the rise of subaltern elites was partly owed to the fact that senior former government officials placed their clients in the NTGL in order to be able to stand in the 2005 elections,[199] and these clients used their positions to accumulate power and independently maintain their newly won status.

By measure of the 2005 and 2011 legislative elections, Charles Taylor's government was the most legitimate of all the armed factions. The former government had commanded resources and consolidated relations of domination for well over a decade, entailing significant institutional continuity. Yet the NPP is best understood as an arena of reciprocal assimilation, not a stable, socially or ideologically homogeneous party. After Taylor was removed from office, centrifugal dynamics took precedence, given intense rivalries and expected negative consequences of openly associating with the former regime. However, relative assimilation during more than a decade of NPFL and NPP rule has created channels of communication and capacities for cooperation that are regularly made use of in Liberia's post-war democracy.

Regional variations in the electoral appeal of warring party elites are instructive concerning the support for warring parties. Judging from the post-war electoral success of its elites, the Charles Taylor government was best implanted in western and central Liberia, in Montserrado, Margibi, Bong, Nimba and Grand Bassa. The area is largely congruous with the core

198 This applies in particular when a president discourages the establishment of comprehensive patronage networks by his clients in order to prevent potential rivals from accumulating power, as Charles Taylor did (cf. Reno 1998; 2000).

199 Interview with senior Taylor government official in Margibi, Mar. 30, 2012.

areas of "Greater Liberia", over which Taylor exercised comparatively stringent control. The only place in the easternmost Counties where the Taylor government enjoyed significant support was Maryland. This can be explained by local rivalries exacerbated during the 1990s war. While large parts of the east sided with forces emanating from the Doe regime, their rivals, among them major clans of Maryland, sided with the NPFL.

The careers of a few prominent war-associated elites are instructive concerning dynamics of electoral success. Jewel Howard-Taylor most strongly profited from Charles Taylor's charisma reflecting on her,[200] but connections and resources dating back to the Taylor regime also proved relevant. Traditional Poro and Sande authorities had recommended voting for her,[201] and Nimba may have been one of the few places where the ex-GOL strategy of occupying the NTGL Interior Ministry in order to maintain privileged relations with Chiefs paid off. Further, Howard-Taylor was appreciated for the relief work she had supported in the County during the Taylor regime. Similar to many other wives of African heads of state, Howard-Taylor represented the compassionate, humanitarian side of the ruler's reign. If she will remain a political force by strengthening these civilian credentials remains to be seen. By contrast, Nimba County Senator Adolphus "General Peanut Butter" Dolo, hailed for having retaken Ganta from LURD, was almost exclusively elected on the basis of military charisma in 2005. As legislator, he earned a reputation for a "military", authoritarian approach to his constituency.[202] In the 2011 elections he came fifth, losing his position to a US diaspora businessman from Prince Johnson's party.

Prince Johnson's Senate landslide election victory in Nimba was probably the most irritating aspect of the 2005 elections to Liberian and outside observers alike. Prince Johnson ran his election campaign "largely on a

200 Focus Group Interviews, Gbarnga, Bong County, Feb. 2–3, 2007

201 Amos Sawyer (2008) emphasized Howard-Taylor's traditional status and relief work in Bong as reasons for the support from traditional authorities. Howard-Taylor's mother's family comes from a chiefly lineage based in Bong. However, as her father hailed from Lofa, focus group respondents did not consider her a native of Bong and did not appear to appreciate her traditional credentials. Matters involving Poro and Sande are not easily disclosed to outsiders and the role of traditional authorities in the elections was thus—unsurprisingly—not discussed. Notwithstanding, there a no reasons to doubt respondents' assertions that they voted for Howard-Taylor because she was considered to represent her husband (Focus Group Interviews, Gbarnga, Feb. 2/3, 2007).

202 Interview with former Dolo legislative office staff, Monrovia, March 7, 2012.

platform of protecting the people of Nimba County against the Krahn" (Ellis 2007b, 116; cf. Sawyer 2008, 195). It is hardly surprising that Johnson's military charisma appealed to voters in this County, which was at the center of armed conflict for sustained periods. At the same time, he adapted to the new situation by partly converting his military into clerical charisma, stressing his religious credentials as a born-again Christian preacher and arguing he was a "transformed man" (IRIN July 28, 2003; Harris 2006, 391). Before the election, Prince Johnson had been making a living as an evangelist preacher in exile in Nigeria. He further campaigned on a populist platform and presented himself as man of the people, denouncing educated people as ineffective or exploitative.[203]

In contrast to most other elites of war, Prince Johnson prospects for a sustained political career were good. He founded his own *National Union for Democratic Progress* (NUDP) political party, ran as presidential candidate in 2011 and obtained 68 percent in Nimba. Johnson fared exceptionally badly in other Counties but Nimba votes sufficed to secure twelve percent and the third place on the national level. In addition, candidates from his party won seven of the ten Nimba seats contested in the election. These, however, generally are locally influential businesspeople not known to have been associated with warring factions. Prince Johnson succeeded to build a powerful network among Nimba elites and is reputed to maintain respectful relations with chiefs. While still widely considered an authoritarian and erratic character, Prince Johnson succeeded much better than "General Peanut Butter" to integrate into civilian politics.[204]

In Grand Gedeh, support for war elites similarly was fading. In 2005, all three representatives and one of the senators elected in Grand Gedeh had their backgrounds in either LURD or MODEL. Since Samuel Doe, the integration of the region into the state of Liberia has taken place through the military, increasing the reputation of violent careers. Being a center of conflict with populations feeling insecure, military power was widely appreciated by grassroots supporters. Further, focus group interviews in Grand Gedeh suggested that the rebel candidates were considered as caring relatively well for their communities in material terms (cf. Sawyer

203 However, House election results in Nimba indicated that careers in the educational and academic sectors were highly valued by the electorate (cf. Konrad Adenauer Foundation 2006).

204 Notwithstanding, NUDP cohesiveness was extremely weak and Prince Johnson's network was vulnerable to fragmentation.

2008, 196).[205] Yet although all rebel representatives stood in the legislative elections of 2011, only one of them was reelected. The individual is a nephew to Samuel Doe, was a "notorious death squad leader" (ICG 2003b, 21) under his presidency, is locally prominent and well-experienced in Liberian politics. However, former MODEL leader Thomas Yaya Nimely obtained 22 percent in Grand Gedeh's Senate election in 2011, coming third. This relative success may have more to do with post-war efforts at building a clientele, probably helped by financial opportunities occasioned by his NTGL position as Foreign Minister. Monrovia-based Nimely is reported to spend much of his time at his small rubber plantation of 45 hectares, establishing himself as a local Big Man.

The lack of cohesion of rebel groups and conflicts within the leadership made themselves felt in parliamentary success, too. The official leaders of both LURD and MODEL used their discretion over appointments to place cronies in the transitional regime or sell positions (cf. Lidow 2011, 193–208). Several lawmakers thus made their way into politics as a consequence of a loose affiliation with warring factions. These included Lofa County Representative Malliam Jallabah, a down-to-earth businesswoman first nominated to the NTLA by the LURD, and Bomi Junior Senator Richard Devine, nominated by MODEL to his previous LPRC Deputy Managing Director post. Both managed to be elected in 2005, Jallabah representing ALCOP and Devine representing COTOL, but lost their position in 2011.

Political success of parliamentarians in Liberia revolves around patronage but cannot be reduced to simple vote buying. Voters essentially elect leaders on the basis of their estimate of how deep ties to the constituency are and how willing they judge elites to care for them. In the process of evaluating candidates, diverse criteria are employed and diverse people of influence intervene, obscuring the overarching dynamics (cf. Sawyer 2008). In most focus group interviews I conducted, interviewees declared their communities had received some kind of assistance through their lawmakers before the election, for instance furniture or zinc roofing for schools. Further, most parliamentarians I interviewed found themselves inundated with requests for assistance and declared to spend more on their constituencies than they received in salary and allowances combined.

---

205 Focus Group Interviews in Zwedru and surrounding areas, Grand Gedeh, March, 13–16, 2007.

Several of the elected "warriors" had had access to significant financial means during the transition period as a result of their NTGL positions, as Table 17 illustrates. A few had access to campaign resources because of private business success. For instance, General Peanut Butter had established his own *North Star* conglomerate, which included a security service with branch offices in several of Liberia's Counties as well as a scrap metal firm active at the former LAMCO mine.[206] Parliamentary office powers further provide access to financial means. Salaries and allowances of lawmakers add up to roughly 10,000 USD for senators and 5,000 USD for representatives. Legislators by law are involved in the—often profitable—management of community forest resources (cf. Panel of Experts 12/2011, 62). Further, it is widely alleged that parliamentary decisions, from confirmation of presidential appointees to ratification of natural resource exploitation contracts, are strongly influenced by cash payments. In one of the most widely discussed cases, the state-owned *National Oil Company of Liberia* (NOCAL) and a foreign company bribed lawmakers in order to have a crude oil concession ratified (Global Witness 2011). Lawmakers in addition have oversight over the notoriously ineffective *County Development Funds* foreign concessions have to establish (cf. Siakor Mar. 1, 2012).

Lawmakers generally should thus have means to establish patronage networks. Yet few could convert their control over resources into sustained electoral success. In 2011, only two of the 15 senators were re-elected (one of whom had been in parliament since 2009 only), although most tried to defend their post. Similarly, only 22 of the representatives elected in 2005 were re-elected in 2011. This translates into turnover rates of 87 and 70 percent, respectively. These are extremely high values, but young democracies often have elevated rates of turnover (e.g. Marenco dos Santos 2006). This indicates weak ties between grassroots and political elites and a lack of legitimacy in Liberia (and young democracies in general).[207] We may as well conclude that electoral defeat of war elites has

---

206 By the lawmakers own account, *North Star* employed some 400 people (Konrad Adenauer Foundation 2006, 91).

207 Generally, turnover rates are positively associated with instable democracies and instable party systems in particular, and these are associated with deficits in legitimacy. Yet there are a number of other factors. The redrawing of constituencies before the 2011 elections contributed to this turnover rate. Further, in some areas of Liberia, there is a pattern of alternating sub-ethnic representation. Clan leaders thus endorse candidates of their own or neighboring clans according to a time-honored formula (Sawyer 2008). Consequently, even well-performing, popular lawmakers may fail to be re-elected, although they often

much to do with general features of Liberia's democracy. It is not only that war elites find it hard to convert military power resources into civilian ones—a process considered particularly challenging (cf. Manning 2004; cf. Zeeuw 2008)—but Liberian elites in general have difficulties in adapting to democratic competition.[208]

However, the major trend between the 2005 and 2011 elections was a drastic rise in representation of the UP, which increased the number of seats in both Houses from twelve to 35 (see Tables 15 and 16). The UP gained strongly when it merged with COTOL in 2009 and emerged even stronger from the 2011 elections. On the part of COTOL, the merger was strongly motivated by the—partly economic—benefits of power. Similarly, the strong showing of the UP in the 2011 legislative elections is most plausibly explained by better access of its candidates to resources. It remains to be seen whether the UP's essentially civilian and often professional elites succeed better to consolidate their positions. The legislature became more favorably disposed toward the executive over time, and it appeared that the economic means and disciplinary opportunities offered by political power allowed the president to expand her network of power. A key turn of events which may be indicative of executive-legislative relations was the removal of the first Speaker of the House of Representatives, Edwin Snowe.

According to the constitution, the position is the third-highest in Liberia. Yet in general, the Houses' leadership positions are powerful and have influence on lawmakers because they allocate positions in the legislature's committees, which define opportunities for the private appropriation of values. Snowe was widely popular in Montserrado, disposed of large financial means, was considered a possible future president of Liberia and an outspoken critic of the president Snowe had won the speakership election with a 2/3 majority, for which his personal wealth quite likely was helpful. Yet hardly a year later in early 2007, 46 representatives or a 2/3 majority signed a resolution declaring Snowe impeached, stating he had "clandestinely attempted to conduct the foreign affairs of the Republic as manifested in engaging in discussions intended to initiate the resumption

try. However, Liberians frequently were indeed deeply disappointed in their lawmakers (Focus Group Interviews in Lofa, Nimba, Bong and Grand Gedeh Counties, Jan. to March 2007).

208 As well, in Liberia's anomic situation, voters may have unrealistic expectations in lawmakers.

[of (sic)] diplomatic ties with Taiwan contrary to the One-China Policy of the Government of Liberia" (House of Representatives Jan. 16, 2007).[209]

A little later, two lawmakers signed a declaration that they had been paid 5,000 dollars each by three other lawmakers "who we know do not have money" in order to impeach the Speaker, and demanded that their signatures be deleted from the resolution.[210] One of the lawmakers alleged to have made the payment was Alex Tyler, who was later elected new Speaker. Two well-placed sources independent of each other reported that up to 250,000 dollars had changed hands before the impeachment of Snowe.[211]

Table 15: Strongest Parties in the 52nd Legislature

Party	Senate (30 Seats)	House (64 Seats)	Both Houses (94 Seats)
CDC	3	15	18
COTOL	7	8	15
UP	4	8	12
LP	3	9	12
Independent	3	7	10
NPP	3	4	7

Source: NEC (2005a)

Table 16: Strongest Parties in the 53rd Legislature

Party	Senate (30 Seats)	House (73 Seats)	Both Houses (103 Seats)
UP	10	25	35
CDC	3	11	14
Independent	2	9	11
NPP	6	3	9
LP	2	6	8
NUDP	2	6	8

Source: NEC (2005a; 2011)

209 While the Taylor government had recognized Taiwan, the Johnson Sirleaf government privileged relations with the People's Republic of China.

210 The declaration was reprinted in, for instance, the Inquirer (March 27, 2007). The two lawmakers declared that they had accepted the money only to serve as evidence to prove that the impeachment was fraudulent.

211 Interviews in Monrovia, February and March 2007.

Already some two weeks earlier, Edwin Snowe had publicly accused Johnson Sirleaf of holding secret meetings with members of the House of Representatives in order to orchestrate his removal (Heritage Dec. 29, 2006), and he maintained his accusations throughout (Africa Confidential Feb. 2, 2007). After the impeachment, the *International Contact Group on Liberia* showed itself deeply worried, and demanded that "all allegations of bribery of the members of the House be investigated in an independent and transparent manner, in accordance with international best practice" (Inquirer Mar. 27, 2007). Despite international pressure and a public outcry, the issue was not conclusively investigated. Snowe eventually resigned a few weeks after the scandal had broken.[212]

A little later, a photo surfaced on the internet showing the Minister of State for Presidential Affairs in a compromising position with two women (cf. Newswatch Apr. 22, 2007). The minister, a key confidante of Johnson Sirleaf, then alleged that Snowe had earlier "unsuccessfully attempted to blackmail me by offering me the photograph [...] if I would [...] stop opposing Mr. Snowe and help find a way to resolve Mr. Snowe's political difficulties" (printed in: Analyst Feb. 20, 2007). He subsequently resigned. Thus, while involvement of the presidency in the impeachment of Snowe was neither seriously investigated nor proven, the central player in the affair clearly believed Johnson Sirleaf to have orchestrated his removal. His successor was affiliated with the COTOL party that later joined the UP.[213]

212 The Supreme Court annulled Snowe's impeachment for procedural errors (cf. Public Agenda Jan. 31, 2007). As lawmakers were about to vote on the resolution for a second time and looked set to respect formal procedures, Snowe resigned.

213 In 2008, the opposition Senate President pro-temp faced impeachment proceedings for his involvement in a dubious car acquisition on behalf of the Senate and he eventually resigned in consequence 2009. His successor was a UP member formerly affiliated with COTOL, too. The Senate President of the 53rd legislature, an independent, was also Johnson Sirleaf's preference among the two contenders.

Table 17: Associates of Warring Parties in the Legislature

#	52nd Legislature	(Re-) elected 2011?	Party (2005/2011)	Association with Warring Parties	NTGL Position
1	Senator	no	ALCOP/ALCOP	ULIMO-K; LURD Major	n/appl.
2	Senator	no	APD/APD	Director of Cabinet	Chairman Advisor
3	Senator	no	CDC/ULD	Ex-GOL; NPFL General, *Bush Marines*; NPP MoP	NTLA MoP
4	Senator (since 2009)	yes	CDC/CDC (since 2009)	NPFL, *Wild Geese* Unit	n/appl.
5	Senator	no	COTOL/UP	INPFL; NPFL; Ex-GOL General, *Strike Force*	n/appl.
6	n/s	Senator	Ind./NPP	NPFL; NPP Sec.-Gen.; Ex-GOL Public Corp. MD	NPA Board
7	Senator	n/appl.	Ind./NUDP	INPFL Leader	n/appl.
8	Senator; pro-temp	n/appl.	NDPL/NDPL	LURD Sec.-Gen.	Comptroller-General; Finance Ministry
9	Senator	n/appl.	NDPL/LP	Ex-GOL; *Anti-Terrorist Unit* Paymaster	Adjutant to AFL *Former Commanding General*

Table 17: Associates of Warring Parties in the Legislature (continued)

#	52nd Legislature	(Re-)elected 2011?	Party (2005/2011)	Association with Warring Parties	NTGL Position
10	n/s	Senator	NPL/NPP	NPP Senator	n/appl.
11	Senator	n/appl.	NPP/NPP	Ex-GOL First Lady; Chair *National Ex-Combatants Commission*	n/appl.
12	Senator	no	NPP/NPP	NPFL; NPP Representative	NTLA MoP
13	Senator	n/appl.	NPP/NPP	AFL (1980s); NPFL; NPP Representative	NTLA MoP
14	n/s	Senator	NPP/NPP	NPFL, NPP Representative	NTLA MoP
15	n/c	Senator	NPP/NPP	Ex-GOL Supt.	Minister of Internal Affairs
16	Senator	no	UP/UP	Ex-GOL Chief Justice	Legal Counsel; Justice Ministry
17	n/c	Senator	–/UP	NPFL Gen., Logging corp. CEO with ex-GOL militia	n/appl.
18	Representative	no	CDC /CDC	NPFL; NPP Assist. Sec.-Gen.	n/appl.

Table 17: Associates of Warring Parties in the Legislature (continued)

#	52nd Legislature	(Re-)elected 2011?	Party (2005/2011)	Association with Warring Parties	NTGL Position
19	Representative	no	CDC/CDC	MODEL General	Insp.-Gen. of Commerce Ministry
20	Representative Speaker	yes	Ind./Ind.	Driver of NPFL Elite; NPP Youth Chair; Ex-GOL LPRC Dep. MD	LPRC MD
21	Representative	yes	Ind./Ind.	AFL (1980s); LURD General	LPRC Dep. MD
22	Representative	no	NDM/NDC	LURD	NTLA MoP
23	Representative	no	NPP/NPP	*NPFL; Ex-GOL Special Operations Division* Director	Assist. Minister of Justice
24	Representative	yes	NPP/NPP	Rubber trader, NPFL protection	n/appl.
25	Representative	yes	NPP/NPP	NPFL; Ex-GOL Assist. Min. Labor	NTLA MoP
26	Representative	yes	NPP/NPP	NPP Activist	NTLA MoP

n/c—not candidate; n/s—not successful; n/appl.—not applicable

Source: Author's Data

4.5. Liberia under Johnson Sirleaf: Rebuilding the State?

The takeover of the presidency by Ellen Johnson Sirleaf constituted a break in Liberia's political history. For about a generation, military actors had occupied the heights of state power. Johnson Sirleaf represented a vastly different segment of Liberian society, i.e. one of international professionals rooted in the historic establishment of Liberia. The basis of her claim to power differed in several respects from that of her recent predecessors, among the most important of which was the form and nature of personal connections. Since 1980, personal political connections had centered on ensuring loyalty of militarized segments of society, who had constituted the most important social forces backing the successive regimes. Johnson Sirleaf's power, in contrast, was largely based on civilian forces, in particular an elite that owed their positions to success in the private, academic, and multilateral public sectors. However, the extent to which Johnson Sirleaf could introduce innovations was restricted. First, forces which had emerged in the past 26 years continued to hold influence. Second, in as much as these forces could be overcome, the direction of changes would not necessarily conform to conventional notions of progress, as social patterns and norms of behavior formed in the last 190 years (or more) continued to shape Liberian politics (cf. Yoder 2003).

This section analyzes patterns of rule that characterized the first term of office of President Johnson Sirleaf. Delivering a comprehensive assessment of the post-war evolution of political patterns in Liberia, however, necessitates reducing complexity and selecting examples that represent the broader trends. In writing this section, I have tried to strike a balance between providing a superficial overview about general developments and narrating events in great detail in order to illustrate dynamics at work. The major arguments of this chapter are structured similar to the analyses of specific configurations of power above. The first part identifies personal patterns in the new administration by investigating practices of staffing of senior executive positions, emphasizing the importance of political loyalty and personal connections. In the second part, I give an overview of major developments relating to the administration of power. In a subsection, anti-corruption efforts of the Johnson Sirleaf government are critically investigated, as these represented the most explicit efforts at bureaucratization. Finally, I investigate patterns of control over the economy and the means of financing political power.

The first part analyses a temporarily very important but transitional phenomenon, i.e. the financing of the state apparatus by tapping donor-related capital imports. The second part analyzes developments in resource control, which are indicative of future patterns of the exercise of political power and access to wealth and privilege.

4.5.1. Anatomy of a Post-War Regime

As has been shown, Ellen Johnson Sirleaf's election victory was to an important extent due to alliances with a variety of individuals representing diverse social forces. Her government strongly reflected these alliances, and was as heterogeneous (and inclusive) as the coalition that had supported her. Johnson Sirleaf took care that her appointments could be justified with respect to qualification. Although poor human capital endowment of Liberia often affected the staffing of senior executive positions, Johnson Sirleaf's government was the most qualified one Liberia ever had.

Yet appointments reflected political realities in that senior political personnel represented important regional constituencies or important segments of Liberian society on the one hand and support Johnson Sirleaf had received during the campaign on the other. For instance, Joseph Korto, who had brought important Nimba votes, was named Education Minister, Jeremiah Sulunteh had helped to win Bong and was made Transport Minister, and Luseni Donzo, a Mandingo with close links to the NMC leadership,[214] was given the Public Works portfolio. Peter Bonner Jallah, a long-time UP member who had been suspected of links to the NPFL in the 1990s and had shortly been Minister of Justice under Charles Taylor, became Minister of National Security. Jackson E. Doe, the relative of Samuel Doe who had held senior positions in the AFL, ULIMO and LURD, was made Minister of Postal Affairs. LURD's Kabineh Ja'neh was appointed Associate Justice at the Supreme Court of Liberia.

Some of those nominated had been prominent civil society activists well connected among Liberia's professionals, in particular the widely respected human rights activists Samuel Kofi Woods named Minister of Labor, Justice Minister Frances Johnson Morris, and Solicitor General

214 Musa Bility, Chairman of the NMC, was made Chairman of the Board of Directors of the NPA.

Tiawon Gongloe. Others were international professionals, for instance former World Bank Country Director Antoinette Sayeh, the first Minister of Finance, and Olubanke King Akerele, a former senior UNDP official given responsibility for the Ministry of Commerce and Industry.

A significant share of government officials had a background in the "Americo-Liberian" segment of society and had been residing in the US for extended periods, which later gave rise to allegations that Johnson Sirleaf brought back to power the old elite and favored friends from the US diaspora. The US diaspora had provided the bulk of Johnson Sirleaf's campaign finances (Johnson Sirleaf 2009, 247). Yet these officials are better understood as international professionals, many of whom had been pushed into exile as a consequence of the 1980s coup. The new LPRC Managing Director Harry Greaves had grown up in Johnson Sirleaf's environment and had later been successful as a financial administration expert in the US. King Akerele was a granddaughter of former President Charles D.B. King and had served in senior government positions before her international career. Johnson Sirleaf's Agriculture Minister Florence Chenoweth (2009–), who had held the same post under Tolbert, had worked in various international positions after the coup. The Mandingo Luseni Donzo had a quite similar background. Previously Minister of Rural Development under Tolbert, he had in exile in the US become a senior manager of a large engineering company. If individuals from Liberia's old establishment re-emerge, it is largely because of the superior opportunities to acquire professional skills and experience their social background had offered.

Against the background of instability, the need to re-build governing capacity and enormous tasks ahead, the president needed a network of personally loyal officials. As the private use of office powers is deeply embedded in Liberian political culture, transgressions were to be expected and a "zero tolerance" policy on corruption would have destabilized the government and eroded trust and support of the officials she needed. Johnson Sirleaf adopted a quiet approach to disciplining officials.

By mid-2007, the Panel of Experts noted that "few civil servants have been penalized [for corruption], and there does not appear to be a strong, coherent policy beyond the President's inaugural address to implement such penalties" (Panel of Experts 06/2007, 9). Failures of officials were dealt with behind closed doors, if at all. In several government reshuffles during the president's first years in office, senior officials lost their positions or were transferred to other ones. By June 2010, only three of the 15 most important ministries were still headed by the same person who had occupied the post in late 2006.[215] Some of these changes in government r-eportedly had their background in abuse of office (cf. Liberian Express Mar. 26, 2007b). In severe cases, the president appeared to "request the resignation of the suspected wrongdoers" (Analyst Feb. 23, 2010). In particular, the resignations of the first Minister for Agriculture and the Minister of Internal Affairs Ambullai Johnson, a cousin of Johnson Sirleaf, were considered such cases (New Democrat Feb. 19, 2010). Indeed, Ambullai Johnson was reportedly sacked on the spot when the president came to his house warming party, realizing he had built a multi-million-dollars mansion incompatible with his income (Africa Confidential July 22, 2011).

In less severe cases, senior officials were given a second chance and merely transferred to less lucrative positions as disciplinary measure. Thus, the first NPA Managing Director was transferred to the post of Deputy Minister of Public Works amid allegations of malpractices. The first Minister of Public Works resigned against speculations of wrongdoing and was subsequently appointed Infrastructure Advisor of the president (Analyst Feb. 23, 2010; Africa Confidential May 14, 2010).[216] Yet in several cases extremely controversial figures were publicly backed by Johnson Sirleaf, e.g. LPRC Managing Director Harry Greaves and Minister of State for Economic and Legal Affairs Morris Saytumah (see below).

Prosecution of accused officials remained the exception and the case of Information Minister Laurence Bropleh, suspended from office in October 2009, is paradigmatic. Bropleh had been one of Johnson Sirleaf's closest confidantes. As an audit by the *General Auditing Commission* (GAC) was ongoing, the president took the initiative for sanctioning and requested the Auditor General to investigate the ministry's payroll (Analyst Oct. 16, 2009). The GAC "concluded that the Minister [was] accountable for misappropriating for his personal benefits the total remuneration of dollars 262,772.73" (New Democrat Feb. 15, 2010). The suspended Minister resigned reluctantly. In spring 2010, Bropleh became the first Minister of

---

215 As most important ministries I consider those led by "key ministers" as specified by the Economist Intelligence Unit (EIU 06/2010, 5). The ministers still in their original positions were Joseph Korto (Education), Brownie Samukai (Defence) and Eugene Shannon (Lands, Mines and Energy).

216 The individual later resigned from this post, too, probably on request of the president (New Democrat Feb. 8, 2011).

the Johnson Sirleaf government to be charged by a court (Analyst Feb. 23, 2010). The prosecution however did not show up for the trial and the minister was found not guilty for lack of evidence (New Dawn Aug. 16, 2012). Liberia's elite, including large parts of the judicial personnel, is organized in social clubs—the Freemasons and the *United Brothers' Friendship* (UBF) in particular—and members shield each other from judicial prosecution or similar sanctions. It is likely impossible to secure convictions against elites *without* the intervention of the president.

Two contradictory tendencies characterized Johnson Sirleaf's human resource management for the first years. On the one hand, reshuffles affecting senior positions in the state administration and in state-owned companies were a pertinent feature. On the other, a core circle of officials was maintained and publicly backed despite significant national and international criticisms. Roughly for the first three years, the core circle of officials was relatively large. The resignations of key Johnson Sirleaf confidantes Christopher Toe and Ambullai Johnson as well as the sacking of Harry Greaves, all between 2009 and 2010, signaled a retrenchment of Johnson Sirleaf's inner circle. By 2010, Johnson Sirleaf's core circle was regarded to have shrunk to a few personalities, in particular comprising her sister "Aunty Jennie" Bernard,[217] her brother-in-law and then-*National Security Advisor* Estrada Bernard, a minister under Tolbert, and Minister of State for Economic and Legal Affairs Morris Saytumah (Africa Confidential May 14, 2010; cf. Johnson Sirleaf 2009).

In sum, Johnson Sirleaf's first government reflected the support she had received during the campaign. The president further tried to create a core of personally loyal officials. Transfers and resignations were the major means to discipline failing officials. In consequence, her government was characterized by much greater continuity than if a "zero tolerance" policy on corruption had been applied. Consolidation of state domination first of all proceeded as the consolidation and extension of a personal network of power. There was hardly any alternative to this approach. In order to establish authority, the president needed loyal officials, and given the dysfunctional state of institutional checks, personal ties had to substitute for them. Personal political networks can be constructed much faster than institutions and they thus respond to the exigencies of post-war situations.

217 Jennie Bernard had been a key member of Johnson Sirleaf's campaign team (cf. Johnson Sirleaf 2009, 246–273).

4.5.2. Major Issues in Institutional Development

It is beyond the scope of this thesis to present a comprehensive review of bureaucratic capacity building efforts in Liberia. Instead, this subsection introduces selected Liberian government efforts—generally financially supported and rewarded by foreign actors—intended to strengthen rationality in state administration. It provides an overview of institutional development by shortly describing efforts and trends in sectors central to the organization of state domination. I start by outlining general issues of public sector development in order to clarify basic problems and provide an idea of the institutional environment for reform. I subsequently portray the evolution of specific institutions and shortly reflect on the security sector before analyzing in greater detail the evolution of official policies intended to strengthen legal-rational administration.

Generally, capacity building programs were concerned with the prerequisites and essentials of bureaucratic governance. From Monrovia's Ministries to hinterland institutions, extensive, mostly UNMIL-led projects to increase administrative capacity were implemented. These included identifying regulations and laws the institutions were formally expected to implement, research internal regulation manuals, compile available information, and train employees accordingly. Significant resources were also spent on equipping offices with the most basic equipment. During the war, most of the essentials of bureaucratic governance had been destroyed, and much of the remaining office equipment was looted by NTGL officials and personnel. Considering Liberia's extremely small base, increases in bureaucratic capacity could only be slight but nevertheless represented relative bureaucratization.

An issue pervading the entire state administration and showing the extent to which patrimonial patterns were engrained was the public sector salary structure. At the takeover of Johnson Sirleaf, the minimum salary in the state administration, effectively the salary of the majority of civil servants, was 15 dollars - an amount insufficient to pay rent, food and transportation for a single person, not to speak of a family. Official basic salaries for senators were about 70 dollars and senior ministers drew substantially less than 100 dollar. On all levels of the administration, salaries may have been considerably increased by allowances granted in non-transparent ways,[218] but there was little doubt that, by and large, public sector wages were considerably below private sector wages for unskilled labor, which varied between 50 and 100 dollars in Monrovia. The attraction of government offices thus lay in the opportunities these offered for extra-legal private gain. Major features characterizing state administration consequently were the exercise of powers according to private interests of civil service personnel (rather than the ruler) and the granting of rights to private appropriation to generate legitimacy among staff, reducing effective powers of the central ruler.

Civil service salaries were significantly raised annually during Johnson Sirleaf's rule. International donors provided means for allowances, increasing income of ministers to competitive levels (cf. IMF 2007, 5). These salary increases constituted a precondition for more rational administration but would need to be backed up by systematic disciplinary action oriented towards meritocracy, which was crucially lacking.

A central piece of Johnson Sirleaf's reforms intended to professionalize the state administration was a reduction in the number of state employees. This reduction, termed "right-sizing" by the government and "down-sizing" by its critics, was deeply unpopular among the politically active population in Liberia. During the NTGL period, public sector employment increased massively. When Johnson Sirleaf took over, the public sector was in a dilapidated state, with hardly any trace of bureaucratic ethos or remnants of meritocracy left. Upon coming into office, Finance Minister Antoinette Sayeh tried to dismiss the entire staff working in the institution. Intense lobbying at the presidency, however, forced her to back down after a few days. In the Finance Ministry, "right-sizing" was then pursued relatively vigorously, and by mid-2007, 372 employees had officially been retired (Government of Liberia July 17, 2007). However, the process of retirement exhibited patrimonial principles. At least some senior executives

218 For instance, allowances for senators were around US$1,500 per month (Panel of Experts 12/2006, 36). In the Ministry of Gender and Development, the Comptroller was allocated allowances of some US$1,000 a month and a middle-level Planning Officer some US$215. A *Liberian Anti-Corruption Commission* (LACC) investigation found that the minister subtracted US$200 from the higher and US$165 from the lower amount. The minister justified her actions by stating that the *Civil Service Agency* had assured her allowances could be allocated in a discretionary way (New Democrat Dec. 20, 2009). Allowances historically played an outstanding role in the organization of Liberian patrimonialism, and were used for personally rewarding and punishing state employees.

sold the privilege not to be dismissed to employees.[219] Yet petty corruption in the Finance Ministry reduced significantly in the coming years.[220]

New civil service employments had to be approved by the *Civil Service Agency* and the *Bureau of the Budget* in order to increase chances that staffing would reflect central government policies. There were numerous attempts to circumvent this regulation but central control over staffing in the public sector increased markedly. Despite adaptability of patrimonial patterns and consequent ambiguous effects of reform, staffing in the public sector was characterized by relative rationalization.

Formalization centered on two sectors indispensable for state power, the security sector and revenue generation. As has been said, the state's police and army had effectively been disbanded. When new security forces were established, former personnel were eligible for recruitment, provided that they met qualification requirements and were not accused of human rights violations. The new *Liberia National Police* (LNP) force was (incoherently) trained by the UN Police. Even high ranking officers of the former police had to undergo basic training. Police salaries were massively increased, from 17 to a 92 dollars minimum (Malan 2008, 51). "Major progress" was that the police was "actually deployed and doing some visible policing without instilling fear in communities" (ibid, 54). The UN Police trainer described the two biggest problems in the new LNP as "low morale and poor discipline, on the one hand, and extremely poor leadership and management, on the other" (ibid., 55).

The new police could quickly be seen extorting bribes from motorists throughout Monrovia and the hinterland, and this highly visible and easily preventable form of corruption went unchallenged. The first Police Chief was dismissed in 2009 for corruption in the purchase of uniforms. The list of police failures is extensive, and large parts of the Monrovian population suspect the police of systematically colluding with armed robbers. In early 2013, the Deputy Police Chief argued that the average police salary of 150 dollars was much too low and invited corruption (New Dawn Jan. 10, 2013). Yet these salaries are competitive and most Monrovian families have to survive on considerably less.[221] As hardly any civil service officials were

---

219 Confidential interview with a civil servant who had paid his boss.

220 Communications with businesspeople, Feb.–Apr. 2012.

221 Liberia's most expensive and best-reputed private security service pays its guards some US$150. It demands higher qualifications of its employees than the police, staff are subjected to comprehensive disciplinary control and and take risks to a similar or greater

penalized for corruption despite widespread reports of administrative malpractices, a similar attitude appeared to pervade the entire state administration. Social acceptance of "corruption" is high in Liberia and standards of bureaucratic discipline are extremely low. When Johnson Sirleaf tried to impose a *Code of Conduct* informed by international standards on public officials, Minister of Foreign Affairs Augustine Ngafuan urged her publicly "not to transform public service into public torture" (Ngafuan 2012). Taking into account that Ngafuan is one of the more reform-minded ministers, the statement indicates that the rationalization of the public sector meets enormous resistance.

The creation of the new *Armed Forces of Liberia* proceeded significantly slower than that of the police force, often due to late, unreliable funding from the US (Malan 2008, 41). Recruitment and training was funded by the US Government (cf. CPA 2003) and outsourced to *DynCorp International* and *Pacific Architects and Engineers* (PAE). Educational, physical fitness and crime record standards for recruits were relatively high; about 75 percent of applicants were rejected, compared to only 10 percent for the LNP force (ibid., 32). There was some progress in the army evolving into a formally regulated institution markedly different from Taylor's system of paramilitaries (Malan 2008; cf. Gberie 2009). However, bureaucratization is a long-term process and there were severe deficits. Soldiers often did not even receive their budgeted rice rations, giving rise to accusations of corruption against the Defense Minister (New Democrat Apr. 25, 2011), lived in squalid conditions, morale was low and the force was hardly functional by 2013. The historic army, were "men, women, and children [were] living as one happy family in the military posts" (Christy 1931, 536) apparently partly informed the minister's and soldiers' vision of the force (New Democrat Feb. 14, 2013). Presidential security continued to be provided by UNMIL and the *State Security Services* (SSS) paramilitary, recruited on the basis of personal recommendations of close Johnson Sirleaf loyalists.

The major success of the government and its showpiece evidence to demonstrate its commitment to strengthen administrative rationality by fighting corruption was a massive increase in state revenue. Johnson Sirleaf's strategy to rationalize governance essentially rested on reducing op-

---

extent than non-elite police forces. Most private security guards in Liberia earn substantially less than police (Askenazi/Boemcken 2011, 47).

portunities for embezzlement by centralizing and better documenting revenue flows, including by computerizing financial administration.

Revenues rose from 77 million dollars in 2005 to an estimated 672 million dollars in financial year 2012/13. The revenue structure remained broadly similar. Internal taxes contributed a little more than half of revenues. About 1/3 of these were corporate taxes, yet a relative decline could be observed. Taxes on international trade provided somewhat less than half of government income, but accrued overwhelmingly from imports. Export duties were negligible (Ministry of Finance 2008; 2009; 2012).

Compared to the previous regimes, management of government finances through formal channels increased tremendously. Further, the revenue structure deviated considerably from the classic Liberian one, and taxing of domestic economic activity was relatively important. While this should increase incentives to build a strong financial administration, the state's post-war revenue base was unsustainable. For one, Liberia had a huge trade deficit, implying that (taxed) imports could not be financed without the capital import occasioned by the intervention force. Further, exports were expected to pick up growth strongly in future and dominate state revenue (cf. EIU 06/2010). Further, domestic production was very low and could, consequently, hardly be taxed. This implies internal taxes were primarily derived from the construction and services sectors fuelled by the international presence. Thus, state revenue was indirectly financed by the donors paying the intervention force. As Liberia's tax structure could be expected to be transformed, it was anything but certain that these successes in tax revenue administration would be sustained. As I will explain later, developments in export commodity management gave hardly any reasons for optimism.

4.5.3. An Anti-Corruption Policy?

The election of Ellen Johnson Sirleaf as president of Liberia raised expectations that reforms introducing transparency, democratic accountability, and rule of law into Liberian politics would be forcefully pursued. When outlining central features of her government's policy upon her inauguration in January 2006, Johnson Sirleaf directly addressed these expectations. In what amounted to a reversal of Liberia's historic political principles, she declared that "Government [would] recognize and support a strong democratic and loyal opposition" while "corruption [...] [would] be the major public enemy" (Johnson Sirleaf 2006). This section takes a closer look at corruption, official anti-corruption policy measures, and resistance to bureaucratic reform. I describe several events in some detail in order to demonstrate the struggles and ambiguities shaping the process of reform.

The first, high profile action of the government in relation to corruption took place between December 2006 and spring 2007, when seven NTGL officials found culpable of embezzlement by the ECOWAS (2005) investigation were arrested and charged. Those charged included former Finance Minister Luseni Kamara, former LPRC Managing Director Edwin Snowe, and former Chairman Gyude Bryant. Dangers of a negative political backlash for Johnson Sirleaf were negligible, as all of the accused had either supported George Weah or had been close to formations supporting him in the 2005 elections. Edwin Snowe further was considered as both eyeing a future presidential candidacy and being a personal foe of Johnson Sirleaf. Given the dilapidated state of Liberia's judicial system as well as the power and wealth of the charged individuals, none of the trials ended in a conviction.

While these isolated cases of juridical prosecution were meant to send a signal to the Liberian public and the International Community. The major initiative to increase capacities for control and certainly the one most trusted by foreign stakeholders was the *Governance and Economic Management Assistance Program* (GEMAP). GEMAP had been concluded in September 2005 under massive international pressure—the European Commission had declared its development assistance efforts contingent on approval of the plan and the US had announced to review its support for security sector reform (Dwan/Bailey 2006, 13–14)—but had remained ineffective under the NTGL. The centerpiece of GEMAP was placing internationally recruited experts in the financially most important government institutions.[222] These experts did share binding co-signature authority with senior management and had a mandate to take a number of initiatives related to rationalizing financial management. GEMAP was headed by a Liberian-International *Economic Governance Steering Committee* (EGSC), the international side being composed of the African Union, the UN, the EU, the ECOWAS, the IMF, the US and the World Bank. Johnson Sirleaf endorsed the Program reluctantly and promised to push a rationalization of

222 Foreign designs to have judges from the sub-region rule on corruption charges as part of GEMAP were successfully blocked by the NTGL.

economic governance that would "render GEMAP non-applicable in a reasonable period of time" (Johnson Sirleaf 2006, 9).

GEMAP met stiff resistance quickly. The first major disagreement between the international stakeholders in the EGSC and the Liberian side arose in mid-2006. Harry Greaves, whose appointment as head of the LPRC had already raised eyebrows among donors because of his role in the NTGL as economic advisor to Bryant, was criticized by the Panel of Experts for bypassing controlling agencies and personally allocating a contract worth 500,000 dollars (Panel of Experts 06/2006, 28). The GEMAP expert at the LPRC was "blamed as the source of the UN report" and was "dismissed for what was termed his lifestyle which was in violation of company policy" a little later (Liberian Express Mar. 26 2007a). A year later, the Panel noted that Greaves had personally allocated a further 21 large contracts without any competitive bidding in violation of the *Public Procurement and Concessions Act* (Panel of Experts 06/2007, 25–26).[223] In 2009 and after much further criticism, Greaves was supposed to be investigated by the Minister of State for Economic and Legal Affairs, Morris Saytumah, for the allocation of a 24.5 million dollars construction contract awarded to a Lebanese company. However, the investigator sent by Saytumah in fact came "to Greaves to demand $300,000 in extortion money" (Africa Confidential May 14, 2010). Both the LPRC head and the investigator were sacked after the former leaked voice recordings of the conversation to the public. Saytumah remained in office and was considered one of the most influential figures in Johnson Sirleaf's government before he was sacked in 2010 for corruption related to the logging industry (see below).

As the controversy about Greaves was ongoing, the next major standoff between international stakeholders in GEMAP and its Liberian counterpart occurred in March 2007. The NPA generally had remained considered one of Liberia's most corrupt institutions (cf. Daily Observer Mar. 26, 2007). Doubts over the new management were reinforced when, despite major growth in imports, profits fell below those achieved during the NTGL period. "In 2006 the port incurred a loss of $70,565, as compared to a profit of $2.041 million the year before. This [might have been] in part because the Freeport shouldered the retrenchment costs of $794,000 over a single year. However, this [was] difficult to verify since NPA has not been audited independently" (Panel of Experts 06/2007, 26).

223 Notwithstanding, "LPRC trebled its profit to $4.76 million in 2006" (Panel of Experts 06/2007, 3).

In this context, there were serious differences between the senior port leadership and the NPA's GEMAP Chief Financial Controller on management of the port. The Managing Director then requested the NPA Board of Directors to relieve the expatriate expert of his duties, arguing that he had failed to submit reports as stipulated in his terms of reference (Heritage Mar. 23, 2007). The US Ambassador, acting in his capacity as Deputy Chair of the EGSC, unconventionally commented publicly and unequivocally on the issue, clarifying that the Controller "was acting within the Terms of Reference of his position" and should not be replaced (Liberian Express Mar. 26, 2007a).

In what appeared to be a turn of events, the two Deputy Managing Directors of the NPA were then dismissed for "administrative" reasons in consideration of "the rapidly deteriorating situation and poor performance at the NPA" (Daily Observer Mar. 26, 2007). The Managing Director at the center of the row was similarly dismissed but instantly transferred to the Ministry of Public Works and instated as Deputy Minister. Two weeks later, the NPA Board of Directors dismissed the GEMAP expert with express approval of the president (New Democrat Apr. 10, 2007).[224] He switched position with the controller at the FDA.

Initially, GEMAP was to last for at least 36 months, i.e. until the end of 2008. Yet the Program was maintained as long as legally possible, until Liberia reached the HIPC completion point in June 2010. This indicated limited confidence of foreign stakeholders in Liberia's own anti-corruption efforts. However, the Program gave foreign actors financing large parts of Liberia's economy access to a wealth of information on state revenue management, and thus increased their capacities for control and intervention.

Two institutions were at the center of the more permanent anti-corruption policy: the *General Auditing Commission* (GAC) and the *Liberia Anti-Corruption Commission* (LACC). The LACC was newly established by the Johnson Sirleaf government and was a project of the president. One of her closest confidantes, her cousin Frances Johnson Morris was chosen to head the institution, indicating the importance attributed to it. The agency was primarily meant to investigate accusations of corruption and was expected to prosecute those accused.

The GAC head John Morlu, had been recruited and his salary was paid by the European Commission. Morlu, only 33 years of age, proved to be

224 Formally, the NPA Board did not have the authority to dismiss the GEMAP expert. The EGSC chaired by Johnson Sirleaf, however, confirmed the Board's verdict.

outspoken and consequently controversial. He clashed with the president for the first time in mid-2007, when he accused the government of inconsistencies in the budget for the coming fiscal year, which created the appearance of "parallel budgets". In the context of a heated exchange, Morlu then accused the Johnson Sirleaf government of being "three times more corrupt" than the NTGL—a claim obviously hard to prove and inviting criticism. Morlu continued to unequivocally accuse senior government officials of corruption. The relation between the executive and the GAC immediately turned sour.

The creation of institutional capacities to rationalize financial administration thus became embroiled in fierce personal battles. The Auditor General was accountable to the European Commission in the first place, disturbed the president's efforts to create a loyal core of senior officials, complicated her cautious approach to rationalization, tarnished her international reputation, and was probably perceived a political rival by her. Johnson Sirleaf did not renew Morlu's contract when it expired in 2011 and the GAC ceased making headlines.

Yet the LACC, the president's official project against corruption, hardly started to make an impact. Chairperson Johnson Morris maintained a less brusque but critical stance and "complained the government lacked the will to prosecute officials linked to corruption" (Africa Confidential Nov. 6, 2009). Although it unearthed some evidence of corruption, by early 2013 it had not concluded a single significant case. The first Police Director was indicted in early 2012 and the LACC was tasked with prosecuting. The trial was announced as the Commission's showpiece case yet by early 2013, no progress had been made. Increasingly, observers considered the LACC "lacking the will or capacity to pursue high-level suspects" (Africa Confidential Sept. 7, 2012).

To sum up, Johnson Sirleaf's efforts at rationalizing governance focused on reducing opportunities for embezzlement and increasing capacities for control. In contrast, hardly any officials faced legal sanctions and few were removed from office. In several cases, Johnson Sirleaf initially publicly backed officials accused of wrongdoing. In several of these cases, the officials had to be removed later in the face of further evidence, considerably embarrassing the president. Johnson Sirleaf had tried to build a core circle of senior officials in which personal loyalty and trust would prevail, and acted accordingly towards her subordinates. Yet corrupt practices are deeply rooted and values promoting trust are in short supply in Liberian society.[225] When the president sacked the Internal Affairs Minister, her cousin, she was reported to have asked: "Who else can I trust?" (Africa Confidential July 22, 2011).

Yet her government stabilized over the years. In several reshuffles and when establishing her second government, Johnson Sirleaf promoted individuals that earlier proved loyal and qualified. Yet few are trusted, and core state institutions continue to be led by close family members. Thus, the *National Security Agency*, effectively an internal intelligence agency, continued to be headed by her stepson Fomba Sirleaf, and the public corporation *National Oil Company of Liberia* (NOCAL) was put under the direction of her son Robert Sirleaf.

The strategy of merely removing but not punishing corrupt officials prevented the alienation of large parts of Liberia's elite and probably consolidated peace and stability. Yet the focus on centralizing revenue flows and better documenting them proved insufficient to reform the natural resources sector. Leniency towards failing officials allowed corrupt networks to expand and accumulate power to the extent that by early 2013, reform of the logging and diamond industries had failed (see below).

4.5.4. New Elections—Reconfigured Alliances

Johnson Sirleaf built a diverse campaign coalition in 2005 that left its imprint on the government. In her first term, she undertook an effort to strengthen effective authority. This resulted in the removal from of officials lacking competence, loyalty and integrity and notably the sidelining of LURD leaders in the government. Over time, the socio-political character of her government as one based on professionals was strengthened. Elites tended to gravitate toward the president yet a number of formerly important supporters who felt they had not been sufficiently rewarded rallied around her main opponent. Yet she comfortably won the 2011 elections against the CDC's candidates, Winston Tubman and his running mate George Weah.[226]

---

225 The core message of most Liberian fairy tales is not to trust anybody while cunning is frequently portrayed as the road to success (cf. Sankawulo n.d.).

226 Johnson Sirleaf obtained 43.9 percent and Tubman 32.7 percent in the first round. She won the run-off, which was boycotted by the CDC, with 90.7 percent yet turnout was only 38.6 percent.

A major trend during Johnson Sirleaf's first terms was the co-optation of established professional elites. Many co-opted elites were linked to the Taylor government, though these had a professional rather than military background.[227] Johnson Sirleaf's overtures towards Emanuel Shaw and Benoni Urey constituted a particular irritant for Western officials. Shaw was appointed Chairman of the Liberian Aviation Authority in 2011 but the president rescinded the decision as a result of US pressure (cf. Executive Mansion May 27, 2011).

The Ureys are an established "Americo-Liberian" family based on a farm in Careysburg outside Monrovia and have long-standing relations to Johnson Sirleaf's family (cf. Johnson Sirleaf 2009, 18). Benoni's brother Clemenceau stood as UP candidate for a Montserrado Senate seat in 2005 and in the 2009 bye-elections. He was vigorously supported by Johnson Sirleaf on his second attempt but narrowly lost against the CDC's candidate. Around the same time, Johnson Sirleaf appointed Benoni Urey Mayor of Careysburg although Urey still was on the UN travel ban and assets freeze lists. He had been seeking the position which, although formally a minor one, symbolized his re-admission into the circles of Liberia's honorable citizens. Benoni Urey was effectively controlling the Careysburg area informally already, and his security personnel are considered the most important security provider in the area. Yet in the 2011 elections, he campaigned for Winston Tubman and George Weah against the background of the CDC-NPP electoral alliance. Little sympathetic to the CDC's grassroots base, his stance was likely to have been informed by economic difficulties under the new regime.[228]

The CDC-NPP alliance was the only tangible outcome of the efforts to establish a broader opposition alliance. These efforts were initially led by Dew Mayson, the Nigeria-based millionaire businessman who had supported Johnson Sirleaf in 2005. Mayson fell out with Johnson Sirleaf during her first term, apparently over lack of government support for his Nigerian business partners (cf. Vanguard Aug. 7, 2011). Yet Mayson did not succeed to rally the opposition behind him as presidential candidate.

227 This distinction is, however, not a clear-cut one and several of Taylor's professionals had played military roles too.

228 Several informants opined that Urey had lost economic protection under Johnson Sirleaf. On visits to his estate by the author in 2012, a large section of the formerly well-running chicken farm was not in use.

He eventually stood alone and with very limited support for his *National Democratic Coalition* (NDC) party.

A major new entrant into the government was Harrison Karnweah, a former NPFL General, successful senior executive of a foreign-owned rubber plantation, and Taylor's Superintendent for Nimba County. He replaced the president's cousin as Minister of Internal Affairs in 2010. Karnweah is popular in Nimba County and the move appeared informed by concerns over the 2011 elections. He was one of the few minister not renominated by Johnson Sirleaf but was made Interim Managing Director of the FDA in August 2012 (see below). Instead, Taylor's former Chief of Cabinet Blamoh Nelson, who had lost his position as senator for Grand Kru in the 2011 elections, was given the portfolio. Nelson had played a leading role in his party not fielding a candidate for the presidential elections and supporting the incumbent instead.

Jewel Howard Taylor's relationship with Johnson Sirleaf suffered when the latter initiated Taylor's extradition. Taylor's wife was selected to be the presidential candidate of the NPP for the 2011 elections but finally did not run, as the NPP supported Tubman. Yet after the elections, Howard Taylor's relationship with the president improved again (cf. Analyst Oct. 1, 2012), demonstrating the president's attempts to enlarge her network and the tendency of lower elites gravitating toward the president.

One of the few NPP stalwarts not supporting the Tubman/Weah duo in 2011 was Lewis Brown, former National Security Advisor and Minister of State for Foreign Affairs under Taylor. After the opposition alliance had faltered, he decided to run ran as an independent for the Senate seat for Montserrado County and support Johnson Sirleaf. He eventually lost the Senate election but came in second and, having demonstrated significant capacity to mobilize votes, he was named Minister of Information.

Yet LURD elites became marginalized over time as the president's network stabilized. Jackson E. Doe, who had been transferred from Posts to Transport in 2008, finally lost his ministerial position in 2009. Soko V. Sackor, who had held two Deputy Minister positions during Johnson Sirleaf's first term, was not re-nominated and given a less lucrative post in the *Constitution Review Committee* in 2012.[229] Aicha Keita (formerly Conneh) continued to support Johnson Sirleaf in the 2011 campaign and established a timber project, partnering with Mandingo businessmen, in 2012. Given

229 Minister of State Morris Dukuly, a prominent ULIMO-K executive, similarly lost his position in 2006 after a mysterious fire incident had destroyed the president's office.

the failure of the reform in the timber sector, her business was likely to benefit from political connections.

After her first election victory, Johnson Sirleaf allocated government positions to elites who had supported her campaign and made hardly any offers to the opposition. Only a few opposition personalities, most importantly CDC campaign manager Milton Teahjay, who was made Superintendent for Sinoe, and CDC Chairman Cole Bangalu, who was named Deputy Labor Minister, were co-opted into the government. While her critics accused the president of not sufficiently promoting national unity and reconciliation, she justified her appointments in terms of qualification (Johnson Sirleaf 2009, 279. In fact, it was hard enough to maintain control over officials who had supported her during the campaign, and integrating elites irrespective of loyalty would have made this task much more difficult. Liberian politics is confrontational and rewarding hostility with political positions neither promotes state nor government consolidation.

Notable among those co-opted into the presidential campaign of 2011 was Lenn Eugene Nagbe, until then CDC Secretary-General. Africa Confidential (Oct. 7, 2011) opined that a major component of the elections strategies of all parties was "bribing effective opponents to change sides" (Africa Confidential Oct. 7, 2011). Nagbe's campaign support was rewarded with the post of Transport Minister. Rufus Neufville, the popular youth activist who had served in the NTLA and the 52nd legislature, ran into conflict with other senior CDC executives and eventually had to give up his CDC representative candidacy. He ran as an independent in 2011 and lost but became a vocal supporter of Johnson Sirleaf. Neufville was appointed Deputy Minister of Commerce in 2012. A particularly notable and difficult supporter was Edwin Snowe, who remained widely popular in his ELWA constituency due to his jovial character and lavish spending. Facing a strong CDC rival in the election, he teamed up with Johnson Sirleaf, supporting her campaign and hoping to benefit from her leverage. Snowe comfortably won his constituency. Yet, elites integrated into her camp would not necessarily be loyal.

Thus, shortly after the elections, a campaign accusing Johnson Sirleaf of nepotism unfolded, starting with a series of newspaper articles, many of which were unmarked "sponsored advertisements". In particular, the appointment of her son Robert Sirleaf as Chairman of NOCAL was criticized. The campaign was a joint project by senior officials from Johnson Sirleaf's own party, i.e. the Speaker of the House Alex Tyler and UP Chairman Varney Sherman, and Edwin Snowe (Africa Confidential Nov. 2012, 16). The latter quickly became the face publicly associated with the campaign. As the president cannot stand for a third term, ambitious elites outside her inner circle positioned themselves against the successor she was suspected to groom.

George Weah continued to pursue a political career in Liberia and remained widely popular among youths, although he spent most of his time abroad—partly in order to study toward a bachelor's degree. Tubman left the NDPL for the CDC to initially become Weah's running mate. In 2011, both switched positions in stage-managed primaries. However, contrary to expectation the take-over of an established, highly educated Big Man did not increase the CDC's appeal to voters and instead led to serious conflicts within the party. As the duo suffered electoral failure, they finally made a bid to be co-opted, boycotting the run-off, arguing that the election had been rigged, and insinuating frustrated CDC supporters could turn violent. The strategy, however, was not successful.[230] Winston Tubman, now over 70 years of age, eventually retired from politics. George Weah was finally integrated by Johnson Sirleaf as "Peace Ambassador"; charged with promoting peace and reconciliation. Weah accepted the post, and considered running for a Senate seat in the 2014 election.

4.6. Political Economy of the New Liberia

4.6.1. A Peacekeeping and Reconstruction Economy

When Johnson Sirleaf took over, Liberia's economy was in an exceptional situation. For one, Liberia's classic natural resource economy was totally devastated. Major mining companies had quit the country and rubber plantations had deteriorated. Further, sanctions against log and diamond exports were in place. Consequently, Liberia had virtually no economic basis to finance a system of state domination.

Yet Taylor's exit raised donors' expectations of policy shifts in Liberia and immediately caused an inflow of significant foreign resources intended

230 There were rumors the CDC leaders were paid a substantial sum to accept the results. However, at the same time, both were under massive international pressure not to resort to violence, and were reminded of the prospect of domestic and international punitive measures.

to support a political transformation. Assistance inflows received another boost after Johnson Sirleaf had assumed the presidency. Johnson Sirleaf's excellent international reputation, coupled with concrete steps demonstrating that Liberia intended to subscribe to more conventional notions of statehood and play a responsible role in the international system of states, immediately paid off economically. Table 18 compares ODA flows to Liberia under the last three Liberian regimes.

Table 18: Official Development Assistance to Liberia,[231] *1997–2010*

Taylor Government		Transitional Government		Johnson Sirleaf Government	
Year	ODA (US$m)	Year	ODA (US$m)	Year	ODA (US$m)
1997	76.20	2003	106.93	2006	260.40
1998	71.98	2004	213.24	2007	687.90
1999	93.95	2005	222.44	2008	684.66
2000	67.42			2009	385,80
2001	38.48			2010	488,11
2002	53.51				
2003	106.93				

Source: OECD (2012)

In the fiscal year 2006–07, the national budget of Liberia only allocated some 18 million dollars, about 14 percent of expenditures, to the security sector.[232] In contrast, the US alone provided almost 50 million dollars just for the establishment of the new army in fiscal year 2007–08 (Malan 2008, 41). The LNP received additional support from several foreign sources. The most important security-related benefits, however, accrued through the UNMIL, as the international force was by far the most important provider of regime security. Table 19 details costs of the UNMIL mission. These underestimate the security benefit to Liberia, as military equipment provided by troop-contributing countries is not included.

231 All data is taken from the OECD (2012) data base. Figures exclude debt relief, amounting to well over US$5 billion in total, leaving Liberia with just about US$150 million of foreign debt. The figures thus underestimate international support to Liberia.

232 The security sector, as defined in the budget, comprised the Judiciary, the Ministry of Justice, the Ministry of National Defense (i.e. the AFL), the National Security Agency, the Special Security Services, the Ministry of National Security, and the National Bureau of Investigation.

Tables 18 and 19 provide an idea rather than absolute figures on financial means mobilized by the International Community. Assistance to Liberia was largely motivated by a desire to provide incentives to pursue and reward a project of state building that would make the country conform to more conventional notions of statehood than had been the case under Taylor. Indeed, capital imports occasioned by the large international presence in Liberia allowed financing huge imports. Taxing of these imports in turn provided the financial basis to the Johnson Sirleaf government. However, Liberia's natural resource exports were expected to grow strongly in the coming years and eventually provide the economic basis for political domination. For this reason, a closer look at trends in natural resource management is worthwhile.

Table 19: UNMIL Budgets August 2003–June 2010

Period	Budget (US$ Million)
August 1, 2003–June 30, 2004	564.494
July 1, 2004–June 30, 2005	821.986
July 1, 2005–June 30, 2006	722.422
July 1, 2006–June 30, 2007	714.613
July 1, 2007–June 30, 2008	688.331
July 1, 2008–June 30, 2009	603.708
July 1, 2009–June 30, 2010	560.979

Source: UN ACABQ 2007–2010

4.6.2. Natural Resources and Political Control

The private, personalized character of political management of natural resources has widely been considered a major structural pattern underlying the Liberian Wars. Consequently, designs for improved natural resource management featured a strengthening of bureaucratic mechanisms. Foreign actors forcefully pushed measures that would increase bureaucratic institutional control over the natural resource economy. In particular, sanctions against diamond and timber exports decided by the UN Security Council were initially maintained when Johnson Sirleaf assumed office. The key question concerning future natural resource management in Liberia was whether the extractive economy would continue to be controlled by opaque, personal networks or to what extent it would be bureaucratically administered. However, it is out of the scope of this thesis to present a comprehensive description and analysis of natural resource management and policies. Introducing the issue, I shortly outline major features of natural resource policy before describing in more detail developments in selected cases.

The Johnson Sirleaf government maintained basic official natural resource policy, i.e. it continued to rely on foreign investors to bring in capital and expertise. The government had inherited a number of contracts with foreign businesses that had been concluded under Taylor. Further, during the rule of the NTGL, a host of foreign firms had signed contracts with the government that would have long-term implications for state finances in general and state revenues from natural resources in particular. A major initiative of the Johnson Sirleaf government was to review contracts concluded by its predecessor, and many were cancelled or renegotiated. Personal connections formed by NTGL officials were devalued, which could promote bureaucratization. The renegotiation of contracts with *Firestone* and *Arcelor Mittal* was considered to have resulted in considerably better terms for the Liberian state. *Mittal Steel* (who little later fused with *Arcelor* to form the world's largest steel producing company) had been awarded the concession to mine the high-grade iron ore reserves in Nimba that should have been exploited by the LIMINCO-MIFERGUI project (see Chapter 4). The *Arcelor Mittal* concession was one of the largest new natural resource ventures in Liberia and expected to have a major impact on future state finances (cf. Global Witness 2006; cf. Global Witness 2007). A project that could have at least as much impact on the future of Liberia was the reform of the logging sector.

4.6.2.1. The Failure of Timber Industry Reform

Executive Order No. 1 of Johnson Sirleaf declared all logging concessions null and void. Earlier in May 2005, a government body established under the NTGL concluded that all active logging corporations had flouted Liberian laws and should consequently have their concessions cancelled (Forest Concession Review Committee 2005). Executive Order No. 1 also interdicted all timber exports until major reforms were implemented, and established the *Forest Reform Monitoring Committee* (FRMC), composed of representatives of the government, the *Liberia Forest Initiative* (LFI)[233] and civil society organizations. The FRMC was tasked with developing forestry reforms and in particular, drafting of a *National Forestry Reform Law*. In June 2006, the UN Security Council lifted the sanctions on timber exports on the condition that the draft forestry law would be passed, which was done soon after in September 2006. The new forestry law was widely considered a suitable legal framework to take bureaucratic control over forestry resources (cf. Panel of Experts 12/2006, 14).

Key provisions of the new forestry law dealt with types of forestry resource exploitation licenses. The law defined four categories of licenses: *Forest Management Contracts* (FMCs), *Timber Sales Contracts* (TSCs), *Forest Use Permits* (FUPs), and *Private Use Permits* (PUPs). FMCs regulated logging in large concession areas between 50,000 and 400,000 hectares. TSCs applied to areas no larger than 5,000 hectares. Concessions that were smaller than 100,000 hectares needed to demonstrate at least 51 percent Liberian ownership. FUPs regulated non-logging activities in forests, while PUPs were intended to license logging on privately owned lands. Other important provisions of the law obliged the FDA to pre-qualify bidders, carry out due diligence and establish a system of documentation of the chain of custody from stump to export (Ministry of Foreign Affairs 2006). This chain of custody tracing mechanism was eventually developed and managed by the foreign company *Société Générale de Surveillance* (SGS). A total of two million hectares of Liberia's forests were opened for commercial exploitation through FMCs and TSCs (FDA 2010). None of the four licenses covered logging on community land, which was subject to specific laws decided later.[234] The *National Forestry Reform Law* further obliged the FDA to work out rules and regulations determining the issuance of PUPs.

By late 2009, six TSCs and seven FMCs were allocated or in the process of being allocated (Panel of Experts 12/2009, 23). Of the FMCs, five were for forest areas of more than 100,000 hectares but the contracts were only advertised in national media (Panel of Experts 12/2008, 22). This approach indicated that well-connected Liberian intermediaries played

233 The Liberia Forest Initiative had been established on the initiative of the US during the NTGL period and comprised various US government agencies as well as multilateral and non-governmental organizations (cf. http://www.fao.org/forestry/lfi/en/).

234 Harvesting timber from community forests is lucrative, and when formulating the law, representatives provided themselves with guaranteed positions in community forestry management that potentially allow access to logging profits. This increases the weight of interests external to the communities in harvesting timber.

an important role in contract allocation. In order to prevent secretive ownership arrangements, the FDA was tasked with undertaking a pre-qualification assessment of bidders and doing background checks on them during later stages of the contract allocation process. Yet, the "FDA [was] often either not aware of the legal requirements or unable to follow them" (ibid., 19). The allocation of TSCs and FMCs was characterized by major irregularities, and the consequences were such that reform of the forestry sector had totally failed by early 2013. When allocating the contracts,

> "FDA appointed an internal committee to conduct due diligence on bidding companies, as legally required. As a result of its investigations of the bidders for the six timber sales contracts and three forest-management contracts, the due diligence committee found problems with all nine provisional winners of contracts. It found that none of the companies bidding on the three forest-management contracts had all of the technical and financial capabilities required by law and that there had been material changes in ownership of three companies, rendering their pre-qualification certificates invalid [...]. The committee also noted that virtually nothing was known about the companies providing almost 100 percent of the financing to two of the bidders that were subsequently named preliminary winners. The committee expressed concern that each of the bidders was to be funded 100 percent by debt. None of the companies had any equity cushion, making the chance of failure high. Nor did any of the companies have any experience with logging." (ibid., 22–23)

The *Inter-Ministerial Concessions Commission* further allocated one of the FMCs against the recommendation of the bid evaluation panel and in violation of the *Public Procurement and Concessions Act* to a company that had made an inferior bid. The president, however, did not sign the contract, and the losing company successfully appealed to the *Public Procurement and Concessions Commission*. Natural resource use contracts need to be passed by the legislature and are subsequently signed by the president.

No reputable, professional firm submitted a bid, which was likely owed to interests and actions of Liberian intermediaries. Starting with the infractions described above, management of the FDA became increasingly patrimonial. This constituted a major impediment to the bureaucratization, as resourceful actors, i.e. a government agency of extreme financial importance and the companies involved in one of Liberia's most lucrative sectors, developed vested interests in challenging legal-rational reform.

In the case of the first three FMCs, the terms of the contracts were altered after they were passed by parliament but before being put to the president. The contracts were for 25 years and stipulated that land rental fees had to be paid every year. The altered version of the contracts, by contrast, said that companies would only have to pay their land rental fee once in the first year. Fees for 24 years amounting to some 50 million dollars were simply forgiven (ibid., 22–24). In reaction to criticism of the Panel of Experts, the FDA Board of Directors changed the terms of the contracts to conform to the original version (Panel of Experts 06/2009, 15). The Minister of State for Economic and Legal Affairs, once one of the president's closest confidantes, much later had to leave his post for making the illegal changes to the contracts (Africa Confidential Jan. 7, 2011). Yet in 2010, following intense "lobbying" of companies, both Houses of the Legislature approved a law converting the annual into a one-time payment (Panel of Experts 12/2012, 38). The president did not sign the law, which prevented it from coming into effect—at least temporarily.

While further investigating the issue, the Panel of Experts was informed by the GEMAP advisor at the FDA that two employees of the agency had promised the companies they would only have to pay their annual fee once if they made a high bid justifying the allocation of the contracts. On the basis of the denial of one of the company representatives and one of the concerned FDA employees, a subsequent investigation by the Board's Administrative Committee concluded that there was "no iota of truth in [...] [this] revelation" (Panel of Experts 06/2009, 15). Two international advisors who had been present at the relevant meeting between the FDA employee and the company representative stated that due to the confidential nature of the conversation, they could not provide information. One of them, the World Bank's FDA advisor, had earlier been instructed by senior World Bank management "to draw back from immediate involvement with such contentious issues in the forestry sector, particularly concerning commercial forestry" (ibid., 19). An internal e-mail from the advisor confirming the dubious agreement was, however, made available to the Panel (ibid., 16). The advisor's earlier intervention in contentious issues had led to considerable tension between the IMF mission and the FDA. Irregular interference undermined competitive bidding to the benefit of one company again when, a little later, the fourth FMC was allocated (Panel of Experts 12/2009, 25).

Foreign intervention into Liberian governance decreased notably over the years. In response to the events described above, the US Government withdrew from financing the commercial forestry sector reform. Further, the GEMAP mission at the FDA ended in June 2009, about a year before the Program should have come to an end.

The irregular allocation of contracts directly implicated the first FDA Managing Director. After a considerable delay, he was eventually dismissed for his role in a dubious carbon credit scheme that guaranteed profits to a foreign company and burdened business risks of some two billion dollars on the Liberian state (Greenbang June 4, 2010; Global Witness Oct. 13, 2010).[235] He was replaced by Moses Wogbeh.

The companies which had won FMCs had made unrealistic bids in order to get the contracts allocated. When, contrary to expectations, the ex-post reduction of fees and taxes was not possible because of international and consequent presidential attention, strictly legal logging could not be profitable. Over the years, companies were sold and changes in ownership occurred that should have invalidated the original pre-qualification. It was eventually revealed that four companies who together had been dominating the timber industry in Liberia were linked to Samling; a resourceful Malaysia-based company notorious for illegal logging worldwide (Global Witness 09/2012).

Under Moses Wogbeh, the FDA started to hand out PUPs to the timber companies *en masse*. Logging under PUPs was minimally taxed and regulations on PUP issuance had not been worked out, which gave FDA management an extreme amount of discretion. Effective February 2012, the Board placed a moratorium on logging with PUPs, but FDA Management ignored it and did not pass the information on to other stakeholders. The Chairperson of the Board (who is simultaneously Minister of Agriculture) was bypassed and documents were signed *per-procurationem* by one of her deputies.[236] In August 2012, the president reiterated the moratorium, ordered an investigation and suspended the Managing Director. Harrison Karnweah was named Interim Managing Director.

PUP allocation, logging and exports, however, continued and by December 2012, 23 percent of Liberia's territory had been licensed for logging under PUPs (Global Witness Dec. 21, 2012). Then, the investigators presented their report and Johnson Sirleaf, by Executive Order, interdicted PUP-covered logging and associated exports (Panel of Experts 12/2012;

235 The quoted Global Witness investigation found evidence that the president's cousin, the former Minister of Internal Affairs, was implicated too.

236 This individual is a confidante of Johnson Sirleaf and is, for instance, on the Board of the NGO *Johnson Sirleaf Market Women Fund*.

Special Independent Investigating Commission 2012; Executive Mansion Jan. 5, 2013).

The scandals exhibited a common pattern. A major feature is the lack of bureaucratically integer officials prepared to apply laws, rules and regulations in their administrative actions. Lengthy delays in sanctioning officials allow networks between the interested parties to expand. Thus company managers, FDA management, government officials (in the PUP case in particular staff of the *Environmental Protection Agency* and the Ministries of State, Agriculture as well as Lands and Mines) and Legislators collude against the presidential reform project. The factionalized character of Liberia's state and government gives private interests great opportunities to influence politics. The president's strategy of establishing facts in lengthy investigations, probably in order to not alienate loyalists and maintain necessary support among elites, often appeared as a lack of commitment to bureaucratic control. Yet even in the case of presidential commitment to reform, rewards for corrupt officials are high and sanctions unlikely. Profits of the logging sector can be huge, and provided few taxes are paid, a significant number of elites can make a fortune in little time while they are effectively immune against legal sanctions because of the powers of secret elite clubs. Thus, it is hardly surprising that staff involved in the carbon credit scheme bore significant responsibility for the issuance of the PUPs.

4.6.2.2. Diamonds

When the Johnson Sirleaf took over, major structures of the diamond trade had been eradicated as the erosion of the RUF entailed a reorganization of the trade in Sierra Leonean diamonds (cf. Pugh et al. 2004, 91–141). Reforms in the diamond sector thus targeted the relatively small Liberian production. Diamond mining was classified into three types: artisanal mining (class C), semi-industrial mining (class B), and industrial mining (class A). The first type historically constituted the major way of mining in Liberia and is obviously difficult to control. Industrial mining, in contrast, is characterized by high capital input of firms controlling large areas and producing large volumes of diamonds. This centralization renders political control easier and the higher profits render control more rewarding. Further, industrial mining is not always feasible or economic. Semi-industrial mining uses limited equipment only and thus bears smaller investment costs, making the industry accessible to domestic entrepreneurs. Operations are flexible and exploit small diamond deposits.

The international diamond embargo imposed in May 2001 was lifted in April 2007 only, and it was highly likely that companies and brokers operating between these dates violated it. One of the most important projects, a semi-industrial mine in Nimba County, was that of *Jungle Waters*.[237] *Jungle Waters* was owned by one of Nimba's most successful businessmen, and active in various sectors ranging from construction over trade in consumer goods to managing the regional fuel depot. The owner further was considered close to Charles Taylor, and "senior officials from the Executive Mansion" were considered to be the investors behind the project (Panel of Experts 10/2002, 30). *Jungle Waters* expanded its activities under the transitional government and was considered to have reached class A proportions in mid-2005 (Panel of Experts 12/2004, 27–28; Panel of Experts 06/2005, 22–23). Activities at the site were ongoing under Johnson Sirleaf (Panel of Experts 12/2006, 9).

About one and a half years after Johnson Sirleaf took over, the site was being prepared for an extension of operations (Panel of Experts 06/2007, 18) and half a year later the Panel of Experts reported increased activity there (Panel of Experts 12/2007, 15). Given considerable international concern about the operation, the government's muted response to the mine indicated reluctance to proactively react against influential personalities. From a technical point of view, stopping the operations would not have posed a problem. UNMIL had a mandate to assist the government in regaining control over its natural resources, a mandate the government made use of in other cases. The mine was well accessible, being located a few kilometers off Nimba's main road, and confiscating a few truckloads of equipment would have stopped semi-industrial mining.

Yet the *Jungle Waters* boss had been well connected politically for considerable time (cf. Panel of Experts 10/2002, 30), and his old contacts continued to hold influence. When Johnson Sirleaf fulfilled her campaign promise of reconstructing the market of Saclepea in Nimba, this businessman was given the contract. Prize money of 100,000 dollars awarded to Johnson Sirleaf by an international NGO and thus personally controlled by her (cf. Hunger Project Oct. 21, 2006), was used to finance construction

237 Jungle Waters operated a second mine of similar dimension in Bahn, Nimba County, on which less information was available (Panel of Experts 12/2004, 28).

costs.[238] The *Jungle Waters* case indicated that the president's strategy to expand authority into the hinterland rested on integrating elites of the Taylor regime, rather than weakening and sanctioning them.

State oversight over diamond operations appeared deficient in several respects, indicating the existence of personal connections preventing legal-rational control. Two large foreign-owned class A projects raised concern. The Panel of Experts regularly reported activities on the sites but could not prove diamond smuggling. One of the companies, *Italgems*, had a license for exploratory activities, which it commenced under the NTGL. However, the Panel of Experts considered *Italgems* to have greatly "exceeded the level of digging associated with bulk sampling of an exploration block" (Panel of Experts 12/2005, 17) and suspected the company of exporting illegally. The company, however, was ordered by the government to cease digging gravel and deposit its finds. *Italgems* eventually deposited a mere 60 carat at the (Italian) *Global Bank* and stopped operations (Panel of Experts 06/2006, 22).

Much more concern caused *American Mining Associates* (AMA), who officially undertook exploratory and preparatory activities. Local artisanal miners clashed with AMA security forces, recruited among Taylor's paramilitaries, on several occasions when the latter chased them of areas not demarcated as belonging to the AMA concession (cf. Panel of Experts 12/2007, 15). Upon a ministerial assessment visit, the AMA manager insisted that although the 1984 concession agreement covered only 66,242 acres, a verbal agreement he had with an NTGL minister entitled AMA to a 215,000 acres concession area. This was remarkable, as virtually all *written* contracts inherited from the NTGL were cancelled or substantially amended by the Johnson Sirleaf government. No action seemed to be taken to restrict or sanction AMA (Panel of Experts 06/2008, 31). The cases of Italgems and AMA indicated that established networks continued to be powerful and the president aimed at co-opting rather than dismantling them. They further corresponded to general parameters of economic policy prioritizing interests of the state, its elites in resource exploitation over local concerns (cf. New York Times Jan. 20, 2012), and relying on private security forces of corporations to establish control over hinterland areas.

---

238 In a public declaration in Saclepea, Johnson Sirleaf declared to use the award money for the market reconstruction (interviews in Nimba, Feb. and March 2007).

For more than three years, the Panel of Experts generally lauded the government's progress in overseeing the diamond economy. Liberian government efforts aimed at becoming a member of the *Kimberley Process* diamond certification scheme and designed its official reforms accordingly. These essentially aimed at making the diamond industry more transparent by strengthening bureaucratic mechanisms documenting production and upstream trade flows of rough diamonds. Indeed, given Liberia's low starting base, documentation of the diamond trade made tremendous progress (cf. Panel of Experts 06/2008, 33–39). However, at no point in time could it reasonably be assumed that the majority of diamond trade was being bureaucratically documented.

There were serious shortfalls from the very beginning. Among the very first nine export shipments after the lifting of sanctions was one parcel suspected of containing smuggled Ivorian diamonds, although Kimberley Process experts had expressly recommended not exporting it.[239] Another of the very first parcels had been issued a certificate although documentation of the origin of diamonds was lacking (cf. Panel of Experts 12/2007, 12–14; Panel of Experts 06/2008, 12).

A major issue of concern was the lack of transparency concerning class C licenses. A few weeks before sanctions were lifted, the Assistant Minister for Mines responsible for issuing class B and C licenses had been dismissed for "granting bogus licenses for mining operations" (Inquirer Mar. 23, 2007). During the first six months of 2009, another three Assistant Ministers of the institution were dismissed for undisclosed reasons, including the new one responsible for Mines. Following patterns described above, the individual was subsequently nominated as Assistant Minister for Energy. The president, however, withdrew the nomination when parliament discussed earlier allegations of corruption against the official (Panel of Experts 06/2009, 11). In late 2008, revenue data suggested that 421 class C licenses had been awarded but the Ministry was unable or unwilling to provide records to the *Kimberley Process* or the Panel of Experts (Panel of Experts 12/2008, 10). Tens of thousands of artisanal miners were estimated to be operating. External assessments of the evolution of the diamond sector turned negative.

---

239 Further, among the first nine exports were five parcels of stockpiled diamonds that had been produced before Kimberley Process procedures were implemented. Documentation on these parcels had inevitably been deficient.

> "Liberia: (a) is in serious danger of non-compliance [with Kimberley Process requirements] in some areas, particularly with respect to the implementation of its system of internal controls; and (b) is not in compliance with provisions regarding data maintenance and sharing [with the Kimberley Process]. The Panel's assessment is more negative than that of the 2009 [Kimberley Process] review visit team, which concluded that Liberia had continued to meet the minimum Kimberley Process requirements but that in some cases it had only barely met those requirements." (Panel of Experts 12/2009, 10)

In 2009, relations between the *Kimberley Process* and the Ministry of Lands, and Mines suffered because authorities had shown little willingness to hand over information during the review team visit. The review team did not engage in providing new input to reforms but considered it necessary that Liberia implement earlier "recommendations" (ibid., 11). The Panel of Experts criticized, inter alia, the obvious use of class C licenses for class B operations without the intervention of Ministry officials, no progress on class C license data, dysfunctional regional offices, and widespread deficient handling of vouchers supposed to document the chain of custody. Further, a large share of Liberian diamonds was traded outside the system yet illegal traders were, according to a police officer, "arrested only when they do not agree to pay officials" (ibid., 20).

The Panel was in particular concerned about "an overall reduction in the political commitment to the [Kimberley Process] Scheme during the past 12 months" (ibid., 13).[240] When it raised the issue of conflict diamonds entering the system, the manager of the *Government Diamond Office* stated that this was the concern of the importers, in direct contravention of *Kimberley Process* principles (ibid., 17). The Deputy Minister opined "that perhaps the Ministry of Lands, Mines and Energy should change its approach in the future and refuse to implement recommendations of the Panel and the Kimberley Process" (ibid., 15). The senior minister, once a close confidante of Johnson Sirleaf and considered untouchable, was among the 20 percent of ministers not renominated after she dismissed the entire cabinet in November 2010 for a reshuffle. He was subsequently

---

240 However, this should not jeopardize *Kimberley Process* compliance, as the organization does not subject the industry to rigorous standards. The Panel itself expressed some concern (12/2009, 21—22). Ian Smillie, one of the founders of the organization, left the Process in 2009 because it had lost credibility. In October 2010, two international banks refused to finance deals in Kimberley-certified diamonds for fear for their reputation (Africa Mining Intelligence Oct. 20, 2010). In December 2011, Global Witness terminated its participation.

side-lined in the UP and did not run for the Senate seat for his Grand Cape Mount County he had sought. His son was candidate for a representative seat but lost the 2011 elections.

Over the years, volumes and value of gems traded through the official system increased. In the first nine months of 2009, the state collected some 222,000 dollars in royalties (ibid., 9) while the figure reached 576,800 dollars for the same period in 2012 (Panel of Experts 12/2012, 77). In particular, high-value gems, often mined by large companies, were increasingly certified. These reap considerably higher prices internationally when certified as being of legal origin. Yet six years after Johnson Sirleaf was first elected, diamond offices outside Monrovia were as dysfunctional as on the first day, with facilities being dilapidated and officials absent. Artisanal diamonds mined in Liberia were more likely to be certified in Sierra Leone than in Liberia, due to better accessibility of the system there. As a comprehensive monitoring system, which would need to include a significant security component for miners, traders and diamond office agents, would be very costly and revenues from diamonds were comparatively low, there were few incentives to establish monitoring capacity.[241] Indeed, it was unlikely that the system as originally envisaged could be viable. As a consequence, informal power holders—loosely structured but hierarchical networks of diamond merchants, mining camp leaders and miners—assumed authority over Liberia's hinterland diamond mining areas (ibid., 28–31).

In general, developments in the timber and diamonds sectors suggested that the state would not be able to assert its control over the hinterland economy without making use of the capacities—in terms of administrative expertise, capital, and private security—of foreign corporations. This corresponds to long-standing dynamics of Liberia's trade-based political economy. It was however uncertain to what extent the state would be able to oversee and regulate the foreign corporations, as the slow progress in bureaucratization and centralizing patrimonialism, reinforced by the fragmentation of its political elite, grant resourceful private actors great opportunities to influence politics. The political economy of Liberia's resource extraction thus suggested that significant weaknesses of legal-rational authority would continue to characterize the state.

241 In response, the US Agency for International Development contemplating to end its funding of the artisanal diamond scheme by mid-2012 (Africa Confidential Sept. 7, 2012).

4.7. From Taylor to Johnson Sirleaf: Major Issues

The major weakness of Taylor's governance was that he did not manage the transition from charismatic warlord rule to a mode of governance more adapted to less turbulent times. Charisma is transient, and Taylor's strategy of increasing patrimonial features of rule under circumstances of severe cash constrains was insufficient to maintain legitimacy among staff and generate it among a wider circle of elites. Cash constraints were related to the strategy of prioritizing political autonomy by foregoing Western donor support and autonomously tapping national and regional resources. Yet aggressive regional policies antagonized both neighbors and important members of the International Community, while substituting repression for legitimacy further eroded authority. Foreign dissatisfaction coupled with the erosion of the patronage networks that were integrating domestic elites eventually proved to be Taylor's undoing.

However, the rebels who had challenged Taylor had not established a viable alternative system of power, and given their political-military and ethnic minority background they stood few chances to successfully do so. More importantly, rebels knew their own limitations and how difficult it would be to maintain an authoritarian grip on power. In return for a guaranteed two-year pay-off, the armed factions consented to massive international intervention and democratic elections to determine who would control power. Institutionally, the transitional period was marked by a significant erosion of central power and increased private appropriation of offices, giving rise to a decentralized patrimonialism characterized by strong personal connections between relatively equal individuals and status groups. That is, patrimonial patterns linked relatively equal partners, and reciprocity served to stabilize a system of cooperation between power-holders rather than to stabilize hierarchies. Cooperative attitudes in the NTGL no doubt supported a transition that meant votes would replace military capacity as a source of power, even if cooperation primarily meant joint embezzlement.

The take-over of Ellen Johnson Sirleaf then signaled and represented major political change. Most importantly, power was re-centralized in a president internationally recognized as representing the sovereign state. The Johnson Sirleaf-led Liberia was a far cry from Taylor's in as much as Liberia accepted basic norms governing the behavior of states in the international system and aspired to take on a responsible role in the region. The

Johnson Sirleaf government further allowed democratic liberties and tolerated a great deal of criticism, if often grudgingly, representing the most important break with the past 185 years or so. Particularly appreciated internationally, Johnson Sirleaf started processes of institution building that would strengthen the bureaucratic, internationally understood (*anschluss-fähige*) element of the state. Yet, re-centralization of domination primarily took place informally in patrimonial fashion, and a priority of the government appeared was the fostering of relations of trust among Liberia's elite. Generally, the building of bureaucratic institutions is a long-term process, and there hardly was an alternative to firstly extending domination through informal networks. In addition, there was widespread resistance to bureaucratic reform among Liberia's elite. Forceful action against corruption would have been likely to spark a backlash that would have had a serious negative impact on the president's ability to direct a process of social change. Capacity building and disciplinary action aimed at reducing levels of private appropriation of offices to financially more sustainable ones. This already could increase the capacity of the state administration to implement central policy, i.e. serve as a tool in the central administration of power.

We should, however, recall that historically state-building all over the world for considerable periods proceeded informally as a centralization of personalized power. Centralization of power in Liberia with an internationally recognized president prepared to accept basic international norms was endorsed and massively supported internationally (for intuitively understandable reasons). Thus, the IMF's insistence that "Liberia initiated profound changes in its governance and economic management" (IMF June 30, 2010) appeared related to the fact that advisors sent by the Bretton Woods Institutions were ordered "to draw back from immediate involvement with such contentious issues" (Panel of Experts 06/2009, 19) that could provoke doubts over the government's commitment to "profound changes".

5. Conclusion

I can no longer see you suffer, you have suffered enough.
I love you from the bottom of my heart;
I will always remember you, wherever I am.
And I say: God willing, I will be back.
God bless you, and save the state!

Charles Taylor, Parting Speech (August 2003)

It may appear ironic that the man widely credited with destroying the Liberian state in pursuit of personal power should quit the presidency with a call to "save the state". Against the background of this study, however, the call is highly plausible. Not only did dynamics of political competition during the wars inadvertently strengthen principles of statehood, "the state" remained an important point of reference in the construction of the systems of domination that different political actors, including Charles Taylor and his NPFL, tried to impose on the Liberian people(s). Conceptions of authority, though, deviated significantly from the legal-rational ideal-type of statehood. The intellectual challenge is to make sense of the resilience of the state as a model of political organization on the one hand and the apparent weaknesses of statehood on the other. This conclusion will address this issue, firstly by explaining the political developments in Liberia that were the subject of this study. In a second step, I will reflect on implications of the Liberian case for democracy in Young States and their international relations.

The question that this study has tried to answer concerned what role the Liberian civil wars played in the trajectory of the Liberian state. In short, the study has shown that the wars were a societal reaction to state power that was increasingly lacking in legitimacy. Historically, the state had extended its reach but the complementary state-building process of the political integration of dominated people had been inadequately slow. One the one hand, the wars then engendered a drastic but temporary retrenchment of state powers. On the other, they overwhelmingly promoted political integration by entailing an unprecedented, charismatically mediated political mobilization of masses, in particular among the numerically dominant youthful segment of society. The political mobilization accompanying the wars was more national in character, and was more directly targeted at sovereign state power than ever before in Liberia's long history of localized conflicts between state forces and indigenous communities. In particular, with Charles Taylor's NPFL the traditional communitarian boundaries were razed, and mobilization explicitly was of a cross-ethnic character and also transcended Liberia's Counties. Though the appeal of his rivals was confined to narrow segments of Liberian society, their organizations vastly transcended the historically small-scale political communities characterizing eastern Liberia, and this mobilization evidently targeted state power too. Eventually, societal upheaval and the quest for ending armed violence opened up opportunities for re-defining relations between state and society. For the time being, these resulted in the extension of centralized, sovereign authority and a more "broad, equal, protective, and consultative" (cf. Tilly 2008, 13–14) arrangement. In a long-term perspective, the wars thus promoted state-building by overcoming elite resistance to political integration of the populace.

I will now present the argument in detail, pointing out key dynamics and steps of state formation that took place during the First War and the associated peace process, and thereafter. This corresponds to reviewing what the empirical chapters contributed to answering the questions of this study.

The First Liberian War engendered a far-reaching disintegration of the Liberian state. State decay reached its zenith when the IGNU government, representing the state, was dissolved, to be replaced by a Council of State staffed by factions controlling and rivaling for non-sovereign fiefs. However, the war continued to revolve around state power. Symbolically, this was expressed, for instance, in the AFL's claim to represent the state, despite it not taking orders from the interim governments, or the ULIMOs' and LPC's refusal to be called "rebels" and their insistence on fighting for "constitutional government". With both symbolic and material effect, Charles Taylor established the NPRA-*Government*, modeled on the institutions of the Liberian state and taking over state bureaucracy offices within its territory.

Beneath the temporary breakdown of sovereign central authority, state formation progressed during the First War by increasing political integration through mobilization of warriors and supporters. The war was accompanied by the greatest political mobilization Liberia ever experienced, and Charles Taylor's NPFL was the largest and most broad-based political movement Liberia had ever had. Warlords, to varying degrees, enjoyed primarily charismatic legitimacy, and assembled youths under their leadership. Through joining or associating with an armed force, more hinterland people than ever before became involved in political organizations pursuing central state power. It is likely that more hinterland people than ever before directly profited from the spoils of political-military power by way of plunder, even though this was accompanied by massive losses among other hinterland civilians.

Re-centralization of power was largely driven by classic monopoly mechanism dynamics. In order to increase the chances of achieving central state power, factions had to extend non-sovereign political authority and, in a closely related phenomenon, to accumulate economic values and opportunities. As there was no paramount authority and anyone's gains were another's losses in the zero-sum game of natural resource exploitation, competition and insecurity were key characteristics of relations between the warring parties, despite numerous instances of collusion. There was thus a tendency towards armed confrontations, which was likely to lead to accumulation of power by one side in the long run. Although, as Reno (1998) has stressed, the object of political control was trade rather than territory, controlling trade required consolidating territorial control. In order to prevent infiltration, and to secure points of extraction of natural commodities as well as the roads needed for evacuating these goods, wider areas had to be secured. When the NPFL regularly posted combatant units to remote hamlets devoid of any attractive economic opportunities, it did so for a purpose.

The NPFL not only possessed the most extensive authority structure, but was also well organized economically. It avoided many of the economic costs of administration by profiting from the exceptional charismatic legitimacy of its leader. Given the dismal organization of its adversaries, it would most likely have been able to quickly take over central state power had foreign powers not decided to intervene and sponsor rival armed groups. This means that the intermittent destruction of the Liberian state was, in essence, a political phenomenon, occasioned by political decisions of foreign governments, and the war economy developed in response to these political decisions.

From a political economy perspective, another mechanism (in addition to the monopoly mechanism) created strong pressures towards conquering sovereign state power. Firstly, features of war associated with insecurity, such as a shortened time horizon, decreasing investments in infrastructure and commodity exploitation, and repeated blockages of important trade routes, led to a decline in war economy profits. As this should, in theory, have concerned all warring parties to a similar extent, relative strength should have remained the same and re-centralization of authority should neither have been prevented nor promoted. The situation should, however, have prevented a temporary "comfortable stalemate" (cf. Zartmann 2003) from consolidating. Declining revenues adversely affect internal command and control of armed actors. This exerts pressures on warring party elites to generate revenues, which, in a zero-sum war economy situation, implies confronting rival armed groups. Declining returns of war economies thus increase competition between armed actors; and it is likely that one of these armed actors will accumulate power and prevail. In Liberia, the crucial contender, the ECOMOG, eventually pulled out of the competition because its Nigerian sponsors were not prepared to shoulder the associated economic and political costs any more, and the new Nigerian president did not consider withdrawal a personal defeat.

However, Charles Taylor's reign as president betrayed his promises of increased political integration. Yet he did start out with an effort to co-opt and consequently integrate major political trust networks centering on important Liberian personalities. This was facilitated by an increase in revenues due to increased logging, increased trade in Sierra Leonean diamonds, monopolistic political oversight over the rubber sector, and other features of the post-war political economy. However, Taylor did not succeed in attracting major new investments, largely because investors estimated Liberia to be too unstable to take the risk. Confirming these fears, major intra-elite conflicts developed over Taylor's refusal to more fundamentally integrate his potential rivals by allowing participation. When patrimonially co-opted elites expressed criticism, they were excluded. Concerns sparked by declining support among Liberia's elite further compelled Taylor to exclude other potential rivals, totally reversing the prior tendency of increasing integration. The effect of this was all the more destabilizing because most of the youths that had fought for armed groups, including the NPFL, were re-marginalized well before the dynamics of exclusion began to prevail in elite circles.

Taylor's problems grew more acute because of the meager revenue occasioned by the lack of reconciliation with regional states and Western donors. Perceiving important donors and relevant regional states as hostile, Taylor abstained from switching to donor funds and regional cooperation as resources to maintain power. Obtaining Western and increased regional support would have required allowing more thorough democratization, undertaking a security sector reform that would have weakened his personal control over security forces, and cutting ties with the RUF, i.e. undertaking actions acutely threatening his power while there would be but uncertain benefits in return. Taylor's dilemma of rule was that the very strategy that had once allowed him to rise eventually provoked enough foreign and domestic opposition to successfully challenge his rule.

The lack of political integration also becomes evident when we confront political developments with Charles Tilly's processes underlying democratization and de-democratization. In this perspective, a major blow to democratization was the failure to gain control over the "major power center" represented by ULIMO-J. This was related to stalling and eventually declining "integration between interpersonal networks of trust [...] and public politics". The two combined to re-emphasize the "major categorical inequalities" around which the war had been organized (cf. Tilly 2008, 23). In conclusion, none of the processes underlying democratization had been executed.

The Second Liberian War then took place under circumstances more amiable to eventual political integration of a broader population. Increasingly, Taylor lost his charismatic appeal, and the disintegration of the NPFL opened up opportunities for integration into alternative networks. On the rivaling side, LURD had learned from previous failures of the ULIMOs. In contrast to their predecessors fighting in the First War, both LURD and MODEL took steps to prevent commanders from autonomously exploiting natural resources, attempted to maintain civilian administrative structures that could liaise with the rebel command, and tried to generate legitimacy by providing services, even if symbolic ones, to populations in their territories. Although there was no definite consensus among the rebels on the post-war political order, a generally agreed rhetorical formula was that democratic elections should determine future governments. Given that, for historical reasons, democratic institutions are widely accepted in Liberia, this framing of the war effort made formal democratization virtually the only plausible outcome of a war settlement. Yet many of the informal practices that historically undermined Liberia's formal democratic institutions form part of a domestic concept of democracy and enjoy similar acceptance.

In the interim, however, a power-sharing government took over. During this period, extraordinary political integration of trust networks and attenuation of categorical inequalities in politics took place. For instance, members of the diverse armed groups and civilian elites joined hands in privately appropriating formally public resources, and state employment surged as elites helped clients to benefit from the spoils of political power. While the political integration dimension of state-building received a boost, central state control over the country remained weak as autonomous elite-centered networks and bands of ex-combatants assumed control over hinterland fiefs and even Monrovian territories (for instance, the Freeport). However, as interim rule was accompanied by a comprehensive disarmament and demobilization process, we can consider all three of Tilly's dimensions of processes of democratization to have been strengthened.

During the reign of democratically elected Ellen Johnson Sirleaf, both state-building dimensions of extension of authority and political integration have reached exceptionally high levels by Liberian standards. This has taken place against the background of major changes in Liberia's political economy. Export of Taylor's most important sources of foreign exchange, diamonds and timber, was initially stopped and had little relevance for financing central authority when it was resumed. These revenues were replaced by a massive, politically motivated influx of foreign resources, both in terms of economic capital and security capacities. The influx and direct, massive military support for the Johnson Sirleaf government was, to a large extent, occasioned by the expectation that she would promote a Liberia tending towards more conventional contemporary notions of statehood. This includes functioning within an international system of states (rather than replacing formal state-state relations with informal state-foreign rebel relations), guaranteeing security of foreign investment, subscribing to some form of democratic competition, and strengthening the bureaucratic rule of law. Other post-war governments, for instance that of Mozambique, have managed to make foreign budget support a major source of government finances over extended periods. Although Liberian revenue from natural resources will rise in the future, foreign support may remain an important component of the finances of power, and become a systemic feature rather than an intermittent phenomenon.

Following Charles Tilly, we can argue that the crises, and in particular the final settlement, offered an (ultimately realized) opportunity to renegotiate state-society relations to the relative benefit of society. As

Acemoglu and Robinson (2009) have stressed, however, long-term democratic quality is dependent on society's ability to consistently make demands on the state. Liberia's political economy fuelled by natural resources and donor assistance is likely to favor the state in state-society negotiations. We will see in the future whether Liberia's relatively vibrant and well-organized civil society will be able to balance adverse political economy conditions. As Mozambique and other examples demonstrate, foreign donors are likely not to take too close a look at democratic quality and the rule of law before disbursing funds if the recipient state continues to tend to conform to expectations and its actions do not become an evident embarrassment to donors.

A priority of the Johnson Sirleaf government is the strengthening and political integration of relations of trust, while rationalization of governance is another, if secondary, objective. For instance, increasing allegations of use of office for private gain against the LPRC boss led to a deteriorating relationship with the president. Yet, the manager was eventually fired for abuse of trust by embarrassing the president in front of the Liberian public and Western donors by leaking the voice recordings, after she had publicly backed him on many occasions. On the other hand, a significant number of long-term, close confidantes of Johnson Sirleaf had to leave their positions, apparently because of abuse of office powers for private gain.

Strengthening and integration of relations of trust are important components of processes furthering democratization, i.e. the integration dimension of state-building. In as much as revenues from natural resources are centrally controlled and could be employed to foster central integration, Liberia's trade-based accumulation could further processes underlying democratization. Central control of revenues was strongest when large, foreign-owned, substantially bureaucratically organized companies such as *Arcelor Mittal* exploited resources.

Yet this was often not the case. In the timber sector, a large, foreign and criminally oriented company dominated, and officials in the sector fully appropriated their office powers. The dismissals of the two Managing Directors demonstrate the difficulties of building networks of trust, as did the fate of the Minister of Lands and Mines. The diamond sector is particularly prone to decentralized control, complicating integration of officials overseeing the industry. The systematic decentralized violations of bureaucratic norms I have shown are not an aberration from general trends.

Rather, the natural resource sector is central to the Liberian state, and the way it is managed tells a lot about the character of the state.

Here, an important caveat concerning Liberia's democracy is in order. As the theoretic chapter outlined, "prebendal patrimonialism" is a borderline case of legitimate authority. Patterns of *decentralized patrimonialism* in Liberia, demonstrated by ubiquitous appropriation of powers by staff and collusion against her reforms, prove that democratic elections are only partially effective in creating the belief of (integrated) elites in the legitimacy of the president. Concomitantly, many of Liberia's elites and significant parts of the populace believe that (some degree of) authoritarian rule is necessary to maintain order. Although there are countervailing tendencies, this diminishes prospects of democratization.

Even centralized (neo-)patrimonial patterns can only partly be reconciled with strengthening of bureaucratic state authority. This implies that legal provisions promoting equity will remain weak. Generation and allocation of state revenues are largely determined by the distribution of power, and are little mediated by law. The non-universal nature of patronage ties (cf. Hyden 2000) may undermine the "broad and equal consultation" (Tilly) characteristic of democratic conditions. On the other hand, broadening the popular base of government is likely to mean relatively more "broad and equal consultation" and thus represent relative democratization. For instance President Johnson Sirleaf has turned "market women", a numerically and economically important but poorly organized and politically marginalized segment of Liberian society, into a constituency of her government.

Post-war Liberia illustrates patterns of private, trans-nationally integrated politics characterizing many Young States. As funds accrue from external actors, we could argue that the government is accountable to external players rather than to internal forces, reducing the powers of domestic society. Yet at the same time, the international system rewards statehood and its most powerful actors advocate democratization. Privatization and internationalization of governance is to some extent compatible with state-building and democratization. The Liberian state is first of all characterized by its contradictions and cannot be reduced to one (e.g. patrimonial) logic.

For the time being, we can conclude that Liberia has made tremendous progress on both the authority-extension and society-integration dimensions of state-building, and that the wars played a major role in this development. However, in so far as Liberia remains democratic, its democracy will deviate considerably from the liberal ideal. This deviation will concern virtually all dimensions of governance. Liberia is likely to feature a system of elite privilege based on privatization of public office, circumvention of bureaucratic processes, and prevention of effective rule of law where it threatens elite interests.

***

Above, I have summarized the dynamics of political development in Liberia. But what are the implications of this study beyond the Liberian case? On the following pages, I will briefly reflect on the dynamics of civil wars and state-building, civil wars and the international system of states, and democracy in states where bureaucracies are weak.

A number of authors have interpreted contemporary civil wars as processes of privatization of politics engendering "state collapse" in terms of both decay of conventional state institutions and replacement of public politics by private racketeering. With slight variations, both Kaldor (1998) and Münkler (2002; 2006) have described these wars as fuelled by private economic interests in criminal activities and symbolically sustained by sectarian identities. Both features appear inimical to re-erection of state rule (cf. Münkler 2006, 142). Collier et al. (2004) lent further support to this thesis by interpreting war as a business that may be viable under certain circumstances; in particular, sufficient natural resource endowments. The present case study of Liberia does not support the thesis of civil war being inimical to dynamics of imposition of state rule. As I have argued, monopoly mechanism dynamics continue to work.

Further, violent competition entails significant costs, and any actor accumulating sufficient power to suppress violence reaps significant rewards, parts of which can be invested to further accumulate power. For superior military actors, it is advantageous to organize as states, because this offers superior access to diplomatic and foreign economic resources, likely outweighing the gains of informal organization.[242] Yet even though I stress the prevalence of classic mechanisms of state-building, Young States clearly do not simply reproduce the European experience.

---

242 Generally, non-sovereign informality offers few benefits, and states even have a competitive advantage in organized crime as occasioned by diplomatic privileges, the ability to define what is legal in the national arena, and ability to influence international law.

Schlichte (2006) tentatively suggested that political economy features—in particular, financing of state domination through taxing of natural resource exports—and the internationalization of governance, understood primarily in terms of foreign support for weak state militaries, were more important causes of weak statehood than was war. As I have made clear, trade-based capitalism is associated with neo-patrimonial rule and this complex constitutes the major *longue durée* pattern in Liberia's political history. This study suggests that natural resource exports help extending state authority and central rulers' interests in controlling appropriation of revenues by subaltern officials may promote bureaucratization. Yet bureaucratization focuses on administrative enclaves of revenue generation. This focus on enclaves from which bureaucratic control may expand has historically been the rule in states, not an exception. By contrast, external military support for weak, illegitimate actors constituted a major impediment to the development of statehood. Yet the UNMIL operation, in turn, strongly supported the recentralization of legitimate authority, indicating that effects of internationalization of security governance are ambivalent (cf. Atkinson 2008).

In a broader perspective, the provision of rents to states in the form of development assistance represents internationalization of governance, and such rents can be expected to have effects similar to those of natural resource rents. In Liberia, the substitution of pro-democracy rhetoric for Cold War-related rhetoric was a precondition for receiving politically motivated Western donor assistance. Contradicting Bayart's (2000) reasoning, external support for democratic state-building may increase the relative importance of society for central authority.[243]

In view of Reno's (1998; 2000) and Lock and Kurtenbach's (2004) argument that neo-liberal reform is associated with internal war, as discussed in the introduction, in the Liberian case refusal to implement democratic reforms had a much more immediate negative impact on state authority.[244] Although some democratic deficits are conveniently overlooked by donors, geopolitically little important recipient states have to respect limits on authoritarian governance. The donor discourse of democ-

243 However, some states may be able to substitute "War on Terror" related assistance for democracy support.

244 This should not be misunderstood as a plea for neo-liberal politics. By contrast, the current crisis of neo-liberal ideology may engender important opportunities for state-building.

ratization thus grants some power to society. It remains to be seen how the growing importance of new players, notably China, affects these developments. As said above, implications of the internationalization of governance are ambivalent.

The economic and political integration of Young State societies into global relations is thus associated both with features that impede and others that promote statehood. Yet we cannot reduce the causes of weak statehood to international factors. Initial conditions in Young States may strongly deviate from those once found in Western societies. The young age of the Liberian state, associated traditional conceptions of authority as a private affair, historical patterns of fragmented authority and associated cultural heterogeneity, all go a long way in explaining weak statehood in Liberia and beyond. Yet the international system tends to reproduce itself by promoting states as principles of political organization. By and large, the contemporary form of international relations is a major factor underlying the spread of states and principles of statehood, rather than one that prevents the latter from being realized.

Finally, what does the Liberian case contribute to theories of democratization? First, it illustrates the intrinsic link between bureaucratic political organization and democracy. Only a bureaucracy can uniformly impose central, democratic decisions on a people. As bureaucratization is a long-term process spanning generations, this would imply that, at best, countries like Liberia can establish some form of "electoral democracy" while democratic decisions have little impact on administrative practices.

It may be more useful to not consider certain fixed characteristics as qualifying a political regime to be democratic, but instead to consider democracy as an ideal of maximally "broad, equal, protective, and consultative" (Tilly 2008, 29) relations between states and their peoples. In polities with weak bureaucracies, comprehensive ties of patronage tending towards patrimonially integrating the whole population may most closely conform to such a situation. The broad and equal character of relations is promoted by multiplying communication channels between the state and citizens. This would imply that even patrimonial parliaments promote democratization, provided legislators are accountable to their constituencies. Where regional cleavages are politically dominant, a majority voting system based on small constituencies may most effectively promote broad representation (cf. Reilly 2005).

Accountability and consultation are promoted by regular, frequent elections. Regular elections further produce pressures on political elites to increase the number of their clients (Bueno de Mesquita et al. 2002). The larger the number of clients, the more cost effective is allocation of patronage in the form of collective goods (ibid.). Inasmuch as collective goods, such as safe drinking water, health and education, promote economic growth, the state may even promote economic development. Generally, neo-patrimonial politics implies prioritizing consumption over investment. However, interests in maintenance of collective goods may promote bureaucratization. Yet globally, effects of democracy on bureaucratic governance are not uniform. Frequent elections may as well promote short-term time horizons reinforcing patrimonial politics.

As I argued in this study, there are many variants of neo-patrimonialism, and neo-patrimonialism is insufficient an explanation for phenomena like civil war, authoritarianism or ubiquitous corruption. The intellectual challenge is to analyze how different types of neo-patrimonialism relate to civil and political liberties or abuse of office powers. A key question of future research should be how and to what extent broad, equal, protective, and consultative relations between peoples and power holders are possible in societies with weak bureaucratic institutions.

Bibliography

Aboagye, Festus B. (1999). *ECOMOG: A Sub-regional Experience in Conflict Resolution, Management and Peace-keeping in Liberia*. Accra: Sedco.

Acemoglu, Daron, and James A. Robinson (2009). *Economic Origins of Dictatorship and Democracy*. Cambridge et al: Cambridge University Press.

Adebayo, Adekeye (2002a). *Building Peace in West Africa: Liberia, Sierra Leone, and Guinea-Bissau*. International Peace Academy, Boulder/London: Lynne Rienner.

Adebayo, Adekeye (2002b). *Liberia's Civil War: Nigeria, ECOMOG, and Regional Security in West Africa*. Boulder/London: Lynne Rienner.

Africa Confidential (May 17, 1991). Sparking Fires in West Africa.

— (Nov. 6, 1992). The Forces in Contention.

— (Mar. 4, 1994). Liberia: Problematic Peacekeeping.

— (May 10, 1996). Liberia: Out of Control.

— (Jan. 22, 1999). West Africa According to Mr. Taylor.

— (Feb 19, 1999). Taylorland Under Siege.

— (May 12, 2000). The Battle for Freetown.

— (June 23, 2000). Godfather to the Rebels.

— (July 21, 2000). Cross-border Crisis.

— (June 29, 2001). Sierra Leone: Precarious Calm.

— (May 16, 2003). Liberia: Horse Trading, Arms-Trading.

— (Apr. 29, 2005a). Double WAMCO.

— (Apr. 29, 2005b). Warlord on the Loose.

— (Oct. 21, 2005). Penalty Shoot Out: Soccer Star George Weah Kept His Election Lead and the Dealmakers Are Hard at Work.

— (Nov. 18, 2005). Off-road Rage.

— (Jan. 20, 2006). Hope at last: The New Government Blends Technocrats, Dodgy Names and Good Intentions.

— (Apr. 14, 2006). Taylor's Trajectories.

— (Dec. 15, 2006). Economy Up, Politics Down: The Post-War Economy Is Easier to Manage than Monrovia's Politicians.

— (Feb 2, 2007). Snowe White-out.

— (Aug. 3, 2007). Rumours and Plots.

— (Oct. 3, 2008). Graft Never Really Went Away.

— (Nov. 6, 2009). A Killing in Kakata.

— (May 14, 2010). A Second Term for Sirleaf.

— (Jan 7, 2011). Johnson Sirleaf Stands on Her Record.

— (July 22, 2011). Honesty: Not the Easiest Policy.

— (Oct. 7, 2011). Ellen Wants First Round Win.

— (Sept. 7, 2012). Not Out of the Woods.

— (Nov. 16, 2012). What Price the Unity Party.

Africa Mining Intelligence (Oct. 20, 2010). Banks Give Thumbs Down to Zimbabwe Diamonds.

AKUF (2003). "Sierra Leone". Ed. Wolfgang Schreiber: *Das Kriegsgeschehen 2002: Daten und Tendenzen der Krieg und bewaffneten Konflikte.* Opladen: Leske + Budrich, by Jérôme Cholet, 101–106.

— (2004). *Das Kriegsgeschehen 2003: Daten und Tendenzen der Kriege und bewaffneten Konflikte.* Ed. Wolfgang Schreiber. Wiesbaden: Verlag für Sozialwissenschaften.

Alao, Abiodun (1998). *The Burden of Collective Goodwill: The International Involvement in the Liberian Civil War.* Aldershot/Burlington: Ashgate.

Amnesty International (1995). *Liberia: A New Peace Agreement–An Opportunity to Introduce Human Rights Protection.* Report AFR 34/0

Anderson, Benedict (2006): *Imagined Communities: Reflections on the Origin and Spread of Nations.* London/New York: Verso.

Anderson, Hilary (1993). "Meeting ULIMO". in: BBC Focus on Africa, reprinted in: *Liberia Newsletter*, Vol. 9, No. 44, Liberia Working Group, Bremen, p.20.

Analyst (Monrovia). (Aug. 5, 2004). Dweh Threatens War, if—Gen. Opande Wheeled Sekou Away.

— (Mar. 7, 2006). UP Accused of Breach of MOU, RULP Threatens to Legal Action.

— (Mar. 13, 2006). RULP Threatens to Sue Unity Party for Refusal to Honor MOU.

— (Feb. 20, 2007). Statement by Willis D. Knuckles, Jr.

— (Oct. 16, 2009). Information Minister Bropleh Suspended.

— (Feb. 16, 2010). Resignation Justice: The Bias, Stigma and Waste in Ellen's Style of Action Against Officials.

— (Oct. 1, 2012). Pres. Sirleaf Mesmerizes Se. Taylor—Performance Enlightened Her.

Ashkenazi, Michael, and Marc von Boemcken (2011). "Liberia". In Marc von Boemcken (ed.). *Commercial Security and Development.* Bonn International Center for Conversion Brief 45, Bonn, pp. 35–48. 02/23/2013 http://www.bicc.de/uploads/tx_bicctools/brief45.pdf

Atkinson, Philippa (1997). *The War Economy in Liberia: A Political Analysis.* Relief and Rehabilitation Network Paper No. 22. Overseas Development Institute, London.

Atkinson, Philippa (2008). Liberal Interventionism in Liberia: Towards a Tentatively Just Approach?. *Conflict, Security and Development*, Vol. 8 , No. 1, 15–45.

Auty, Richard M. (ed.). (2001). *Resource Abundance and Economic Development.* Helsinki/Oxford: Oxford University Press.

Barr, Tyron (1993). The ECOMOG Initiative in Liberia: A Liberian Perspective. *Issue: A Journal of Opinion*, Vol. 21, No. 1–2, 74–83.

Basedau, Matthias (2003). *Erfolgsbedingungen von Demokratie im subsaharischen Afrika: ein systematischer Vergleich ausgewählter Länder.* Opladen: Leske+Budrich.

Bayart, Jean-François (1993). *The State in Africa: Politics of the Belly.* London: Longmann.

— (2000): Africa in the World: A History of Extraversion. *African Affairs*, Vol. 99, No. 395, pp. 217–267.

BBC (Oct. 25, 1999). Liberia Peace Cost Nigeria 8 Billion Dollars. 08/19/2010 http://news.bbc.co.uk/2/hi/africa/485191.stm

— (May 2, 2008). Taylor "Had Billions" in US Bank. 05/02/2008 http://news.bbc.co.uk/2/hi/africa/7379536.stm

— (July 28, 2009). African View: Memories of Charles Taylor, by Elizabeth Ohene. 07/28/2009 http://news.bbc.co.uk/2/hi/africa/8171244.stm

Bendel, Petra, and Michael Krennerich (2003). "Einleitung: Staat und Rechtstaat in jungen Demokratien: eine Problemskizze". In Petra Bendel, Aurel Croissant, and Friedrich Rüb (eds.). *Demokratie und Staatlichkeit: Systemwechsel zwischen Staatsreform und Staatskollaps*, 9–34. Opladen: Leske + Budrich.

Berg-Schlosser, Dirk (2005). "Korruption und Entwicklungsforschung". In Ulrich von Alemann (ed.). *Dimensionen politischer Korruption: Beiträge zum Stand der internationalen Forschung*, 311–327. PVS-Sonderheft 35, Wiesbaden: Verlag für Sozialwissenschaften.

Berkeley, Bill (1992). Between Repression and Slaughter. *The Atlantic* (Washington, D.C.), Dec., 53–64.

Billon, Philippe Le (2001). The Political Ecology of War: Natural Resources and Armed Conflict. *Political Geography* 20, 561–584.

Blair, Robert (2009). In Defense of Charles Taylor. Huffington Post, (29.6.). 19.09.2009 http://www.huffingtonpost.com/robert-blair/in-defense-of-charles-tay_b_246744.html

Blake, Charles, and Christopher Martin (2006). The Dynamics of Political Corruption: Re-examining the Influence of Democracy. *Democratization*, Vol. 13, No. 1, 1–14.

Blunt, Elizabeth (1990). The BBC's War. *Focus on Africa* (BBC Magazine), Vol. 1, No. 3, 5–8.

Bøås, Morten, and Anne Hatløy (2008). 'Getting In, Getting Out': Militia Membership and Prospects for Re-integration in Post-war Liberia. *Journal of Modern African Studies*, Vol. 40, No. 1, 33–55.

Boyd, Richard (2006). "The Making of State-Bureaucracy Relations in Japan". In Richard Boyd and Ngo Tak-Wing (eds). *State Making in Asia,* 53–90. New York/Abingdon: Routledge.

Brabazon, James (2003). *Liberia: Liberians United for Reconciliation and Democracy.* Royal Institute for African Affairs, Armed Non-State Actors Project, Briefing Paper No. 1. 05/10/2007.
http://www.chathamhouse.org.uk/pdf/research/africa/Brabazon%20BP.pdf

Bratton, Michael, and Nicholas van de Walle (1994). Neopatrimonial Regimes and Political Transitions in Africa. *World Politics,* Vol 46, No. 4.

— (1997). *Democratic Experiments in Africa: Regime in Transitions in Comparative Perspective.* Cambridge: Cambridge University Press.

Braudel, Fernand (1984). "Geschichte und Sozialwissenschaften: Die 'longue durée'". In Hans-Ulrich Wehler (ed.). *Geschichte und Soziologie,* 189-215. Königstein/Ts: Athenäum.

Brewer, Herbert Jr., and Ezekiel Pajibo (1995). More Thoughts on the Liberian National Conference. *Liberian Studies Journal,* Vol. 20, No. 1, 126–130.

Bueno de Mesquita, Bruce, James D. Morrow, Randolph M. Siverson, and Alastair Smith, (2002). Political Institutions, Policy Choice and the Survival of Leaders. *British Journal of Political Science,* Vol. 32, No. 4, 559–590.

Burrowes, Carl Patrick (1995). Democracy or Disarmament: Some Second Thoughts on Amos Sawyer and Contemporary Politicians. *Liberian Studies Journal,* Vol. 20, No. 1, 117–125.

Chabal, Patrick (2009). *Africa: The Politics of Suffering and Smiling.* London: Zed Books.

Chabal, Patrick, and Jean Pascal Daloz (1999). *Africa Works: Disorder as Political Instrument.* Oxford et al: James Currey.

— (2006). *Culture Troubles: Politics and the Interpretation of Meaning.* London: Hurst & Company.

Christy, Cuthbert (1931). Liberia in 1930. *Geographical Journal,* Vol. 77, No. 6, 515–540.

Clapham, Christopher (1985). *Third World Politics: An Introduction.* Landon/Sidney: Croom Helm.

Cohen, Herman J. (2000): *Intervening in Africa: Superpower Peacemaking in a Troubled Continent.* New York: St. Martin's Press.

Collier, Paul (2000). "Doing Well out of War: An Economic Perspective". In Mats Berdal and David M. Malone (eds.). *Greed & Grievance: Economic Agendas in Civil Wars,* 91–111. Boulder/London: Lynne Rienner.

Collier, Paul, and Anke Hoeffler, (2004). Greed and Grievance in Civil War. *Oxford Economic Papers* Vol. 56, No. 4, 563–595.

Conrad, Burkhard (2006). Informal Politics. *Hamburg Review of Social Sciences,* Vol. 1, No. 3, 256–272.

Consortium Agrifor Consult (2004). *FDA: Management and Financial Review. Final Report,* Vol. 1/Main Report, commissioned by the European Commission Institutional Support Programme Liberia.

CPA (2003). *Comprehensive Peace Agreement Between the Government of Liberia and the Liberians United for Reconciliation and Democracy (LURD) and the Movement for*

Democracy in Liberia (MODEL) and Political Parties. Accra 18th Aug., 2003. 01/21/2004. http://www.usip.org/files/file/resources/collections/peace_agreements/liberia_08182003.pdf

Dahl, Robert A. (1998). *On Democracy.* New Haven: Yale University Press.

Daily Observer (Monrovia) (Mar. 22–26, 1996). Panic Grips Monrovia.

— (Aug. 1, 2005). PRODEM Elects Damate Conneh as it's (sic) Standard Bearer.

— (Mar. 26, 2007). Bombshell at NPA: Managing Director, 2 Deputies Relieved.

Daniels, Anthony (1991). Ears For Souvenirs. *The Spectator,* (20.4), 16–18. http://www.diamondintelligence.com/magazine/magazine.aspx?id=7895

Dolo, Emmanuel (1996). *Democracy Versus Dictatorship: The Quest for Freedom and Justice in Africa's Oldest Republic.* Lanham et al: University Press of America.

Dwan, Renata, and Laura Bailey (2006). *Liberia's Governance and Economic Management Assistance Programme* (GEMAP: A Joint Review by the Department of Peacekeeping Operations' Peacekeeping Best Practices Section and the World Bank's Fragile States Group. UN DPKO/World Bank, (May). 30.05.2007. http://www.peacekeepingbestpractices.unlb.org/PBPS/Library/DPKO-WB%20joint%20review%20of%20GEMAP%20FINAL.pdf

Easton, David (1953). *The Political System: An Inquiry into the State of Political Science.* New York: Knopf.

ECOWAS (1990). "Decision A/DEC.1/8/90 of the ECOWAS Standing Mediation Committee on the Cease-Fire and Establishment of an ECOWAS Cease-Fire Monitoring Group for Liberia, taken in Banjul, 7 August 1990". In Marc Weller (ed.). (1994). *Regional Peace-Keeping and International Enforcement: The Liberian Crisis,* 67–69. Cambridge: Cambridge University Press.

ECOWAS (2005). *Final Report of the ECOWAS Team of Investigators on Financial Crime in Liberia.* Unpublished document prepared in Monrovia.

EIU (Economist Intelligence Unit) (1996). Guinea, Sierra Leone, Liberia: Country Profile 1996–97.

— (07/1996). Guinea, Sierra Leone, Liberia: Country Report 3rd Quarter, July.

— (10/1997). Guinea, Sierra Leone, Liberia: Country Report 4th Quarter, October.

— (04/1998). Guinea, Sierra Leone, Liberia: Country Report 2nd Quarter, Apr..

— (07/1998). Guinea, Sierra Leone, Liberia: Country Report 3rd Quarter, July.

— (1999). Guinea, Sierra Leone, Liberia: Country Profile 1999–2000.

— (01/1999). Guinea, Sierra Leone, Liberia: Country Report 1st Quarter, January.

— (08/1999). Guinea, Sierra Leone, Liberia: Country Report 3rd Quarter, August.

— (06/2010). Liberia: Country Report, June.

Eisenstadt, Shmuel N., and René Lemarchand (eds.). (1981). *Political Clientelism, Patronage and Development.* Beverly Hills/London: Sage.

Elias, Norbert (1999). *Über den Prozess der Zivilisation: Wandlungen der Gesellschaft - Entwurf zu einer Theorie der Zivilisation* (Vol. 2). Frankfurt am Main: Suhrkamp.

— (2006a). *Was ist Soziologie?* Gesammelte Schriften, Vol. 5, Frankfurt am Main: Suhrkamp.

— (2006b): "Über den Rückzug der Soziologen auf die Gegenwart (I) (1983)". In Norbert Elias. *Aufsätze und andere Schriften II,* 389–408. Gesammelte Schriften, Vol. 15, Frankfurt am Main: Suhrkamp.

Ellis, Stephen (2007a): *The Mask of Anarchy: The Destruction of Liberia and the Religious Dimension of an African Civil War.* Third Impression. London: Hurst & Company.

— (2007b). "Liberia". In Andreas Mehler, Henning Melber and Klaas van Walraven (eds.). *Africa Yearbook: Politics, Economy and Society South of the Sahara in 2006,* 115–121. Leiden/Boston: Brill.

— (2008): "Liberia". In Andreas Mehler, Henning Melber and Klaas van Walraven (eds.). *Africa Yearbook: Politics, Economy and Society South of the Sahara in 2007,* 117–124. Leiden/Boston: Brill.

Ellis, Stephen, and Gerrie ter Haar (2004). *Worlds of Power: Religious Thought and Political Practice in Africa.* London: Hurst & Company.

Elwert, Georg (1989). Nationalismus und Ethnizität: Über die Bildung von Wir-Gruppen. *Kölner Zeitschrift für Soziologie und Sozialpsychologie,* Vol. 41, No. 3, 440–464.

Erdmann, Gero (2003). "Apokalyptische Trias: Staatsversagen, Staatsverfall und Staatszerfall". In Petra Bendel, Aurel Croissant and Friedrich Rüb (eds.). *Demokratie und Staatlichkeit: Systemwechsel zwischen Staatsreform und Staatskollaps,* 267–292. Opladen: Leske + Budrich.

Erdmann, Gero, and Ulf Engel (2007). Neopatrimonialism Reconsidered: Critical Review and Elaboration of an Elusive Concept. *Commonwealth & Comparative Politics,* Vol. 45, No. 1, 95–119.

Ernst & Young (2005a). *Liberia Petroleum Refining Company "LPRC": Executive Audit Report, Audited Period from October 2003 to June 2004,* Volume 1. Commissioned by the European Commission Institutional Support Programme Liberia.

— (2005b). *Liberia Petroleum Refining Company "LPRC". Detailed Audit Report, Audited Period from October 2003 to June 2004,* Volume 2. Commissioned by the European Commission Institutional Support Programme Liberia.

— (2005c): *National Port Authority (NPA): Systems and Financial Audit.* Executive Report, Volume 1. Commissioned by the European Commission Institutional Support Programme Liberia.

— (2005d). *National Port Authority (NPA): Systems and Financial Audit.* Detailed Report, Volume 2. Commissioned by the European Commission Institutional Support Programme Liberia.

Eye, The (Monrovia) (1992). $ 350,000 Market for Caldwell, New Georgia, Oct. 15.

Executive Mansion (May 27, 2011). *Appointment of Emanuel Shaw as LAA Chairman Withdrawn over Sanctions.* Press Release. 06/15/2011. http://www.emansion.gov.lr/2press.php?news_id=1903&related=7&pg=sp

— (Jan 5, 2013): *Liberian President Issues Executive Order No. 44, Declaring Moratorium On Private Use Permits to Protect Nation's Forests.* Press Release, 02/23/2013.

http://allafrica.com/stories/printable/201301142016.html
Fahnbulleh, Henry Boima (2002). Now They Know!. *The Perspective*, (2.9.). 6/11/2010. http://www.theperspective.org/nowtheyknow.html
Farah, Douglas (2005). *Following Taylor's Money: A Path of War and Destruction.* Coalition for International Justice Report (May), Washinton, D.C.
Farah, Douglas, and Stephen Braun (2007). *Merchant of Death: Money, Guns, Planes, and the Man Who Makes War Possible.* Hoboken: Wiley & Sons.
FDA (Forestry Development Authority) (2010). *Commercial Forestry Department.* 10.06.2010. http://www.fda.gov.lr/content.php?sub=Commercial%20Forestry&related=Commercial%20Forestry
Financial Times (July 22, 1997): Liberian Warlord Heads for Poll Victory, by Mark Huband.
Foucault, Michel (1994). *Überwachen und Strafen: Die Geburt des Gefängnisses.* Frankfurt am Main: Suhrkamp.
Forest Concession Review Committee (2005). *Report of the Forest Concession Review Committee.* Review Phase III, June. 8/19/2010.
http://www.fao.org/forestry/lfi/29664
Frankfurter Rundschau (Mar. 1, 1993). Keiner spricht von Liberia,.
— (Aug. 9, 1995). Hinter den Kautschukbäumen lauert der Tod, by Wolfgang Kunath,.
— (Sept. 23, 1996). Böse Ahnung für die Zukunft: Ist Liberias neue Staatschefin eine Marionette der Warlords?, by Wolfgang Kunath.
Frontline World (May 2005). A Political Survivor: Interview With Daniel Chea,. 1/20/2007 http://www.pbs.org/frontlineworld/stories/liberia/chea.html
Gberie, Lansana (2002). *War and Peace in Sierra Leone: Diamonds, Corruption and the Lebanese Connection. Partnership Africa Canada, Diamonds and Human Security Project*, Occasional Paper #6. 10./20/2004.
http://www.pacweb.org/Documents/diamonds_KP/6_War-Peace_sierraleone_Eng-Nov2002.pdf
— (2009). "Liberia". In Andreas Mehler, Henning Melber and Klaas van Walraven (eds.). *Africa Yearbook: Politics, Economy and Society South of the Sahara in 2008,* 117–122. Leiden/Boston: Brill.
Gerdes, Felix (2006). *Forced Migration and Armed Conflict: An Analytical Framework and a Case Study of Refugee-Warriors in Guinea.* Research Unit of Wars, Working Paper 1/06, University of Hamburg, Hamburg. 01/18/2009. http://www.sozialwiss.uni-hamburg.de/publish/Ipw/Akuf/publ/AP2006–1.pdf
— (2009). "Militärputsch in Guinea. Hintergründe der aktuellen Entwicklungen". *AKUF-Analysen* Nr. 3, Januar 2009. 01/18/2009
http://www.sozialwiss.uni-hamburg.de/publish/Ipw/Akuf/publ/AKUF-Analysen-03.pdf
— (2010). "Die Militarisierung liberianischer Flüchtlinge in Guinea". In Grete Misselwitz and Klaus Schlichte (eds.). *Politik der Unentschiedenheit: Die*

internationale Politik und ihr Umgang mit Kriegsflüchtlingen, 135–161. Bielefeld: Transcript.

— (2011). *Liberia's Post-war Elite. A New Era of Inclusive Ownership or Old Wine in New Bottles?* Working Paper 1/2011, Research Unit of Wars, University of Hamburg. 04/15/2013. http://www.wiso.uni-hamburg.de/fileadmin/sowi/akuf/Text_2010/AP_Liberia_Elite-Gerdes_2011_1.pdf

— (2013). *The Evolution of the Liberian State. Neo-patrimonialism, Charismatic Authority and Institutional Change through War and Peace*. Working Paper 1/2013, Research Unit of Wars, University of Hamburg. 04/15/2013 http://www.wiso.uni-hamburg.de/fileadmin/sowi/akuf/Text_2010/AP_Evolution_State-Gerdes_2013_1.pdf

Gifford, Paul (1993). *Christianity and Politics in Doe's Liberia*. Cambridge: Cambridge University Press.

Global Witness (2001): *Taylor-made: The Pivotal Role of Liberia's Forests and Flag of Convenience in Regional Conflict*. Report, London. 10/20/2010. http://www.globalwitness.org/media_library_detail.php/97/en/taylor_made

— (2002). *Logging Off: How the Liberian Timber Industry Fuels Liberia's Humanitarian Disaster and Threatens Sierra Leone*. Report, London. 10/20/2010. http://www.globalwitness.org/media_library_detail.php/662/en/logging_off

— (2003a). *The Usual Suspects: Liberia's Weapons and Mercenaries in Côte d'Ivoire and Sierra Leone: Why it's Still Possible, How it Works and How to Break the Trend*. Report, London. 10/20/2010. http://www.globalwitness.org/media_library_detail.php/96/en/the_usual_suspects

— (2003b). *For a Few Dollars More: How Al Quaeda Moved into the Diamond Trade*. Report, London. 10/20/2010. http://www.globalwitness.org/media_library_detail.php/109/en/for_a_few_dollars_more

— (2004). *Back to the Future: What is the Future of Liberia's Forests and its Effects on Regional Peace?*. Report, London. 10/20/2010.http://www.globalwitness.org/media_library_detail.php/116/en/liberia_back_to_the_future

— (2005). *Timber, Taylor, Soldier, Spy: How Liberia's Uncontrolled Resource Exploitation, Charles Taylor's Manipulation and the Re-recruitment of Ex-Combatants are Threatening Regional Peace*. Report (June), Washington, D.C. 10/20/2010. http://www.globalwitness.org/media_library_detail.php/137/en/timber_taylor_soldier_spy

— (2006). *Heavy Mittal: A State Within a State*. Report, Washington, D.C. 10/20/2010.http://www.globalwitness.org/media_library_detail.php/156/en/heavy_mittal

— (2007). *Update on the Renegotiation of the Mineral Development Agreement between Mittal Steel and the Government of Liberia*. Briefing Paper. 10/20/2010. http://www.globalwitness.org/media_library_detail.php/156/en/heavy_mittal

— (Oct. 13, 2010). *Global Witness Welcomes Decisive Action by Liberian President Regarding Carbon Fraud Investigation.* Press Release, 02/23/2013. http://www.globalwitness.org/library/global-witness-welcomes-decisive-action-liberian-president-regarding-carbon-fraud

— (2011). *Curse or Cure: How Oil Can Boost or Break Liberia's Post-war Recovery.* 02/23/2013 http://www.globalwitness.org/curse_or_cure/curse_or_cure_lowbw.pdf

— (2012). *Signing their Lives Away: Liberia's Private Use Permits and the Destruction of Community-Owned Rainforest.* Report, Sept.. 02/23/2013. http://www.globalwitness.org/sites/default/files/library/Signing%20their%20 Lives%20away%20–%20Liberian%20Private%20Use%20Permits%20–%204%20Sept%202012%20U_0.pdf

— (Dec. 21, 2012). *Logging Company Flouts Liberian President's Timber Export Ban and Drives Breakdown in Rule of Law,* Press Release, 02/23/2013. http://www.globalwitness.org/library/logging-company-flouts-liberian-president%E2%80%99s-timber-export-ban-and-drives-breakdown-rule-law

Government of Liberia (July 17, 2007). *Retired Finance Ministry Workers Praise President Sirleaf for Bringing Honor and Dignity to Pension Programme.* Press Release. 11/10/2008. http://www.emansion.gov.lr/press.php?news_id=314

Government of Liberia (2008). *Summary of the Main Changes Brought About by the Government of Liberia's Review of the 2005 Concession Agreement with Firestone Liberia Inc.*, Monrovia. 11/10/2008. http://www.emansion.gov.lr/doc/Firestone AgreementComparison20052008.pdf

Greenbang (2010): *Anti-Corruption Group Warns of 'Carbon Cowboy' Crimes.* June 04. 02/23/2013. http://www.greenbang.com/anti-corruption-group-warns-of-carbon-cowboy-crimes_14462.html

Gunston, John (Dec. 2, 1990). Welcome to My Bloodbath: Prince Johnson's Reign of Terror. *Mail on Sunday – You Magazine* (2.12.), pp. 44–48

Harris, David (1999). From 'Warlord' to Democratic President: How Charles Taylor Won the 1997 Liberian Elections. *Journal of Modern African Studies*, Vol. 37, No. 3, 431–455.

— (2006). Liberia (2005): An Unusual Post-conflict Election. *Journal of Modern African Studies*, Vol. 44, No. 3, 375–395.

Hayner, Priscilla (2007). *Negotiating Peace in Liberia: Preserving the Possibility for Justice.* Henry Dunant Centre for Humanitarian Dialogue & International Center for Transitional Justice Report (Nov.), Geneva. 08.01.2010 http://www.ictj.org/static/Africa/Liberia/HaynerLiberia1207.eng.pdf

Hensell, Stephan (2009). *Die Willkür des Staates: Herrschaft und Verwaltung in Osteuropa.* Wiesbaden: Verlag für Sozialwissenschaften.

Heritage (Monrovia). (Dec. 28, 2005). Cuffing, Looting and Thieves, by John S. Morlu, II.

— (Dec. 29, 2006): Pres. Sirleaf Breaks Silence on Speaker Snowe's Removal Claim.

— (Mar. 23, 2007): GEMAP Expert at NPA Risks Removal.

Hoffman, Daniel (2004). The Civilian Target in Sierra Leone and Liberia: Political Power, Military Strategy, and Humanitarian Interventions. *African Affairs*, Vol. 103, No. 411, 211–226.

— (2006). "Despot Deposed: Charles Taylor and the Challenge of State Reconstruction in Liberia". In Henning Melber and Roger Southall (eds.). *Legacies of Power: Leadership Change and Former Presidents in African Politics*, 308–331. Cape Town: HSCR Press.

House of Representatives (2007). "Resolution Affecting the Removal of Hon. Edwin Melvin Snowe, Jr. as Speaker of the House of Representatives of the 52nd Legislature of the Republic of Liberia" (16.1.). Reprinted in: *Public Agenda* (Monrovia), Jan. 31, 2007.

Huband, Mark (1999). *The Liberian Civil War*. London et al: Cass.

Human Rights Watch (1993). *Waging War to Keep the Peace: The ECOMOG Intervention and Human Rights*. Africa Watch Report, Vol. 5, No. 6, New York. 09/12/20006 http://www.hrw.org/legacy/reports/1993/liberia/

Hunger Project, The (Oct. 21, 2006). Africa's First Elected Woman President Receives Africa Prize for Leadership. 1/8/2010 http://www.thp.org/what_we_do/key_initiatives/honoring_africa_leadership/prizes_recent/2006

Hyden, Goran (2000). "The Governance Challenge in Africa". In Goran Hyden (2000). *African Perspectives on Governance*, 5–32. Trenton: Africa World Press.

Hyman, Lester (2003). *United States Policy Towards Liberia, 1822–2003: Unintended Consequences?*. Cherry Hill: Africana Homestead Legacy.

ICG (International Crisis Group) (2002a). The Key to Ending Regional Instability" *Africa Report* No. 43, Freetown/Brussels. 22.04.04 http://www.crisisweb.org/home/index.cfm?id=1533&l=1

— (2002b): Liberia: Unravelling. *Africa Briefing* (19.8), Freetown/Brussels. 22.04.2004 http://www.crisisweb.org/home/index.cfm?id=1533&l=1

— (2003a): Côte d'Ivoire: The War is not yet Over. *Africa Report* No. 72, Freetown/Brussels. 22.04.2004 http://www.crisisgroup.org/library/documents/africa/072__cote_d_ivoire_war_not_yet_over.pdf

— (2003b). Tackling Liberia: The Eye of the Regional Storm. *Africa Report* No. 62, Freetown/Brussels. 22.04.2004 http://www.crisisgroup.org/~/media/Files/africa/west-africa/liberia/Tackling%20Liberia%20The%20Eye%20of%20the%20Regional%20Storm.ashx

— (2005). Liberia's Elections: Necessary but Not Sufficient. *Africa Report* N°98, Dakar/Brussels. 08.09.2006 http://www.crisisgroup.org/~/media/Files/africa/west-africa/liberia/Liberias%20Elections%20Necessary%20but%20Not%20Sufficient.ashx

IMF (International Monetary Fund) (2000a). Liberia: Selected Issues and Statistical Appendix. *IMF Staff Country Report* No. 00/50. 15.06.2006 http://www.imf.org/external/pubs/ft/scr/2000/cr0050.pdf

— (2000b). Liberia: Staff Report for the 1999 Article IV Consultation and Staff-Monitored Program. *IMF Staff Country Report* No. 00/52. 18.12.2006 http://www.imf.org/external/pubs/ft/scr/2000/cr0052.pdf

— (2003a). "Liberia: 2002 Article IV Consultation, Overdue Financial Obligations to the Fund – Review Following Declaration of Ineligibility, and Decision on Suspension of Voting and Related Rights- Staff Report". Staff Statement, Public Information Notice and Press Release on the Executive Board Discussion; and Statement by the Executive Director for Liberia, *IMF Country Report* No. 03/274. 18.12.2006 http://www.imf.org/external/pubs/ft/scr/2003/cr03274.pdf

— (2003b). Liberia: Selected Issues and Statistical Appendix. *IMF Country Report* No. 03/275. 15.06.2006 http://www.imf.org/external/pubs/ft/scr/2003/cr03275.pdf http://www.imf.org/external/pubs/ft/scr/2005/cr05167.pdf

— (2006). Liberia: Selected Issues and Statistical Appendix. *IMF Country Report* No. 06/167– 15.06.2006 http://www.imf.org/external/pubs/ft/scr/2006/cr06167.pdf

— (2007). Liberia: Interim Poverty Reduction Strategy Paper—Joint Staff Advisory Note. *IMF Country Report* No. 07/313.

— (2010). *IMF and World Bank Announce US$ 4.6 Billion Debt Relief for Liberia.* IMF Press Release No. 10/267. 29.06.2010 http://www.imf.org/external/np/sec/pr/2010/pr10267.htm

— (2010). *Liberia: Life After Debt.* By John Lipsky, First Deputy Managing Director, International Monetary Fund. 30.06.2010 http://www.imf.org/external/np/speeches/2010/063010.htm

Inegbedion, E. John (1994). "ECOMOG in Comparative Perspective". In Timothy M. Shaw, and Julius Emeko Okolo, (eds.) (1994). *The Political Economy of Foreign Policy in ECOWAS.* New York: St. Martins Press, pp. 218–244.

International Rubber Study Group (2002). *World Rubber Statistics Handbook: 1975–2001* (Vol. 6). London.

Inquirer (Monrovia). (Dec. 2, 1993): Fresh Fighting May Delay Troops' Arrival.

— (Jan. 25, 1995). ECOWAS Patience Running Out–Sanni Abacha Tells Factional Leaders in Ghana.

— (Aug. 23, 1995). Why How Sankawulo.

— (Mar. 22, 1996). ECOMOG Takes over Kakata: No NPFL Men in Dixville.

— (Feb. 16, 1998). Roosevelt Johnson in Unusual Return: President Expresses Concern.

— (May 16, 2005). Port Operations Delayed.
— (May 25, 2005). Matthews Wants Liberia National Alliance.
— (Aug. 23, 2005). New Diamond Mine Discovered in Sinoe - Eviction Begins in Sapo Park.
— (Sept. 12, 2005). LPRC Press Release: LPRC Reacts to Baron (sic) Tarr's New Dem Article.
— (Mar. 23, 2007). Ellen Begins Cleaning Up: Dismisses Two at Lands & Mines.
— (Mar. 27, Mar. 27, 2007). Bribery Allegation: What Evidence Does the Lower House Need.
— (Nov. 12, 2008). Alhadji Kromah and Armah Youlo Lied to TRC, 8/20/2010 http://www.concern-liberians.org/chat_room/view_topic.php?id=48663&forum_id=1&highlight=alhaji
International Herald Tribune (1996). Amid Chaos, Liberia's Feisty Press Endures, Aug. 20.
IRIN (July 28, 2003). Former Warlord Prince Johnson Seeks Political Career. 6/20/2005 http://www.irinnews.org/Report.aspx?ReportId=45188
— (Apr. 8, 2004). Exiled Taylor Deserted by Followers as Hard Times Bite. 5/18/2005 http://www.irinnews.org/report.aspx?reportid=49457
Itano, Nicole (2003). *Liberating Liberia: Charles Taylor and the Rebels Who Unseated Him*. ISS Paper 82, Pretoria: Institute for Security Studies. 2/9/2004 http://www.iss.co.za/pubs/papers/82/Paper82.pdf
Jackson, Robert H. (1990). *Quasi-states, Sovereignty, International Relations and the Third World.* Cambridge: Cambridge University Press.
Johnson, Prince Yomi (2003). *The Rise and Fall of President Samuel K. Doe: A Time to Heal and Rebuild Liberia.* Ed. Wa Hne, Jr. Lagos: Soma Associates.
Johnson Sirleaf, Ellen (2006). *Inaugural Address of H.E. Ellen Johnson Sirleaf. Repulic of Liberia, Executive Mansion*, (held on 1/16) 16/18/2007 http://www.emansion.gov.lr/doc/inaugural_add_1.pdf
— (2009). *This Child Will Be Great: Memoir of a Remarkable Life by Africa's First Woman President.* New York: HarperCollins.
Johnston, Patrick (2004). Timber Booms, State Busts: The Political Economy of Liberian Timber. *Review of African Political Economy*, Vol. 31, No. 101, 441–456.
Jung, Dietrich (1995). *Tradition – Moderne – Krieg: Grundlegung einer Methode zur Erforschung kriegsursächlicher Prozesse im Kontext globaler Vergesellschaftung.* Münster: Lit.
Jung, Dietrich (ed.). (2003). *Shadow Globalisation, Ethnic Conflicts and New Wars: A Political Economy of Intra-State War.* London/New York: Routledge.
Kaldor, Mary (1999). *New and Old Wars: Organized Violence in a Global Era.* Cambridge: Polity Press.
Kamara, Tom (n.d.): Charles Taylor's Threat of "Ferocity" Over Veep Dogolea's Death. Perspective Website. 5/18/2006 http://www.theperspective.org/ferocity.html
Kaplan, Robert (1994): The Coming Anarchy. *Atlantic Monthly* 273/2, 44–76.

Keen, David (1998). *The Economic Functions of Violence in Civil Wars*. International Institute of Strategic Studies, Adelphi Paper No. 320, Oxford.

— (2000). "Incentives and Disincentives for Violence". In Mats Berdal and David M. Malone (eds.). (2000). *Greed & Grievance: Economic Agendas in Civil Wars*, 19–41. Boulder/London: Lynne Rienner.

Kelsall, Tim (2005). "History, Identity and Collective Action: Difficulties of Accountability". In Ulf Engel and Gorm Rye Olsen (eds.). *The African Exception*, 53–67. Aldershot/Burlington: Ashgate.

Kilson, Martin (1966). *Political Change in a West African State: A Study of the Modernization Process in Sierra Leone*. Cambridge: Harvard University Press.

Konrad Adenauer Foundation (2006). *A Profile of Members of the 52nd Legislature of Liberia*. Konrad Adenauer Foundation Monrovia/European Commission Office in Liberia, Monrovia. 1/5/2009
http://www.kas-benin.de/liberia/Profiles_2005_52nd_Legislature-Liberia.pdf

Körner, Peter (1996). *Macht- und Interessenpolitik in der ECOWAS-Region und der Krieg in Liberia: Die politische Dimension regionaler Integration in Westafrika*. Institut für Afrika-Kunde, Hamburger Beiträge Nr. 51, Hamburg.

Kulah, Arthur F. (1999). *Liberia Will Rise Again*. Nashville: Abbington.

Kurtenbach, Sabine, and Peter Lock (2004). "Kriege als (Über)Lebenswelten: Schattenglobalisierung, Kriegsökonomien und Inseln der Zivilität". In Sabine Kurtenbach and Peter Lock (eds.). *Kriege als (Über)Lebenswelten: Schattenglobalisierung, Kriegsökonomien und Inseln der Zivilität, 20*–37. Berlin: Dietz.

Liberian Dialogue (Aug. 5, 2005). Who's Amelia Ward? She Must Say More to Win Me Over, by Tewroh-Wehtoe Sungbeh. 6/25/2006
http://www.theliberiandialogue.org/articles/c080505tws.htm

— (Sept. 15, 2005). An Open Letter to Madam Ellen Johnson-Sirleaf, by Tom Woewiyu. 25/6/2006 http://www.theliberiandialogue.org/articles/c091505tws.htm

Liberian Express (Jan. 2–5, 2006). UP Accused.

— (Monrovia) (Mar. 26–28, 2007a). GEMAP: Failing or Smear Campaign.

— (Monrovia) (Mar. 26–28, 2007b). Fear Grips Cabinet Officials over Pending Changes in Gov't.

LiberianSoccer.com (n.d.) [2009]. Periscoping Liberian Soccer: Merits and Demerits, by Bill B. Blamo. 6/3/2010
http://www.liberiansoccer.com/Periscoping%20Liberian%20Soccer.htm

Liberty, Clarence E. Zamba (1998). Butuo: A Lilliputian Testament to a Struggle – The NPFL Journey to State Power: How Charles Taylor Upset the Bowl of Rice and Took Home the Whole Hog. *Liberian Studies Journal*, Vol. 23, No. 1, 135–207.

Lindberg, Staffan I. (2003). »It's Our Time to 'Chop«: Do Elections in Africa Feed Neo-Patrimonialism rather than Counteract it?. *Democratization*, Vol. 10, No. 2, 121–140.

— (2006). The Surprising Significance of African Elections. *Journal of Democracy*, Vol. 17, No. 1, 139–151.

Lock, Peter (2004). "Gewalt als Regulation: Zur Logik der Schattenglobalisierung", In Sabine Kurtenbach and Peter Lock (eds.). *Kriege als (Über)Lebenswelten: Schattenglobalisierung, Kriegsökonomien und Inseln der Zivilität*, 40–61. Berlin: Dietz.

MacKinlay, John (2000). Defining Warlords. *International Peacekeeping*, Vol. 7, No. 1, 48–62.

Malan, Mark (2008). *Security Sector Reform in Liberia: Mixed Results from Humble Beginnings*. Strategic Studies Institute, U.S. Army War College. 10.01.2009 http://www.strategicstudiesinstitute.army.mil/pubs/display.cfm?pubID=855

Manning, Carrie (2004). Armed Opposition Groups into Political Parties: Comparing Bosnia, Kosovo, and Mozambique. *Studies in Comparative International Development*, Vol. 39, No. 1, 54–79.

Marenco dos Santos, André (2006): *Comparing Houses of Representatives: Parliamentary Recruitment in Argentina, Brazil, Chile and Mexico*. 23.02.2013 http://socialsciences.scielo.org/pdf/s_tsoc/v2nse/scs_a04.pdf

Marx, Karl (1987). *Das Kapital: Kritik der Politischen Ökonomie*. Berlin: Dietz.

Mauss, Marcel (1954). *The Gift: Forms and Functions of Exchange in Archaic Societies*. London: Cohen & West.

Médard, Jean-François (1982). "The Underdeveloped State in Tropical Africa: Political Clientelism or Neo-patrimonialism?". In Christopher Clapham (ed.). *Private Patronage and State Power: Political Clientelism in the Modern State*, 162–192. London: Frances Pinter.

Médecins Sans Frontières (2002). "Populations Affected by War in the Mano River Region of West Africa: Issues of Protection". MSF Report (May). 22.04.2004 http://www.msf.org/countries/page.cfm?articleid=EB07B3BF-3442–4FDE-A1D6E36464BB6EA9

Midweek Concord (Lagos). (1991). A Tale of Two Capitals: Monrovia and Gbarnga, by Razak Yusuf, Dec. 2.

Mihatsch, Moritz (n.d.) [2005]. *Preview of the Liberian Special Elections 2005*. Konrad Adenauer Foundation Monrovia/European Commission Office in Liberia, Monrovia.

Ministry of Finance (2008). *Fiscal Outturn (FY 2007/08)* (unaudited). Republic of Liberia (Oct.), Monrovia. 6/10/2010 http://www.mof.gov.lr/doc/FISCAL%20OUTTURN%202007–2008.pdf

— (2009). *Fiscal Outturn: Fiscal Year 2008/09* (unaudited). Republic of Liberia (Oct.), Monrovia. 6/10/2010 http://www.mof.gov.lr/doc/PUBLISHED%20FISCAL%20OUTTURNS%20FOR%20FISCAL%20YEAR%202008–09.pdf

— (2012). *National Budget for Fiscal Year 2012–13*, Republic of Liberia, Monrovia. 2/23/2013. https://sites.google.com/a/mopea.gov.lr/mtef-budget/home

Ministry of Foreign Affairs (2006). *An Act Adopting the National Forestry Reform Law of 2006*. Republic of Liberia, Monrovia.

Monrovia Daily News (Mar. 30, 1995). ULIMO-J, ULIMO-K: Fighting at Po River.

Montclos, Marc-Antoine de (1999). "Liberia oder die Ausplünderung eines Landes". In François Jean, and Jean-Christophe Rufin (eds.). *Ökonomie der Bürgerkriege*, 219–242. Hamburg: Hamburger Edition (IFS).

Moran, Mary (2006). *Liberia: The Violence of Democracy*. Philadelphia: University of Pennsylvania Press.

Mungiu-Pippidi, Alina (2006). Corruption: Diagnosis and Treatment. *Journal of Democracy*, Vol. 17, No. 3, 86–99.

Münkler, Herfried (2002). *Die neuen Kriege*. Hamburg: Rowohlt.

— (2006). "Was ist neu an den neuen Kriegen? Eine Erwiderung auf die Kritiker". In Anna Geis (ed.). *Den Krieg überdenken: Kriegsbegriffe und Kriegstheorien in der Kontroverse*, 133–150. Baden-Baden: Nomos.

Murphy, William (2003). Military Patrimonialism and Child Soldier Clientelism in the Liberian and Sierra Leonean Wars. *African Studies Review*, Vol. 46, No. 2, 61–87.

Nass, Innocent Asubike (2000). *A Study in Internal Conflicts: The Liberian Civil Crisis*. Enugu: Fourth Dimension.

National Chronicle (Monrovia). (2005): Weah: Academic Standards vs. Real Issues, Sept. 14.

— (2005). On Transfer of Gov't. Properties: NTLA Challenges U.S. Government, Nov. 21.

NEC (2005a). *National Tally Center Progressive Results Report for the Election of the President, Vice-President, Senate and House of Representatives on 11 October 2005*. National Elections Commission of Liberia, Monrovia. 20.10.2005 http://www.necliberia.org/

— (2005b). *National Tally Center Results Report for the Runoff Election of the President and Vice-President on 8 November 2005*. National Elections Commission of Liberia, Monrovia. 20.10.2005 http://www.necliberia.org/

— (2011). *National Tally Center Tally Report for the Presidential and Legislative Elections on 11 October 2011, as of 25 Oct. 2011*. 20/1/2012 http://www.necliberia.org/results2011/

Neue Zürcher Zeitung (1995). Triumphaler Einzug Charles Taylors in Monrovia: Vereidigung einer neuen Übergangsregierung für Liberia, Sept. 2–3.

New African (1993). Killing of Brian Garnham, Apr.

— (1995). Liberia on a Knife Edge, by Baffour Ankomah, Mar.

— (1997). At Last, Liberia Has a President; by Baffour Ankomah, Sept.

New Dawn (Monrovia). (Aug. 16, 2012). Indictment Hooks Bropleh. By Winston Parley, 2/23/2013. http://allafrica.com/stories/201208161049.html

— (Jan. 10, 2013). Police Chief Backs Corrupt Cops. By Winston Parley. 2/23/2013 http://allafrica.com/stories/printable/201301100505.html

New Democrat (Monrovia). (Jan. 13, 1994a). 22 Gates to Reality: A Journey to Gbarnga, by Lindsay Barret.

— (Jan. 13, 1994b). SELF Elections.
— (Jan. 27, 1994). Voices From Behind the Lines, by Lindsay Barret.
— (June 23, 1994). Taylor's Greater Liberia: The Other Side of Gbarnga, by John H.T. Stewart,.
— (Aug. 18, 1994). The Woewiyu Story: A Catalogue of Deaths, Deception and Double-Crossing. Interview with Tom Woewiyu, by Tom Kamara.
— (May 11, 1995a). Difficult Choice: What After the Gun? An Encounter With NPFL Fighters, by Charles A. Jackson.
— (May 11, 1995b). Justice Min: US Man's Murder Well-Planned.
— (Sept. 5, 2005). Bonanza at LPRC.
— (Sept. 9, 2005). TLA: "We're Corrupt".
— (Apr. 10, 2007). NPA's GEMAP Agent Fired.
— (July 1, 2007): GOL Barters. 7/3/2007 http://www.newdemocratnews.com/news_details.php?recordID=1648
— (Dec. 20, 2009). Gender Boss Booked for "Theft, Exploitation, Abuse of Office". 2/16/2010 http://allafrica.com/stories/200912290958.html
— (Feb. 15, 2010). Bropleh, Others, Casusalties of President's Zero Theft Tolerance. 2/16/2010 http://allafrica.com/stories/201002151721.html
— (Feb. 19, 2010). I was not Fired, 7/21/2011 http://allafrica.com/stories/201002190712.html
— (Feb. 8, 2011). The Era of "Omerta". 21/7/2011 http://allafrica.com/stories/201102090849.html
— (Apr. 25, 2011). Army Rice Scandal. 2/23/2013 http://allafrica.com/stories/201104251090.html
— (Feb. 14, 2013). Liberia: Samukai Slips - On Army's Plight. 2/23/2013 http://allafrica.com/stories/201302141277.html
New York Times (2012). A Nobel Laureate's Problem at Home by Silas Siakor and Rachael Knight, Jan. 20. 2/23/2013 http://www.nytimes.com/2012/01/21/opinion/in-liberia-a-nobel-laureates-problem.html?_r=0
Newswatch (Apr. 22, 2007). Liberia: Minister's Naughty Threesome with State, Press and Free Speech, by Rohan Jayasekera. 7/28/2008 http://oldcontent.newswatch.in/news-analyses/ethics-and-freedom/7397.html
Ngafuan, Augustine (2012). *Remarks by H.E. Augustine K. Ngafuan, Minister of Foreign Affairs and Dean of the Cabinet, at Program Marking the Official Commissioning of Members of the Liberian Cabinet, March 16.* Printed in New Democrat (Monrovia) Mar. 22.
O'Donell, Guillermo A. (1994). Delegative Democracy. *Journal of Democracy*, Vol. 5, No. 1, 55–69.
OECD (2012): *OECD.Stat Extracts Database.* 7/30/2012 http://stats.oecd.org/index.aspx

Panel of Experts (12/2000). *Report of the Panel of Experts Appointed Pursuant to Security Council Resolution 1306 (2000), Paragraph 19, in Relation to Sierra Leone.* Document S/2000/1195

— (10/2001). *Report of Panel of Experts on Liberia Submitted in Accordance with Resolution 1343 (2001).* Document S/2001/1015.

— (04/2002): *Report of the Panel of Experts Pursuant to Security Council Resolution 1395 (2002), Paragraph 4, in Relation to Liberia.* Document S/2002/470.

— (10/2002): *Report of Panel of Experts on Liberia Submitted in Accordance with Resolution 1408 (2002).* Document S/2002/1115.

— (04/2003). *Report of the Panel of Experts on Liberia Submitted in Accordance with Resolution 1478 (2003).* Document S/2003/937.

— (10/2003). *Report of the Panel of Experts on Liberia Appointed Pursuant to Paragraph 4 of Security Council Resolution 1458 (2003).* Document S/2003/498.

— (06/2004). *Report of the Panel of Experts Pursuant to Paragraph 22 of Security Council Resolution 1521 (2003) Concerning Liberia.* Document S/2004/396

— (12/2004). *Report of the Panel of Experts Pursuant to Paragraph 2 of Security Council Resolution 1549 (2004) Concerning Liberia.* Document S/2004/955

— (06/2005). *Report of the Panel of Experts Submitted Pursuant to Paragraph 8 (e) of Security Council Resolution 1579 (2004) Concerning Liberia.* Document S/2006/360.

— (12/2005). *Report of the Panel of Experts, Submitted Pursuant to Paragraph 14 (e) of Security Council Resolution 1607 (2005) Concerning Liberia.* Document S/2005/745.

— (06/2006). *Report of the Panel of Experts Submitted Pursuant to Paragraph 9 (e) of Security Council Resolution 1647 (2005) Concerning Liberia.* Document S/2006/379.

— (09/2006). *Report of the Panel of Experts Submitted Pursuant to Paragraph 5 of Security Council Resolution 1689 (2006) Concerning Liberia.* Document S/2006/976

— (06/2007). Report of the Panel of Experts Submitted Pursuant to Paragraph 9 (e) Of Security Council Resolution 1521 (2007) Concerning Liberia. Document S/2007/340

— (12/2007). *Report of the Panel of Experts Submitted Pursuant to Paragraph 1 (e) of Security Council Resolution 1760 (2007) Concerning Liberia. Document S/2007/689.*

— (06/2008). *Report of the Panel of Experts On Liberia Submitted Pursuant to Paragraph 5 (e) of Security Council Resolution 1792 (2007) Concerning Liberia.* Document S/2008/371.

— (12/2008). *Report of the Panel of Experts on Liberia Submitted Pursuant to Paragraph 1 of Security Council Resolution 1819 (2008) Concerning Liberia.* Document S/2008/785

— (06/2009). *Midterm Report of the Panel of Experts on Liberia Submitted Pursuant to Paragraph 4 of Security Council Resolution 1854 (2008).* Document S/2009/290. Zeitpkt. Fehlt http://www.un.org/sc/committees/1521/liberiaPOE.shtml

— (12/2009). *Final Report of the Panel of Experts on Liberia Submitted Pursuant to Paragraph 4 (e) of Security Council Resolution 1854 (2008).* Document S/2009/640.

PBS (2002). Liberia: America's Stepchild. Transcript of Grain Coast Production for WGBH Boston. Broadcast on PBS, Oct. 10. 23.02.2013 http://www.pbs.org/wgbh/globalconnections/liberia/pdfs/liberiatranscript.pdf

Pech, Birgit (2009). *Korruption und Demokratisierung: Rekonstruktion des Forschungsstandes an den Schnittstellen zu Institutionenökonomik und politischer Transformationsforschung.* INEF-Report 99, University of Duisburg-Essen, Duisburg. 18.02.2010 http://inef.uni-due.de/cms/files/report99.pdf

Perspective, The (Atlanta). (n.d.) [ca. 1998/99]: Measuagoon: How Rural Liberians Are Rebuilding Their Communities, by Harry Greaves. 9/14/2005 http://www.theperspective.org/measuagoon.html

— (Apr. 9, 2000). Teahjay Executed?, by our Staff. 10/27/2007 http://www.theperspective.org/miltonteahjay.html

— (Oct. 25, 2000). Alhadji Kromah: Disappointment and Denials (An Interview), by Siahyonkron Nyanseor & J. Kpanneh Doe. 29/25/2005 http://www.theperspective.org/kromah.html

— (May 07, 2004). Liberia's Mining Minister Threatens to Resign Over Bribery Allegation If Proven Guilty, by Josephus Moses Gray. 5/18/2005 http://www.theperspective.org/2004/may/bribery.html

Pham, Peter (2004). *Liberia: Portrait of a Failed State.* New York: Reed.

Porte, Albert (1974). *Liberianization or Gobbling Business?* Crozierville: Porte (self-published).

Prkic, François (2005). "The Phoenix State: War Economy and State Formation in Liberia". In Klaus Schlichte (ed.). *The Formation and Crisis of State Domination*, 115–136. Aldershot/Burlington: Ashgate.

Public Agenda (Monrovia). (Jan. 31, 2007). Supreme Court Ruling Queried - Ambiguity Looms.

Pugh, Michael Neal Cooper, and Jonathan Goodhand (2004). *War Economies in a Regional Context: Challenges of Transformation.* Boulder/London: Lynne Rienner.

Reilly, Benjamin (2005). "Does the Choice of Electoral System Promote Democracy? The Gap between Theory and Practice". In Philip G. Roeder, G., and Donald Rothchild (eds.) (2005). *Sustainable Peace: Power and Democracy after Civil Wars*, 159–171. Ithaca/London: Cornell University Press.

Reinhard, Wolfgang (1999). "Einführung: Moderne Staatsbildung – eine ansteckende Krankheit?". In Wolfgang Reinhard. *Verstaatlichung der Welt: Europäische Staatsmodelle und außereuropäische Machtprozesse*, VII–XIV. München: Oldenbourg.

Reno, William (1993). Foreign Firms and the Financing of Charles Taylor' NPFL. *Liberian Studies Journal*, Vol. 18, No. 2, 175–187.

— (1995). Reinvention of an African Patrimonial State: Charles Taylor's Liberia. *Third World Quarterly*, Vol. 16, No. 1, 109–120.

— (1998). *Warlord Politics and African States.* Boulder/London: Lynne Rienner

— (2000). "Shadow States and the Political Economy of Civil Wars". In Mats Berdal, Mats and David M. Malone (eds.). *Greed & Grievance: Economic Agendas in Civil Wars*, 43–67. Boulder/London: Lynne Rienner.

— (2002). La "sale petite guerre" du Liberia. *Politique Africaine*, No. 88, 63–83.
— (2007). "Liberia: The LURDs of the New Church". In Morten Bøås, Morten, and Kevin C. Dunn (eds.). *African Guerrillas: Raging Against the Machine*, 69–80. Boulder/London: Lynne Rienner.
— (2008). Anti-Corruption Efforts in Liberia: Are they Aimed at the Right Targets?. *International Peacekeeping*, Vol. 15, No. 3, 387–404.
Richards, Paul (1995). "Rebellion in Liberia and Sierra Leone: A Crisis of Youth?". In Oliver Furley (ed.). *Conflict in Africa*, 134–170. London/New York: Tauris.
— (1996). *Fighting for the Rain Forest: War, Youth and Resources in Sierra Leone.* London: James Currey.
Ross, Michael (1999). The Political Economy of the Resource Curse. *World Politics*, Vol. 51, Jan., 297–322.
— (2005). *Booty Futures.* Manuscript, UCLA Department of Political Science. 20.08.2010 http://www.sscnet.ucla.edu/polisci/faculty/ross/bootyfutures.pdf
Roth, Guenther (1968). Personal Rulership, Patrimonialism, and Empire Building in the New States. *World Politics*, Vol. 20, No.2, 194–206.
Sankawulo, Wilton (n.d.): *The Marriage of Wisdom and Other Stories.* Monrovia (Self-published)
Sawyer, Amos (2008). Emerging Patterns in Liberia's Post-conflict Politics: Observations From the 2005 Elections. *African Affairs*, Vol. 107, No. 427, 177–199.
Schaffer, Frederic C. (1998). *Democracy in Translation: Understanding Politics in an Unfamiliar Culture.* Ithaca: Cornell University Press.
Schlichte, Klaus (1998). *Why States Decay: A Preliminary Assessment.* Research Unit of Wars, Working Paper No. 2/98, University of Hamburg, Hamburg.
— (2003). "State Formation and the Economy of Intra-state Wars". In Dietrich Jung (ed.) (2003). *Shadow Globalisation, Ethnic Conflicts and New Wars: A Political Economy of Intra-State War.* London/New York: Routledge, pp. 27–44.
— (2005). *Der Staat in der Weltgesellschaft: Politische Herrschaft in Asien, Afrika und Lateinamerika.* Frankfurt am Main: Campus.
— (2006). "Staatsbildung oder Staatszerfall? Zum Formwandel kriegerischer Gewalt in der Weltgesellschaft". *Politische Vierteljahresschrift*, Vol. 47, No. 4, pp. 547–570.
— (2009). *In the Shadow of Violence: The Politics of Armed Groups.* Frankfurt/New York: Campus.
Schönberger, Christoph (2007). "Max Webers Demokratie: Utopisches Gegenprinzip zur bürokratischen Herrschaft". In Andreas Anter and Stefan Breuer (eds.). *Max Webers Staatssoziologie*, 157–173. Baden-Baden: Nomos.
Schreiber, Wolfgang (2009). *Krieg und bewaffnete Konflikte 2009: Ein erster Überblick.* AKUF Analysen No. 8, University of Hamburg, Hamburg. 1/15/2010 http://www.sozialwiss.uni-hamburg.de/publish/Ipw/Akuf/publ/AKUF-Analysen-08.pdf

Schwidrowski, Arnim, and Saji Thomasi (2005). *Forestry Taxation in Africa: The Case of Liberia.* IMF Working Paper 05/156. 25.06.2006 http://www.imf.org/external/pubs/ft/wp/2005/wp05156.pdf

Siakor, Silas (Mar. 12012). Where Is the Money? Citizens Demanding Government and Arcelor Mittal Account for US$ 16 Million County Social Development Fund. In *FrontPageAfrica* (Monrovia).

Siegelberg, Jens (1994). *Kapitalismus und Krieg: Eine Theorie des Krieges in der Weltgesellschaft.* Münster: Lit

— (2000). "Staat und internationales System: Ein strukturgeschichtlicher Überblick". In Jens Siegelberg, and Klaus Schlichte (eds.). *Strukturwandel internationaler Beziehungen: Zum Verhältnis von Staat und internationalem System seit dem Westfälischen Frieden*, 11–56. Wiesbaden: Westdeutscher Verlag.

Smillie, Ian, Lansana Gberie, and Ralph Hazleton (2000). *The Heart of the Matter: Sierra Leone, Diamonds, and Human Security* (Complete Report), Partnership Africa Canada, Insights Series. 20.10.2004 http://www.pacweb.org/Documents/diamonds_KP/heart_of_the_matter-full-2000–01–eng.pdf

Smillie, Ian (2007). *Diamonds, the RUF and the Liberian Connection: A Report for The Office of the Prosecutor, The Special Court for Sierra Leone.* 10.09.2008 http://charlestaylortrial.files.wordpress.com/2008/01/p-19–report-ian-smillie.pdf

Special Independent Investigating Commission (2012). *Special Independent Investigating Body Report on the Issuance of Private Use Permits (PUPs).* Reprinted in *Heritage* (Monrovia) 11. Jan. 2013. 23.02.2013 http://allafrica.com/stories/printable/201301130166.html

Staines, Nicholas (2004). "Economic Performance over the Conflict Cycle". In Jean A.P. Clément (ed.). *Post-conflict Economies in Sub-Saharan Africa: Lessons from the Democratic Republic of Congo*, 129–176. Washington, D.C: IMF.

Steinberg, John (2010). Briefing: Liberia's Experiment with Transitional Justice. *African Affairs*, Vol. 109, No. 434, 134–144.

Tangri, Roger, Andrew M. Mwenda (2006). Politics, Donors, and the Ineffectiveness of Anti-Corruption Institutions in Uganda. *Journal of Modern African Studies*, Vol. 44, No. 1, 101–124.

Taz.de (July 7, 2009). Wahrheitsfindung, die keine war: Liberischer Bürgerkrieg "aufgearbeitet". 7/10/2009 http://www.taz.de/1/politik/afrika/artikel/1/wahrheitsfindung-die-keine-war/

Theobald, Robin (1982). Patrimonialism. *World Politics*, Vol. 34, No. 4, 548–559.

Therkildsen, Ole (2005). "Understanding Public Management Through Neopatrimonialism: A Paradigm for all African Seasons?". In Ulf Engel and Gorm Rye Olsen (eds.). *The African Exception*, 35–51. Aldershot/Burlington: Ashgate.

Tilly, Charles (ed.) (1975a). Western State-Making and Theories of Political Transformation. In Charles Tilly (ed.). *The Formation of National States in Western Europe*, 601–638. Princeton: Princeton University Press.

— (1975b). "Reflections on the History of European State-Making". In Charles Tilly (ed.). *The Formation of National States in Western Europe*, 3–83. Princeton: Princeton University Press.

— (1985). "War Making and State Making as Organized Crime". In Peter B. Evans. Dietrich Rueschemeyer and Theda Skocpol (eds.). *Bringing the State Back In*, 169–191. New York: Cambridge University Press.

— (1992). *Coercion, Capital, and European States: AD 990–1992*. Malden et al: Blackwell.

— (2008). *Democracy*. Cambridge et al: Cambridge University Press.

TRC (Truth and Reconciliation Commission) (2009). *Consolidated Final Report*. Vol. II. Republic of Liberia Truth and Reconciliation Commission, Monrovia. (6/30/2009). 8/15/2010
https://www.trcofliberia.org/reports/final/volume-two_layout-1.pdf

Tuck, Christopher (2000). «Every Car or Moving Object Gone»: The ECOMOG Intervention in Liberia. *African Studies Quarterly*, Vol. 4, Issue 1, 1–16. 29.02.2003 http:\\web.africa.ufl.edu/asq/v4/v4ia1.htm

UN ACABQ (2007–2010): UNMIL Financial Performance Reports, for years 2007–2010.6/10/2010
http://www.un.org/ga/acabq/reports.asp?type=search&desc=unmil

UN Secretary General (02/1995). *Ninth Progress Report of the Secretary-General on the United Nations Observer Mission in Liberia*. Document S/1995/158. 8/15/2003
http://www.un.org/Docs/secu95.htm

UNMIL (2006). *Human Rights in Liberia's Rubber Plantations: Tapping into the Future*. UN Mission in Liberia, Human Rights and Protection Section Report, Monrovia.

US Department of State (1996): *Testimony of William Twaddell, Assistant Secretary of State for African Affairs*. Hearing on Liberia before the House International Relations Committee.

US Embassy (n.d.) (2006). *Doing Business in Liberia*. Economic/Commercial Section of the US Embassy in Monrovia Information Report. Monrovia.

Utas, Mats (2003). *Sweet Battlefields: Youth and the Liberian Civil War*. Uppsala: Uppsala University Dissertations in Cultural Anthropology.

Vanguard (Lagos). (2011). *Why Liberians Are Ready to Vote Out Sirleaf-Johnson (sic)*. Interview with Dew Mayson, Aug. 7. 23.02.2013
http://www.vanguardngr.com/2011/08/why-liberians-are-ready-to-vote-out-sirleaf-johnson-by-prof-dew-mayson-opposition-presidential-candidate-2/

Washington Post (April 25, 2005): A Protected Friend of Terrorism, by Douglas Farah

Washington Post (June 5, 2005). The Man Who Would Be President, by Jonathan Ernst.

Weber, Max (1978a). *Economy and Society: An Outline of Interpretive Sociology*. Vol. 1, ed. by Guenther Roth & Claus Wittich, Berkeley et al: California University Press.

— (1978b). *Economy & Society: An Outline of Interpretive Sociology*. Vol. 2, ed. by Guenther Roth and Claus Wittich, Berkeley et al: California University Press.

Weissman, Fabrice (1996). Le Liberia, ôtage des seigneurs de guerre. In Médecins Sans Frontières (ed.) (1996). *Populations en danger*. Paris: La Découverte.

West Africa (June 24, 1991). Recourse to Arms?, by James Butty.

— (July 22, 1991). Life under Taylor, by John Momoh.

— (Oct. 14, 1991). War is Far From Over, by Janet Fleischman.

— (Dec. 16, 1991). Confusion in Gbarnga, from a Correspondent.

— (Oct. 5, 1992). Of Arms and Legitimacy, by Lindsay Barrett.

— (Nov. 16, 1992). The US State Department Files.

— (Apr. 5, 1993): The Firestone Factor, by Lindsay Barrett.

— (Mar. 1, 1993). The Nimba Equation, by Lindsay Barrett,.

— (Apr. 12, 1993). Firestone Comeback.

— (July 26, 1993). Charles Taylor's Psyche, by James Butty.

— (Sept. 5, 1994). Taylor's NPFL in Disarray.

— (Oct. 10, 1994). Liberia: Easy Prey, by Isaac Bantu.

— (Dec. 26, 1994). Taylor Return to Gbarnga, by Lindsay Barrett.

— (Feb. 13, 1995). New Dangers Emerge, by Lindsay Barrett.

— (May 29, 1995). A Flicker of Hope, by Lindsay Barrett.

— (Feb. 19, 1996). Deep Doubts about Peace, by Lindsay Barrett.

— (Mar. 18, 1996). The Vicious Circle in Liberia.

— (Oct. 14, 1996). Human Tragedy in Bomi, by Davidetta Browne.

— (Nov. 18, 1996). The 'Coup' that Failed, by a Special Correspondent.

— (Dec. 9, 1996). The Moment of Truth, by a Special Correspondent.

— (Mar. 17, 1997). Liberia: Kromah under Arrest.

— (Aug. 4, 1997). A Resounding Victory, by James Butty.

— (Feb. 23, 1998). The Media under Attack, by James Butty.

Wikileaks (2007). *Former Rebel Leader Denies Harboring Fighters*. US Embassy Monrovia Cable, Nov. 30. 2/23/2013 http://wikileaks.org/cable/2007/11/07MONROVIA1375.html

Yoder, John Charles (2003). *Popular Political Culture, Civil Society, and State Crisis in Liberia*. Lewiston (NY): Edwin Mellen Press.

Youboty, James (2004). *A Nation in Terror: The True Story of the Liberian Civil War*. Philadelphia: Parkside I.E.

Zartmann, William (2003). "The Timing of Peace Initiatives: Hurting Stalemates and Ripe Moments". In John Darby and Roger MacGinty (eds.). *Contemporary Peacemaking: Conflict, Violence and Peace Processes*, 19–29.New York/Basingstoke: Palgrave Macmillan.

Zeeuw, Jeroen de (2008): "Understanding the Political Transformation of Rebel Movements". In Jeroen de Zeeuw (ed.). *From Soldiers to Politicians: Transforming Rebel Movements after Civil War*, 1–32. Boulder/London: Lynne Rienner

Index

Abacha, Sani 49, 119, 121
Abuja Agreement 49, 58, 108, 127, 187
Agriculture; Ministry of 53, 134, 182, 193, 219, 220, 242, 243
American Mining Associates (AMA) 245
Americo-Liberian 31, 61, 65, 192, 197–199, 202
Anti-Terrorist Unit (ATU) 138, 139, 142, 158
Appropriation 13, 15, 18, 28, 30, 69, 74, 110, 125, 131, 150, 151, 153, 177, 179, 188, 189, 211, 223, 249, 250, 258, 260
Arcelor Mittal 238, 257
Armed Forces of Liberia (AFL) 34–47, 52–63, 70, 105–119, 124, 129, 131, 135, 140, 155, 157, 174, 175, 192, 201, 214–218, 236, 252
Assets freeze 178, 232
Association for Constitutional Democracy in Liberia (ACDL) 197

Babangida, Ibrahim 118–120, 122
Bangalu, Cole 234
Bility, Musa 193, 199, 218
Blah, Moses 159, 168, 194, 203
Boakai, Enid Tupee 61
Boakai, Joseph 199, 204
Bockarie, Sam "Mosquito" 142, 161, 162, 164
Boigny-Houphouët, Félix 62
Boley, George 36, 42, 52, 56, 58, 59, 107, 108, 123, 128–131, 192
Bomi 42, 69, 126, 158, 170, 184, 200, 209
Bong 7, 52, 91, 98, 113, 182, 193, 196, 199, 200, 206, 207, 218
Bong Defense Force 38
Bong Mines 53
Bong Mining Company (BMC) 98
Bowen, Hezekiah 52, 107, 108, 129, 131, 155
Bretton Woods Institutions 250
Bropleh, Laurence 220
Browne, Lewis Garseedah 233
Brumskine, Charles 135, 136, 160, 195, 204
Bryant, Gyude 178, 179, 188–190, 195, 196, 227, 228
Buchanan 43, 55, 81, 83, 85, 87, 90, 98, 122, 129, 130, 166, 187
Bureau of Maritime Affairs (BMA) 134, 148, 150, 174
Bureau of the Budget 174, 224
Burkina Faso 35, 61, 62, 118, 161
Burkinabé soldiers 41, 61, 63, 66, 77
Bush Marine Strike Force 47, 48, 139, 214

Capitalism, trade–based 30, 248, 260
Carter, Jimmy 70, 112
Centre for Democratic Empowerment (CEDE) 138

Charismatic administration 14; legitimacy 17, 132, 134, 136, 158, 253
Chea, Daniel 168
Cheapoo, Chea 129
Christian churches 195; see also St Peter Lutheran
Christianity 72, 195
Civil Society 7, 36, 40, 42, 52, 60, 108, 114, 138, 173, 174, 179, 187, 190, 197, 199, 203, 218, 239, 257
Clarke, Charles 178
Clientelism 12, 16, 27, 206
Coalition for the Transformation of Liberia (COTOL) 182, 196, 197, 204, 209, 211–214
Cocoa 96, 97, 103, 172
Coffee 96, 97, 103, 172
Commerce and Industry; Ministry of 174, 216, 219; Minister of 187, 195, 234
Compaoré, Blaise 61, 62, 77, 161, 164
Comprehensive Peace Agreement (CPA) 172–175, 179, 183, 187
Congress for Democratic Change (CDC) 199, 202–205, 212–216, 231–235
Conneh, Aicha 169, 171, 183, 184, 185, 192, 193, 199, 233
Conneh, Sekou Damate 169, 170, 183–184, 192, 203, 204
Contracts and Monopolies Commission 180
Cooper, Oscar 139
Council of State 44, 52, 55, 56, 108, 127, 131, 252
Crane, David 177
Cuttington University College 196, 200

De Beers 92
Defense; Ministry of; Minister of 140, 168, 184, 225
Democracy, neo–patrimonial 6, 18, 28, 248
Dennis, Cucoo 139, 177
Development assistance; 23, 25, 98,101, 227, 236, 260
Diah, Ophorie "Iron Jacket" 185
Doe, Chayee 184
Doe, Jackson Eddo 193, 218, 233
Doe, Jackson Fiah 63
Doe, Samuel Kanyon 31, 34–36, 40, 45, 52, 58, 60, 61, 71, 80, 106, 107, 114, 128, 184, 192, 193, 195, 201, 203, 204, 208, 209, 218
Dogonyaro, Joshua 120, 131
Dokie, Samuel 138, 156, 159
Dolo, Adolphus "Peanut Butter" 177, 182, 196, 200, 201, 207
Dukuly, Morris 233
Duo, Roland 139
Dweh, George 201, 203

ECOWAS 33–35, 40, 77, 109, 117, 118, 121, 141, 167, 174, 183, 188, 226, 227
ECOWAS Cease–Fire Monitoring Group (ECOMOG), 34–59, 71, 76, 77, 83, 89, 94–109, 112–142, 154–157, 160, 164, 255; Field Commander of 40, 56, 107, 119–121, 124, 131, 154
ECOWAS Mission in Liberia (ECOMIL) 167, 168, 173, 174
Elections, legislative 59, 182, 206, 208, 210
Elections, presidential 58, 59, 181, 191, 194, 198, 204, 232
Embargo 100, 143, 144, 161, 162, 165, 180, 243
European Commission 227, 229
Executive Outcomes 94, 140
Exports 36, 44, 80, 83–98, 104, 122,

130, 141, 143–148, 162, 166, 167, 226, 235–239, 242, 246, 260
Extraversion 23, 172
Fahnbulleh, Henry Boima 199
Farley, Kai 186
Firestone (Tire and Rubber Company) 43, 49, 87–90, 112, 148, 194, 195, 199, 238
Forestry Development Authority (FDA) 65, 134, 145, 173, 186, 229, 232, 240–244
Freemasons 220

Garlawolo, Francis 182, 193, 199
Gaye, Nixon "Striker" 47, 76
Gbalah, Joe 183, 184
Gbandi 170
Gbarpolu 199
General Auditing Commission (GAC) 220, 229, 230
George, Martin 180
Gerontocratic authority 11
Ghana 61, 108, 117, 118, 120, 141, 159
Gio 32, 63, 75, 106, 115, 117
Global Bank 194, 245
Gola 196
Gongloe, Tiawon 199, 218
Gould, Orishall 202
Governance and Economic Management Program (GEMAP) 228–230, 242
Grand Bassa 44, 56, 87, 136, 159, 186, 195, 206
Grand Cape Mount 126, 196, 247
Grand Gedeh 31, 42, 44, 171, 185, 203, 208, 210
Grand Kru 232
Greaves, Harry 198, 199, 218, 220, 221, 227, 228
Guinea 35–38, 41, 42, 45, 59, 81, 82, 113, 117–128, 132, 141, 143, 156, 157, 160, 162–164, 168–171, 182, 183
Guthrie Rubber Plantation 126
Guthrie Rubber Plantation 126

House of Representatives 59, 186, 191, 198, 205–216, 234, 241
Howard–Taylor, Jewel 181, 199, 200, 206, 207

Ideal–type 4, 10, 11, 15–18, 21, 64, 251
Independent National Patriotic Front of Liberia (INPFL) 35, 36, 39, 40, 43, 89, 105, 115, 116, 117, 119, 120, 213, 214
Inienger, John Mark 121
Inland Logging Company (ILC) 139, 160
Interim Government of National Unity (IGNU) 36, 40, 41, 44, 45, 105, 109–117, 131, 132, 252
Internal Affairs 173, 175, 219, 230, 232, 242
International Contact Group on Liberia (ICGL) 174, 183, 212
International Monetary Fund (IMF) 1, 85, 227, 241, 250
Internationalization (of authority) 180, 259–261
Iron ore 23, 43, 64, 80–84, 103, 188, 238
Italgems 245

Ja'neh, Kabineh 184, 193, 218
Jacobs, Cassius 77
Jallah, Peter Bonner 218
Johnson Morris, Francis 218, 229, 230
Johnson Sirleaf, Ellen 1, 6, 59, 160, 175, 178, 181, 192, 193, 195–203, 211, 212, 216–258
Johnson, Prince Yormie 35, 39, 40, 43, 61–63, 70, 106, 107, 115–119, 203, 207, 208
Johnson, Roosevelt 38, 45, 52–55, 103, 124–128, 135, 155, 156

Johnson, Wesley 187
Julu, Charles 108, 200
Jungle Waters 244

Kaine, Roland Cooper 203
Kamara, Luseni 183, 188, 226
Karnweah, Harrison 232, 242
Karpeh, Albert 42, 107, 124, 199
King Akerele, Olubanke 218
Kissi 37, 68, 126, 170, 199
Knuckles, Willis 199
Korto, Joseph 199, 200, 218, 219
Kpelle 45
Kpomakpor, David 44
Krahn 31, 32, 34, 36, 38, 42–45, 55, 56, 70, 106, 107, 125, 127–131, 139, 155, 156, 184, 185, 192, 207
Kromah, Alhadji 37, 38, 42, 45, 48, 52, 53, 55, 57, 58, 59, 108, 124–128, 156, 159, 192, 203
Kru 124, 196, 201, 232

Lands, Mines and Energy 58, 116, 173, 180, 207, 219, 239, 243, 247, 258
Lebanese 145, 149, 150, 177, 178, 195, 228
Legal–rational authority 4, 10, 13, 18, 28, 64, 179, 184, 190, 222, 240, 245, 248, 251
Legislature 59, 135, 136, 204, 205, 211–216, 234, 240, 241, 272, 275
Liberia Action Party (LAP) 58, 187, 195
Liberia Agricultural Company (LAC) 87–90, 130, 147, 194
Liberia Anti–Corruption Commission (ACC) 229, 230
Liberia Equal Rights Party (LERP) 199
Liberia Mining Company (LIMINCO) 64, 81–83, 98, 123, 239
Liberia Peace Council (LPC) 35–37, 42–48, 52–57, 67, 76, 89, 119–131, 192, 253
Liberia Petroleum Refining Company (LPRC) 149, 174, 178–180, 188–190, 193, 209, 215, 218, 220, 226–229, 257
Liberian Unification Party (LUP) 196
Liberians United for Reconciliation and Democracy (LURD) 126, 157, 159, 163, 165–174, 179–189, 192, 200–204, 207–210, 213–216, 218, 231, 233, 255
Liberty Party (LP) 204
Libya 41, 62–66, 159, 168
Lofa 7, 37, 42, 45, 47, 68, 91, 97, 99, 125, 126, 157, 159, 166, 170, 171, 172, 192, 199, 202, 207, 209, 210
Lofa Defense Force (LDF) 37, 45–48, 52, 57, 105, 127, 135, 159
Logging 86, 130, 135, 137, 139, 140, 144–147, 160, 166, 166, 215, 228, 231, 238–243, 254
Loma 37, 45, 47, 126, 159
London International Bank 180, 181
Longue durée 30, 260
Looting 37, 55, 68, 74, 78, 88, 98, 99–104, 107, 123, 126

MacIntosh, Toga 198
Malu, Victor 56, 131, 155
Mandingo 34, 38, 42, 45, 99, 106, 107, 124–126, 128, 156, 157, 185, 192, 193, 201, 218, 219, 233
Mano 63, 75, 106
Mano River Women Peace Network (MARWOPNET) 195
Margibi 43, 200, 206
Maryland 44, 56, 140, 196, 200, 206
Maryland Wood Processing Industries (MWPI) 139

Massaquoi, François 48, 52, 135, 159
Massaquoi, Roland 134, 182, 193, 200, 204
Matthews, Gabriel Bacchus 58, 135, 202
Mayson, Dew 177, 199, 200, 232
Measuagoon 198
Mende 71
Mesurado Group of Companies 177, 198
Milton, Ruth "Attila" 129, 160, 192
Mines de Fer de Guinée (MIFERGUI) 81, 238
Minor, Grace 197
Mittal Steel 238
Montserrado 32, 196, 197, 201, 204, 206, 211, 232, 233
Movement for Democracy in Liberia (MODEL) 161, 165, 167–174, 180–187, 191, 202, 208, 209, 216, 255
Movement for Justice in Africa (MOJA) 31, 40, 160, 199
Movement for the Redemption of Muslims (MRM) 124
Muslim 45, 124
Musu–Scott, Gloria 200

Nagbe, Lenn Eugene 202, 234
National Commission for Disarmament, Demobilization, Rehabilitation and Reintegration (NCDDRR) 188
National Democratic Party of Liberia (NDPL) 58, 192, 195, 199, 204, 205, 214, 215, 234
National Investment Commission (NIC) 180
National Mandingo Caucus (NMC) 192, 193, 218
National Patriotic Front of Liberia (NPFL) 5, 32–167, 181, 197, 202–206, 213–219, 232, 251–256; G-2 unit 140
National Patriotic Front of Liberia-Central Revolutionary Council (NPFL-CRC) 45, 47, 52, 58, 75, 76, 77, 127, 135, 138, 156, 159
National Patriotic Party (NPP) 58, 59, 71, 136, 138, 159, 179, 182, 193, 194, 197–206, 213–216, 232, 233
National Patriotic Reconstruction Assembly Government (NPRAG) 64, 66, 69, 71, 86, 134
National Ports Authority (NPA) 139, 174, 184–186, 215, 218, 220, 228, 229
National Transitional Legislative Assembly (NTLA) 179, 187–191, 203, 209, 214–216, 234
National Union for Democratic Progress (NUDP) 208, 212, 214
Nationalism 22, 26, 71, 79, 151
Neo–liberalism 2, 3, 262
Neo–patrimonialism 4, 17–19, 24, 28–30, 64, 65, 133, 154, 182–183, 260, 262
Ngafuan, Augustin Kpehe 224
Nigeria 5, 35–59, 76, 108–132, 141, 142, 161, 168, 176–178, 180, 181, 199, 207, 232, 254
Nimba 7, 32–39, 44, 47, 61–70, 74–82, 97, 98, 106–108, 137, 155, 181, 196–210, 218, 232, 244
Nimely, David 107
Nimely, Thomas Yaya 165, 185, 202, 208
Non–Governmental Organization (NGO) 70, 91, 101, 194, 198, 242, 244

Oriental Timber Company (OTC) 135, 140, 144, 146

Patriarchal authority 11, 67
Patrimonialism; decentralized 13, 18, 69, 132, 150, 259
Pennue, Zoe 180, 204
People's Democratic Party of Liberia (PDPL) 196
Political Parties (bloc) 168, 172–174, 180, 187, 193
Poro 37, 72, 135, 138, 206, 207
Progressive Alliance of Liberia (PAL) 31, 58, 135
Progressive Democratic Party (PRODEM) 192, 205
Progressive movement 31, 32, 35, 36, 40, 42, 52, 92, 109, 115, 129, 135, 160, 192, 196–204; see also MOJA, PAL
Public Works 218, 220

Quainoo, Arnold 120
Quiah, Oscar 52
Quiwonkpa, Thomas 31, 32, 35, 61, 115

Rapp, Stephen 80
Rationalization 223, 224, 227, 230, 257
Refugees 37, 42, 45, 110, 124, 157, 163, 169, 171, 172, 185, 187
Revolutionary United Front (RUF) 38, 41, 42, 78, 92–96, 104, 124, 139–144, 157, 161–166, 180, 243, 255
River Cess 44, 56
Rubber 7, 53, 72, 86–91, 97, 103, 112, 126–131, 134, 147–151, 186, 208, 213, 232, 235, 254
plantation, 7, 147, 187, 232, 235
Rubber Planters Association of Liberia (RPAL) 112

Saint Yrian, Michel 180
Sanctions, international 167, 176, 180–182, 186, 235, 237, 238, 246
Sande 206, 207
Sankara, Thomas 62
Sankawulo, Wilton 52, 230
Sankoh, Foday 41, 61, 141–143, 162
Sarpo 36, 43, 44, 52, 129
Sarpo National Park (SNP) 186
Sawyer, Amos 40, 41, 45, 58, 108–110, 124, 138, 190, 197, 199, 206
Security sector 133, 138–141, 145, 154–157, 165, 175, 188, 221–224, 227, 236, 255
Senate 59, 135, 136, 190–203, 205–209, 213–216, 231, 233, 235, 247
Shannon, Eugene 219
Shaw, Emanuel 150, 178, 231
Sherman, Varney 182, 195, 203, 204, 234
Sinoe 7, 44, 52, 56, 129, 160, 161, 172, 187, 202, 203, 233
Sinoe Rubber Plantation 187
Small Boys Unit (SBU) 67, 78
Snowe, Edwin 178–180, 189, 193, 211, 212, 226, 234
Special Court for Sierra Leone 80, 160, 175, 177
Special Emergency and Life Food Program 114, 115, 135
Special Operations Division (SOD) 156, 215
Special Security Services (SSS) 139, 158, 159, 160, 225
Spencer, Edward 199
St Peter Lutheran Church massacre 70
State; Ministry of 36, 42, 61, 62, 107, 123, 192, 212, 220, 221, 228, 233, 241
State; Ministry of 36, 42, 61, 62, 107, 123, 192, 212, 220, 221, 228, 233, 241
Sulunteh, Jeremiah 195, 199, 204, 218
Supuwood, Laveli 45, 47, 58, 159

Taylor, "Chuckie" Emanuel 138
Teahjay, Milton 160, 203, 233
Timber; see Logging
Tipoteh, Togba Nah 203
Tolbert, Carmina 178
Tolbert, Stephen 178, 197
Tolbert, William 31, 62
Travel ban 176, 179, 233
True Whig Party (TWP) 31, 40, 196, 197
Truth and Reconciliation Commission (TRC) 197
Tubman, William 192, 195
Tubman, Winston 192, 195, 203, 204, 231, 232, 235
Tubmanburg 53, 158, 171, 183

United Brothers' Friendship (UBF) 220
United Liberation Movement for Democracy in Liberia (ULIMO) 35–38; -Kromah 37, 38, 45–48, 53, 57, 68, 105, 125–131, 157, 184, 214, 234, -Johnson 38, 45–47, 52–57, 106, 125–131, 135, 137, 155, 156, 164, 276
United Nations Mission in Liberia (UNMIL) 175, 185–191, 222, 225, 236, 237, 244, 260
United Nations Observer Mission in Liberia (UNOMIL) 100
United States of America (US) 31, 43, 55, 61, 70, 80, 111, 112, 119, 212, 138, 147, 156, 178, 186, 190, 225, 227, 228, 231, 236, 238, 241, 248
Unity Party (UP) 58, 178, 191, 194, 199, 204, 205, 211–215, 218, 232, 234, 248
University of Liberia 40, 109, 193
Urey, Benoni 134, 150, 198, 232
Urey, Clemenceau 232
US diaspora 61, 82, 157, 186, 188, 199, 207, 218, 219

Ward, Amelia Ward 194, 204
Warlord politics 16, 17, 75, 76, 79, 129
Weah, George 160, 192–204, 227, 231–235
Wesseh, Conmany 199
West African Mining Corporation (WAMCO) 180, 181
West Oil 149, 150, 178
Wilson, Eugene 186
Wogbeh, Moses 242
Wollokollie, Dusty 199
Woods, Kofi Samuel 199, 218
Wylie, Joe 183

Yeaten, Benjamin 66, 139, 160
Young States 252, 259–262
Yuan, Harry 197

Zwedru 172, 209